REPRODUCING DOMINATION

CARIBBEAN
STUDIES
SERIES

ANTON L. ALLAHAR AND NATASHA BARNES
Series Editors

REPRODUCING DOMINATION

On the Caribbean Postcolonial State

Edited by Percy C. Hintzen with
Charisse Burden-Stelly and
Aaron Kamugisha

University Press of Mississippi / Jackson

The University Press of Mississippi is the scholarly publishing agency of
the Mississippi Institutions of Higher Learning: Alcorn State University,
Delta State University, Jackson State University, Mississippi State University,
Mississippi University for Women, Mississippi Valley State University,
University of Mississippi, and University of Southern Mississippi.

www.upress.state.ms.us

The University Press of Mississippi is a member
of the Association of University Presses.

First printing 2022
∞

Library of Congress Cataloging-in-Publication Data

Names: Hintzen, Percy C., editor. | Burden-Stelly, Charisse, editor. |
Kamugisha, Aaron, editor.
Title: Reproducing domination : on the Caribbean postcolonial state /
edited by Percy C. Hintzen with Charisse Burden-Stelly and Aaron Kamugisha.
Other titles: Caribbean studies series (Jackson, Miss.)
Description: Jackson : University Press of Mississippi, 2022. |
Series: Caribbean studies series | Includes list of publications
by Percy C. Hintzen. | Includes bibliographical references and index.
Identifiers: LCCN 2022034871 (print) | LCCN 2022034872 (ebook) |
ISBN 9781496841513 (hardback) | ISBN 9781496841520 (trade paperback) |
ISBN 9781496841537 (epub) | ISBN 9781496841544 (epub) |
ISBN 9781496841551 (pdf) | ISBN 9781496841568 (pdf)
Subjects: LCSH: Postcolonialism—West Indies. | Postcolonialism—Social aspects.
Classification: LCC F1628.8 .R46 2022 (print) | LCC F1628.8 (ebook) |
DDC 972.905/3—dc23/eng/20220824
LC record available at https://lccn.loc.gov/2022034871
LC ebook record available at https://lccn.loc.gov/2022034872

British Library Cataloging-in-Publication Data available

Dedicated to the Caribbean subaltern subjects perpetually engaged in struggle against colonial reason and to the scholars who chronicle their reasonings.

CONTENTS

ACKNOWLEDGMENTS

Because this is a collection mostly of work that was already published over the past twenty-five years, there are multitudes of people who should be acknowledged, more than I can mention here. Importantly, however, this volume would not have been thought of, not to mention published, without the insistence, efforts, and work of its coeditors Aaron Kamugisha and Charisse Burden-Stelly. All thanks go to them. I would like to thank the group of scholars with whom I had the pleasure of presenting and discussing preliminary versions of these chapters at annual meetings of the Caribbean Studies Association, as well as at conferences hosted by the Sir Arthur Lewis Institute of Social and Economic Studies. I took you all seriously. Finally, I would like to acknowledge the significant contributions of my students, particularly those for whom I served as adviser, and those who enrolled in my graduate seminars at the University of California, Berkeley, and most recently at Florida International University. You will recognize yourself in many of the chapters and in the development of the overall thesis of the volume. These include Aaron Kamugisha and Charisse Burden-Stelly, who deserve mention again and who wrote the introduction and epilogue to the volume, and, in the case of Charisse, coauthored one of the chapters.

COVER IMAGE

Sunday Morning in Port of Spain
Illustrated by Richard Bridgens in the 1830s
Restored by Peter Shim in 1984 from a screen print of the original lithograph for Paria
     Publishing Co. Ltd
Reproduced with kind permission of Gerard Besson

ARTICLES

The editors would like to acknowledge the permission of the following presses to reproduce the previously published essays: Duke University Press, Ian Randle Publishers, SUNY Press, University of the West Indies Press, *Social and Economic Studies*, *Social Identities*, *Small Axe*, *The C. L. R. James Journal*, *Transition* (Guyana).

1. "Reproducing Domination: Identity and Legitimacy Constructs in the West Indies." *Social Identities* 3, no. 1 (1997): 47–75.

2. "Afro-Creole Nationalism as Elite Domination: The English-Speaking West Indies." In *Foreign Policy and the Black (Inter)National Interest*, edited by Charles P. Henry, 185–218. Albany: State University of New York Press, 2001.

3. "Structural Adjustment and the New International Middle Class." *Transition*, no. 24 (February 1995): 53–73. University of Guyana Press.

4. "Rethinking Democracy in the Post-Nationalist State." In *New Caribbean Thought: A Reader*, edited by Brian Meeks and Folke Lindahl, 104–26. Mona, Jamaica: University of the West Indies Press, 2001.

5. "Race and Creole Ethnicity in the Caribbean." In *Questioning Creole: Creolisation Discourses in Caribbean Culture*, edited by Verene A. Shepherd and Glen L. Richards, 92–110. Kingston, Jamaica: Ian Rande Publishers, 2002.

6. "Creoleness and Nationalism in Guyanese Anticolonialism and Postcolonial Formation." *Small Axe* 8, no. 1 (March 2004): 106–22.

7. "Rethinking Democracy in the Post-Nationalist State: The Case of Trinidad and Tobago." In *Modern Political Culture in the Caribbean*, edited by Holger Henke and Fred Reno, 395–423. Mona, Jamaica: University of the West Indies Press, 2004.

8. "Diaspora, Globalization and the Politics of Identity." In *Culture, Politics, Race and Diaspora: The Thought of Stuart Hall*, edited by Brian Meeks, 233–86. Kingston, Jamaica: Ian Randle Publishers, 2006.

9. "Nationalism and the Invention of Development: Modernity and the Cultural Politics of Resistance." *Social and Economic Studies* 54, no. 3 (September 2005): 66–96.

10. "Culturalism, Development and the Crisis of Socialist Transformation: Identity, the State, and National Formation in Thomas's Theory of Dependence." *C. L. R. James Journal* 22, nos. 1–2 (Fall 2016): 191–214.

11. "Towards a New Democracy in the Caribbean: Local Empowerment and the New Global Order." In *Beyond Westminster in the Caribbean*, edited by Brian Meeks and Kate Quinn, 173–98. Kingston, Jamaica: Ian Randle Publishers, 2018.

THE ARC OF THE POSTCOLONIAL

PERCY C. HINTZEN

From the inception, I have always been unconvinced that the postcolonial arc bent in the direction of a transformative agenda for justice (to borrow a phrase from Martin Luther King Jr.). As a student studying marine radio in England in 1968, I was forced to confront (more, open my eyes to) the integral and entangled relationship between racial injustice and imperialism while grappling with a vicious and violent anti-immigrant campaign organized around the slogan "Keep Britain White" and a US-led campaign to keep Southeast Asia, inter alia, pro-American and capitalist at any cost. At the time, the American imperium seemed to be withering in the face of generalized protests occurring everywhere, including in Great Britain. These protests mirrored challenges to the racial, capitalist, imperial order (singly or in combination) occurring in the United States itself. The military campaign in Vietnam appeared to many as an immoral one aimed, if necessary, at the total destruction of a people whose history spans from at least 200 BCE and who had endured and prevailed against colonization by China and France. In the year 1968, capitalism, racism, and imperialism were under siege. The project of global domination by white Western men seemed to be faltering under the weight of protest and challenge. Cuba appeared to be a beacon of hope. My engagement in the praxis of anti-imperialist critique led me to the choice, in my required nontechnical course in liberal studies, to a variant of "Politics, Economics, and Philosophy"—a transdisciplinary field of study first developed at Oxford, which had spread to other major universities. In that one single course, I became somewhat familiar with Marxist analysis, even though in a very superficial way. This was my entrance into the arena of radical critique, and the beginning of my discomfort with forms of orthodoxy that refuse challenge. Troubled by the narrowness and limited possibilities of a technical education, and disturbed by its instrumentality in technologies of exploitation, expropriation, and dispossession, I came to the conclusion that sociology was the best route forward, notwith-standing the structural functionalism of Talcott Parsons that was preeminent in the United States. I had somewhat of an innate orientation to what I came to realize later was a neo-Marxist variant of radical sociology, the version that was highlighted, at least in my circles in Britain, in what came to be known as the Birmingham School of Cultural Studies. Ironically, in the very year of my decision to switch my field of study, the directorship of the school was transferred to a fellow West Indian, Jamaican Stuart Hall. My intention to remain in Great Britain was stymied by the unwillingness of the Guyanese high commissioner to entertain the thought of a "radical" transition to a new field of engagement, deeming "technical and professional training" to be more relevant to the country's development needs. So, I decided to return to Guyana, a country that proved refreshingly open to radical critical practice. I became a high school teacher while awaiting admission to the University of Guyana. It was the hardest and in retrospect the most rewarding pursuit that I have ever undertaken. I was the worst and most ineffectual teacher in the school, and this sparked inner reflection. The teachers were employing a "problem pos-ing" pedagogical method, even before it became publicized and specified by Paulo Freire in 1970. This had much to do with the history of radical critique, which had infused anticolonial politics in Guyana from the beginning of the twentieth century, relatively unencumbered by the influence of a small and politically insignificant nationalist capitalist class in the political economy of the country. This fed into a particular social equalitarianism that translated into the pedagogy of the classroom. Many of the country's teachers had moved up from apprenticeships in their local primary schools as "pupil teachers," to achieve professional status after attending the Teacher's Training College. Those who attended high school were selected predominantly from the lower strata based on performance in national examinations. They became the pool from which the country's high school teachers, bureaucrats, and overseas university students were drawn, for the most part. High school teachers and their students shared identical interests and experiences, hence the former's effectiveness. Having grown up in Barbados, with its rigidly racialized class divisions, I was more comfortable with a hierarchal order that demanded obedience. And this informed my approach to teaching. This recognition had a profound impact on my later scholarship.

Colonial Guyana was dominated by multinational capital organized around the agro-industrial production of sugar and later mineral extraction of bauxite. Trade and commerce were almost exclusively controlled by the sugar-producing multinationals. This left very little room for the emergence of a significant influ-ential, wealthy group of national capitalists. Popular consciousness, shaped by the structural order, pervades institutional practice. I came to this conclusion in my comparative analysis of the political economies of Guyana and Trinidad for my dissertation and later my book *The Costs of Regime Survival*. The influential presence of a national capitalist class in the latter and its relative absence in the former explain differences in the ideologies of the two postcolonial regimes.

I enrolled at the University of Guyana in 1969 in the Sociology Department. The university was forged out of the ferment of the nationalist movement. It was established as a deliberate challenge to colonialism by the leadership of the movement's radical anticapitalist, anti-Western wing. Its specified intent was to provide tertiary education to the Guyanese masses. The university began with evening classes conducted at one of the few high schools in the country. Its curriculum was somewhat of a hybrid between the almost exclusively disciplinary focus of British universities and the broad liberal arts approach of those in the United States. Everyone, irrespective of major, was required to take courses in literature, Caribbean history, pure and applied mathematics, economics, and social biology. We were forced to see the connections among multiple disciplines. This approach pervades my scholarship.

Despite the radicalism and anti-Westernism of its nationalist movement, postcolonial Guyana could not escape its colonial legacy. The country's lower strata were divided between a predominantly Indo-Guyanese agro-proletariat and peasant faction of South Asian origin and a predominantly Afro-Guyanese and mixed-creole urban proletariat and rural subsistence peasantry. Guyana's anticolonial (in the true sense of the term) nationalist movement was forged out of an anticapitalist, anti-imperialist, multiracial alliance of these segments. In the late 1940s, the racial (and class) divide between the leaders of the two became congealed in anticolonial practice. But, by 1955, the project of transforming anticolonialism into decolonial praxis became entrapped in a regime of coloniality. The challenge to racial capitalism and its association with Westernism became undermined by the colonial racial order. The support base of the primary avatars of radical decolonization was drawn exclusively from the Asian Indian segment of the population, by virtue of racial identity. The nationalist movement became racialized, opening the pathway to creole nationalist formations tied to the ambivalent anticolonialism of the United States. These formations undergirded the independence movements in the Anglophone Caribbean in their rejection of British colonialism. Like the rest of the British West Indies, Guyana transitioned to independence under the control of Afro-creole middle class functionaries of a rapidly unfolding neocolonial global order, with the support of commercial minorities and white and near-white members of the class of national capitalists. This is the root cause of postcolonial crisis in the region.

The University of Guyana was formed as a decolonizing project. Its faculty took on the mantle of intellectual vanguards in anticolonial, anticapitalist nationalist praxis. And it suffered the identical fate of forms of vanguardism divorced from the structural order. The university and its promise were torn asunder by a student movement that organized into two racial camps. This negated its liberatory promise, as its potential role in the project of decolonization became nullified in a politics of cultural (racial) identity that divided the student body. Many organizational efforts aimed at challenging colonial legacy were neutered by the cultural politics of race.

In 1970, students at University of the West Indies in Saint Augustine, Trinidad, became the pivotal center of a challenge to racial capitalism that eventually spread into a national rebellion against the country's Afro-creole neocolonial regime. The challenge began as support for arrested West Indian students at Sir George Williams (now Concordia) University in Montreal who had joined a Black power movement there and occupied a computer center, which was eventually destroyed. Two groups at the University of Guyana, Ratoon and the Movement against Oppression (MAO), joined in support of the students in Canada and eventually of those engaged in the attempted rebellion against the Trinidad postcolonial regime. As a student at the University of Guyana at the apogee of these movements, I became fully aware of the promise and pitfalls of student activism and of the potential role of the university in the project of liberation. Upon reflection, this was probably the basis of my decision to become a university instructor. Ratoon and MAO laid the groundwork for an eventual even though unsuccessful challenge to Afro-creole nationalism in Guyana, morphing into a movement called the Working People's Alliance directed at re-creating the radical promise of the country's nationalist movement.

Thus, the foundations of my academic career and praxis were laid in my experiences, broadly cast, that preceded a decision to enroll in a master's program in international urbanization and public policy at Clark University in Worcester, Massachusetts. My mentor at Clark, Professor Cynthia Enloe, was working on a comparative project on the relationship among race, ethnicity, and politics in the Global South that had taken her to Guyana. Her work fit perfectly with the fundamental and initial concerns that were to become the basis for my early published work. I followed her advice and urging and enrolled in the Sociology Department of Yale University to do doctoral studies in comparative political sociology with a focus on political economy. These topics framed the work I undertook for my dissertation project and for my first book, *The Costs of Regime Survival: Racial Mobilization, Elite Domination and Control of the State in Guyana and Trinidad*, which was an extension of research I conducted for my master's thesis. I was concerned with the seeming unimportance of ideology in predicting differential outcomes in postcolonial political economy. In comparing Guyana and Trinidad, I concluded that, invariably, postcolonial authority rested in the representatives of the middle strata who were its beneficiaries, however well or poorly the economy performed. This, I began to see, was a global phenomenon. The question for me became, then, how did the representatives of these middle strata maintain their authorial control of national governance? I concluded that it rested in their ability to use foreign exchange transfers from transnational flows to ensure regime survival. They did so by deploying techniques of co-optation, control, and coercion to mobilize support and to suppress and punish challenges and dissent. This came at considerable cost. The distinction between the newly independent Global South and the metropolitan Global North rested in capital accumulation. The Global North allowed for a "social democratic alliance" of capital, labor, and government for the manufacture of loyalty, consent, and consensus. My thesis was developed through comparative analysis of Guyana and Trinidad and Tobago. I conducted research for the project in the immediate postcolonial "national development" phase of independence. Then came the debt crisis, neoliberalism, Thatcherism, and Reaganomics. These were accompanied by the beginnings of the collapse of Eurocommunism and by significant technological breakthroughs in computer, information, communication, and transportation technology. These processes were becoming concretized during the 1980s while I was teaching at the University of California, Berkeley, in the African American Studies Department. They directed a shift in my scholarly attention to a concern with globalization, which precipitated a profound transformation in my thinking. Perhaps the fundamentals of capitalist power were, from the inception, always rooted in global flows. National boundaries served, primarily, the imperative of a division of labor along a global axis. This division was specified in racial/cultural terms. And this explains its reproduction within national boundaries in a fractal-like manner. So, everywhere that they occurred, racialized differences within national boundaries served global capitalist interests through the transnationalization of identities. It all had to do with the axial division of labor, which, following Immanuel Wallerstein, is the foundational condition of capitalist accumulation, nationally and internationally. I began to look at creole identity in the Caribbean in these terms, as a basis of exclusion rather than hybridized inclusion. The creole order seemed to be one of the most important elements in the postcolonial co-optation of the region into the agenda of global capital. It was specified by the developmentalist trope of a promise of upward movement from African savagery to white enlightenment. And the latter conferred upon its holder claims to a global order, unfettered by territorial boundaries. Upward mobility in the creole order enhanced such claims. I began to understand the desire for convergence with the West to be based on aspirations to membership in a globalized order of whiteness. Its realization came to be understood as the condition of escape from the racial division of labor. Under these terms, there could be no national consensus. Citizenship in this global order was always and everywhere conferred by exception and flexibility based on where one was located in the cultural order of whiteness.

Thus began the second phase of my work, articulated through a focus on diaspora, an engagement that led to the development of a PhD in African diaspora studies at Berkeley instituted when I was department chair of African American studies. I saw racialization as elemental for understanding the appeal of development (understood as material accumulation), because the latter offered an escape from a racial order characterized by material (in the broadest sense as capabilities) dispossession. I turned my attention to global flows of people forged out of the imperatives of capital accumulation. Capitalism was always and essentially constituted out of these global flows. Its inextricable ties to racial formation rested in notions of places of origin that sustained the racialized axis in the division of labor everywhere. I conducted research on West Indian presences in the United States to make this point, even though obliquely.

There has been a profound shift in the conditions of global capital accumulation. It has come in the wake of rapid technological developments that are reducing transaction and remuneration costs in the Global South. The shift is changing the axis of the division of labor by catapulting populations previously excluded from accumulation on racial terms into the mainstream of capitalist production and consumption. This has been accompanied by shifts in the centers of accumulation to emerging economies in the Global South and an intensification of global flows of people, finance, technology, and information. It is characterized by forms of transnational class formation. The result has been a "Third Worldization" of the Global North, accompanied by an intensification of racial and class contestations within national borders, as the division of labor loses its racial characteristics. My current work is focused on analyzing the implications of this respecification. It has led me to rethink "the state" as always a global rather than a national formation. The Westphalian form of national authority and sovereignty appears merely to be an instrumentality for the management of global flows for capitalist accumulation. The state reveals itself to have always been a global imposition upon national territories, organizing inflows and outflows of people, finance, resources, technology, and information in keeping with the needs of capital. Such flows have become unhinged from national authority. They have become tied to transnational processes and practices that harness the utility of people and things. These processes and practices challenge or ignore national authority, or conscripts it to the demands of transnational capital. My current work in the Caribbean focuses on the manifestations of this phenomenon, ranging from analysis of the globalized "all inclusive" as a new form of tourism, to the development of new regional formations, to new social forces organized outside the jurisdiction of national authority, to national dependence on these globalized forces, to the failure of projects of transition, to new conditions of precarity. In all of this, what is reflected are the forms capitalism takes in keeping up with new forces of production and with the rapid transformations that these are eliciting. The fundamental question remains, at what point will the forces of capitalism become unsustainable, producing conditions for transformation to noncapitalist forms? In the final analysis, it relates to a quest to understand the failure of the promise of the postcolonial nationalist movement, particularly as articulated in Guyana, my country of birth.

REPRODUCING DOMINATION

REPRODUCING DOMINATION

Percy Hintzen and Theories of the Caribbean Postcolonial State[1]

AARON KAMUGISHA

> Why are relations of domination and conditions of economic exploitation that are little different, and sometimes more severe, than those suffered under colonialism understood and interpreted differently in the postcolonial era? What explains the universal predisposition of those who engaged in and supported anticolonial struggles to accept the conditions of postcolonial repression and exploitation?
> —PERCY HINTZEN, "RETHINKING DEMOCRACY IN THE POSTNATIONALIST STATE"

Reproducing Domination: On the Caribbean Postcolonial State collects key essays on the Caribbean by Percy Hintzen, the foremost political sociologist in Anglophone Caribbean studies. For the past forty years, Hintzen has been one of the most articulate and discerning critics of the postcolonial state in Caribbean scholarship, making highly influential contributions to the study of Caribbean politics, sociology, political economy, and diaspora studies. His work on the postcolonial elites in the region, first given full articulation in his first book, *The Costs of Regime Survival: Racial Mobilization, Elite Domination and Control of the State in Guyana and Trinidad* (1989), is unparalleled, and is the most important guide for persons concerned with tracing the consolidation of power in a new elite in the Anglophone Caribbean following independence in the 1960s. *Reproducing Domination* collects some of Hintzen's most important Caribbean essays over a twenty-five-year period, from 1995 to the present. These works have broadened and deepened his earlier study on the postcolonial elites in *The Costs of Regime Survival* to encompass the entire Anglophone Caribbean; interrogated the formation and consolidation of the postcolonial Caribbean state; and theorized the role of race and ethnicity in Caribbean politics.

The central concern and distinctive contribution of Hintzen's work of the past forty years is captured well in the above epigraph from his landmark essay on democracy in the postindependence Anglophone Caribbean. The interest here is not merely in the well-traveled terrain of studies of structural adjustment, the vulnerabilities of small open economies, and internal class oppression in the Caribbean neocolonial state but in the *meaning* ascribed to these phenomena in the minds of Caribbean citizens. This ability to resemanticize the perspective of anticolonialism, which would have condemned the very same set of conditions as incompatible with Caribbean self-determination and freedom, and the uncovering of this ideological puzzle mark Hintzen's signal contribution to Caribbean social and political thought. His body of work contains compelling contributions to Caribbean social theory through his distinctive assessment of creolization, Caribbean political economy, and globalization, and at its most revelatory, through his particularly discerning critique of the Anglophone Caribbean postcolonial state. Hintzen's work represents the finest response by an Anglophone Caribbeanist to the critical questioning of the postcolonial state advanced by Frantz Fanon in *The Wretched of the Earth*, giving his work immense value two generations after the advent of independence.

Anglophone Caribbean radical social and political thought in the era post the collapse of the Grenada revolution can be conceived as occupying two overlapping traditions of thought. The first tradition, with its institutional center the Department of Government at the University of the West Indies, Mona campus, developed an arsenal of theories committed to an interrogation of the character of the Caribbean postcolonial state. This work resulted in a conceptual terminology, including "plantation society," "clientelism," "false decolonization," "peripheral capitalism," and "hegemonic dissolution," that has become widely utilized by Caribbean scholars and been highly influential for those interested in comprehending the nature of the Caribbean postcolonial state.[2] This interest in creating a theory of the Anglophone Caribbean postcolonial state emerged prior to flag independence in the form of the New World Group, but it was sharpened and radicalized by the emergent crises of the late colonial and newly independent Caribbean polities, from Jamaica to Guyana, and the decisive turn to socialism of the Caribbean Left between 1968 and 1983. Another set of theorists, located within both regional and transnational circles and emergent since the turn of the twenty-first century, have been more consciously concerned with theorizing citizenship and its denials within the Caribbean state, not only expanding previous understandings of the character of the colonial and postcolonial state but posing searching questions about the limits of human freedom under coloniality. This focus on citizenship has been influenced by many theoretical sources including critical race theory and African diaspora studies, with the work of Caribbean feminists, in brilliant depictions of the heteronormative and sexist impulses of the Caribbean state, constituting the leading work that has exposed the realities of the coloniality of citizenship in the Caribbean (Alexander 1994, 6–23; Robinson 2000, 1–27). Neither of these traditions exists in isolation from the other, although the shift toward theorizing Caribbean neocolonial citizenship is in part influenced by the decline in Caribbean socialism and state-centered projects of liberation following the collapse of the Grenada revolution.

The work of Percy Hintzen represents a moment of convergence of both traditions. *The Costs of Regime Survival* (1989) is a rare *comparative* study by a social scientist of power and subordination in two Anglophone states, while the ethnographic account in *West Indian in the West* (2001c) advances an argument about racialization and community formation in a previously little-studied location of the Caribbean diaspora. Between these two monographs, and since then, Hintzen has published several discerning essays on the contemporary Caribbean, a number of which constitute this collection. Hintzen's work seeks to comprehend why Caribbean nationalist discourse resulted in "even more egregious forms of domination, super-exploitation, and dependency" (Hintzen 1997, 48). This reading of the postcolonial Caribbean suggests that it cannot be understood without an appreciation of the interplay between cultural and political frames of reference, identity, and legitimacy constructs.

ELITE DOMINATION IN THE CONTEMPORARY ANGLOPHONE CARIBBEAN

The recounting of preindependence Anglophone Caribbean nationalism is crucial in any attempt to formulate a history of the present, for the class ideologies established in this period, the bases of their legitimacy constructs, and the forms of regimentation introduced at that time still haunt the Caribbean today. Here, Hintzen draws a distinction between anticolonial thought and struggle—a sentiment present in the masses and the radicalized intelligentsia—and "Afro-creole nationalism," the mobilizing ideology of the Caribbean middle classes. Afro-creole nationalism is here seen as a convoluted mixture of Garveyism and Black consciousness, Fabian socialism, twentieth-century trade unionism, and recognition of the shifting relationship between the colonizing power of Britain and the new superpower, the United States; all filtering into the ideology of the Black middle classes (Hintzen 2001a). The middle-class participation in the nationalist movement, complicated and influenced by a variety of sources as it was, was also a response to colonialism's inability to maintain power and fully accommodate the material and self-governing demands of this class. The middle-class critique of colonialism was a contestation over whites' right to rule, making the nationalist claim that "the colonial condition of inequality and white superiority was artificial and imposed. Once removed, a 'natural state' of equality would assert itself." Anticolonial nationalism, a broad-based sentiment encompassing large parts of the population, must thus be distinguished from Afro-creole nationalism, the ideology of the middle classes. By Hintzen's reckoning, "anticolonial nationalism was, first and foremost, an expression of the general will for equality. This expression was transformed by petit bourgeois ideology into demands for sovereignty and development" (Hintzen 2001b, 105–21). The poverty of creole nationalism is that it "left intact the racial order underpinning colonialism while providing the ideological basis for national 'coherence.' It left unchallenged notions of a 'natural' racial hierarchy" (Hintzen 2004, 113).

Colonial and postcolonial bureaucratic formations are of considerable import here, as the wresting of control of these away from the colonizer in the immediate preindependence period opened up pathways for postindependence regime consolidation. The transfer of this bureaucratic structure, with little interrogation of its underlying premises, allowed Caribbean states to gain control over revenue-generating activities, the surpluses of which were now under their direction and which grew with postcolonial state expansion (Hintzen 1993, 13).[3] State bureaucracies (and potential state largesse) also expanded further with the new responsibility for defense and foreign affairs, which allowed governing elites to engage in "violent coercive retaliation against those challenging their authority and legitimacy" and avail themselves of "direct access to international resources necessary for regime survival" (Hintzen 1993). The middle classes' basis of power in unions and political parties after the 1930s rebellions and the social and cultural capital they possessed facilitated their ascendancy to the head of the nationalist movements. In Hintzen's reading: "[B]y the time adult suffrage was introduced . . . the lower class was firmly organized into political and labour bureaucracies dominated by middle-class leadership. Where they were not, Britain showed extreme reluctance to move the constitutional process along to full independence" (Hintzen 1993). The Anglophone Caribbean postcolonial state was, in part, a gift of the British to the Caribbean middle classes, who were seen as possessing the social and cultural capital, and commitment to Western capitalism, that made them fit to rule.

The collapse of the West Indies Federation resulted in the advent of independence in the 1960s for a number of the territories within the Anglophone Caribbean and the arrival of associated statehood for others.[4] The moment of independence was simultaneously a moment of recolonization, as "all the leaders who came to power during the sixties did so while announcing their commitment to a moderate ideological position and to a pro-capitalist program of development for their respective countries" (Hintzen 2001a, 200). Further, the United States' post–World War II dominance resulted in the annulment of the possibility of any authentic decolonization within Anglophone Caribbean states. The postcolonial elites' demand for "sovereignty and development," allied to an "industrialization by invitation" developmental strategy, led to discourses of modernization taking center stage in debates about the future of the Caribbean state. Nationalism demanded the local utilization of surpluses previously appropriated by metropolitan imperialism. Its leaders' disinterest in linking colonial abjection to capitalism meant that development programs predicated upon capitalist modernization could gain hegemony without a contest. The decline of the radical movements of the late 1960s and 1970s that had contested this postindependence neocolonial condition, and the rise of an even more predatory neoliberal globalization, has meant that the postcolonial elite's dream of the equality of nation-states and its liberal ideal of the equality of citizens within Caribbean nation-states looks more like a nightmare than anything else:

> Once the condition of equality becomes asserted in the postcolonial context, everything associated with postcolonial inequality is rendered irrelevant and subject to different interpretations, irrespective of the objective conditions. What once was exploitation becomes sacrifice. What was domination becomes functional organization. What was privilege becomes reward. What was discrimination becomes strategic allocation. These transformations are explained by the logic of equality embedded in the meaning of nationalism. Presuppositions of postcolonial equality become the force driving predispositions toward the acceptance of conditions of extreme inequality. (Hintzen 2001b, 106)

In the late colonial period, Euro-American modernization was advanced as the only future for the region, with Western modernity becoming the litmus test of equality (Hintzen 1997, 63). For a Caribbean elite that sought to define itself on the standards of a global bourgeois class, this meant adopting the consumption patterns of the West and acquiring its cultural capital—a surrender to neocolonialism critiqued by every Caribbean radical movement from the New World Group to the Grenadian Revolution (Hintzen 1997, 70). Today, to critique the desire for those tastes risks incomprehension, as "such tastes are no longer understood as 'foreign,' 'white' or 'colonial.' They are the 'styles' and 'tastes' of development, and *modernity's prerequisites for equality*" (Hintzen 1997, 70).

What, then, does this mean for attempts to theorize the Anglophone Caribbean postcolonial state? To trace the rise of the Afro-creole elites, as Hintzen does, is to pose serious questions about the nature of democracy and citizenship in polities still structured in dominance. It reveals again the deep limitations of the "cultural citizenship" offered (often hesitantly) to the postcolonial masses by the middle-class elites, a citizenship often bereft of the revolutionary potential of anticolonial nationalism after it has gone through the organizational rationalities of the middle class. Like all of the most pervasive systems of power, which operate by rendering their guises invisible, "creole culture serves to hide a racialized division of labor and a racialized allocation of power and privilege" (Hintzen 2002a, 493). Race, color, and culture, and the bifurcations they cause in class formations in the postcolony, suggest that the Caribbean postcolonial state is a racial state as much as it is simultaneously a neocolony that expresses its political-economic interests based on the hegemony of a global elite's norms and values (Goldberg 2002).[5]

For Hintzen, creole nationalism is the cultural ideology that legitimates middle-class domination in the Anglophone Caribbean. Claims to belonging and citizenship in the Anglophone Caribbean postcolonial state have for two generations turned on arguments about creolization. First popularized as a theory of Caribbean culture by Edward Kamau Brathwaite in his *The Development of Creole Society in Jamaica*, creolization has become *the* theory of Caribbean multiculturalism—but with proponents unwilling to subject it to the same critique levied against liberal multiculturalism in its North American guises (Brathwaite 1971; Bannerji 2000). Brathwaite's work was a creative response to both the social stratification of M. G. Smith and the anomie of Orlando Patterson, perceiving instead society as a complex whole—riven by force, subversion, and abduction, but despite itself also constituted through intercultural understanding, style, and possibility.[6] A generation after Brathwaite's intervention, and with the culturalist turn in Caribbean scholarship, creolization would become merely a theory of Caribbean cultural expressivity and creativity, emphasizing the latter of Kamau's take on the clash of African and European cultures in the New World—"cruel, but also creative" (Brathwaite 1971, 307; Baron and Cara 2011). With the decline of movements and scholarship firmly tied to uncovering the political economy of Caribbean racism, creolization became merely a sign of the multicultural Caribbean. However, for Hintzen, while it may well be that "to be 'Caribbean' is to be 'creolized' and within this space are accommodated all who, at any one time, constitute a (semi)permanent core of Caribbean society" (Hintzen 2002b, 92), creole identity, far from being a harmonious multicultural nirvana of mixed identities, is instead one thoroughly and unashamedly colonial:

> Creole discourse has been the bonding agent of Caribbean society. It has functioned in the interest of the powerful, whether represented by a colonialist or nationalist elite. It is the identific glue that bonds the different, competing, and otherwise mutually exclusive interests contained within Caribbean society. It paved the way for accommodation of racialized discourses of difference upon which rested the legitimacy of colonial power and exploitation. (Hintzen 2002a, 477)

The colonial provenances of "creoleness" are to be found not only in the power relations it reinscribes but in the centrality of European and African culture to its frame of reference. Thus:

> The combination of racial and cultural hybridity determines location in between the extremes. For the European, this pertains to the degree of cultural and racial pollution. It implies a descent from civilization. For the African, creolization implies ascent made possible by the acquisition of European cultural forms and by racial miscegenation whose extensiveness is signified by color. This, in essence, is the meaning of creolization. It is a process that stands at the center of constructs of Caribbean identity. (Hintzen 2002a, 478)

Here we see again the limitations of the criticism of colonialism fashioned by the Caribbean nationalist elites. At times, Africa occupied a significant space in their thoughts, but this was invariably "associated with the freedom and transcendence denied the colonized" rather than a repudiation of its image as a "space for exploitation and for the exercise of paternalism" (Hintzen 1997, 55). The reproduction of domination onto those now considered to *be* Black, namely the poor, or in Jamaican parlance "the sufferers," who are the newly condemned of the Caribbean, could thus be facilitated without contradiction by the postcolonial Afro-creole elites.

Hintzen's work allows us to theorize "creole neocolonialism" as the operative condition of a Caribbean wedded still to anti-Blackness and comfortable with colonial arrangements of power. It represents a specifically Caribbean contribution to the scholarship now grouped under the title "critical race theory," a Fanonian interpretation of contemporary Caribbean experience and a discerning extension of the field of study on racial capitalism.[7] *Reproducing Domination* resumes the conversation between Caribbean thinkers and their global counterparts on colonialism, capitalism, and the future of humanity begun by Hintzen's predecessors Frantz Fanon, C. L. R. James, Claudia Jones, Eric Williams, and Walter Rodney, and, given the recent global resurgence of interest in elite ownership patterns and their relationship to power and governance, it will be widely celebrated and appreciated.

NOTES

1. This introduction draws on my reading of Percy Hintzen's work in *Beyond Coloniality: Citizenship and Freedom in the Caribbean Intellectual Tradition* (Kamugisha 2019, 41–44).

2. I am thinking here particularly of the work of George Beckford (1971, 7–22); Carl Stone (1980, 91–110); Lloyd Best (1967, 13–34); Trevor Munroe (1972); Brian Meeks (1993, 124–43);

Norman Girvan (1976, 200–228); Clive Thomas (1984); and Paget Henry (1985). See also Kamugisha 2013.

3. Hintzen cites Max Weber's well-known observation that "once it is established, bureaucracy is among the social structures which are the hardest to destroy," with clear resonances for the Caribbean's contemporary predicament.

4. Jamaica (1962), Trinidad (1962), Barbados (1966), and Guyana (1966) achieved their independence in this decade, while associated state status, which meant local self-government with Britain retaining control of foreign affairs and defense for the territory, came to Antigua, Dominica, Grenada, and Saint Lucia in 1967. Full independence came to most of these territories in the 1970s and early 1980s: Antigua (1981), the Bahamas (1973), Belize (1981), Dominica (1978), Grenada (1974), Saint Kitts and Nevis (1983), Saint Lucia (1979), and Saint Vincent (1979).

5. On the racial state, see Goldberg 2002. This global elite is hegemonically white but far from solely so, as it is perfectly willing to admit members who possess European cultural capital and a neoliberal capitalist ethos, or what Walter Rodney, among others, once called the "comprador elite of the Third World."

6. For a longer reading of Brathwaite, see Kamugisha 2019, 81–85.

7. See the epilogue to this volume by Charisse Burden-Stelly.

BIBLIOGRAPHY

Alexander, M. Jacqui. 1994. "Not Just (Any) *Body* Can Be a Citizen: The Politics of Law, Sexuality and Postcoloniality in Trinidad and Tobago and the Bahamas." *Feminist Review*, no. 48 (Autumn): 5–23.

Bannerji, Himani. 2000. *The Dark Side of the Nation: Essays on Multiculturalism, Nationalism and Gender*. Toronto: Canadian Scholars' Press.

Baron, Robert, and Ana C. Cara, eds. 2011. *Creolization as Cultural Creativity*. Jackson: University Press of Mississippi.

Beckford, George. 1971. "Plantation Society." *Savacou*, no. 5 (June): 7–22.

Best, Lloyd. 1967. "Independent Thought and Caribbean Freedom." *New World Quarterly* 3, no. 4: 13–34.

Brathwaite, Edward Kamau. 1971. *The Development of Creole Society in Jamaica, 1770–1820*. Oxford: Oxford University Press.

Girvan, Norman. 1976. "Expropriation and Compensation from a Third World Perspective." In *Corporate Imperialism: Conflict and Expropriation*, by Norman Girvan, 200–228. New York: Monthly Review Press.

Girvan, Norman. 1984. "Swallowing the IMF Medicine in the Seventies." In *The Political Economy of Development and Underdevelopment*, edited by Charles K. Wilber, 169–81. New York: Random House.

Goldberg, David Theo. 2002. *The Racial State*. Malden, MA: Blackwell.

Henry, Paget. 1985. *Peripheral Capitalism and Underdevelopment in Antigua*. New Brunswick, NJ: Transaction Publishers.

Hintzen, Percy C. 1989. *The Costs of Regime Survival: Racial Mobilization, Elite Domination and Control of the State in Guyana and Trinidad*. Cambridge: Cambridge University Press.

Hintzen, Percy C. 1993. "Democracy and Middle-Class Domination in the West Indies." In *Democracy in the West Indies: Myths and Realities,* edited by Carlene J. Edie, 9–24. Boulder, CO: Westview Press.

Hintzen, Percy C. 1997. "Reproducing Domination: Identity and Legitimacy Constructs in the West Indies." *Social Identities* 3, no. 1: 47–75.

Hintzen, Percy C. 2001a. "Afro-Creole Nationalism as Elite Domination: The English-Speaking West Indies." In *Foreign Policy and the Black (Inter)National Interest,* edited by Charles P. Henry, 185–218. Albany: State University of New York Press.

Hintzen, Percy C. 2001b. "Rethinking Democracy in the Postnationalist State." In *New Caribbean Thought: A Reader,* edited by Brian Meeks and Folke Lindahl, 104–26. Mona, Jamaica: University of the West Indies Press.

Hintzen, Percy C. 2001c. *West Indian in the West: Self-Representations in an Immigrant Community.* New York: New York University Press.

Hintzen, Percy C. 2002a. "The Caribbean: Race and Creole Ethnicity." In *A Companion to Racial and Ethnic Studies,* edited by David Theo Goldberg and John Solomos, 475–94. Malden, MA: Blackwell.

Hintzen, Percy C. 2002b. "Race and Creole Ethnicity in the Caribbean." In *Questioning Creole: Creolisation Discourses in Caribbean Culture,* edited by Verene A. Shepherd and Glen L. Richards, 92–110. Kingston, Jamaica: Ian Randle Publishers.

Hintzen, Percy C. 2004. "Creoleness and Nationalism in Guyanese Anticolonialism and Postcolonial Formation." *Small Axe* 8, no. 1 (March): 106–22.

Kamugisha, Aaron. 2013. *Caribbean Political Thought: Theories of the Post-Colonial State.* Kingston, Jamaica: Ian Randle Publishers.

Kamugisha, Aaron. 2019. *Beyond Coloniality: Citizenship and Freedom in the Caribbean Intellectual Tradition.* Bloomington: Indiana University Press.

Meeks, Brian. 1993. "The Political Moment in Jamaica: The Dimensions of Hegemonic Dissolution." In *Radical Caribbean: From Black Power to Abu Bakr,* by Brian Meeks, 124–43. Mona, Jamaica: University of the West Indies Press.

Munroe, Trevor. 1972. *The Politics of Constitutional Decolonization: Jamaica, 1944–62.* Mona, Jamaica: Institute of Social and Economic Research.

Robinson, Tracy. 2000. "Fictions of Citizenship, Bodies without Sex: The Production and Effacement of Gender in the Law." *Small Axe,* no. 7 (March): 1–27.

Stone, Carl. 1980. *Democracy and Clientelism in Jamaica.* New Brunswick, NJ: Transaction Publishers.

Thomas, Clive Y. 1984. *The Rise of the Authoritarian State in Peripheral Societies.* New York: Monthly Review Press.

Chapter 1

REPRODUCING DOMINATION IDENTITY AND LEGITIMACY CONSTRUCTS IN THE WEST INDIES

PERCY C. HINTZEN

ANTICOLONIAL NATIONALISM

The complex of ideas that has had the most significant and profound impact on twentieth-century West Indian political economy is that contained in the ideology of anticolonial nationalism. This form of nationalism became the basis for the rejection of colonialism and for the development of a political strategy for overthrowing colonial domination. It has also served as the basis for legitimizing the transformation of the political economy in the postcolonial era. The blueprint for such transformation was fashioned and formulated by an ascendant anticolonial elite and was justified on the grounds of an argument for self-determination, racial equality, and developmental transformation.

Embedded in nationalist discourse were two distinct sets of constructs. One was directed at the intensification, clarification, and crystallization of identity. These are what I term "identity constructs." The other was directed at the legitimation of forms and structures of postcolonial political authority. These I choose to call "legitimacy constructs." Idioms of identity encoded in nationalist constructs came to be integrally linked to notions of "self-determination." These idioms became the basis for organizing and channeling the participatory experiences of those engaged in contesting the colonial order. They also became the basis for the "invention" of the "imagined political communities" (Anderson 1983, 15) that were to be the independent nations of the British West Indies.

Political parties in the Caribbean became the organizational (power) instrument through which the "images" of the new nations were hegemonically imposed. Democratic participation and developmental transformation emerged as legitimizing constructs authenticating the authorial power of an educated elite. This elite came to be vested with the legitimate right to create the new postcolonial society. Such a right was justified through what French philosopher Michel Foucault terms a regime of "political rationality" (Foucault 1979; Dreyfus and Rabinow 1983, 128–42). It was exercised through the postcolonial state as the "proper subject matter of [a] new technical and administrative knowledge" (Dreyfus and Rabinow 1983, 137). In other words, the technical and administrative knowledge possessed by this new elite came to be employed, through the mechanisms of the state, in the exercise of what Foucault calls "disciplinary power" (1979, chap. 7).

The language of liberation is central to the ideology of anticolonial nationalism. Explicit in this formulation is liberation from domination, with colonialism becoming *the* universal metaphor for all forms of domination. Colonialism became, as well, a symbolic reference for poverty and want. Anticolonialism came to signify, then, liberation from domination, poverty, and want. As it turns out, the nationalist discourse was not, however, a "narrative of liberation."[1] Historically, postcolonial political economies have failed to reflect the ideological promise of self-determination, development, and de facto democratic participation. The promise of liberation has failed to materialize in postcolonial social constructions. Instead, colonialism has been replaced by even more egregious forms of domination, super-exploitation, and dependency.

Embedded in notions of self-determination in nationalist discourse was the idea of sovereignty and the autonomy of the state. The semiotic codes contained in anticolonial nationalism (with references to liberation) were central to efforts by the nationalist elite to capture control of the governing institutions and share state power with nongovernmental elites from the international and domestic sectors. Once in control of governmental institutions, state power was employed by these elites for the intensification, deepening, and widening of their access to economic, social, and cultural capital. Thus, the power of the state was employed for the accumulation of wealth, income, status, and prestige.

Nationalism as an ideology has shown itself to be quite amenable to those whose interests rest in the ownership and control of economic capital. As a construct, it has accommodated the changing technical and social conditions of economic capital without losing its symbolic power. These changing conditions have accompanied the demise of colonialism. They have been incorporated into a newly emergent postindependence neocolonial formation. What this means is that nationalism has been accompanied by the maintenance and expansion of relations of affinity with dominant class actors internationally, particularly those in the northern industrial countries. This includes relations with elites in the colonial states against which the discourse of nationalism was directed. The focus of new relations of affinity was the United States, where there has been an undisputed concentration of ownership of economic capital during the post–World War II era. Historically, the United States played a central role in maintaining the anticolonial credentials of nationalist elites. It participated in a discursive challenge to European colonialism during the Franklin D. Roosevelt administration. This challenge helped to cement US relations with leaders of nationalist movements fighting European colonialism throughout the world. The position of the United States as an ally in efforts at national liberation freed subsequent relations between that country and the newly emergent nations from the taint of colonial imposition. This, more than anything else, allowed the transfer of affinities from colonial Europe to the United States in the postcolonial era. The anticolonial credentials of the United States allowed nationalist elites to retain symbols of self-determination as the driving force in their ideologies while establishing neocolonial forms of international relations with the new dominant power in the international arena. This was very much the case for the English-speaking West Indies (Fraser 1994).

Domestically, nationalism served to authenticate the position of dominance of the educated elite. The social and cultural assets possessed by this elite came to be elevated to a privileged position in the social hierarchy. It was power and privilege that created the conditions for these assets to be converted into social and cultural capital. Along with economic and symbolic capital, Pierre Bourdieu (1977, 1984) has identified social and cultural capital as the basis for location in the class structure in any society.[2]

Nationalism, as symbolic capital, was employed by this emergent postcolonial elite to authenticate its cultural style as the dominant form, to legitimize its position of dominance in the social hierarchy, and to legitimize its preferential access to the economic surplus. It is through the appropriation of symbolic capital that this ascendant elite was able to formulate, fashion, and hegemonically impose nationalist ideology as the dominant ideology. Such appropriation was made possible when this elite seized the opportunity to "define the situation" during a period of crisis in colonial political economy.

THE REPRODUCTION OF DOMINATION
IN THE WEST INDIES

The Structural Context

The Middle-Strata Elite

Pierre Bourdieu has made a trenchant criticism of the structuralist approach in social sciences. At the critical center of such an approach is a reification of the "objectifying glance" of the social scientist (Bourdieu 1984). His criticism is particularly relevant to the frameworks employed for analyzing and understanding the political economy of the West Indies. Evident in analytical constructs such as "plantation society," "plural society," and those emerging out of neo-Marxist formulations of class employed in "West Indian" social science is the notion that social behavior is confined to or "determined" by objectively observed "social facts." The latter are considered to exist independently of human volition and agency.[3] There is an alternative approach to the understanding of social behavior. Social reality may be considered to constitute a complex of "imagined" social groups, aggregates, and categories that are socially manufactured.[4] Those employing this framework see such groups, aggregates, and categories as products of cognitive constructs. Even though understood in essentialist terms, they are not "real" in any sui generis sense. One needs to be careful, nonetheless, lest such an approach leads to a disentanglement altogether from social structure, objectively defined, or to a phenomenological challenge to any notion that social reality can be apprehended (Bourdieu 1984).

Cognitions and objective social facts must be considered to be integrally related. Like Marx, Bourdieu sees the core of the latter to be objective social classes in which individuals are located and that "constrain and circumscribe volition" (J. Turner 1991, 508). At the same time, class positions are understood interpretively. These interpretations are at the root of social action. Ultimately, for dominant groups, they reflect objective class interests. Such interests are protected and advanced against the interpretive actions of others in different class positions. At the root of such interpretations are cognitive constructs that constitute the "image of their communion" (Anderson 1983, 15) and of the communion of others. In this particular context, such constructs constitute the ideologies that legitimate class interests and the interpretive actions associated with these interests (Bourdieu 1977, 21; Bourdieu 1984).

Social classes are the social groups organized around competition for the various forms of capital defined earlier. Thus, class interests can be conceptualized as the resources of economic, social, cultural, and symbolic capital available to a particular social class. It makes considerable analytical sense to consider the primacy of economic capital (primarily international) as reflective of the reality of West Indian social formation. This leads to formulations that take into account the relationship to the means of production. As such, those who own and control the means of production are grouped together in the upper strata of the bourgeoisie. Those who do not own or control the means of production and who rely exclusively on the sale of their labor power or on noncapitalist subsistence production are grouped into the lower strata of the proletariat, semiproletarian "segmented" labor, and subsistence peasantry. In between are the middle strata who own very little economic capital but who are neither proletarian labor nor engaged in subsistence activity as a primary occupation. In terms of their composition, these three strata are permeable and in constant flux. They have no inherent integrity. This is true even of the factions that make up these strata. In reality, these factions resemble social aggregates or categories.[5]

Almost universally in postcolonial society there have emerged these intermediate middle-strata groups between proletarian workers and peasants on the one hand and elites directly connected to international capital and its administration on the other.[6] In their historical production and reproduction, these strata came to constitute

> owners of medium and small enterprises, medium and small farm-
> ers, merchants and artisans ... [and] administrative officials, military
> people, teachers, other intellectuals, and salaried employees at various
> levels ... [as well as] lawyers, medical doctors, writers, artists and so
> forth who function as independent enterprisers or freelancers. (Rude-
> beck 1991, 33–34)

The link among these disparate groups was and continues to be the common beneficence of development and modernization in the colonial and postcolonial eras. The privilege and benefits that members of these groups enjoy derive from their "capacity and willingness to rationalize their economic and social behavior along Western lines" (Galli 1991, 2). They are the modernizers with "government officials, military, [and] international bureaucrats" among them playing a strategic economic and political role for national and international economic capitalists (Galli 1991, 2).

At any one time, factions of these middle strata can be engaged in collective defense of their specific interests (social, cultural, economic, symbolic). For the most part, however, there tends, except during periods of mass mobiliza-tion, to be a relative absence of collective class behavior *across* factions of the middle strata. In terms of their interests, there is little that is common among the various segments except in a broad economic sense. What was common among the factions in the colonial West Indies was the quest to challenge the colonial power and the quest for or in defense of their own interests.

This chapter examines the process through which these middle strata transformed themselves into the dominant social group in postcolonial political economies. The eventual composition of the dominant groups that succeeded the colonial elite or its local representatives came to differ over time and place largely in response to differences in the technical and social conditions of capitalist production. Changes over time within a historically changing social formation created the conditions for the reconstitution of elite social formations, the emergence of new structures of social organization, and the reformulation of cognitions.

Elite Formation in Twentieth-Century West Indian Political Economy
During the twentieth century in the English-speaking West Indies, the strategic importance of the middle strata increased with the growth of state administration and with the infusion of foreign economic capital. New investments were made in large-scale plantation agroproduction, agro-industry, mining, assembly and packaging operations, refining, import substitution, and the like. A new concentration on development planning and opportunities opening up for domestic private sector activity in the retailing, service, and assembly and packaging industries reinforced the growing strategic importance of members of these strata. This increasing importance combined with a growing demand for functionaries at the intermediate levels of colonial bureaucracy to lay the groundwork for leaders of these middle strata to mount a successful challenge to colonial domination.

The challenge to colonial domination emanated from those factions of the middle strata that had little access to economic capital. Characteristically, they worked as clerical and bureaucratic employees of the state and in the private sector. Their members came to constitute the educated and skilled of the country. They were the salaried urban workers and professionals within the middle strata.

Under colonialism, the construction of identities was forged out of a hegemonically imposed discourse of race that allocated historically constructed and racially identified groups to exclusive socioeconomic sectors of the political economy. In most of the English-speaking West Indies, three distinct groups were historically produced over time. "Blacks" were constituted from the descendants of the enslaved population transported from West Africa. "Whites" comprised the groups of plantation owners, colonial officials, former indentures, small-scale peasant landholders, and workers who came, primarily, from Britain. "Coloreds" were those whose ancestry could be traced to both the "Black" and the "white" group. There were some deviations from this pattern. The most notable were in Guyana and Trinidad, where indentureship replaced the system of slavery. Indentureship brought with it groups who came to be racially identified by their regions of origin. Most important were the "East Indians," followed by "Portuguese" and "Chinese." In Trinidad, a preexisting group of whites comprising persons with origins in Spain (the former colonial power) and France (via Haiti) was historically differentiated from the British colonial whites in colonial reproduction. In these two colonies, the group of domestic entrepreneurs came, almost exclusively, from this population of "local" whites (Spanish, French, and Portuguese in Trinidad and Portuguese in Guyana). In the latter half of the twentieth century, middle-strata East Indians became associated, also, with the entrepreneurial class. In Trinidad, the white entrepreneurial group was joined by a small but important group of Lebanese and Syrians. Local whites and East Indians came to be heavily represented also in professional occupational groups.

Emerging in the historical process of identity construction in all the colonies was a "colored" middle strata that had become distinguished from other racially defined intermediary groups. A "Black" group was located somewhat lower in the hierarchy of the middle strata. The difference between the two rested in differential access to social and cultural capital by virtue of their "biological distance" from the colonial elite. The colored group enjoyed considerably more access out of its claims to an ancestry that was "mixed" between European and African. The Blacks could make no such claim. Thus, in its social reproduction, the characteristic pattern assumed by colonial society in the West Indies was a preponderance of Blacks in the lower strata, a racialized hierarchy of Blacks, coloreds, and whites occupying middle-strata positions, and white exclusivity in the upper strata. This was true, with minor modifications, for all of the colonies except Guyana and Trinidad.

By the third decade of the twentieth century, relations of affinity began to develop between the two racialized communities of Blacks and coloreds in the middle strata. This was the outcome, quite possibly, of increasing access to social and cultural capital by the Black group as a result of opportunities opening up in the wake of the changing social and technical conditions of colonial capitalist production. It led, eventually, to the forging of a common social identity, idiomatically identified in both racial and class terms. A number of factors combined in this reformulation of their identity.

Middle-strata coloreds had managed to gain financial security and class standing just below the white elites and subelites even before the abolition of slavery in the third decade of the nineteenth century. However, they found the barrier of race and Anglo-Saxon ethnic exclusivism impenetrable.

Access to higher incomes and to economic capital allowed an increasing number of those in the middle strata to meet the qualifications to vote and to hold elective office under electoral franchises that were limited by income and property qualifications. By the second decade of the twentieth century, there were enough voting members from the middle strata to elect from their own group a few representatives to legislative and local government bodies in their respective colonies. Despite these gains, power continued to rest with a colonial administration headed by a British governor and directed by the British Colonial Office. In Barbados, Bermuda, and the Bahamas, this power was shared somewhat with the remnants of a local white English planter class.

The increase in the numbers of middle-strata voters resulted more from agitation against the colonial government to reduce property and income qualifications than from increased abilities to meet preexisting ones. This reflected the greater strategic importance of the middle strata for the maintenance of colonial order, in purely functional terms. At the same time, colonial society, dependent as it was upon a racial discourse for its legitimacy, could not accommodate the incorporation of a non-European colonized group. That became quickly evident in the refusal of the colonial governing elite to allow those elected to office from the middle strata any effective say in governance. The reformulation of the terms of election to allow their representation, as it turned out, was a mere palliative aimed at co-optation. This left them little option but to contest the colonial order and to agitate for independence from Britain. The effort was led by professionals, intellectuals, and nonproletarian workers who embarked upon the organization of nationalist movements. This was the historical context within which occurred the fusion of Black and colored middle-strata groups and the reformulation of their respective social identities.

Colonial Crisis and Elite Formation

A "crisis of colonialism" created the conditions for the ascendance of the middle strata into positions of dominance in the West Indies. The crisis was evident in a prolonged international recession during the 1920s and 1930s. The recession fueled a developing sociocultural crisis in which "the complementarity between the requirements of the state apparatus and the occupational system, on the one hand, and the interpreted needs and legitimate expectations of members of society, on the other, is disturbed" (Habermas 1973, 48). The result was a negation of the legitimacy of the colonial order.

The negation of colonial legitimacy created the historical conditions for the middle strata to seize authorial power. Professionals and intellectuals within these strata used the economic crisis to formulate an ideology of transformation. Embedded in this ideology were notions of democratic participation and sovereignty proposed as solutions to the sociocultural crisis that undermined the legitimacy of colonial rule. These solutions were proposed within and constrained by the realities of colonial domination and colonial social structure. Such realities dictated the imperative of accommodating the privileged position of capitalist forms of production. The solutions had to be formulated within the context of the valorization of European "taste" and European symbolic forms, these being the bases of claims to authority by the middle-strata elite. Such claims were being made even while challenging the legitimacy of colonial authority.

The symbiosis between colonialism and white supremacy created fertile ground for a challenge to be mounted against the former by rejecting the latter.[7] The semiotics of colonialism, and its legitimacy, were firmly rooted in a discourse of racial superiority and inferiority. Once challenged on racial grounds, colonialism loses its legitimacy. The use of the racial idiom was, thus, the sole effective means of bringing together the lower- and middle-strata social groups.

The appropriation of symbolic capital from the colonizers allowed the professional and intellectual strata to fashion and impose a legitimizing ideology of anticolonialism in the West Indies. The defining characteristic of this ideology involved the construction of an Afro-creole identity. Afro-creole nationalism became the instrument of anticolonial mobilization. Once imposed as an ideology, it became the symbolic condition of power.

The social capital derived from their strategic position in the colonial political economy provided the middle strata with access to the material conditions of power. Symbolic capital provided the means of formulating Afro-creole nationalism. It was through the combination of social and symbolic capital that factions within these strata catapulted themselves to positions of domination by legitimizing their claims to authorial power.

White Supremacy and Afro-Creole Identity

The problem faced by colonialism was the need to integrate the economic activities of the colonial and colonized populations under extreme conditions of economic exploitation. The dilemma was resolved in colonialism's racially constructed reality. Race, as an organizing idiom, became the centerpiece of colonial social formation and the primary element in identity construction. The idiom of race assumed primacy in the dominant discourse of colonialism legitimizing a social reality historically produced out of mythic constructs of white supremacy. Social constructions of class, based on possession of social, cultural, economic, and symbolic capital by segments of the colonized population, somewhat modified an exclusive reliance on racial discourse. This modification was the basis for the stratification of the colonial dominant class as much as it was for the stratification of groups of the dominated colonized population.[8] Racial constructions of colonial society produced differences in participatory experiences and differences in "core cultural patterns" among the various groups. These differences provided meaning to perpetual efforts directed at contesting the hegemonically imposed colonial order. Such contestations led eventually to mobilization against colonial domination.

Afro-creole identity received clarification, sustenance, and support from ideological currents emanating out of challenges to white supremacy throughout the non-European world during the first half of the twentieth century.[9] Among these historical developments were the Pan-African movement, the new understandings of Black nationalism that emanated from Booker T. Washington through his institute in Tuskegee, Alabama, and the emergence of Marcus Garvey and his Universal Negro Improvement Association.

These were manifestations of a new development of racial consciousness on an international scale that continued unabated during the third decade of the century. In 1927, the League against Imperialism was formed, followed, in 1931, by the League of Coloured Peoples (LCP). These two organizations were represented as the "non-white counterforce to the League of Nations." They were formed as a reaction to the latter's steadfast refusal to address the issue of racial equality in its charter and deliberations (Lauren 1988, 76–101). Branches of the LCP began to show up throughout the West Indies.

There was also the rising tide of fascism. Benito Mussolini's invasion of Ethiopia in 1935 and the reluctance of European and North American governments to take action against the invasion galvanized Black opinion throughout the world. Garvey declared Mussolini to be the "arch barbarian of our times." The American Committee for Ethiopia and the International African Friends of Abyssinia were formed and joined with the LCP and the Pan-African movement to condemn the invasion. In the West Indies, the Rastafarian movement was established. The movement took its name from Ras Tafari, the given name of Haile Selassie (Lauren 1988, 118–22).

These developments and contentions fed into a new conceptualization of identity informed by images of a new commonality of African "diasporic intimacy" (Gilroy 1993). Nonetheless, the new identity was fashioned out of middle-strata intellectual discourse and constituted of bastardized forms of images of the colonizers. This is the source of its creole component, because what is indicated in the term "creole" is a polluted version of white forms. Middle-strata intellectuals employed their appropriated symbolic capital and their access to social and cultural capital, derived as rewards for their close approximation to "whiteness," in the historical construction of Afro-creole identity. The image of "Africa" in Afro-creole identity was associated with the freedom and transcendence denied the colonized in the construct of colonialism (Chude-Sokei 1995, 1–30). Not contested was the image of Africa that existed in the minds of Europe as a space for exploitation and for the exercise of paternalism (Chude-Sokei 1995, 16). This image continued to inform the "understandings" that the ascendant middle-strata elite applied in their visions of the Black lower-strata population.

Identity Formation and Class Mobilization

The development internationally of class ideology was also influencing identity and organization among lower-strata social groups in the West Indies. As early as the first decade of the twentieth century, proletarian workers in the West Indies had begun to follow the lead of their European counterparts in mobilizing for labor reform. The Bolshevik Revolution of 1917 gave their efforts added impetus.

In British Guiana (now Guyana), the modern trade union movement was started by a Black dock worker, Hubert Nathaniel Critchlow. Critchlow converted his national prominence as one of the colony's top sportsmen into social capital. In 1906, he joined a nascent movement of labor protest and used his position to mobilize urban workers. By 1919, inspired by the Russian Revolution and the rise of the British Labour Party, he formed the British Guiana Labour Union (BGLU) (Chase 1964, 50–53).

The BGLU and a counterpart union in Trinidad, the Trinidad Workingmen's Association (TWA), grew dramatically during the 1920s to be the dominant political movements in the entire West Indies (Oxaal 1968, 50–55). They were joined in 1924 by the Barbados Democratic League formed by socialist physician Charles O'Neale and progressive journalist Clennell Wickham, who had returned from World War I after serving in the West Indies Regiment between 1914 and 1919 (Hoyos 1972, 107–24).

During the 1920s, Black West Indian leaders of working-class movements were engaged in the development of intraregional and international alliances centered around labor and workers' organizations. In 1924, Critchlow attended the International Workers' Education Conference in Oxford, England, accompanied by the head of the TWA. The next year, both were present at the British Commonwealth Labour Conference held in London. In 1926, political and labor leaders from the entire English-speaking West Indies met in Georgetown, British Guiana, at a conference attended by representatives from the British Labour Party. There, they formed the Guyanese and West Indian Federation of Trade Unions and Labour Parties. This was, in effect, the formalization of a regional political and labor alliance.

Identity, Class, and Crisis: The Crystallization of Afro-Creole Politics
During the 1930s, class contestations combined with anticolonialism, antiwhite sentiment, and Black pride to produce labor mobilization. Afro-creole identity began to provide the symbolic impetus for a mass political movement. Pressures for nationalism were increasing. Internationally, the Soviet Union was taking an intense interest in Europe's colonial possessions. A Black Trinidadian, George Padmore, was appointed by the Kremlin to head the Negro Bureau of the Red International of Labor Unions in the USSR. Padmore served, concurrently, as secretary of the International Trade Union Committee of Negro Workers. In the West Indies, Critchlow affiliated his union with the Socialist International and, by 1930, was calling for a workers' struggle to overthrow capitalism and for socialist reconstruction. In 1932, he visited the Soviet Union (Chase 1964, 50–53).

Thus, there was a conflation during the 1930s of the idioms of race, class, and anticolonialism in the ideological constructs that gave meaning to and became the basis for interpreting the struggles of the lower strata of social groups in the West Indies. It is this conflation that laid the groundwork for the historical production of Afro-creole nationalism.

The objective conditions for worker mobilization at the time were emerging in the process of urbanization. The descendants of former slaves, many of whom had settled in rural areas after emancipation in 1838, were now migrating to urban areas, particularly in the larger colonies. Their identity as "Black" was forged in the racial constructs of colonialism. As urbanized workers, they were subjected much more intensely to the "organizational rationality" of the colonial state. This produced a more intensive incorporation into the colonial political economy. With their migration, the newly urban workers could no longer participate in social, cultural, and economic activities in the rural areas that preserved and reinforced notions of racial separateness. Thus, urbanization produced an erosion of the social basis for preserving and maintaining "difference" as it served to satisfy the new social and technical conditions of capitalist production. Jürgen Habermas comments on this contradiction. "While organizational rationality spreads," he argues, "cultural traditions are undermined and weakened" (1973, 47). It produced a dilemma for colonial society, dependent as it was upon the maintenance of distinctive "cultural traditions" (or core cultural patterns) for its integrity. The implications are noted by Habermas: "Traditions important for legitimation," he observes, "cannot be regenerated administratively. Furthermore, administrative manipulation of cultural matters has the unintended side effect of causing meanings and norms previously fixed by tradition and belonging to the boundary conditions of the political system to be publicly thematized" (1973, 47).

The problem posed for colonial authority by urbanization related to the need to maintain the boundary conditions of racially constructed culture while incorporating the disparate groups created by this culture more intensely into the organizational rationality of the colonial state. The inherent contradictions quickly became manifest in conditions of crisis. The reaction in the West Indies was the "public thematization" of cultural traditions in the form of a politicized Afro-creole identity. Even in Guyana and Trinidad, with their large and growing East Indian populations, the Black lower strata was the first to mount racialized challenges to colonial authority. Black proletarian and semiproletarian mobilization was fed by the economic crisis of the Depression. Beginning in Saint Kitts in 1935, dissatisfaction finally exploded into debilitating riots throughout the English-speaking West Indies (West India Royal Commission 1945; Fraser 1994, 37–50).

A liberal Royal Commission formed to examine the causes of the riots and disturbances came to the conclusion that they represented "a revolt of

West Indian peasant and worker against a society in which, despite formal emancipation, they were still regarded merely as supplies of cheap labor" (G. Lewis 1968, 88). Habermas points to the effectiveness of the "symbolic use of hearings, expert judgments, juridical incantations and also the advertising techniques (copied from oligopolistic competition) that at once confirm and exploit existing structures of prejudice" (1973, 70). In this case, the strategy proved temporarily effective.

As an effective challenge to colonial domination, racialized political mobilization became subjected, almost immediately, to the organizational rationality of middle-strata elites. The instrument of this subjugation was the trade union. Much of the rioting was orchestrated through trade union mobilization, with the middle-strata leaders using such mobilization and the ensuing riots to demand participation in colonial decision-making. Acknowledgment of exploitation and proposals for remedies were one thing; restructuring the colonial political system was quite another. The Royal Commission found itself divided on granting the demands by the middle-strata Black and colored leadership for universal suffrage. The two issues of independence and self-determination that were to dominate postwar political discourse and contestation were never even considered (G. Lewis 1968, 108–9). The challenge to colonial authority was in and of itself a challenge to white supremacy. The confrontation that ensued, once cast in these terms, could never be resolved by administrative fiat. This was the failure of the commission. Its recommendations were confined to issues of de facto colonial administration. It failed to recognize white supremacy as being at the heart of the problem. This set the stage for the nationalist struggle through which the factions of the middle strata, employing racialized nationalist ideology, came to gain control of the governing institutions of the state.

Afro-Creole Nationalism: Organizational Rationality and Middle-Strata Domination

During the first half of the twentieth century, middle-strata groups concentrated their politics on mobilization for representative government. The strata that prevailed were those that were able to channel their politics into the development of an ideology of anticolonial nationalism. The idiom of race was central to this effort. New racial constructs were at the core of the symbolic arsenal employed for the defeat of formal colonialism. These constructs were employed to make meaningful the demand for liberation from colonial domination and exploitation. Liberation was to be achieved by seizing control of the governing institutions of the colony, including its bureaucratic apparatus. This formulation was quite consistent with the realities of colonial political economy. The Crown Colony system, introduced in the nineteenth century, gave absolute control of colonial government to a British administrative elite headed by the governor. Before its introduction, control was shared between a shrinking white plantocracy and colonial officials. With the introduction of the Crown Colony system, colonial bureaucracy, developed during the period of industrial colonialism, replaced the plantation as the primary instrument of accumulation and domination (i.e., of power).[10] Bureaucratic function expanded considerably during the "golden era" of later colonialism. In the wake of this shift in the structure of governance, "white" domination became synonymous with "foreign" domination. Domination and control came to be located in the governing institutions of the colonial state rather than directly in the institutions of production. This explains the connection that developed between ideas of sovereignty and democracy on the one hand and the contestation of white supremacy on the other. The former were directed against institutions of governance. Both were incorporated into the complex of symbols and meanings that came to constitute Afro-creole nationalism.

The educated factions of the middle strata employed their legitimacy derived from possession of social, cultural, and symbolic capital to authenticate their claims to leadership. These claims allowed them to impose their own organizational rationality on a developing lower-class movement. The subjugation of the lower strata to middle-strata rationality came without the problems that inhered in colonial political economy. Indeed, the very rationale for the development of trade unions and nationalist organizations, headed by middle-strata elites, was to mount a challenge to the organizational rationality of the colonial state against which lower-strata mobilization was directed. Afro-creole nationalism and the nationalist movement that it legitimated became the ideology and organization for the public thematization of the cultural tradition of difference. The organizational rationality of the middle class brought with it the promise of an "Afro-creole nation" where the contradiction between race and statist incorporation, inherent in colonial organization, was negated.

The incorporation of the racialized lower strata into the organizational rationality of the middle-strata elite served two functions. The first was strategic. Proletarian labor and rural agricultural producers constituted by far the largest segment of the populations of the English-speaking West Indies in numerical terms. They were also the most widely dispersed of all the social groups under colonialism and the most predisposed to challenge colonial hegemony. They provided sheer numbers and were the most motivated in the conduct of the anticolonial campaign.

The second function of formal organization was regimentation. It placed professionals and intellectuals in positions of control over the activities of proletarian and peasant resistance. Additionally, regimentation allowed the regulation by the middle-strata leadership of relations between proletarian workers and peasants on the one hand and other social groupings on the other.

Relations of affinity between proletarian and peasant groups and the middle-strata groups of professionals, intellectuals, and nonproletarian wage and salaried workers were established and cemented in formal organizations developed and led by the latter. Afro-creole identity, newly constructed out of a diasporic image of African commonality, provided the symbolic basis for the development of these relations. In the West Indies, this new image of Africa fed upon proletarian movements of protest creating the conditions for successful incorporation of the latter into trade union and protonationalist political parties. The renewed construction of Africa as an image of "freedom, utopia, transcendence" (Chude-Sokei 1995, 14) combined with lower-strata demands for economic justice to legitimize the calls of the middle strata for national sovereignty. All of these were encoded in the developing ideology of Afro-creole nationalism.

Calls for representative government were heard as early as the second decade of the twentieth century. The Representative Government Association was founded in Grenada by Theophilus Marryshow, a journalist who came to be known as the father of West Indian nationalism. The ultimate aim of the association was securing independence for the West Indian colonies under a federal arrangement. In 1919, Marryshow's inspiration led to the founding of a similar organization in Dominica under the leadership of attorney Cecil Rawle. In 1926, under the initiative of the two leaders, a conference on West Indian nationalism was organized in British Guiana. It was attended by political and labor leaders from throughout the West Indies. The organizational and ideological roots of West Indian Afro-creole nationalism were fashioned and formulated at this conference. By the latter half of the 1930s, demands for independence were being made by all of the major middle-strata political leaders. These included Barbadian attorney Sir Grantley Adams; Jamaican colored businessman Alexander Bustamante, the son of a white planter; colored Jamaican attorney Norman Manley; Portuguese Trinidadian publisher Albert Gomes; and Black oil worker Uriah Butler of Trinidad. The identities of all but Gomes, who was Portuguese, were rooted in the Black and colored racial group. All of the leaders involved in the growing nationalist movement, with the exception of Critchlow of British Guiana and Butler of Trinidad, were from the middle strata. Significantly, by the 1950s, Gomes, Butler, and Critchlow had all faded from the political scene, now dominated by the Black and colored political elites engaged in the reformulation of racial identity.

The strategy of the nationalist elites to place themselves in leadership positions of worker movements had an enormous impact on colonial policy and practice. Colonial reform had to take its cue from the developing ideology of Afro-creole nationalism, constructed and imposed by these leaders. Soon, representative government, around which their political efforts were organized, became the watchword of colonial civil practice. The currents of international developments were chipping away at colonialism's legitimacy. Racially, the fratricide of two world wars in Europe and Japan's challenge to the North Atlantic nations dealt severe blows to the ideology of white supremacy upon which colonialism rested. Colonial hegemony suffered a setback from the replacement of European colonial states by the Soviet Union and the United States as postwar superpowers in the international arena.[11] Both countries actively supported decolonization, albeit for strategic and exploitative reasons. The newly formed United Nations gave credence to the principle of equality of sovereign states. All these developments combined to erode the legitimacy of the colonial system. In the newly emerging world view, colonialism appeared to violate the very tenets of self-determination for which World War II had been fought.[12]

In this confluence of circumstances, any lingering effort by members of the colonial middle strata to identify with a defunct and illegitimate system lost credence and instrumental appeal. In its place came the quest to be included among the elites in a new world order of independent sovereign nations.

In their historical construction and reproduction, the social identities of lower-strata social groups were shaped by struggles of resistance to domination and hegemonic imposition. Once the struggles of the middle strata became anticolonial and anti-European, the basis was laid for the development of an ideology of racial solidarity against white colonial domination.

Thus, the ideology of Afro-creole nationalism came to incorporate lower-strata challenges to colonial and European domination. There were also ritualistic components of Afro-creole nationalism. The movement embraced ritually the more universal forms of expressive culture of the Black lower strata, including speech, dress, visual and performing arts, forms of worship, and the like. These became the symbolic ritual forms of nationalism. They signaled the loss of legitimacy of colonial elite forms. At the same time, they signaled the willingness of the Black and colored middle strata to embrace images of "Africa" in their new myths of origins and to incorporate these images into national culture. Ritualistic embrace symbolized the rejection of colonial and racial domination in nationalist discourse.

I mentioned earlier the contradiction between incorporation into the colonial state and the need to preserve racial discourse as a means for maintaining the boundary conditions of colonialism. The incorporation of Afro-creole identity into the definition of the new nation-states eliminated this contradiction in all but Guyana, Trinidad, and Belize. In these political economies, the social construction of race was considerably more complex. The discourse of difference applied to other social constructions of race rooted in identities shaped by the interaction of colonial political economy with postemancipation migration and, in Belize and Guyana, with precolonial presence. New identities were forged out of images rooted in notions of "diaspora" and in constructs of indigenousness. For the most part, however, once the authorial power of the ruling class of the British colonial state and the governing class of colonial elites were removed with independence, the discourse of the postcolonial political economy shifted away from the idiom of race. Legitimacy, in the postcolonial era, became separated from the maintenance of racial boundaries. With the elimination of the contradiction posed by the discourse of racial difference, the intensive incorporation of the lower strata into the statist constructs of the nationalist elite could proceed apace. This was accomplished by an extension of the latter's organizational rationality from political parties and trade unions to the governing institutions of the state.

The cognitive linking of "nation-ness" with Afro-creole identity was universal, even in Trinidad and Guyana, where the postemancipation histories had produced more complex racial constructions. In these two countries, large segments of the population whose identities were constructed as historical products of postemancipation diasporic discourses were excluded from the conceptualization of the "nation." The largest of these diasporic "communities" was the East Indian population. Efforts at including these diasporic communities in nationalist constructs failed miserably in both countries. The reason was obvious. The anticolonial movement could not accommodate a discourse of racial difference and maintain its challenge to white supremacy. The nationalist challenge was, in its conceptualization, a contestation of difference. It demanded the embracing of the inferior as equal. Any attempt to incorporate into nationalist ideology notions of difference among the colonized brought with it the contradiction of acceptance of colonial discourse upon which white supremacy was rooted. This discourse of difference legitimized and rendered meaningful not only the constructs of white and Black but constructs of difference within the colonized population itself. In rejecting a colonial discourse of difference, the nationalists were forced to reject claims to nationhood by those whose identities were fashioned out of this very discourse. Thus, the elites who led both countries to independence were forced by the logic of their challenge to colonialism to embrace unequivocally the Afro-creole constructs of the region's nationalist movements. These constructs were dependent upon an image of Africa associated with "freedom, utopia, and transcendence." As such, images of the national community came to incorporate only those whose identities were located in "memories" of an African past.

Legitimacy Constructs and Authorial Power

Democracy

Democracy, as a metaphor for freedom and equality, became a legitimizing construct of elite authorial power in the West Indies (Best 1969; Oxaal 1968;

Bell 1964, 1967). The task of the postcolonial elite was to secure the transfer of its authorial power from anticolonial organizations, in the form of the nationalist political parties and trade unions, to the governing institutions of the state. Trade unions and nationalist political parties were organized to contest colonial authority and challenge the institutions of colonial governance. They had to be converted into institutions of support for governmental authority once independence was achieved under a nationalist government. The incorporation of the ideology of representative government into the framework of Afro-creole nationalism laid the groundwork for such a conversion by legitimizing the adoption of the Westminster form of parliamentary democracy in postcolonial political economy. Its adoption gave added force to democracy as an allegorical form of freedom and an index of racial equality, since it was the form of government practiced by the colonial power. It came to constitute a powerful symbol of the equality of the postcolonial state with those of the former colonizers.

Westminster democracy resolved the contradiction between equality and middle-strata authorial power. It legitimized control of the legislative and executive branches of the government by nationalist political parties. In these parties were incorporated diverse movements of protest, including trade unions, ethnic and cultural organizations, and other politicized voluntary organizations. The integral link between party and government facilitated the incorporation of these organizations of nationalist protest into the governing structures of the state. As a result, the state became synonymous with national liberation. As the representatives of the "Afro-creole nation" through their leadership of institutions of nationalist protest, middle-strata elites secured and legitimized their authorial power. This was important in another sense. During colonialism, the valorized social and cultural forms of the colonizers, acquired through socialization, authenticated the dominant position of the middle-strata elite. Nationalism rejected the colonizer's claims to superiority and to the superiority of its social and cultural forms. This rejection came with the threat of undermining the claims to authority by the middle strata. With Westminster democracy, images of African commonality, incorporated into rituals of anticolonial protest, were transferred to institutions of government, thereby negating the latter's symbolic relationship with colonial forms. This was true also for nongovernmental institutions of state power. As an example, through a process of "localization," middle-strata elites began to fill positions of authority in the foreign-owned sectors of the economy. This was in response to subtle, and not so subtle, demands for localization by the new nationalist governments. In some ex-colonies, most notably Guyana and Trinidad, nationalist governments embarked on a process of expansion into and nationalization of the private sector.

Development

It was the image of equality that drove the quest for development. Industry and the consumptive styles of Europe and North America were the pervasive symbols of white supremacy. The symbolic power of development rests in the essentiality of its relationship with equality. Developmental transformation brings in its wake the promise of industrial production and consumptive styles typical of the metropolitan "North." The power of the ideology of development, embedded in nationalist discourse, was its transformative guarantee of modernity. Implied in the latter was the notion of racial equality. To be modern was to be equal. For the community of Afro-creole nationalists, equality (with Europeans) came with the material life conditions and productive technology of western Europe and North America. This was the promise of development.

In the West Indies, the institution of government became the engine of developmental transformation. As "modernizers," the task fell to the national governmental and nongovernmental elites to assert the equality of the postcolonial nation-state in the international arena. Implied by such equality was the equality of the formerly colonized with their erstwhile white colonizers. National elites became the agents of modernity and the instruments of equality. The ideology of development, therefore, came to justify the authorial power of managers, professionals, technicians, and bureaucrats who possess the skills, capacities, credentials, and education needed for developmental planning and its implementation (Hintzen 1993). Developmental planning was incorporated, firmly, into the functions of government (Hintzen 1995; A. Lewis 1949). It is in this manner that development was transformed into a legitimacy construct.

As an ideology, development contributed to the legitimization of the authorial power of the new elite. Its force, as a legitimacy construct, was enhanced by its promise of an end to economic crisis. Indeed, it was the search for a solution to the economic crisis of the 1930s that spawned the nationalist movement in the West Indies. Out of this search, an integral link was forged between development and nationalism.

Sovereignty

In the colonies, there was an inherent contradiction between the quest for sovereignty and the continued maintenance of exclusive economic relations with Europe. Continued economic dependence upon the colonial power was inconsistent with ideas of national self-determination as a critical component of sovereignty. The emergence of the United States as the dominant global economic power led the way out of this dilemma. A symbolic shift in the focus of economic and political relations from Britain to the United States became one of the central elements in nationalist assertions of sovereignty. It allowed the newly independent countries to retain relations of economic dependency in the global capitalist economy while freeing such relations from the taint of colonial domination.

The establishment and intensification of economic and political ties with North America were justified also in terms of developmental transformation. As the dominant, richest, and most technologically advanced economic power, the United States offered opportunities for transformation. This was underscored in the quest by nationalist leaders to secure US investments in their economies. Beginning in the 1950s, there was a gradual shift to more representative governments in the English-speaking West Indies. Nationalist politicians were being elected to lead governments under constitutions that provided greater degrees of autonomy from the dictates of colonial administration. These leaders used their autonomy to begin to reorientate their economies toward the United States and Canada and to develop firmer political ties with these two North American countries. Efforts to attract North American investments intensified. An increasing flow of North American visitors to the West Indies began to fuel a developing tourist industry. Ties with North America became even stronger with the willingness of the United States and Canada to absorb an increasing number of West Indian migrants. The effects of these migratory flows to North America were becoming evident in the alleviation of persistent problems of unemployment and underemployment.

Nationalist leaders in the West Indies soon began to establish links of support with North American political and economic interests in their local political campaigns (Fraser 1994, 110–17). These relations with North America set the stage for intensification of the integration of the West Indies into the political economy of global capital.

Bureaucracy and the Structural Conditions
of Middle-Strata Authorial Power

Once established in any sphere of activity, bureaucratic structures are almost impossible to destroy. In the Caribbean, as elsewhere in the former colonies of Europe, middle-class functionaries became responsible for organizing and running colonial and postcolonial bureaucracies. This followed in the wake of significant expansion in the governmental, welfare, and productive functions of the state. There was a parallel expansion in nongovernmental bureaucracies in the private sector, and the development and expansion of voluntary organizations of mass participation, particularly political, labor, and cultural organizations. When the English-speaking former colonies became independent beginning in the 1960s, authorial power in the colonial bureaucracies passed from colonial to nationalist elites. As organizations of nationalist protest were absorbed into postcolonial institutions of government, the latter became the new mechanisms for imposing the organizational rationality of the middle strata upon the population. Opportunities for transforming institutions of protest into regimented institutions of elite authority increased significantly with governmental expansion. There was significant growth in police forces, defense forces, militias, and national guard units in the West Indies even before independence was achieved. Everywhere there was the addition and expansion of new governmental bureaucracies to perform new international and domestic functions of government. The addition of ministries of trade and commerce, ministries of development, finance ministries, and their equivalents became de rigueur for the newly independent governments. Their addition and growth were justified by their role in administering the process of developmental transformation and in establishing and maintaining "sovereign" relations (Hintzen 1993).

Nationalism and the End of Racial Discourse

Before national liberation, relations between the colony and the outside world were inseparable from colonial relations of racial dominance. The symbolic transition to "independence" frees these relations from the discourse of racial domination. As "sovereign nations," new states enter the system of international relations as political equals (at least in de jure terms). Equality becomes particularly meaningful with reference to the "white" nations of the world. Sovereignty brings with it an implication of racial equality, now defined in nationalist terms (since race comes to be embodied in nationalist definitions).

At the same time, the dilemma of inequality fails to be resolved by sovereignty alone. Instead, the dilemma shifts to a discourse of development. In the new universe of the sovereign, nations are separated (i.e., rendered unequal) by their respective positions on the continuum of development. Such separation gives pertinence to the connection between development and equality in postindependence discourse. At the same time, because of its association with "freedom," sovereignty provides the opportunity for the realization of equality. It allows the exercise of choice in international relations. Choice frees new nations to pursue development, this being the basis of a new conceptualization of equality. With sovereignty, therefore, a new narrative of equality, embodied in developmental transformation, is thrust upon postindependence discourse. In the process, the semiotics of equality shifts to the international arena and away from intranational divisions of race or class. Developmental transformation, in the pursuit of equality, is catapulted to a position of primacy.

The new discourse of sovereignty, by representing international relations as national choice, provides legitimation for a more intensified integration of the West Indies into the international capitalist political economy. International relations have come to be understood in terms of choices for development. Foreign relations policy is explained by governments in terms of the need to secure advances in technology, to acquire the means for the development of industry, and to provide to the population the wherewithal for mass consumption. Relations with North America, particularly the United States, are explained as offering the best opportunity for acquiring the prerequisites for development. All countries in the region have dramatically increased their relations of trade, aid, and development cooperation with Canada and the United States. This is true even of Guyana, Jamaica, and Grenada, which, for various lengths of time, had established symbolic and nominal relations accompanied by some developmental assistance with Cuba and, to a lesser extent, with eastern Europe and China. During the 1980s, there was an intensification of political relations between the United States and all the countries of the English-speaking Caribbean except Guyana and, to a lesser degree, Trinidad and Tobago. With the United States as the focal point in an intensifying pattern of economic relations, there was a dramatic increase in the penetration of international capital in the political economies of the West Indian countries.

The discourse of development embedded in nationalism camouflages the real conditions of power in postcolonial political economy. In the West Indies, development has replaced claims of Afro-creole representation in the ideology of nationalism. Now, elite domination is legitimated by what Foucault terms the "speaker's benefit." This pertains to claims by the "universal intellectual" to speak for humanity and to base assertions of privilege on appeals to the ability to create a future that is unquestionably better. Typically, such claims are made under circumstances in which the conditions of power are masked and, as a result, rendered more tolerable (Foucault 1980; Dreyfus and Rabinow 1983, 130–31). In the West Indies, the speaker's benefit has come to legitimize the domination of that group of educated elite represented to have the technical qualifications necessary for development transformation.

The conflation of intellectualism and political power is very much part of the postcolonial reality of the West Indies. Intellectualism and political leadership are inextricably linked in popular consciousness. A universal understanding of politics as "intellectual discourse" has had consequences in the exclusive presence of intellectual elites in positions of governmental authority and state power. This phenomenon has been noted by scholars such as Lloyd Best (1969) and Ivar Oxaal (1968, 1971). It was Best who coined the term "Doctor Politics" to characterize West Indian political reality. This term has become an integral part of popular political parlance throughout the Caribbean. In the postcolonial construction of political reality, there is an overwhelming representation of national scholarship winners among the political leaders in the Caribbean. In Barbados, for example, every single prime minister elected to office has been the holder of an Island Scholarship, the highest academic award in the country.

The Primacy of Development

As development gains primacy in postcolonial nationalist discourse, there is an inevitable undermining of the symbolic power of ethnic nationalism. Authorial power, authenticated merely through claims to ethnic representativeness, begins to lose its salience. To legitimize their continued domination, postcolonial elites increasingly come to rest claims to authority upon their ability to secure development and manage the transition to modernity.

Development brings with it a shift in conceptualizations of equality. Nationalism, in its essence, is a discourse of race. Development is integrally linked to the valorization of industrialization, technology, and mass consumption. These become the yardsticks of modernity employed in definitions of difference among sovereign national entities.

Once development replaces nationalism, the constellations of "difference" (ethnicity, race, class, region, etc.) within the geographic boundaries of national postcolonial entities become less meaningful. Development must incorporate the efforts and economic resources (and sacrifices) of every group within these boundaries. This had particular implications for Afro-creole nationalism in the West Indies. There has arisen an inevitable contradiction between the legitimizing claims of the latter and the demand for development. Those whose identities were not embedded in images of an African diasporic community were excluded from the community of the nation. This exclusion and its contestation intensified relations of antipathy between their own identific communities and the community of Afro-creoles. These identific communities included whites and near-whites everywhere, and East Indians, Chinese, and Portuguese in Guyana and Trinidad. There were also small but important communities of Lebanese and Syrians in Trinidad and Jamaica. Many in these excluded communities had managed to acquire the economic capital, skills, and education deemed necessary for development transformation.

Developmentalism authenticates the dominant role of those with economic capital and cultural capital derived from education and training. It legitimizes the differential distribution of power as a prerequisite for transformation to modernity, and hence for the achievement of equality with the northern industrial countries. Everything comes to be subordinated to and encapsulated by the quest for developmental equality. This includes understandings of the character of the nation.

There is considerable evidence of a shift away from an Afro-creole definition of the nation in the West Indies. In Jamaica, the shift was marked by the election of Lebanese businessman and scholar Edward Seaga as prime minister in 1979. His qualification for the office was predicated, almost exclusively, upon his reputation as a "development wizard" (Edie 1991, 115–42). The inherent contradiction of "Lebanese" leadership of the "Afro-creole" nation was resolved in the ascension of development to primacy in the national consciousness. The shift has had identical and much more profoundly dramatic implications in Guyana and Trinidad. It allowed the election in Guyana in 1992 and in Trinidad in 1995 of prime ministers who were not merely from the identific community of East Indians, but who in popular consciousness were understood to represent these communities in the political arena. An "East Indian" government is incompatible with conceptualizations of an Afro-creole nation. The former would have to endure the inevitability of a persistent and pervasive challenge to its legitimacy on ethnic grounds. Its legitimacy could only be established after successful efforts to redefine the nation symbolically as "East Indian." No significant challenge to the legitimacy of the "East Indian" governments occurred in either Guyana or Trinidad. Neither engaged in systematic efforts at ethnic redefinition of the nation. That neither challenge nor redefinition occurred is proof of a transformation in the meaning of the nation from the vessel of Afro-creole identity to the instrument of modernity. The People's Progressive Party (PPP) in Guyana came to power in the wake of a developing consensus that the ruling Afro-creole People's National Congress had violated the conditions of democracy. A pervasive and chronic economic crisis was blamed on the failure of the latter to guarantee "free and fair" elections. This can be explained by the shift in nationalist discourse from ethnicity to development. The changing conceptualization failed to be signaled by Afro-creole support for the PPP. Voting patterns remained ethnically bound. Rather, it was indicated by the willingness of the community of Afro-creoles to entertain the possibility of an "East Indian" government and to accept its legitimacy once elected. The same is true for Trinidad. In both countries, East Indian elites own a significant share of domestic economic capital. Additionally, particularly in Trinidad, East Indian professionals and intellectuals are popularly identified with the technical and managerial professions and disciplines. It is the possession of economic and cultural capital, understood as prerequisites for development, that has come to authenticate the authorial power of this new elite.

Thus, the combination of bureaucratic statism, Westminster parliamentary democracy, and developmentalism has allowed a postcolonial elite with economic and social capital to reproduce structures of domination characteristic of a colonial order. Here lies the explanation for the crisis experienced in the region today with such devastating consequences for the poor, the powerless, and, in every country, that segment of the population whose identity is constructed out of images of its African roots. The crisis is also affecting groups formerly incorporated into the middle strata. Government workers, teachers, and clerical and supervisory workers are among segments of the colonial middle strata who have been dispossessed of the economic and social benefits and privileges they enjoyed during the waning years of colonialism and the beginning years of postcolonial governments. This is a consequence of the logic of the discourse of development and its role in the erosion of the welfare state. Development has rendered obsolete the welfarism that emerged in the West Indies as a reactive response to the economic crisis of the 1930s. The welfare state was erected in the face of an ethnically defined nationalist challenge to white supremacy. Ethnic nationalism allowed the colonized to make claims, rooted in a discourse of racial exclusion and exploitation, to social and economic redress. Development acts as a negation of these claims. It negates, also, the moral basis of ethnic clientelism, legitimized in the symbolic identification of the state with the Afro-creole population. This form of clientelism derived from racially articulated moral claims against the white colonizers to distributive justice and to the resources of the nation. In effect, welfarism and clientelism were mechanisms for distributing widely among the population a significant portion of the economic surplus. With developmentalism's new credo of neoliberalism, the role of the governing institutions of the state is shifting to managing the financial and manufacturing interests of domestic and international capital and to creating and maintaining conditions of superexploitation (Hintzen 1995).

The cultural, social, and symbolic capital of the postcolonial elite derived from privileged access to the resources of the colonial metropole. These elites accumulated social capital primarily through their European education and training. The acquisition of cultural capital derived from their socialization into the dominant European forms. The authorial power of these elites in the postindependence state created the conditions for the reauthentication of European forms now incorporated into their "style" or "taste." The social construction of this dominant group as a "nationalist" elite negated the force of challenges to their legitimacy based on claims of the perpetuation of white (colonial) supremacy. In the 1960s and 1970s, such challenges were attempted by university-based groups such as Abeng in Jamaica (Nettleford 1972; Rodney 1969), the African Society for Cultural Relations with Independent Africa (ASCRIA) in Guyana (Hintzen 1989, 170–72), and the National Joint Action Committee in Trinidad (Oxaal 1971), with very little success. This was despite appeals from these protest groups for "Black power" directed against the Afro-creole nationalist elite (see esp. Rodney 1969).

CONCLUSION

Bureaucratic statism, intellectual authority, and regimentation of the population in bureaucratized parties, trade unions, and voluntary organizations all combined to create, maintain, and support the conditions of domination for those of the region's middle strata, organized around Afro-creole constructs of identity. Their positions as bureaucrats, administrators, managers, and professionals derived largely from the legacies of colonial privilege. The claims to position and status made by those most willing to embrace the cultural values and social norms of their European masters were authenticated in colonial discourse. In the postcolonial political economy, they found themselves best placed to assume control of the governing apparatus. This control became their "source of power" (Trimberger 1978, 7). The image of "diasporic intimacy" represented in Afro-creole nationalist discourse combined with Westminster parliamentarianism to preserve the myth of representative participatory government. The adoption of the Westminster democratic form ensured party political representation in government. It ensured, also, the de jure incorporation of organizations of nationalist protest into party structures and thus into the system of government. In this way, popular aspirations for Afro-creole nationalism came to be realized through the fusion of government and nation in popular consciousness.

The end of white colonial domination resolved the sociocultural crisis out of which Afro-creole nationalism emerged. This crisis was spawned out of a fundamental contradiction inherent in colonial society. Colonial legitimacy, dependent upon the maintenance of racial privilege, proved to be incompatible with changes in the technical and social conditions of colonial economic production. These changes demanded a more intensive incorporation of the colonized into the organizational rationality of the colonial state. The response was ethnic nationalism with demands for independence. With sovereignty, a shift was effected away from domestic challenges to racial supremacy, to a quest for modernity as the new condition of equality. Development became the legitimizing construct authenticating the authorial power of a newly emergent "modernizing" technocratic and managerial elite.

As the ideology of development assumed increasing primacy in nationalist discourse, it set the stage for the authoritative diffusion of the rapidly changing values, behaviors, beliefs, and practices typical of highly developed industrialized economies. The penetration of these forms has been reflected in a number of ways. There has been an escalation of demand for the modern consumer goods of mass consumption. These new consumption patterns have proven quite devastating, given their incompatibility with local and regional resources and productive capabilities. They have contributed to the intensification of the incorporation of West Indian political economies into global capital. Another contributing factor is the valorization of the "style" or "taste" of the new postcolonial elite. Even though patterned after their elite counterparts in western Europe and North America, such tastes are no longer understood as "foreign," "white," or "colonial." They are the styles and tastes of development, and modernity's prerequisites for equality.

Thus, the "North" as a construct has come to be popularly glorified. The quest for equality has become a quest for the acquisition of its cultural capital. Images of the North are now pervasive throughout the Caribbean. These include the pathologies of Western capitalism such as drug consumption, gang violence, environmental degradation, the cult of individualism, and the glorification of profit over welfare and social security. As a consequence, and in response, there has been an avalanche of out-migration, particularly to North America, especially of the skilled and educated and their families. Domestic capital and savings have been exported abroad, legally and illegally, to purchase and support northern lifestyles and to increase returns on investment (McAfee 1991). Meanwhile, the grouping of governing elites has become constricted. It includes, almost exclusively, managers and technocrats with the skills and expertise to oversee the interests of international finance and manufacturing capital. Its members have become devoid of any nationalist allegiance Domestically, the logical end product of development is the absorption of this elite into the class of international managerial and technical elites whose members have become incorporated into the structure of the state. There, they are joined by a group of local capitalists whose operations are becoming increasingly internationalized in globalized productive, financial, and service activities. Developmentalism is exposing itself as the negation of ethnic nationalism (Hintzen 1995). The latter emerged as mechanisms for accommodating Western capitalism in the face of claims by lower-strata groups against colonialism rooted in images of proletarian communality. These contestations of colonialism were evident particularly during the second, third, and fourth decades of the twentieth century. Developmentalism has intensified the incorporation of the West Indies into global capital.

NOTES

1. For a discussion of the notion of a "narrative of liberation" as it applies to the work of Frantz Fanon, see Taylor 1989. The narrative points to the role of symbolic communication in the transformation of social reality from a "Manichean dualism" to one of true and authentic "freedom."

2. Economic capital refers to the ownership and control of productive resources. Social capital refers to the relative positions of social groups, aggregates, and/or categories and the social networks associated with them. Cultural capital refers to the "interpersonal skills, habits, manners, linguistic styles, educational credentials, tastes, and lifestyles" (J. Turner 1991, 512) of those occupying various class positions. Finally, symbolic capital has to do with the symbolic content of legitimating discourse. In this sense, it pertains to the means of determining and defining symbolic content and its meaning (J. Turner 1991, 512–18; Bourdieu 1977; Bourdieu 1984).

3. See J. Turner 1991, 508–18, for an excellent summary of the constructivist structuralism of Pierre Bourdieu from which this criticism of structuralism derives.

4. Benedict Anderson applies the notion of an "imagined community" specifically to the nation. He recognizes, however, that "all communities larger than primordial villages of face-to-face-contact (and perhaps even these) are imagined" because "in the minds of each [member] lives the image of their communion" (Anderson 1983, 15).

5. See, for example, the contributions in Galli 1991.

6. Here, a thin line needs to be traversed between the structuralist and constructivist frameworks. To the extent that the "images" of these groups appear as real and are acted upon as if they were real by social actors, then a structuralist framework is most appropriate for analysis. It is for this reason that these groups are considered to be historically produced and reproduced. At the same time, to the extent that the groups exist as cognitive constructs, they cannot be considered to be real. For the sake of analysis, these groups (class, ethnic, racial, etc.) are treated in this chapter "as if" they were real at any historical moment because they are manifested in social structure. At the same time, the fact that they are "images" subject to contested interpretations places severe limitations on the use of a purely structuralist analysis.

7. Here, I use the term "white supremacy" following George Fredrickson, referring to "the attitudes, ideologies, and policies associated with the rise of blatant forms of white, or European dominance over 'nonwhite' populations." The consequences are "the restriction of meaningful citizenship rights to a privileged group characterized by" its whiteness (Fredrickson 1981, xi).

8. This is the argument of theorists who propose a "reticulated" model of "color/class" colonial organization. For a thorough discussion of these challenges, see Paul Gordon Lauren (1988, 44–87), who details the historical events that contributed to growing challenges to colonial and racial domination throughout the world beginning in the last decade of the nineteenth century.

9. For a full discussion of this, see Hintzen 1993.

10. The support of the United States for anticolonial movements was somewhat tenuous. Before the end of World War II, the administration of President Franklin Roosevelt strongly advocated for the West Indian nationalist cause. After the war, there was some reversion to support for Europe's colonial claims. Support for anticolonial movements, when forthcoming, was conditioned upon the anticommunist credentials of the leadership. See Fraser 1994.

11. This is one of the central arguments of Paul Gordon Lauren (1988, 102–65) as an explanation for the emergence and success of anticolonial nationalist movements in less developed countries after World War II.

12. A problem emerges when nationalist discourse retains its ethnic exclusivity and comes to be directed against groups within national boundaries. Under these circumstances, nationalist claims become contested on communal (racial, ethnic) grounds, which could lead to prolonged and violent confrontation.

BIBLIOGRAPHY

Anderson, Benedict. 1983. *Imagined Communities: Reflections on the Origin and Spread of Nationalism.* London: Verso Books.

Ashley, Richard K. 1984. "The Poverty of Neorealism." *International Organization* 38, no. 2 (Spring): 225–86.

Bell, Wendell. 1964. *Jamaican Leaders: Political Attitudes in a New State*. Berkeley: University of California Press.

Bell, Wendell. 1967. *The Democratic Revolution in the West Indies: Studies in Nationalism, Leadership, and the Belief in Progress*. Cambridge, MA: Schenkman.

Best, Lloyd. 1969. "Doctor Politics in the Caribbean, parts 1, 2 and 3." *Trinidad Express*, May 1.

Bourdieu, Pierre. 1977. *Outline of a Theory of Practice*. Translated by Richard Nice. Cambridge: Cambridge University Press.

Bourdieu, Pierre. 1984. *Distinction: A Social Critique of the Judgement of Taste*. Translated by Richard Nice. Cambridge, MA: Harvard University Press.

Braithwaite, Lloyd. 1953. "Social Stratification in Trinidad: A Preliminary Analysis." *Social and Economic Studies* 2, no. 2: 5–175.

Brereton, Bridget. 1979. *Race Relations in Colonial Trinidad, 1870–1900*. Cambridge: Cambridge University Press.

Cardoso, Fernando H., and Enzo Faletto. 1970. *Dependencia y desarrollo en América Latina*. Mexico City: Siglo Veintiuno Editores.

Chase, Ashton. 1964. *A History of Trade Unionism in Guyana, 1900 to 1961*. Georgetown, Guyana: New Guyana Company.

Chilcote, Ronald H., and Joel C. Edelstein. 1974. *Latin America: The Struggle with Dependency and Beyond*. New York: John Wiley and Sons.

Chude-Sokei, Louis. 1995. "The Incomprehensible Rain of Stars: Black Modernism, Black Diaspora." PhD diss., University of California, Los Angeles.

Cox, Robert W. 1983. "Gramsci, Hegemony and International Relations: An Essay in Method." *Millennium* 12, no. 2: 162–75.

Daly, Vere T. 1966. *A Short History of the Guyanese People*. Georgetown, Guyana: Daily Chronicle.

Dos Santos, Theotonio. 1970. "The Structure of Dependence." *American Economic Review* 60, no. 2 (May): 231–36.

Dreyfus, Hubert L., and Paul Rabinow. 1983. *Michel Foucault: Beyond Structuralism and Hermeneutics*. 2nd ed. Chicago: University of Chicago Press.

Edie, Carlene J. 1991. *Democracy by Default: Dependency and Clientelism in Jamaica*. Boulder, CO: Lynne Rienner.

Feld, Steven. 1988. "Aesthetics as Iconicity of Style, or 'Lift-Up-Over Sounding': Getting Into the Kaluli Groove." *Yearbook for Traditional Music* 20: 74–113.

Foucault, Michel. 1979. *Discipline and Punish: The Birth of the Prison*. Translated by Alan Sheridan. New York: Vintage Books.

Foucault, Michel. 1980. *The History of Sexuality*. Vol. 1: *The Will to Knowledge*. Translated by Robert Hurley. New York: Vintage Books.

Frank, Andre Gunder. 1967. *Capitalism and Underdevelopment in Latin America: Historical Studies of Chile and Brazil*. New York: Monthly Review Press.

Frank, Andre Gunder. 1969. *Latin America: Underdevelopment or Revolution*. New York: Monthly Review Press.

Frank, Andre Gunder. 1972. *Lumpenbourgeoisie and Lumpendevelopment: Dependence, Class, and Politics in Latin America*. New York: Monthly Review Press.

Fraser, Cary. 1994. *Ambivalent Anti-Colonialism: The United States and the Genesis of West Indian Independence, 1940–1964*. Westport, CT: Greenwood Press.

Fredrickson, George M. 1981. *White Supremacy: A Comparative Study in American and South African History*. New York: Oxford University Press.

Galli, Rosemary E., ed. 1991. *Rethinking the Third World: Contributions toward a New Conceptualization*. New York: Crane, Russak.

Geertz, Clifford. 1973. *The Interpretation of Cultures*. New York: Basic Books.

Gilroy, Paul. 1993. *The Black Atlantic: Modernity and Double-Consciousness*. Cambridge, MA: Harvard University Press.

Goldberg, David Theo. 1990. "The Social Formation of Racist Discourse." In *Anatomy of Racism*, edited by David Theo Goldberg, 295–318. Minneapolis: University of Minnesota Press.

Gramsci, Antonio. 1971. *Selections from the Prison Notebooks*. Translated by Quintin Hoare and Geoffrey Nowell Smith. New York: International Publishers.

Habermas, Jürgen. 1973. *Legitimation Crisis*. Translated by Thomas McCarthy. Boston: Beacon Press.

Harris, Nigel. 1976. *The End of the Third World*. Harmondsworth, Middx., England: Penguin.

Hintzen, Percy C. 1989. *The Costs of Regime Survival: Racial Mobilization, Elite Domination and Control of the State in Guyana and Trinidad*. Cambridge: Cambridge University Press.

Hintzen, Percy C. 1993. "Democracy and Middle-Class Domination in the West Indies." In *Democracy in the West Indies: Myths and Realities*, edited by Carlene J. Edie, 9–24. Boulder, CO: Westview Press.

Hintzen, Percy C. 1995. "Structural Adjustment and the New International Middle Class." *Transition*, no. 24 (February): 52–74. University of Guayana Press.

Hintzen, Percy C., and Ralph Premdas. 1982. "Coercion and Control in Political Change." *Journal of Interamerican Studies and World Affairs* 24, no. 3 (August): 337–54.

Hintzen, Percy C., and W. Marvin Will. 1988. "Garvey, Marcus Mosiah." In *Biographical Dictionary of Latin American and Caribbean Political Leaders*, edited by Robert J. Alexander, 180–82. Westport, CT: Greenwood Press.

Hoyos, F. A. 1972. *Builders of Barbados*. London: Macmillan Caribbean.

Lauren, Paul Gordon. 1988. *Power and Prejudice: The Politics and Diplomacy of Racial Discrimination*. Boulder, CO: Westview Press.

Lewis, Arthur. 1949. "The Industrialization of the British West Indies." *Caribbean Economic Review* 11, no. 1: 1–53.

Lewis, Gordon K. 1968. *The Growth of the Modern West Indies*. New York: Monthly Review Press.

MacDonald, Scott B. 1986. *Trinidad and Tobago: Democracy and Development in the Caribbean*. New York: Praeger.

McAfee, Kathy. 1991. *Storm Signals: Structural Adjustment and Development Alternatives in the Caribbean*. London: Zed Books.

Nettleford, Rex. 1972. *Identity, Race, and Protest in Jamaica*. New York: William Morrow.

Noguera, Pedro. 1990. "The Basis of Regime Support in Grenada from 1951 to 1988: A Study of Political Attitudes and Behavior in a Peripheral Society." PhD diss., University of California.

Oxaal, Ivar. 1968. *Black Intellectuals Come to Power: The Rise of Creole Nationalism in Trinidad and Tobago*. Cambridge, MA: Schenkman.

Oxaal, Ivar. 1971. *Race and Revolutionary Consciousness: A Documentary Interpretation of the 1970 Black Power Revolt in Trinidad*. Cambridge, MA: Schenkman.

Rapkin, David P. 1990. "The Contested Concept of Hegemonic Leadership." In *World Leadership and Hegemony*, edited by David P. Rapkin, 1–19. Boulder, CO: Lynne Rienner.

Rodney, Walter. 1969. *The Groundings with My Brothers*. London: Bogle-l'Ouverture.

Rudebeck, Lars. 1991. "Conditions of People's Development in Postcolonial Africa." In *Rethinking the Third World: Contributions toward a New Conceptualization*, edited by Rosemary E. Galli, 29–88. New York: Crane, Russak.

Ryan, Selwyn D. 1972. *Race and Nationalism in Trinidad and Tobago*. Toronto: University of Toronto Press.

Ryan, Selwyn D. 1989. *The Disillusioned Electorate: The Politics of Succession in Trinidad and Tobago*. Port of Spain: Inprint Caribbean.

Ryan, Selwyn D. 1991. *The Muslimeen Grab for Power: Race, Religion, and Revolution in Trinidad and Tobago*. Port of Spain: Inprint Caribbean.

Scott, James C. 1972. "Patron-Client Politics and Political Change in Southeast Asia." *American Political Science Review* 66, no. 1 (March): 91–117.

Segal, Daniel. 1992. "'Race' and 'Color' in Pre-Independence Trinidad and Tobago." In *Trinidad Ethnicity*, edited by Kevin A. Yelvington, 81–115. London: Macmillan Caribbean.

Stone, Carl. 1980. *Democracy and Clientelism in Jamaica*. New Brunswick, NJ: Transaction Publishers.

Taylor, Patrick. 1989. *The Narrative of Liberation: Perspectives on Afro-Caribbean Literature, Popular Culture, and Politics*. Ithaca, NY: Cornell University Press.

Trimberger, Ellen Kay. 1978. *Revolution from Above: Military Bureaucrats and Development in Japan, Turkey, Egypt, and Peru*. New Brunswick, NJ: Transaction Publishers.

Turner, Jonathan H. 1991. *The Structure of Sociological Theory*. Belmont, CA: Wadsworth.

Turner, Victor. 1974. *Dramas, Fields, and Metaphors: Symbolic Action in Human Society*. Ithaca, NY: Cornell University Press.

Wallerstein, Immanuel. 1980. *The Modern World-System II: Mercantilism and the Consolidation of the European World-Economy, 1600–1750*. New York: Academic Press.

Wallerstein, Immanuel. 1984. *The Politics of the World-Economy: The States, the Movements and the Civilizations*. Cambridge, MA: Harvard University Press.

Weaver, Frederick Stirton. 1991. "Toward an Historical Understanding of Industrial Development." In *Rethinking the Third World: Contributions toward a New Conceptualization*, edited by Rosemary E. Galli, 107–52. New York: Crane, Russak.

West, Cornel. 1982. *Prophesy Deliverance! An Afro-American Revolutionary Christianity*. Philadelphia: Westminster Press.

West India Royal Commission (1938–1939). 1945. "Statement of Action Taken on the Recommendations." London: Her Majesty's Stationery Office.

Chapter 2

AFRO-CREOLE NATIONALISM AS ELITE DOMINATION

The English-Speaking West Indies

PERCY C. HINTZEN

BACKGROUND

Political nationalism has provided the ideological underpinnings for overthrowing colonial domination. It has provided, also, the blueprint for the development of a postcolonial society. Its legitimacy was argued on the basis of the rights of the colonized population to sovereignty, national autonomy, self-determination, and freedom from repressive domination. At its heart, it was a contestation of colonial constructions of difference.

Those suffering under the yolk of colonial domination in the English-speaking Caribbean were, for the most part, descendants of slaves transported originally from Africa. In Guyana and Trinidad, they were replaced on the plantation by indentured servants brought primarily from India after emancipation in 1838.[1] Today, East Indians constitute an absolute majority in Guyana and the largest racial group in Trinidad and Tobago. Everywhere else in the English-speaking Caribbean, with the exception of Belize with its large indigenous Amerindian population, descendants of African slaves constitute over 90 percent of the population. This number includes the group of colored descendants of unions between Black slaves and white colonizers.

During the sixteenth century, a system of European domination and absolute control quickly established itself, unhindered by indigenous challenge. The native populations of Caribs and Taíno-Arawaks were quickly decimated to the point of total extinction in most island territories very soon after their first contact with European explorers and conquerors. Their disappearance was hastened by continued resistance to European conquest, by the spread of new European diseases for which they had no natural protections, and by the consequences of land seizure for colonial production. Thereafter, the European colonial plantocracy and officials easily prevailed against the persistent, even though localized and discontinuous, rebellions organized by the African slave population throughout the period of plantation enslavement. East Indian workers mounted similar challenges to the terms of their contractual obligations in Trinidad and Guyana.

ANTICOLONIALISM AND THE INTERNATIONAL CHALLENGE TO WHITE SUPREMACY

Mobilization against the colonial administrative, managerial, and ownership elite became more persistent and organized during the twentieth century. The terms of nationalist contestation were shaped by the reality of the overwhelming predominance of the Black descendants of enslaved West Africans in the island territories under British colonial control. West Indian nationalism was shaped by the latter's struggles for self-definition and self-determination. It was informed by the internationalization of a newly developed racial consciousness during the first three decades of the twentieth century. The imposed assertions of white supremacy that legitimized European colonial domination were being challenged in new international discourses of racial identity.

Racial struggle and the quest for racial equality took on a new urgency in the twentieth century after the defeat by Ethiopia in 1896 of an Italian conquering army in the Battle of Adowa. This was followed by the victory of the Japanese over the armies of czarist Russia in 1904. These two events gave impetus to ongoing localized challenges to white supremacy that were occurring among the colonized populations of Africa, Asia, and the Caribbean. Europe's predispositions to war and conquest were beginning to erode claims of the superiority of white civilization. In the eyes of the colonized, the distinctions emerging in a new discourse of scientific racism between the "civilized" and the "savage" were being contradicted by these predispositions. The fratricidal tendencies of European "civilization," which became particularly glaring in the conduct of the First World War, contributed much to the corrosion of the myth of white supremacy as a basis for legitimizing colonial domination.

An emerging Black universal consciousness began to take institutional form in the organization of the fledgling Pan-African Congress in London in 1900. It grew quickly, under the inspired leadership of the American W. E. B. Du Bois. In 1919, the congress was able to mount a highly successful and credible alternative to the Paris Peace Conference, which had convened to set the terms of peace after World War I. The intention of the congress was to force the insertion of issues of racial domination into international policy making.

Challenges to colonial domination in the West Indies contributed integrally to the new international currents informing the development of a new consciousness of African universal identity. During the first decade of the twentieth century, direct connections were established between Black West Indians and Booker T. Washington in the United States. A number of Black West Indians attended a world conference held at Washington's Tuskegee Institute in 1912. There, they were highly influenced by Washington's ideas. Some, including Augustus Parkinson of Barbados, began to directly advocate for a modification of the educational systems of their colonies in keeping with the Tuskegee model (Hoyos 1972, 98–100).

The Jamaican Marcus Garvey was perhaps most influential in the development of African identific consciousness during the first three decades of the twentieth century. Between 1909 and 1914, Garvey became exposed to labor radicalism during stints in Panama, Costa Rica, and London as a West Indian migrant laborer. After being introduced to Pan-Africanism in London, he returned to Jamaica in 1914 to form the Universal Negro Improvement Association (UNIA). The association received its philosophical underpinnings from a combination of ideas gleaned from the labor movement of Europe, from Pan-Africanism, and in particular from the influence of Booker T. Washington. The UNIA grew rapidly, developing branches in the West Indies, the United States, and Africa. At the invitation of Washington, Garvey traveled to the United States, where, between 1916 and his deportation in 1927, the UNIA developed into a formidable international Black nationalist movement. Total membership exceeded five million in 1927. At the UNIA's convention held in Harlem in 1920, attended by twenty-five thousand delegates, a Declaration of Rights of Negro People of the World was drafted demanding self-determination, political and legal equality for Blacks, and the liberation of Africa (Hintzen and Will 1988). More than anything else, the UNIA became an organizational manifestation of a new universal understanding of diasporic intimacy among the Black populations of the world. It was this understanding that began to inform the development of nationalist consciousness at the various levels of sociopolitical organization.

The development of racial consciousness on an international scale continued unabated during the third decade of the century, fueled by the formation of new race-based international organizations. The League against Imperialism was launched as a "non-White counterforce to the League of Nations" in 1927 at an international conference held in Brussels. It was developed in response to the steadfast refusal by the League of Nations to address the issue of racial equality in its charter and deliberations. The delegates to the conference represented a multinational multiracial alliance opposed to the principle of racial domination in national and international affairs. Opposition to the League of Nations also came to be reflected in race-specific organizations such as the League of Coloured Peoples (LCP), formed in London in 1931. Both organizations mounted calls for racial equality, challenging white racial superiority at the national and international levels (Lauren 1988, 76–101). They formalized efforts aimed directly at challenging colonial domination. By the end of the 1930s, branches of the LCP began to show up throughout the West Indies.

International currents against colonialism were being fed during the 1930s by the two emerging superpowers of the Soviet Union and the United States. The Soviet Union had begun to take an intense interest in Europe's colonial possessions indirectly through the Red International of Labor Unions, of which a Black Trinidadian, George Padmore, was a leading official. It developed an even more direct involvement through the Negro Bureau of the Red International of Labor Unions, which Padmore headed, and through the International Trade Union Committee of Negro Workers, an offshoot of the Red International, for which Padmore served as secretary (Howe 1993, 84–89). The development of an international alliance of Black labor fed directly into anticolonial nationalist organizations in the West Indies. West Indian leaders of an increasingly powerful labor movement began to develop strong ties of affiliation with socialist and communist labor organizations in Europe. These affiliations, developed largely through West Indian intellectuals in London, led eventually in 1945 to the founding of the Caribbean Labour Congress (CLC) as a broad association of trade unions and their affiliated parties in the English-speaking Caribbean. The parent body of the CLC was located in London; an influential segment of its leadership, many with direct ties to the Communist Party of Great Britain, began advocating an anticolonial agenda of radical social change for the West Indies. Its affiliates included Britain's socialist Trade Union Congress and the British Labour Party. The main thrust of the CLC was in the securing of an independent Federation of the West Indies.

It becomes clear, therefore, that, in combination, anticolonial sentiments in Europe, particularly among socialist and communist political organizations in Britain, and the activism of the Soviet Union had influenced the nationalist efforts in the region in deep and profound ways. The willingness of both to recognize and acknowledge the integral ties between racial domination, international capitalism, and the structure of colonial exploitation appealed to the nationalist leadership. In British Guiana, one of the central figures in labor organization in the region, Hubert Nathaniel Critchlow, affiliated his union with the Socialist International, and, by 1930, he was calling for a socialist reconstruction based on the workers' struggle to overthrow capitalism. In 1932, Critchlow visited the Soviet Union (Chase 1964, 50–53).

The profound effect of the socialist and communist challenges to capitalism on the development of West Indian nationalism is unquestioned. Many of the region's leaders who went on to head postindependence governments were members of the CLC. These included Grantly Adams of Barbados (who went on to become prime minister of a West Indian federation), Michael Manley of Jamaica, and Cheddi Jagan and Forbes Burnham of Guyana (Howe 1993, 210–13). But racial nationalism led to an inevitable conflict between the articulation of this form of nationalism and international socialism. The multiracial vision of an international proletariat that stood at the heart of socialist ideology conflicted sharply with the emerging development of a universal Black consciousness. Once the latter became the basis of the anticolonial struggle in Africa and the Caribbean, then the door was open for a rejection of socialism. In the 1930s, international events were to bring the contradiction to a head in a way that profoundly shaped the development of West Indian nationalism. Ultimately, these had the effect of curbing radical expression and bringing to the center of nationalist discourse new conceptualizations of identity informed by images of an African "diasporic intimacy" (Gilroy 1993). The appeal in the colonies of arguments for a class struggle began to erode with the rising tide of fascism in Europe. The new racial discourse strengthened the appeal of those advocating the contestation of colonialism on racial grounds. It contributed also to an erosion of the appeal of white morality and its claim to occupancy of the center of civilized discourse. The class-based challenges to capitalism emanating from Europe began to lose their appeal. The weak reaction of radical Europe to Mussolini's invasion of Ethiopia in 1935 confirmed that the paramount basis of identity was race. This notion was reinforced by the complicity of white governments in their failure to act in the League of Nations against Italy. The invasion galvanized Black opinion throughout the world. Marcus Garvey, the preeminent Black political leader in Jamaica, declared Mussolini to be the "arch barbarian of our times." The American Committee for Ethiopia and the International African Friends of Abyssinia were formed and joined the LCP and the Pan-African movement to condemn the invasion. In the West Indies, the invasion gave birth to a new Black "Rastafarian" nationalist movement, which took its name from Haile Selassie's given name, Ras Tafari (Lauren 1988, 118–22).

The profound shift in ideological direction and affinities from class to race was immediately evident among those West Indian intellectuals in Britain who had become the driving force behind the development of nationalist thought. Particularly important in this regard were C. L. R. James and George Padmore from Trinidad. Before the invasion of Ethiopia, the two were deeply involved in British left-wing politics. They had become very influential in efforts to develop and support the anticolonial agendas of socialist and communist political organizations in Britain. Padmore's communism had led to a particularly close relationship with the Soviet Union. Even before Mussolini's invasion, both had begun to develop suspicions about the commitment of the European left to colonial liberation. The reaction of the Left to the invasion brought these concerns to a head. Padmore broke with the Soviet Union over its refusal to observe sanctions against Italy. Eventually, the break extended to communism itself. Joined by James, Jomo Kenyatta of Kenya, and other Black immigrants from Britain's colonies, Padmore formed the International African Friends of Abyssinia. This signaled the beginning of a new ideological direction that placed Africa at the center of a discourse of identity and nationalism. The intellectuals most responsible for shaping the character of West Indian nationalism were at the very center of this development. Their new understandings translated directly into the reformulation of West Indian nationalist expression. The shift to notions of a universal African consciousness as the basis of the struggle against colonialism was institutionalized in the formation of the International African Service Bureau, and later the Pan-African Federation (Howe 1993, 84–86). It signaled a new emphasis on international Black organization in efforts to secure national sovereignty for Black countries. The shift was formalized in 1945 at the Pan-African Congress held in Manchester. Many of those in attendance, including Jomo Kenyatta and Kwame Nkrumah, were to return to their respective countries to lead independence movements. Thus, by the late 1930s, the basis was laid for the insertion of Pan-Africanism into the development of nationalist consciousness in the predominantly Black colonies of Europe located in Africa and the Caribbean. From then on, nationalist campaigns were to be based on the independent organization of persons of African descent. Activists in London began to emphasize country-focused independence movements. In the colonies themselves, attention shifted to racial mobilization. Radical left movements such as the Movement for Colonial Freedom, formed in 1954, mounted generalized challenges to colonialism itself. This was the culmination of efforts by disparate anticolonial movements in Britain to mobilize for independence for Britain's colonies. Included among the groups represented in the movement were labor unions, students' groups, and socialist and communist organizations. They were joined by progressive members of the British Labour Party, who gave the movement clout in the British Parliament. The aim was to bring an end to British colonialism as a "moral" imperative (Howe 1993, 234). This internal campaign against colonialism in Britain created space for the development of racialized nationalist challenges. The nationalist movements in the colonies and their country-based metropolitan organizations were freed from the burden of making strategic racial compromises with metropolitan allies. Such alliances would have been rendered imperative without the independent development of ideological challenges to colonialism that drove British anticolonial opposition.

It was the influence of Pan-Africanism as defined and shaped by the Pan-African Congress and its predecessors that informed the development of Afro-creole nationalism in the West Indies. Pan-Africanism became the basis for the contestation of white supremacy as the linchpin of European colonialism (Lauren 1988, 118–22; Hintzen 1997, 47–45). Its influence gave rise to a conceptualization of the West Indian state as the institutional embodiment of Black nationalist aspirations for sovereignty and self-determination.

Pan-Africanism provided the ideological framework for the contestation of white supremacy upon which rested colonial legitimacy. The growing institutional and ideological separation from the radical movement in the metropole had profound consequences for the direction taken by the nationalist movement. The relationship between colonialism and capitalism itself went largely uncontested among the large majority of the nationalist leaders. This allowed the United States to begin to exercise the most profound influence upon West Indian nationalism. American involvement with West Indian nationalism emerged out of a combination of strategic concerns, economic interests, and domestic political calculations. These propelled the United States into a dominant role in a developing tripartite relationship that included Great Britain and its West Indian colonies. It is out of this relationship that the character and limits of West Indian nationalism were established (Fraser 1994).

US NATIONALIST INVOLVEMENT

During the interwar years, the United States became firmly convinced that the emergent pattern of neomercantilism in European colonial relations was detrimental to its economic interests. Support for the anticolonial movements in the region was seen as a means of breaking this mercantilist hold. There were also domestic political pressures for US intervention. Economic crisis and political turmoil in the West Indies were creating pressures for the migration of West Indians to the United States. Many of the new migrants settled in New York, attracted by opportunities in the service and commercial sectors of that city. They quickly became inserted into American racial politics at a time of growing strategic dependence by the Democratic Party on the Black vote. Their very presence engendered deep concern and sympathy among African American voters for the plight of West Indians who remained at home under the yolk of British imperialism, and the aforementioned economic crisis and resultant turmoil in the region. Strategic geopolitical considerations also weighed heavily on US policy in the region. The growing political turmoil in Europe that preceded World War II compelled the United States to increase its strategic presence in the Caribbean for its own protection. All of these concerns propelled the United States to take a special and active interest in the region and to pay particular attention to Britain's West Indian colonies (Fraser 1994, 9–53).

American direct intervention in policy making in Britain's West Indian colonies was formalized during World War II. It came in the wake of the US administration's decision in August 1940 to provide destroyers to an embattled Britain in support of that country's war with Nazi Germany. In exchange, the United States demanded the right to locate military bases in the colonies. Direct US influence was exercised through the Anglo-American Caribbean Commission, formed in 1942. The establishment of the commission was part of a broader effort to place ultimate responsibility for the protection of the entire hemisphere directly in US hands in the event of a German victory in Europe. An agreement to this effect was signed with leaders of the independent states of the hemisphere. It gave the United States the right to assume, unilaterally, trusteeship of the colonies of any European power defeated by Germany should the latter attempt to transfer to itself sovereignty of such colonies.

The United States used the Anglo-American Caribbean Commission effectively to further its anticolonial interests. Immediately it embarked upon a campaign of intense criticism of Britain's colonial policies. Such criticism was informed less by enlightenment and more by profound concerns over the destabilizing consequences of resentment against European rule. In the view of the US administration, it was this very resentment that explained the rapidity of Japan's advance into Europe's Asian colonies. The anticolonialism of the United States stemmed also from domestic political and security concerns. There were fears that civil disorder in the West Indies would trigger civil unrest at home among the West Indian population and their African American supporters, particularly in New York (Fraser 1994, 55–89).

Thus, the United States was inserted into West Indian colonial discourse as a defender of nationalism. Its involvement began to have a profound effect upon the orientation and ideological character of the West Indian nationalist movement. The Democratic administration positioned itself to shape the political currents of the region and establish strategic political ties with its nationalist leaders. With this involvement, opportunities for surveillance and intelligence gathering increased considerably.

With the defeat of Germany, US foreign policy had to respond to a new and different set of concerns. The strategic and economic considerations that drove the earlier policy of anticolonialism began to disappear rapidly in the face of profound changes occurring in the postwar international environment. Developing postwar economic relations between the United States and Europe began to eat away at US anticolonial predispositions. Anticolonialism in the prewar era was driven by the desire of American policy makers to gain access to the markets of Europe's colonies and exploit their investment opportunities. At the end of the war, mercantilist barriers were dismantled as the United States assumed the major role in the postwar reconstruction of Europe. Increasingly, US economic interests were becoming tied to the ability of Europe to maintain its exploitative relationships with its colonies. The economic devastation of the war led the colonial powers to become increasingly dependent on economic surpluses. A strong, stable, and resurgent western Europe was central to the ability of the United States to assert its superpower status as the leader of the capitalist world. US capital invested in postwar western Europe thus became increasingly vulnerable to decolonization. With this, the economic motivation for US anticolonial policy vanished (Fraser 1994, 93–121).

Profound changes were also occurring in US domestic politics that acted to significantly diminish Black influence on national decision-making. The new postwar Republican administration was not dependent on the African American vote, as was its Democratic predecessor. Moreover, it had very few ties to the African American community. There was little incentive, therefore, to consider the concerns of the Black population in shaping postwar foreign policy. Anticolonialism was also affected by a resurgence of racist views that were beginning to hold sway in the United States. Such views began to feed into generalized notions about the unfitness for rule of non-European peoples. Additionally, the Joseph McCarthy era of virulent anticommunism at home began to affect negatively anticolonial policy abroad by provoking extreme intolerance for nationalist movements that were even mildly critical of Western capitalism or of the United States.

All the above factors signaled an end to the economic, strategic, and domestic political considerations that had driven the anticolonial policies of the Democratic administrations of the 1930s and 1940s. As the United States asserted its role as leader of the free world in the postwar environment, the containment of communism became the driving principle of US foreign policy. It also became the basis of support for or opposition to nationalist movements in the former colonies.

Nonetheless, any predisposition for intervention against anticolonial movements in Europe's colonies was constrained by the realpolitik of the emerging Cold War. New considerations were beginning to impinge on US foreign policy. The emergent Soviet Union was providing considerable support to anticolonial movements in Europe's former colonies. The United States was cast, in a new ideological campaign aimed at winning the hearts of the new nationalist movements and regimes, in the role of a repressive reactionary power. In this climate, any support provided by the United States for a return to the colonial status quo had to be tempered by geopolitical and geostrategic calculations. Such support came with the real possibility of confirming the role of the United States as a neocolonial power. What emerged in US foreign policy was the practice of supporting those nationalist leaders with an explicit commitment to anticommunism and a pro-Western agenda. At the same time, the United States embarked on an aggressive policy of active intervention against radical and progressive leaders of anticolonial campaigns in Europe's colonies.

Historian Cary Fraser argues persuasively that it was within the context of this new US policy of communist containment that the boundaries of West Indian nationalism came to be defined. A potential conflict with Britain over support for the nationalist aspirations of its West Indian colonies was defused in the face of the colonies' declining economic importance. With the economic burden of supporting these colonies growing, Britain began making preparations for ending its colonial responsibilities in the region. It began to promote a plan for federation as a formula for securing their political independence. With independence inevitable, US policy in the region shifted to ensuring an anticommunist agenda for the postindependence governments. It did so through active intervention.

US intervention in the region was justified on a number of counts. Washington had become acutely aware of the role of radicals, many of them known Marxists, in the region's nationalist movements. Avowed socialists had managed to gain political power through elections in British Guiana in 1953 and again in 1957. The left wing of the political leadership in Trinidad had become highly influential in the shaping of political policy. It had managed to shape a campaign to force the United States to give up a portion of one of its remaining military bases on the island for the location of the capital of a proposed West Indian federation. Undergirding all of this was the turn taken by the Cuban revolution in 1961. America was unprepared to brook another Cuba in the Western Hemisphere.

Concerned over the presence and influence of the radical Left in the region, the United States began to act decisively to define the limits of West Indian nationalism. With the active support of Great Britain, a campaign was mounted to expunge any hint of radicalism and anti-Americanism from the nationalist agendas of West Indian political movements. With US policy driving Britain's actions and decisions, the West Indian nationalist movement took on a decidedly anticommunist and pro-West character. This phase of US interventionism, Fraser argues, marks the passage of the British West Indies into the US sphere of influence.

THE CLASS BASIS OF AFRO-CREOLE NATIONALISM

West Indian nationalism was also shaped by the historical unfolding of the domestic political economy. At the beginning of the 1930s, urbanization and proletarianization were creating conditions for the development of a trade union movement. Trade unions were being organized out of massive mobilization campaigns for better working conditions. Even in Guyana and Trinidad, with their large and growing East Indian populations, the African population was at the center of these mobilization efforts. The movement was fed by the economic crisis of the Depression. Beginning in 1935, worker dissatisfaction finally exploded into debilitating riots that persisted throughout the English-speaking West Indies until 1939 (West India Royal Commission 1945).

Developments in Europe were acting to legitimize the role of professionals and intellectuals in the organization and leadership of the growing working-class movements. West Indian intellectuals residing in Britain had become allied with their European counterparts as champions of progressive causes. The emergence of the British Labour Party provided a great deal of legitimacy to these causes. Progressive members of the West Indian middle class were encouraged to support similar mobilization efforts in their respective colonies.

During the twentieth century, the size and strategic significance of the West Indian middle strata increased considerably. This was partly in response to an infusion of foreign capital for large-scale plantation agroproduction, agro-industry, mining, assembly and packaging operations, refining, import substitution, and the like. The expansion of the middle strata was spurred also by the growth of state administration. The demand for an intermediate strata of functionaries engendered by these developments provided Blacks and coloreds who had managed to acquire skills and education with the wherewithal for their eventual emergence as a powerful political force for change. Most important among this intermediary group were the professional and salaried urban workers holding state and private-sector jobs.

The assumption of leadership positions in worker movements was a considerable departure from the historical practice of this colonized middle strata. It represented a shift from the prior strategy of seeking inclusion in the circle of the colonial elite as a basis of increasing the power and influence of its members. With colonialism and its system of white supremacy under attack, efforts to be included at the apex of a defunct and illegitimate system lost credence and instrumental appeal. Such efforts were replaced by strategies aimed at capturing positions of leadership in a new world order of independent sovereign nations. This was to be acquired through constitutional means. Self-determination became the new focus of political behavior among the politically active segment of this domestic middle strata.

As early as the second decade of the twentieth century, members of the middle strata were making demands for the devolution of power to representatives of the colonized populations. Organized efforts began with the formation of the Representative Government Association in Grenada. Founded by Theophilus Marryshow, a journalist, the association embarked on a campaign for an independent West Indies. In 1919, Marryshow's inspiration led to the founding of a similar organization in Dominica under the leadership of attorney Cecil Rawle. These efforts spurred the development of a regionwide movement launched at a conference in British Guiana in 1926. The conference was attended by political and labor leaders from throughout Britain's colonized West Indian territories. It was at this conference that the ideology and organization of West Indian Afro-creole nationalism was fashioned and formulated.

By the latter half of the 1930s, local political leaders were making strident calls for self-government and eventual independence. These leaders came predominantly from the ranks of the middle-strata elite. They were also predominantly Black and colored. They included Barbadian attorney Sir Grantley Adams, Jamaican colored businessman Alexander Bustamante (the son of a white planter), colored Jamaican attorney Norman Manley, and Black oil worker Uriah Butler of Trinidad. The sole racial exception was Portuguese Trinidadian publisher Albert Gomes. Butler and Nathaniel Critchlow from Guyana were the only nationalist leaders attending the conference with working-class backgrounds. Significantly, by the 1950s, Gomes, Butler, and Critchlow had all faded from the political scene.

This leadership quickly established itself as a vanguard of the new ideology of nationalism. Its strategic insertion into the politics of anticolonialism rested almost exclusively on its ability to mobilize support from among the lower strata of workers and peasants. With the exceptions of Guyana and Trinidad, with their large, predominantly rural East Indian population, these lower strata were overwhelmingly Black. An appeal to racial identity, under such circumstances, made political and strategic sense. Fashioned by an increasingly anticolonial and antiwhite middle-class leadership, it was such an appeal that began to shape the character of the nationalist movement in the region (Hintzen 1995).

In its formulation, therefore, the ideology of Afro-creole nationalism came to integrate lower-strata challenges to colonial and European domination with the aspirations to power of the middle-strata elite. The "racial understandings" that informed this nationalist movement differed in significant respects from the ideologies of Pan-Africanism developing in Europe and North America. In the West Indies, there was little by way of commitment to notions of the new commonality rooted in an African "diasporic intimacy" (Gilroy 1993). The emerging context of the struggle was different in the colonies. So were the prerequisites for mounting a successful anticolonial campaign. Increasingly, these campaigns became dependent on strategic support provided by one or the other of the two emerging superpowers. A rejection of colonialism on purely racial grounds was incompatible with strategic dependence on either of these white superpowers.

Afro-creole nationalism was critical if mass support for the political agenda of the emergent elite was to be secured. It was to the understandings of this Black working class that the nationalist appeal was pitched. As such, the rituals and symbols that were embraced by the movement were not explicitly antiwhite.

They incorporated instead aspects of the expressive culture of this domestic lower strata, including their patterns of speech and dress, their forms of worship, and the like. Ritualistic embrace of these local forms served as a visible indicator of the willingness of the middle strata to reject their own aspirations for colonial elite status, thereby legitimizing their anticolonial credentials.

NATIONALISM AND NEOCOLONIAL ACCOMMODATION

In the postwar era, new forms of capitalist organization were beginning to signal the demise of colonialism and the emergence of neocolonialism. Through its challenge to colonial domination, nationalism was creating conditions for the insertion of these new forms into the domestic political economy of the former colonies. The United States was located at the undisputed center of an emerging neocolonial reality. In the West Indies, Afro-creole nationalism became the legitimizing principle for the penetration of these neocolonial forms. Colonialism was rapidly becoming an impediment to the development of more intensive forms of exploitation in the peripheral economies. This, more than anything else, explained the prewar attack mounted against colonialism by the United States. New developments in global capital were engendering new patterns of international capitalist relations. These demanded significant changes in the political economies of the colonies. The emergence of the United States as the financial and technological superpower within the industrialized capitalist world and as the world's major market was the force driving these transformations. The relations of empire between the European colonial powers and their non-European colonies were being replaced, rapidly, by a new focus of international relations centered upon the United States.

In numerous respects, the nationalist movements paved the way for accommodating the new demands of neocolonialism. Sovereignty freed the new postcolonial leadership from obligations imposed and maintained by colonial power. There were enormous benefits to be derived from a reorientation of their countries' economic relations away from the colonial metropole and toward the United States. The latter had catapulted to a position as the world's dominant economic and financial power.

During the 1950s, West Indian nationalist leaders began to employ their increasing autonomy to effect a reorientation in their international relations. They began a gradual shift in their economic and political relations toward the United States. A potent signal of this shift was the formulation of plans to implement a "Puerto Rican" model of development patterned after the model of "industrialization by invitation" that informed the bootstrap policies of the United States in Puerto Rico (Mandle 1996, 57–71). Such a development was the predictable outcome of the deepening ties of dependence with the United States. It was intensified by a developing tourist industry based on North American visitors that was becoming indispensable to the economic well-being of islands such as Barbados and Jamaica. Additionally, the United States was beginning to absorb a growing number of West Indian immigrants under conditions of growing unemployment and underemployment in the region. North American migration was becoming critical to the region's efforts at poverty alleviation. Remittances from these migrants were proving important as additional sources of income and economic support.

The nationalist leaders were faced with the reality of raised expectations promised in their anticolonial campaign. Popular participation in politics, engendered by the nationalist campaign and institutionalized by the insertion of democratic representative government, brings with it demands for economic betterment. Those at the bottom come to expect, therefore, significant improvements in their life conditions. Such expectations of improvement give considerable legitimacy to nationalist leaders attempting to institute changes in economic and political arrangements in pursuit of modernity. Thus, the development of ties with the world's economic superpower made considerable sense.

Nationalist ideology and aspirations produced a governing elite whose position of power came to be legitimized increasingly by their qualifications as "modernizers." As the embodiment of Afro-creole aspirations, these elites came to be popularly understood to represent the "will of the people." In exercising this "will," understood in terms of the need for development, they entered into a new pattern of neocolonial domination and dependency. This became manifest in a shift in relations of dependency to the new global superpower, the United States. Such a shift in orientation served more than pragmatic functions. It was also a powerful symbol of self-assertiveness for each country's new and emergent nationalist leadership. A new, neocolonial reality was hidden under the symbolic camouflage of the exercise of the sovereign right of international association (Hintzen 1995).

NATIONALISM AND THE COLD WAR AGENDA

Economic pragmatism led, naturally, to the development of political ties with North America. The new pattern of neocolonial dependency brought in its wake an imposed pro-capitalist agenda that placed severe limits and imposed strict conditionalities on domestic and international policy. This came with profound ideological implications as the nationalist leaders lined up behind the United States across the Cold War divide. Anticommunism became a justification for the constriction of freedom and for the setting of limits on democratic participation. This emergent postcolonial construction began to take shape even before the granting of independence. Once inserted into the Cold War discourse, nationalist leaders in the region quickly imposed the litmus test of anticommunism as a legitimizing principle of political participation at any level. Without exception, it was anticommunist leadership that led the governments of the region to independence during the 1960s and 1970s. Radical members of the nationalist movement found themselves isolated and abandoned as the new anticommunist agenda began to unfold. Those who attempted to break out of the ambit of the United States and the strictures of anticommunism all found themselves suffering from a near consensus of opposition among the postcolonial leadership of the region. Moreover, persistent and pervasive efforts at destabilization by the United States received the covert, and sometimes overt, support of the region's nationalist leadership.

In pursuit of their ideological agenda, nationalist leaders were prepared to violate the very principles of democracy and self-determination for which they had fought in their anticolonial campaign. They rallied around an anticommunist coalition of the People's National Congress and the United Force in British Guiana in the early 1960s. These two parties had become engaged in a violent campaign against the colony's legitimate, democratically elected government of the People's Progressive Party (PPP). The campaign against the government was conducted with the orchestrated support and intervention of the United States and Great Britain. Both governments had declared the leadership of the ruling party to be communist. Reeling from a combination of covert activity, constitutional fiat, and violent confrontation, Cheddi Jagan, the colony's prime minister, was forced to yield to demands for an imposed settlement that guaranteed the ouster of his party from power. A change in government in 1964 ushered in a period of brutal undemocratic rule that lasted until 1992 and left in its path economic ruin and racial turmoil (Hintzen 1989, 52–56; Sheehan 1967; Pearson 1964; Lens 1965, 779).

In Trinidad, the People's National Movement (PNM)'s explicit rejection of socialism at its formation in 1956 proved not enough to satisfy the litmus test of anticommunism. While in office, its leadership became embroiled in a conflict with the United States over the use of the naval base at Chaguaramas for the capital of the West Indies Federation. The intervention of Britain on behalf of the United States forced a purging by the ruling party of its radical leadership and secured a denunciation of communism by its leader, Eric Williams (Ryan 1972, 197–208). In exchange, a constitutional arrangement was signed with Britain that guaranteed the party's continued political power and the country's independence, which was quickly granted in 1962. The PNM remained in power until 1986 before losing in elections to a coalition of moderate and right-wing parties in the face of an ongoing economic crisis.

Thus, the insertion of Cold War ideology into Afro-creole nationalism created the conditions for control of governing institutions by anticommunist political leaders, supported by powerful international actors. All the leaders who came to power during the 1960s did so while announcing their commitment to a moderate ideological position and a pro-capitalist program of development for their respective countries. In 1961, Alexander Bustamante came to power in Jamaica by engaging in a virulent attack on communism, Cuba, and the West Indies Federation. In the process, he swept the socialist-leaning government of Norman Manley out of power. He was rewarded with full self-government. In 1962, Eric Williams was granted independence for Trinidad and Tobago after declaring communism as "one of the evils facing his country" (Ryan 1972). With independence came an explicit commitment to capitalist development linked to North America. The governments of Barbados, Guyana, Jamaica, and Trinidad and Tobago, all of which were granted independence in the 1960s, embraced the credo of "industrialization by invitation" as the basis for their development. They aggressively pursued efforts to attract foreign industry while opening their economies to free trade and providing guarantees of profit repatriation and protective legislation to foreign investors.

The pattern of support by Britain and the United States for leaders embracing moderate and pro-Western ideological positions was replicated throughout the region. Such support allowed Vere Bird in Antigua and Barbuda to dominate the colony's politics. In 1967, Bird became its first premier under a constitution of self-government. His economic program was based on the attraction of foreign investors in light industries and tourism. Support for anticommunists allowed the moderate George Price in Belize to continue to dominate the colony's domestic political affairs. In Dominica, such support led to the success of moderate Edward LeBlanc in ousting the committed socialist Phyllis Shand Allfrey from the leadership of the Dominica Labour Party. LeBlanc led the party to electoral victory in 1961. Immediately, the government was given increased powers. In 1967, under a new self-governing constitution, Dominica was granted associated statehood with Britain. It was British support for conservative Herbert Blaize that allowed him to dominate the legislative affairs of Grenada after gaining power in 1962. In 1967, Blaize became the colony's first premier after the granting of associated statehood with Great Britain. In Montserrat, William Bramble's change in strategy from agitation against the colony's economic elite to one of accommodation was rewarded with a political victory for his Labour Party in 1961. He immediately instituted a program of economic development based upon the active promotion of foreign-financed tourism and the attraction of foreign capital. In Saint Lucia, conservative George Compton's United Workers Party won an electoral victory in 1964. Under his leadership, the country was granted associated statehood in

1967. His economic program, like that of the others, embraced the aggressive attraction of foreign investment.

Thus, in the 1960s the political leaders heading every single government of the British West Indies were uniform in their declared willingness to tow the line imposed by the United States. They fully embraced a pro-Western, vehemently anticommunist ideology. Were they not prepared to do so, they would have found themselves facing formidable international opposition directed from and dictated by the United States. This reality sparked the observation by Eric Williams, the former prime minister of Trinidad and Tobago, in pointing to Vietnam and the Dominican Republic, that a campaign would have been mounted against any leader who espoused views that were antithetical to the plans of the United States for the region (Williams 1974, 28).

THE CHALLENGE OF THIRD WORLDISM

During the 1960s, the legitimacy of the governing elite was integrally tied to discourses of development and sovereignty. The meaning of independence was shaped by expectations of modernity contained in popular understandings. It was shaped also by expectations of self-determination and racial equality. When such expectations remain unrealized, legitimacy is threatened. Conditions in the domestic and international environment at the end of the 1970s began to pose precisely such a threat.

Various actors, both domestic and international, reasserting discourses of race and imperialism, were raising new challenges to the policies and practices of the United States. Such challenges were beginning to manifest themselves in the civil rights movements of the 1950s and 1960s within the United States. Internationally, challenges were being raised in the wake of US Cold War interventionist policies. These were occurring during a period when the rigidities of Cold War demarcations were being compromised by new understandings and interpretations of "North-South" relations. Cold War ideology was being superseded by discussions of a new "Third World" commonality. With this, the issue of racial domination was telescoped onto the stage of international relations between the northern and southern countries. International relations were collapsing into discourses of racial domination and subordination.

The insertion of Third World understandings into the ideological debate, and of racial understandings into the arena of international relations, was increasingly evident. The development of Arab socialism under the Nasser regime in Egypt was beginning to legitimize challenges to Western capitalism on racial grounds. The direct intervention of US troops in Vietnam in 1965, and the subsequent bombing of Laos and Cambodia, served symbolically as a manifestation of a new, racialized imperialism. This was the most visible of a pattern of ubiquitous involvement of the United States against popular Third World challenges to colonialism and imperialism.

Popular opinion in the newly constructed Third World quickly turned against the United States, which was beginning to be viewed as the architect of the new racial imperialism. All the signs in the new "North-South" confrontation began pointing to the moral and strategic superiority of the South. The signs were everywhere and were becoming particularly evident in the growing success of progressive nationalist movements in Africa, in the defeat of the French by Vietnamese nationalists in 1954, and in the victory of the National Liberation Front against the French in Algeria in 1962. Almost everywhere there were indications of an escalating and winnable struggle against a racialized neocolonialism. This was highlighted particularly by the initiation of armed struggle in the Portuguese colonies of Guinea-Bissau and Angola. The Sharpeville massacre in South Africa underscored the continued paramountcy of race in human relations (Chaliand 1978, 17–24). This evidence of a newly racialized struggle was not confined merely to instances of Western interventionism. The split from the Soviet Union by China in 1960 and the emergence of the latter as an international power in its own right began to complicate notions of communist solidarity. It inserted issues of race into radical debate as China became a major force in the new "Third World international."

Such were the ingredients that went into the construction of a new Third World common identity. It emerged out of a newly reconstructed sense of a common history rooted in colonialism and other forms of racialized domination by the white industrialized North. The common experience of domination forged a unity of interests among the countries of the South. This experience demanded the development of a common strategy of confrontation as the new prerequisite for solving endemic social, economic, and political crises of the newly understood Third World. The ideology of Third Worldism signaled a growing consensus that the problems facing less developed countries were directly attributable to their historical relations with the industrial North.

The emergence of Third Worldism was not independent of political challenges to capitalism in the colonial metropole. The victory of the socialist Labour Party in Britain in 1964 and its period of tenure until 1970 was mirrored in political developments throughout western Europe. Progressive governments capturing power in western Europe embarked on a reorganization of their respective societies along anticapitalist principles. As democratic socialism began to sweep western Europe, demands by the United States for strict adherence to anticommunism began to lose their moral force. Anti-imperialist currents were being felt in the United States as well. Anticommunism as a justification for a policy of intervention in the Third World was under increasing challenge in the growing popular opposition to the Vietnam War and military intervention in Southeast Asia more generally.

The practice of racial segregation in the United States was beginning to telescope onto the international arena in the debate on racial imperialism. US international intervention was linked with increasing assertions by America's people of color for civil rights. Racial imperialism abroad and racism at home began to underscore and support allegations of the existence of a racialized international division of labor.

Third World solidarity was given an additional boost by the growing rapprochement between the superpowers across the ideological divide. In 1971, President Richard Nixon visited the Soviet Union to signal the beginning of US-Soviet détente. In 1972, he visited China to cement a year-long effort out of which emerged a normalization of relations. With détente, the barriers of ideology that may otherwise have foreclosed the development of political and economic relations among Third World countries began to erode.

The West Indies was being inserted into this new international climate of Third Worldism at a time when Caribbean leaders were questioning the benefits of the developing relationship with the United States. Economic and political ties with the United States were not producing the anticipated returns in developmental transformation. Indeed, the period of nationalist assertion was accompanied by growing unemployment and poverty (Mandle 1996, 79–92). The new international climate combined with dashed expectations for economic betterment to cast doubt on the strategy of linkage with the United States at a time when new arguments of racial imperialism were beginning to challenge claims that such a strategy was a demonstration of self-determination.

By the late 1960s, there was in the West Indies a discernible swing in mass opinion toward alternative understandings of sovereignty and self-determination. It was fueled by Black power and antiwar demonstrations raging in the United States. The foreign policy of the United States soon came to be understood, popularly, as an extension of its practice of racial oppression against its Black population at home. West Indian governments advocating continued ties with the United States and uncritical support of Western capitalism soon found themselves under attack by advocates of Black power in the region. In 1968, the government of Jamaica was forced to take action. Walter Rodney, a citizen of Guyana, had gained regionwide prominence for his rejection of capitalism and neocolonialism. In his writings and speeches, he explained the roots of both in an internationalized racial division of labor. While a lecturer at the University of the West Indies in Jamaica, he began to conduct a Black power campaign against the government by organizing segments of the Jamaican lower classes. Fearing his growing popular appeal, the government of Jamaica revoked his right to work in the country. The decision provoked debilitating riots that almost crippled the conservative regime of the Jamaica Labour Party (Gray 1990, 145–65).

By 1970, Black power challenges to pro-US governments seemed to be sweeping the region. In Trinidad, radical trade unionists joined university students to create a mass movement that mounted a severe challenge the moderate pro-capitalist regime of Eric Williams. Their campaign of mass mobilization escalated when factions of the army, led by radical junior officers, mutinied in support of their cause. The Williams government survived the crisis only after the intervention of a loyalist coast guard and veiled threats of a US military intervention (Hintzen 1989, 78–84).

Radical nationalist leaders throughout the Third World were given considerable breathing room with the election of Jimmy Carter to the presidency of the United States in 1976. A commitment to human rights placed the Carter administration in conflict with corrupt right-wing regimes being opposed at home by radical insurgency movements. The pronouncements of the Carter administration against civil rights violations provided tacit support for the leaders of these movements. With the appointment of Andrew Young as US ambassador to the United Nations, there was less strident opposition to Third World socialist movements fighting campaigns of national liberation.

The reduction of this stridency came at a time of a discernible shift in the policies and programs of political leaders in the West Indies, leading to a mass rejection of the capitalist policies of the 1960s and of the practice of establishing exclusive ties with the United States. After 1971, the Forbes Burnham government in Guyana increasingly and publicly identified itself with the nonaligned movement and with Third World socialism. Guyana's foreign policy position became stridently anti-American, and the Burnham regime developed strong ties with Cuba and China. By 1975, a series of nationalizations of foreign concerns had contributed to acquisition by the state of 80 percent of the country's economic assets (Hintzen 1989, 65–69). Elsewhere in the region, governments intransigent to calls for change were swept out of power. In Jamaica, the People's National Party under Michael Manley won a landslide victory over the conservative Jamaica Labour Party (JLP). The victory was secured in a campaign that promised fundamental socioeconomic change informed by the principles of democratic socialism. Manley pledged the elimination of class barriers and class privilege, "real" sovereignty and self-determination at the international level free from the dictates of external powers, and local control of the domestic economy that would be free from the dictates of foreign investors (Manley 1982, 25–91). In 1970, Maurice Bishop returned to Grenada and joined with radical activist Kenrick Radix to forge a popular movement against the corrupt right-wing government of Eric Gairy. In 1979, his socialist New Jewel Movement seized power from the Gairy regime and established relations with Cuba and eastern European nations.

The yet-to-be-independent smaller islands were also swept away in the tide of Third World radicalism. In Dominica, the government of Patrick John had to resort to a brutal campaign against popular political dissent to maintain power against calls for radical reform. In Saint Lucia, the Saint Lucia Labour Party (SLP) began a process of internal radicalization after George Odlum returned from Great Britain to eventually become the country's deputy prime minister. The party was able to attract enormous popular support.

During the 1970s, there was growing space for the exploration of alternative political and economic strategies in an international environment that challenged US hegemony. Increasingly, the United States was cast as the international leader of a new form of racialized neocolonialism. During the second half of the 1970s, an economic recession added to the United States' weakened international position despite a growing conservative climate within that country that favored a more aggressive international policy to combat the spread of radicalism.

GLOBALIZATION AND THE END OF NATIONALISM

By the beginning of the 1980s, an international debt crisis, generalized conditions of economic recession, and a resurgence of the Cold War created a new environment that forced a reformulation of nationalist discourse. The economic crisis was fueled by an inflationary explosion during 1973–1974 that produced a doubling of commodity prices and a quadrupling of oil prices. The crisis contributed to a 43 percent increase in the cost of Third World imports from industrialized countries. Serious declines in the price of commodity exports and significant drops in demand began to place severe pressure on the ability of the Third World economies to earn foreign exchange (Girvan 1984, 169). The accumulation of huge current account deficits forced drastic cutbacks in imports, and considerable declines in incomes and economic activity. Huge deficits accumulated during the period were offset by relatively easy access to foreign exchange support made available through the accumulated financial surpluses of oil-exporting countries. Foreign exchange support was made available by the International Monetary Fund (IMF) through an oil facility set up to fund oil-related balance of payment deficits. For the English-speaking Caribbean, foreign exchange surpluses accumulated by Trinidad and Tobago, an oil producer, became available for the deficit financing of current account imbalances for most countries in the region.

During 1979–1980, a second "oil shock" produced another series of dramatic increases in oil prices, fueling another international recession that rocked the Western economies. The resulting escalation of interest rates in international financial markets and decreased demand for export commodities placed enormous additional pressure on foreign exchange. Debtor countries, borrowing at flexible interest rates or seeking to refinance loans, were faced with enormous, unpredictable interest payments. Under the threat of default by major borrowers in 1982, international banks made a decision to suspend or limit loans to many beleaguered Third World economies. Countries in the region, rocked by severe economic crises, were forced to turn to the IMF as the agency of first resort for financing balance of payments deficits. Quickly, the IMF was joined by the World Bank in making demands for enormous concessions in exchange for assistance in a program of structural adjustment. These adjustments imposed a regime of strong controls on domestic demand, cuts in state expenditure, devaluation, export promotion, economic liberalization, and concessions aimed at attracting foreign investors.

The burgeoning middle classes and urban lower classes, who had emerged as the most strategic political force in the English-speaking Caribbean, were most profoundly affected by the ensuing economic crisis. As their lifestyles became threatened, their support shifted to leaders whose programs seemed to have the best chance of attracting foreign investment and foreign exchange support. Popular support shifted to those political leaders willing to aggressively pursue a program aimed at attracting foreign financing. A consensus emerged that the leaders best suited to run these countries were those able to develop strategic ties with international actors who were in a position to deliver badly needed economic assistance.

In the early 1970s, the democratic socialism of Jamaica's Michael Manley came to typify new understandings of nationalist self-determination. Manley was the first to suffer the consequences of the changes in the international economic and political environment. Soon after 1976, his People's National Party became the target of political and economic destabilization efforts by the United States. President Jimmy Carter's dovish approach to the Third World was coming under increasing attack by a resurgent conservative movement led by Ronald Reagan. In Jamaica, escalating debt, capital flight, and divestment of foreign capital from the domestic economy was fueling a growing economic crisis. In its efforts to secure balance of payments support, the Manley government was forced to approach the IMF and accept conditions of economic reorganization that were anathema to the party's espoused ideological position. The conditionalities imposed were more stringently applied by the IMF as a means of ensuring a reversal of policies rooted in the principles of socialism (Girvan 1984, 149–209; Anderson and Witter 1994). In the process, wittingly or unwittingly, the IMF became another component in an interventionist campaign aimed at supporting the pro-capitalist, pro-Western opposition.

The program of "stabilization" called for by the IMF demanded a devaluation of Jamaica's currency and massive cuts in state expenditure. These exacerbated economic conditions, causing further erosion in popular support for the ruling party particularly among the country's middle classes. A propaganda campaign succeeded in placing the blame for the crisis on Manley's socialism and his ties with Cuba. Quickly, a majority of the voting population became convinced that strengthening relations with the United States offered the best hope for crisis resolution. Majority support shifted to the Jamaica Labour Party headed by conservative Edward Seaga. The archetypal conservative pragmatist, Seaga had assumed the leadership of the party in 1974 with a reputation as an economic wizard that he had earned during a stint as minister of finance and planning between 1967 and 1972. He was unequivocally committed to the capitalist model of development based on the attraction of foreign private investment. He was strongly pro-Western and pro-American. And he was able to rely on the support of the Carter administration as well as American conservatives, particularly Ronald Reagan, who, as a presidential candidate, took special interest in Jamaica's affairs.

Seaga's JLP won an electoral victory on December 15, 1980, after a violent and ideologically charged campaign. The victory presaged the demise of the nationalist agenda, as West Indian political leaders in the 1980s were forced to deal with the realities of a new globalism. The conditions of participation in this new international political economy conflicted fundamentally with the principles of nationalism forged earlier in the century. Political leaders were forced to make a number of concessions that were anathema to this nationalist agenda. These concessions struck at the heart of notions of sovereignty and self-determination.

The new globalism was accompanied and supported by a resurgence of US interventionism. This came with the end of rapprochement and the heating up of the old bipolar rivalries of the Cold War. Cold War interventionism in the region strengthened the positions of conservative political leaders who could now anticipate, expect, and demand US support. Those unwilling to accept the new conditions imposed on domestic and international policy making had to be prepared to face the consequences of US retaliation aimed at demobilizing leftist groups, neutralizing leftist political leaders, and destabilizing leftist governments in the region.

The conservative tide became evident throughout the English-speaking Caribbean as politicians strongly devoted to export-oriented capitalism, strong ties with the United States, and liberal economic policies came to dominate the region's political systems. In Antigua, George Walter's welfare- and labor-oriented Progressive Labour Movement (PLM) was voted out of power in 1976 despite winning the popular vote. His successor was veteran politician Vere Bird, who headed the rival Antigua Labour Party (ALP). Bird's economic policies emphasized the attraction of foreign investment, particularly in the tourist and export-oriented sectors of the economy. In April 1980, Bird's popularity gave his party an overwhelming victory at the polls. He continued to dominate the country's affairs after leading it to independence in November 1981.

In Barbados, Tom Adams's strong advocacy of capitalist policies and a staunchly pro-American foreign policy while leader of the parliamentary opposition paved the way for a dramatic electoral victory by the Barbados Labour Party in 1976. His government vigorously pursued policies based on the attraction of foreign capital and the development of local capitalism.

In Belize, the government of the moderate George Price was buffeted by an economic crisis that had become particularly severe by 1979. His People's United Party managed to hold on in that year's elections and took the country to independence in 1981. But in 1980, the opposition United Democratic Party (UDP) made the decision to elect to its leadership the conservative pro-American Manuel Esquivel, whose ideology placed heavy emphasis on free enterprise and the encouragement of foreign investment. Under Esquivel's leadership, the UDP won a sweeping victory in the country's first postindependence elections, held in 1984.

In Dominica, political chaos, caused partly by declining economic conditions and partly by the brutal repression of political radicals, resulted in the collapse of the regime of Patrick John in 1979. Out of an ideological amalgam of dissidents emerged the extremely conservative and pro-American Mary Eugenia Charles, who led her Dominica Freedom Party to electoral victory in July 1980. Like other regional conservatives, her political platform was grounded in a firm commitment to private enterprise, the attraction of foreign investors, and a strong aversion to socialism.

In Montserrat, despite a successful economic program and a commitment to welfare policies, the government of Percival Bramble lost power in 1978 to John Osborne. Osborne's victory came in the wake of a blistering attack on his predecessor's welfare program, which he berated as socialist. His ardent support for the free enterprise system and for the attraction of North American investors to Montserrat galvanized the country's local business community around him.

In Saint Kitts and Nevis, the dominance of progressive Robert Bradshaw from the 1940s until his death in 1978 was not enough to stop the conservative tide. In 1980, a coalition government of the People's Action Movement (PAM) and the Nevis Reform Party sent Bradshaw's Labour Party to its first electoral defeat since its formation in 1946. Under the premiership of conservative Kennedy Simmonds, there was a decidedly more moderate turn to the policies of the colony, which was granted independence in 1983.

In Saint Lucia, the government of George Compton suffered a defeat in 1979 after fifteen years in power. Compton's loss to the Saint Lucia Labour

Party (SLP), whose guiding light was the radical George Odlum, appeared to be one instance (along with Guyana and Grenada) in which the conservative tide was bucked in the region. Nonetheless, ideological factionalism within the SLP, under the leadership of moderate Allan Louisy, provoked a political crisis that forced a 1982 election. This time, the electorate turned, once again, to Compton, attracted by his policies of industrialization by invitation and the attraction of foreign investments in the tourist sector.

The appeal of the conservative leaders was bolstered by a propaganda campaign that highlighted the demonstrated political and economic failures of the region's two socialist governments: the Burnham regime in Guyana and the Manley regime in Jamaica. There was abundant evidence of the demonstrated resolve of the United States to oppose, neutralize, and destabilize progressive governments, organizations, and groups and to provide support for their pro-capitalist, pro-Western counterparts. The ties between these conservative regimes and the United States were so complete that many joined the latter in a military invasion of Grenada to oust its radical government in 1983.

The United States made abundantly clear its willingness to provide economic and political support to its regional allies. In return for its strong and unwavering support for the policies advocated by Reagan's administration, the JLP government in Jamaica became the recipient of a tremendous amount of US bilateral assistance. US support and backing cleared the way for the transfer of a considerable amount of multilateral assistance to the country, particularly from the IMF. Additionally, the Reagan administration poured significant amounts of resources into the development of a program of economic assistance for its Caribbean allies. Using the argument of supporting its "vital interests" in the region, the US administration pushed through Congress the Caribbean Basin Economic Recovery Act. Known as the Caribbean Basin Initiative (CBI), the act was signed into law in August 1983. Included in its provisions were duty-free access for the products of selected countries to US markets. Apparel assembled in these countries was provided with special access to US markets through a textile initiative. Special tax benefits and investment incentives were made available to potential and actual US investors in the region. And the United States provided backing for bilateral support for the region from other countries, particularly Canada, Mexico, and Venezuela (Shultz 1983). The United States also doubled its aid to the region, as reflected in an increase from 6.6 percent to 13.6 percent of its overall economic assistance budget, between 1980 and 1984 (Shultz 1983). Most of the increased allocations were targeted for use by the private sector, to provide critical balance of payments support, for infrastructure projects, and to support training and scholarship opportunities. The choice of countries to be included in the CBI was determined on strictly ideological grounds. Guyana, Grenada, and Nicaragua were pointedly excluded.

The United States used the might of its economic power to generate, sustain, and deepen economic crises in those countries that retained progressive governments during the 1980s. It was precisely such a strategy that forced a change in ideological direction upon the socialist People's National Congress regime in Guyana. Desmond Hoyte, succeeding President Forbes Burnham after the latter's death in 1985, adopted economic and foreign policies that were more consistent with US designs for the region. By 1987, Hoyte's change of ideological direction began paying dividends in the form of bilateral and Western multilateral assistance, which was in short supply during the Burnham presidency.

The carrot of economic and developmental assistance was accompanied by the stick of the threat of military intervention. The United States increased its military presence in the region and publicized this increase by holding military exercises (Big Pine I and II) and joint maneuvers with some of the region's armed forces. The infrastructure for this significantly expanded US military presence was constantly upgraded after 1981 particularly at its bases in Honduras. It provided support for a guerrilla campaign against the Sandinista government in Nicaragua. It invaded Panama in 1989 to oust the intransigent government of Manuel Noriega. And in 1983 it mounted an invasion to oust the radical pro-Cuban and pro-Soviet government of Grenada. The invasion was the culmination of retaliatory efforts by the United States aimed at political and economic destabilization during the entire term in office of the radical New Jewel Movement, which had come to power by coup d'etat in 1979.

The United States, demonstrating willingness to intervene in support of its ideological allies, provided massive amounts of military assistance to conservative governments in the region under challenge by guerrilla campaigns. This was particularly the case for the governments of El Salvador and Guatemala, both under siege by radical guerrilla groups. Honduras became a staging ground for a guerrilla campaign mounted by the US-supported contras against the radical Sandinista regime in Nicaragua. Military intervention and support became visible indicators of the reassertion by the United States of its hegemonic role in the Caribbean and Central America and its return to a vigorous assertion of its national and regional interests.

The policies of the new conservative leadership have focused on the development of export-oriented activities, many in specially erected industrial parks and export processing zones (EPZs). Domestic agriculture has plummeted, and there has been an increasing emphasis on the export of traditional agricultural commodities. There has also been a heavy emphasis on tourism. The result has been a more intense integration of the political economies of the region into the global system of manufacturing and finance and a deepening reliance on experts with technical and managerial competence by both the public and private sectors. This has produced significant changes in the composition of the governing elite. Located at the center of this new elite is a political executive that has become highly dependent upon the transfer of resources from Western international governmental and economic actors for its power. It relies on technical experts to establish and manage the new realities of economic globalism. They have become responsible for securing resource transfers from private and public international financial institutions, both bilateral and multilateral, into the domestic political economy. These experts are indispensable to any government's efforts to reorganize and manage a political economy in the process of neoliberal transformation. They are recruited from a growing group of international elites with unrestricted means of geographic and even sectoral mobility. Their employment opportunities depend upon their willingness to be constantly on the move, seeking the salaries, privileges, prerequisites, and chances of promotion provided by multilateral agencies and transnational organizations with seemingly limitless access to resources. The political, technocratic, and managerial elites are joined by a new grouping of merchants involved in importation and wholesale and retail activities. Local manufacturers are forced to turn their attention to export processing activity, producing on a subcontracting basis for companies based in the industrialized economies. Tied increasingly to the international system of manufacturing as subcontractors, they are forced to undertake the labor-intensive aspects of a disaggregated system of international manufacturing. To make a profit, they are forced to maintain low labor costs, wages, and salaries in their own peripheral political economies.

The new global agenda has intensified further with the escalating dependence of Caribbean political economies on tourism. Its success depends upon the attraction of foreign investment in growing tourist industries, the reorganization of economic activity, the retraining of the workforce to cater to international, particularly Western, tastes, the destruction of local architectural forms and their replacement with "modern" Western forms for tourist accommodations, and the commodification of local culture to suit Western palates.

All of the above act to create conditions for the undermining of the nationalist agenda. As the focus of the new elite shifts to sectors of the political economy that cater to the demands of international finance and manufacturing, resources are diverted from satisfying the needs of the local population. Governments turn to international NGOs as they seek to reduce spending on health, education, welfare, and social security. These NGOs attempt to fill in the breach as workers become displaced from wage-earning activities, and as real wages become significantly depressed.

Those without formal connection to this new global reality are forced to rely increasingly on their own efforts to secure access to international resources, directly and indirectly. Many become heavily reliant on remittances transferred from abroad by relatives. Others begin to engage in small-scale, semilegal or illegal activities in the "informal sector," servicing the needs of the new domestic and international elite or filling in gaps left in the process of economic transformation. Typically, the informal sector comes to include an enormous amount of nonconventional activities including petty trade, smuggling, gambling, thieving, outworking, personal services, and the like. Most important in the West Indies is involvement in the local and international drug trade and in male and female prostitution. These activities are directly associated with the tourist industry.

Thus, nationalism, with its aspirations for sovereignty and self-determination, becomes meaningless and irrelevant. It is replaced by popular glorification of the behavior and practices of the North Atlantic, particularly North America. These include the pathologies of Western capitalism such as drug consumption, gang violence, environmental degradation, and the privileging of profit over welfare and social security. There has been an avalanche of out-migration, particularly to North America, especially of the skilled and educated. Domestic capital and savings have been, legally and illegally, exported abroad to purchase and support northern lifestyles (McAfee 1991). As a consequence and for all intents and purposes, the nationalist domestic agenda has been abandoned (Hintzen 1993). The explanation for its abandonment is that it no longer serves the interests of the regional elites who were its ideologues.

NOTE

1. Slavery was abolished in the British colonies in 1833. Emancipation was followed by a five-year period of "apprenticeship" during which former slaves were required to remain on the plantation under conditions similar to indentureship.

BIBLIOGRAPHY

Anderson, Patricia, and Michael Witter. 1994. "Crisis, Adjustment and Social Change: A Case Study of Jamaica." In *Consequences of Structural Adjustment: A Review of the Jamaican Experience*, edited by Elsie Le Franc, 1–55. Kingston, Jamaica: Canoe Press.

Chaliand, Gerard. 1978. *Revolution in the Third World: Myths and Prospects*. New York: Penguin.

Chase, Ashton. 1964. *A History of Trade Unionism in Guyana, 1900 to 1961*. Georgetown, Guyana: New Guyana Company.

Fraser, Cary. 1994. *Ambivalent Anti-Colonialism: The United States and the Genesis of West Indian Independence, 1940–1964*. Westport, CT: Greenwood Press.

Gilroy, Paul. 1993. *The Black Atlantic: Modernity and Double-Consciousness*. Cambridge, MA: Harvard University Press.

Girvan, Norman. 1984. "Swallowing the IMF Medicine in the Seventies." In *The Political Economy of Development and Underdevelopment*, edited by Charles K. Wilber, 169–81. New York: Random House.

Gray, Obika. 1990. *Radicalism and Social Change in Jamaica, 1960–1972.* Knoxville: University of Tennessee Press.

Hintzen, Percy C. 1989. *The Costs of Regime Survival: Racial Mobilization, Elite Domination and Control of the State in Guyana and Trinidad.* Cambridge: Cambridge University Press.

Hintzen, Percy C. 1993. "Democracy and Middle-Class Domination in the West Indies." In *Democracy in the West Indies: Myths and Realities,* edited by Carlene J. Edie, 9–24. Boulder, CO: Westview Press.

Hintzen, Percy C. 1995. "Structural Adjustment and the New International Middle Class." *Transition,* no. 24 (February): 52–74. University of Guyana Press.

Hintzen, Percy C. 1997. "Reproducing Domination: Identity and Legitimacy Constructs in the West Indies." *Social Identities* 3, no. 1: 47–75.

Hintzen, Percy C., and W. Marvin Will. 1988. "Garvey, Marcus Mosiah." In *Biographical Dictionary of Latin American and Caribbean Political Leaders,* edited by Robert J. Alexander, 180–82. Westport, CT: Greenwood Press.

Howe, Stephen. 1993. *Anticolonialism in British Politics: The Left and the End of Empire, 1918–1964.* Oxford: Clarendon Press.

Hoyos, F. A. 1972. *Builders of Barbados.* London: Macmillan Caribbean.

Lauren, Paul Gordon. 1988. *Power and Prejudice: The Politics and Diplomacy of Racial Discrimination.* Boulder, CO: Westview Press.

Lens, Sidney. 1965. "American Labor Abroad." *Nation,* July 5.

Mandle, Jay R. 1996. *Persistent Underdevelopment: Change and Economic Modernization in the West Indies.* Amsterdam: Gordon and Breach.

Manley, Michael. 1982. *Jamaica: Struggle in the Periphery.* London: Third World Media.

McAfee, Kathy. 1991. *Storm Signals: Structural Adjustment and Development Alternatives in the Caribbean.* London: Zed Books.

Pearson, D. 1964. "U.S. Faces Line Holding Decision." *Washington Post,* May 31.

Ryan, Selwyn D. 1972. *Race and Nationalism in Trinidad and Tobago.* Toronto: University of Toronto Press.

Sheehan, Neil. 1967. "C.I.A. Men Aided Strikes in Guiana against Dr. Jagan." *New York Times,* February 22.

Shultz, George. 1983. "Caribbean Basin Economic Recovery Act." Statement before the Senate Finance Committee, April 13.

West India Royal Commission (1938–1939). 1945. "Statement of Action Taken on the Recommendations." London: Her Majesty's Stationery Office.

Williams, Eric. 1974. "Economic Transformation and the Role and Vision of the PNM." Address to the Sixteenth Annual Convention of the People's National Movement, Port of Spain, Trinidad.

Chapter 3

STRUCTURAL ADJUSTMENT AND
THE NEW INTERNATIONAL MIDDLE CLASS

PERCY C. HINTZEN

Nationalist politics, rooted in statism and driven by an ascendent educated elite in their quest for control of the state, is on the decline. This has to do with its rooting, exclusively, in the satisfaction of power and the accumulative interests of this elite. Their exclusive ascendance to authorial national power has created the conditions for the current state of crisis and collapse. The patronage, control, and coercive functions of the nationalist state that formed the basis of domination have eroded. What is left is the state's international functions, namely the pattern of international alliances with powerful international actors (public, private, and multilateral) as a basis for the transfer of international resources to serve national interests. With the collapse of the nationalist state, popular interests have become neutralized and eliminated from the power equation. Now, international actors are able to define, dictate, and determine state policy without regard to its effect on the postcolony. The end product has been structural adjustment and liberalization.

The role of the state in this process is shifting to the technical management of international interests. It is to those managers and technocrats with the expertise to effect this shift that the latter have turned. These new elites are devoid of any nationalist allegiance. They are insulated from the domestic consequences of their policies because of their international mobility. They have become, in effect, absorbed into the group of international managerial and technical elites. This explains the current abandonment of a domestic agenda in the state policies of underdeveloped societies. It also explains the attendant domestic crises that have become universal. This chapter will explore the structural explanations for such a development.

Frederick Stirton Weaver (1991) has identified three broad phases in this historical unfolding of capitalism: (1) the comparative capitalist phase, (2) the financial capitalist phase, and (3) the monopoly capitalist phase. There is some uniform agreement that the second phase corresponds to the "statist" phase of capitalist development in the industrialized centers, characterized by "welfarist" structures of state organization. Nigel Harris sees only a quantitative distinction among the various forms of *etatiste* corporatism that characterize this phase, be it in "its Russian or Stalinist guise or in the milder Keynesianism of Western managed economies" (1976, 160). In the capitalist economies of the West, the emergence of this phase is explained as a response to crisis (particularly of the 1930s). Such response incorporated an intensified opposition to the "anarchy of the market" by elements of the bourgeoisie. Anarchy was to be replaced by "the guidance of experts and professional managers" (Harris 1976, 158).

In the new formulation, fundamental differences emerged between the socialism of the West and Eastern Europe's brand of "communism." Referring to the postwar period, Samir Amin points to the continuing reality of relations of expropriation between the industrialized North on the one hand, and colonies and former colonies of Europe's quickly crumbling colonial empire on the other. Thus, the development of corporatism in the bourgeois democracies cannot be understood outside of the reality of the "superexploitation" of the colonies and former colonies and of the intensifying expropriation of their surpluses. It allowed, according to Amin, the fashioning of a "social democratic alliance" between capitalists and workers in the metropolitan centers. The alliance was sustained and supported by the expropriation of the social surplus from the periphery (Amin 1976). In other words, the welfarism of the northern industrialized states cannot be understood outside the context of the intensification of relations of dependency between the industrialized centers and their peripheries. The result is neocolonialism, with the international extension of corporatism to the peripheral economies of the South.

State-organized corporatism acted to change the objective conditions of class exploitation everywhere. In the metropole, there emerged an ascendent elite comprising members of an ever-expanding nonproletarian working class. This elite developed alliances with an ever-increasing "aristocracy of labor" organized in political parties and industrial unions. The political unification of this alliance was orchestrated and controlled by the professional and intellectual elite.

The rise of this elite social grouping and its relations of affinity with others had to do with changes in the technical and social conditions of capitalist industrial production. These changes led directly to statist corporatism in the organization of the political economy. In the industrialized centers, what emerged was a state-controlling, bureaucratic, managerial, and technical elite who, in turn, mobilized the increasingly strategic workers in intermediate and capital goods industries and in clerical and semiprofessional occupations. This mobilization explains the success of the newly emergent elite social formation in challenging the dominance of the industrial bourgeoisie.

The changes in Europe had profound but different effects upon its actual and former colonial possessions. These became quite evident in the post–World War II era. In the major economies of Latin America, most evidently in Brazil and Mexico, the historically cumulative process of change in the technical conditions of capitalist production resulted in import substitution industrialization (ISI).[1] Later, it combined with a changing international division of labor and changing international conditions of capitalist accumulation to produce the "four tigers" of South Korea, Taiwan, Hong Kong, and Singapore. Structural changes in the world economy during the 1970s generated the conditions for exceptional growth in these countries. In Taiwan and South Korea, growth focused on export-led manufacturing. To this was added, in the city-states of Hong Kong and Singapore, exceptional growth in the tertiary service sectors. These sectors came to be dominated by entertainment, transport, retailing, and office and banking activities (Drakakis-Smith 1992, 14–15).

Hong Kong and Singapore were glaring exceptions among the group of countries that retained their status as European colonies at the beginning of the Second World War. In the latter, the technical conditions of capitalist production remained relatively unchanged during the postwar era. For the most part, colonies retained their "terminal" economic structures even as international conditions of production and social conditions in Europe were changing. These changes led to the granting of independence to the colonies beginning in the 1950s and escalating during the 1960s (Best 1968; Hintzen 1989a, 14–15).

The formal economies of the colonies and the newly independent nations, with a few notable exceptions, continued their reliance on exports to the northern industrialized countries of one or a few primary agricultural, food, and/or mineral products. Export earnings supported huge propensities to import wage and luxury (modern consumer) goods, intermediate goods, and some (limited) capital goods. There were, of course, considerable differences in the sizes of the subsistence and informal sectors across these societies.

The new social conditions of peripheral capitalism became evident in the reformulation of the elite social grouping and the assumption of control of the colonial state by its political representatives. The emergence and persistence of this elite were directly related to changes in international capitalism and the bifurcation of international power contentions between a US-dominated Western bloc and a Soviet-dominated communist bloc. To a certain extent, these post–World War II developments in international relations and exchange provided the political leadership in the former colonies with opportunities to cater to a much broader array of domestic interests. Nonetheless, the paramount objective of this political leadership was the maintenance of power on behalf of, and in the exclusive service of, the accumulative claims made by this newly reconstituted elite upon the postcolonial political economy (Hintzen 1989b). Cold War contentions allowed these leaders to do so while maintaining social and political order. They created the conditions for absorbing a larger number of the proletariat and semiproletarian peasantry into the group of nonproletarian workers and for the latter's incorporation into the elite social grouping. In addition, they allowed access to resources that were employed to expand the largess of patronage available for distribution to proletarian workers and semiproletarian peasants. Accommodation and patronage provided the political elite with the means to maintain social and political order without resorting to coercion. All of this was accomplished through the state allocation of resources derived internationally through relations of trade and exchange.

The emergence of the idea of "Third Worldism" in the semantic history of international politics proved important in strategic terms. It became critical to the organization of social conditions of peripheral capitalism and their refor-mulation in the former colonies after World War II. Independent India played a leading role in this development through its prime minister, Jawaharlal Nehru. He became a prime mover in the organization of the Asian-African (Bandung) Conference held in Indonesia in April 1955. This conference set the stage for the development of strategic international alliances among primarily southern former colonies. Out of this conference emerged the Non-Aligned Movement, formed in 1961. The leaders of the movement were Nehru himself, joined by President Josip Broz Tito of Yugoslavia, Prime Minister Gamal Abdel Nasser of Egypt, and President Julius Nyerere of Tanzania (Kothari 1978, 338–92).

The Non-Aligned Movement (NAM) was specifically tailored to sustain and enhance the power and accumulative interests of the newly ascendent elites in the former colonies. Its goal, according to Harris (1976, 177) was to create and sustain the conditions "to retain full control [of the state] in the hands of the [elite] leadership and yet offer enough to a wide enough segment of the population to sustain a politically significant movement." The NAM did so in a number of ways. One was by playing off the superpowers against each other in their competition for control of the "South." Another was by expanding state autonomy. The significance of this derives from the opportunities such autonomy provided to state-controlling elites to embark upon policies and programs that supported their own power. They were able to pursue these opportunities even in violation of actual or perceived interests (economic, political, strategic, etc.) of the superpowers and their allies. In this, they were able to call upon the protective alliances and support engendered in the notion of nonalignment.

Elite interests were also served through the opportunity provided to member states by the NAM to support each other's right of access to resources from either of the contending power blocs. This mitigated fear of retaliatory and punitive action particularly from Western nations against countries establishing relations of trade and aid with Eastern-bloc countries.

The greatly expanded access to international resources engendered by the NAM allowed members to wield much greater autonomy to formulate and implement domestic policies consistent with the power interests of the elite social grouping. Consequently, there was a dramatic expansion of the state into private sector activity. Much of this was accomplished by outright nationalization, by the development of joint ventures with the private sector, and by the expansion of the state's welfare functions. All of these served to strengthen the state, to enhance the power of the political representatives of the ascendent elite, and to expand the latter's opportunities for accumulation.

In the English-speaking West Indies, there were other factors at play that acted to strengthen this pattern of social formation. The victory of the socialist Labour Party in Britain in 1964 and its period of tenure until 1970 was important. Labour Party rule provided progressive governments with opportunities to erect and expand the welfare state with the support and assistance of Great Britain. The adoption of European welfarist policies allowed the elites to expand opportunities for their own accumulation and for distributing patronage to proletarian workers and nonproletarian peasants (Hintzen 1989b). Welfarism was supported by increased access to resources from progressive European governments. Regional developments also supported the process of social reformulation. The Cuban revolution of 1959 and the US trade embargo that followed in its wake proved highly beneficial. It gave West Indian sugar producers preferential access to the highly lucrative US market. Allocation of quotas and prices that far exceeded those prevailing on the world market filled the fiscal coffers of West Indian states. The combined effect of all of these was increased access to foreign exchange and increased state revenues. This proved highly beneficial to the power and accumulative interests of the ascendent elites.

The stable order was shattered in the early 1970s. An inflationary explosion that followed the first oil shock of 1973–1974 had profound effects on the economies of the South. For the oil-importing countries among them, it produced a doubling of (import) commodity prices, a quadrupling of oil prices, and a 43 percent increase in their imports (by value). This was followed by an international recession in 1975–1976 that severely depressed the prices and export volumes of these southern economies (Girvan 1984, 169). The consequences of the second oil shock of 1979–1980 were even more devastating. Once again, the economies of the industrialized North were rocked by recession, while international oil prices skyrocketed. This time, foreign exchange surpluses from oil-exporting countries that were lodged in eurocurrency markets were not available in the abundant supplies of the earlier period following the first oil shock. Countries in the region, shaken by severe economic crises, turned to the International Monetary Fund (IMF) as the agency of first resort for balance-of-payments supports.

IMF assistance to these beleaguered countries came with the upper-credit-tranche conditionalities that were later formalized in structural adjustment programs. The Fund's program of stabilization typically insisted upon a shift from fiscal to monetary controls. Successive phased drawings on lines of credit established by the IMF were determined by a country's performance in the achievement of usually quantitative monetary targets established with the Fund in standby arrangements (Dell 1984, 163–66). Structural adjustment programs proceeded from the conditionalities derived from such arrangements. To these were added stringent conditions for access to loans, investment funds, and aid specified and stipulated in the form of targets set primarily by the World Bank and US funding agencies. These included: (1) strong curbs on domestic demand through credit contraction; (2) the lowering of state expenditures aimed at reducing public sector deficits, particularly through cuts in subsidies and health, education, and welfare allocations; (3) revenue increases through tax reform programs that increased personal income taxes and through the reorganization of income tax administration; (4) currency devaluations; (5) programs of export promotion; (6) programs of economic and trade liberalization; (7) support for foreign investors involving the granting of liberal concessions (including tax holidays and the elimination of tariffs on imported inputs), and for investment in infrastructural supports; and (8) the alignment of domestic prices with world market prices (Bienen and Waterbury 1992, 376–85).

These new conditions for access to international economic resources were very much in keeping with the need to transform the parameters of peripheral capitalist production. They had profound effects on the social conditions in the political economies of the southern countries. Given these effects, there was the need to secure the absolute compliance of state-controlling elites if the necessary transformations were to be accomplished. In the West Indies, the ability to secure the compliance of the political leadership was directly related to an escalation of policies of direct interventionism in the region by the United States. This became most evident after the election of Ronald Reagan in 1980. Interventionist policies included direct support for political leaders with neo-conservative agendas. It also entailed efforts to demobilize groups, neutralize political leaders, and destabilize governments that opposed the new conservative agenda.

Jamaica under the government of Michael Manley had come to typify the social conditions of peripheral capitalism of the 1960s and 1970s. It was the first country to suffer the consequences of changes in the international economic and political environment. Even before Reagan's election, Jamaica had to bear the brunt of political and economic destabilization efforts by the United States, during a period when President Jimmy Carter's dovish approach in international affairs was coming under increasing attack by a resurgent conservative movement represented in Reagan's bid for the presidency. The ensuing economic crisis, produced by the combined effects of international stagflation and US interventionist efforts, forced Manley to agree to upper-credit-tranche conditionalities in standby arrangements for balance-of-payments supports with the IMF (Girvan 1984; Manley 1982, 149–203). At the same time, the Reagan campaign actively provided assistance to the political opposition led by neoconservative Edward Seaga, who had long signaled his support for the new agenda of structural adjustment. Such policies of interventionism and support for the conservative opposition resulted in Seaga's election to power in December 1980 (Manley 1982).

There is an essential link between programs of structural adjustment and international interventionism of the type described above. The former entails a dissolution of the nationalist elite alliance of professionals, intellectuals, and nonproletarian wage and salary workers. It also entails the dissolution of the welfarist structure of statist organization. The consequences are a dramatic reduction in the state's massive patronage largess and a curtailment of efforts at income redistribution to proletarian workers and the semiproletarian peasantry.

Transformation of social conditions leads to the demise of the nationalist coalition. The ideology of nationalism that undergirded the ascendence of the existing elite to power came under critical scrutiny and challenge by multilateral organizations such as the IMF and the World Bank, which were engaged in developing a new neoliberal consensus with strong support from Western governments. Nationalist ideology was replaced with support for programs of international interdependence that are consistent with the changing demands of international manufacturing and finance capital. The groundwork for programs of transformation in keeping with these demands was laid by international political and economic intervention in the form of structural adjustment. This program also involves strategic political support for sympathetic leaders, intense efforts to oppose unsympathetic ones, and, of course, direct and indirect (low-intensity) military intervention.

Henry Bienen and John Waterbury have labeled this process a "neoconservative transformation" (1992, 382). It occurs when "a political leadership sets out to fundamentally reorganize social and political as well as economic agreements. The aim is to change a pattern of political and social power in a country directly" (1992, 382). Fundamental change is necessitated by the conflicting demands of international manufacturing and finance capital on the one hand, and the welfarist social formations of the period of Third Worldism and nationalism on the other. The new interventionism that undergirded the neoconservative transformation is called forth by the changing structure of international capitalism. High mobility provides capital, in its reconstituted form, with the means of escape from national contexts that are unfavorable. Such mobility is accompanied by the development of a highly integrated global system of manufacturing, creating, in its wake, a single global labor market. There is also a process of disaggregation of manufacturing. Production of various component parts and different processes of production are becoming highly specialized. They are undertaken in multiple locations, one of which is engaged solely in the assembly of the finished product. All of this increases the autonomy of capital. In its reformulated state, international manufacturing and finance capital is separated from dependence upon the means of any single powerful state to create, protect, and maintain the social conditions of exploitation (Harris 1976, 187–203). Every state, in turn, is forced to succumb to internationalizing demands even in the face of highly negative consequences for its national political economy. The state is forced to succumb in efforts to meliorate the negative effects of internationalization. Alternatively, the state willingly does so when the demands of internationalized capital provide spinoff opportunities for the domestic economy.[2]

The consequences of the new interventionism in the peripheral political economies of the South are seen immediately in the reformulation of the elite social grouping. No longer are state-controlling elites able to protect and support the accumulative interests of the larger social grouping of elites historically produced during the era of nationalist politics and anticolonial struggle. Many of their constituent segments are sloughed off in a process of elite reformulation. The new internationalization and its related program of structural adjustment require drastic reductions in the public wage bill, achieved through the lowering of real wages (through, for example, delinking them from inflation). It is also achieved through the firing of public employees. These efforts are matched by drastic reductions in public sector perquisites. These measures come with profound implications for elite social formation. A large segment of public sector bureaucrats is cast aside. No longer are their accumulative interests served by state policies and programs. Their separation is compounded by the divestment of public assets to the private sector and the complete elimination of many of the remaining public enterprises. Cuts in consumer subsidies and state-provided services, including health, education, welfare, and social security, have a much more generalized effect on the elite (Bienen and Waterbury 1992, 382–86). During the nationalist era, these services formed the basis of elite reproduction.

Other segments of the elite alliance are affected just as profoundly. The import substitution industry is faced with the escalating cost of foreign and domestic inputs and competition from relatively cheap imports. This competition is enhanced by a sophisticated advertising campaign. National capitalists faced declining domestic demand for their products because of the ongoing and intensifying effects of the recessionary crisis.

There is a decline in the power and influence of elites in formal political organizations, particularly political parties and trade unions. Such decline comes in the wake of the increasing power of the central executive, called upon to assume exclusive control of policy implementation. State policies are defined and dictated increasingly by international financial institutions (IFIs) through programs of structural adjustment. The cadre of leaders in politically significant voluntary organizations find themselves locked out of the corridors of power. Their access to state resources has become severely limited. It is upon such access that their elite status relies. Access provides them with the opportunity to satisfy their accumulative interests and to deliver patronage to their support base.

The international penetration of the economy is also felt among the professional, technical, and managerial groupings. They are displaced not merely by the economic transformations that are occurring but by the increasing employment of international consultants and experts funded by multilateral and bilateral agencies. Many migrate to the industrialized North, attracted by lucrative offers, leading to significant brain drain.

What this leaves is a reformulation and constriction of the elite social grouping that had originally grown out of the anticolonial nationalist struggle. At the center of the reformulated grouping is a political executive that is highly dependent upon international intervention (including military intervention) for its power. This executive relies upon a group of technical experts engaged in international negotiations with private and public sector IFIs (bilateral and multilateral) that involve setting the terms of structural adjustment. The central executive also relies heavily upon a managerial elite to reorganize and manage the political economy, which is in the process of neoconservative transformation. Part of this reorganization entails the prerequisites for meeting the targets stipulated in structural adjustment agreements. The political, technocratic, and managerial elite is joined by a new grouping of merchants involved in importation and wholesale and retail activities. More importantly, they are joined by a new group of local industrialists engaged in export-oriented and export-processing activity "producing orders on a subcontracting basis for trading and manufacturing firms" based in the industrialized economies (Crow, Thorpe, et al. 1988). Tied to the international system of manufacturing as subcontractors, they undertake the labor-intensive parts of the disaggregated system of international manufacturing. They exploit the low labor costs, wages, and salaries in their own peripheral political economies.

Structural adjustment forces proletarian workers and the semiproletarian peasantry to adapt; they must rely on their own efforts to secure access to international resources, directly and indirectly. Some become heavily reliant on remittances transferred from abroad by relatives. Others are increasingly reliant on small-scale, semilegal or illegal activities in the informal sector. Many of these activities entail servicing the needs of the new domestic and international elites, or filling in gaps left in the process of economic transformation at all levels of demand. Typically, the informal sector involves nonconventional activities including petty trade, smuggling, gambling, thieving, outworking, personal services, and the like. Most important in the West Indies are the local and international drug trade, and male and female prostitution. These activities are directly associated with the tourist industry.

In the formal sector, the displacement of the organized male labor force is offset by the employment of women in export-oriented activities as part of a process of global feminization of labor. The increasing use of women workers is accompanied by a weakening of income and employment security (Standing 1992). There is also an intensification of women's participation in the informal sector.

In the Caribbean, structural adjustment was accompanied by the development of export-oriented activities in specially erected industrial parks and export processing zones (EPZs). Domestic agriculture has plummeted, and there has been an increasing emphasis on the export of traditional agricultural commodities. There has also been a heavy emphasis on tourism (McAfee 1991).

The reconstitution of the elites is accompanied by their absorption into the international system of manufacturing and finance. This is based on the technical and managerial competence required of both public and private sector elites. Industrialist investors in the system of global manufacturing must themselves possess these capabilities or must be in a position to hire those who do, to organize and run their businesses. With these capabilities, they become part of an international elite with unrestricted means of geographic and even sectoral mobility.[3] Thus, their commitment to any one nation-state is weakened as they seek opportunities to enhance their power and accumulation internationally. Domestic investors are constantly on the lookout to expand their operations overseas and, if need be, to relocate when conditions prove unfavorable. The technical and managerial elites are constantly on the move, seeking out the privileges and perquisites, ultimately, of employment in multilateral agencies with limitless access to foreign exchange.

The concern of this new elite becomes confined increasingly to sectors of the political economy that cater to the demands of international finance and manufacturing. To fill the gap, there is a growing reliance on nongovernment organizations (NGOs) to cater to the needs of those who have been discarded and are no longer formally or fully integrated into this international system. This has profound and new implications for those located in such sectors. For the first time since the development of industrial colonialism,[4] these persons have access to forms of organization that are not under the hegemonic control of international capitalism or of the domestic elite. There is, of course, intense pressure for the co-optation of NGOs by local and foreign state actors, by international capital, and by IFIs (McAfee 1991, 217–19). Indeed, as state functions becomes more exclusively tied to international capital, there is pressure to transfer the task of reproduction of labor and the functions of control and regimentation to NGOs. This serves to allow governments "pressed by economic constraints and structural adjustment conditionalities" (McAfee 1991, 217) to reduce spending on health, education, welfare, and social security. NGOs fill in the breach as people become displaced from wage-earning activities, and as real wages become significantly depressed. They are frequently encouraged to take over the functions abandoned by the welfare state using resources raised outside of the public sector, and not infrequently derived from the efforts of the local communities that they service.

Nonetheless, many NGOs have transformative agendas rooted in empowering the poor and powerless and supporting efforts at self-determination. They are able to penetrate the space vacated by the state to pursue such agendas. This is the essential contradiction of the developing system of international "monopoly" capitalism. As its control of the international means of production intensifies and becomes increasingly concentrated, it is forced to abandon control of the social and cultural order in areas where a growing number of persons are sloughed off in the process. This leaves such persons free for revolutionary and transformative organization. It is this fundamental contradiction in the development of the global system of manufacturing and finance "monopoly" capitalism that may very well prove its downfall.

NOTES

1. See Harris 1976, 12–18, 70, 92, for an explanation and description of the process and the reasoning from which it derived. For a discussion of the implications for social and political relations, see Weaver 1991, 121–35.

2. For instance, the need for military intervention can engender an increase in military spending with spinoff benefits for the domestic political economy. In the United States, this is accomplished through deficit spending. While it was justified in Cold War terms, the new military technology and the buildup of forces have been employed in peripheral political economies, particularly in the Persian Gulf region (against Iraq and Iran), in Lebanon, in Grenada, and in Panama.

3. These elements in the "social and cultural order" are identified by Frederick Stirton Weaver (1991) as characteristics and conditions of the "monopoly capitalist" phase of industrial development. This phase corresponds to the process of internationalization of manufacturing and finance capital here identified.

4. This is defined by David Drakakis-Smith as the period of colonial expansion in search of cheap raw materials and food, and extended markets. It is characterized by the restructuring of the colonies into national states and away from control of limited areas involved in colonial mercantilist trade by merchants, planters, and trading companies. Its beginnings are traced roughly "to the industrial or high colonial era [of] the mid-nineteenth century when European, primarily British, industrial capital began to look for ways of expanding production to retain profitability (Drakakis-Smith 1992, 27).

BIBLIOGRAPHY

Althusser, Louis. 1971. *Lenin and Philosophy and Other Essays*. Translated by Ben Brewster. New York: Monthly Review Press.

Amin, Samir. 1976. *Unequal Development: An Essay on the Social Formations of Peripheral Capitalism*. Translated by Brian Pearce. New York: Monthly Review Press.

Ashley, Richard K. 1984. "The Poverty of Neorealism." *International Organization* 38, no. 2 (Spring): 225–86.

Best, Lloyd. 1968. "The Mechanism of Plantation-Type Economies: Outlines of a Model of Pure Plantation Economy." *Social and Economic Studies* 17, no. 3 (September): 283–326.

Bienen, Henry, and John Waterbury. 1992. "The Political Economy of Privatization in Developing Countries." In *The Political Economy of Development and Underdevelopment*, 5th ed., edited by Charles K. Wilber and Kenneth Jameson, 376–402. New York: McGraw Hill.

Crow, Ben, Mary Thorpe, et al. 1988. *Survival and Change in the Third World*. New York: Oxford University Press.

Dell, Sidney. 1984. "Stabilization: The Political Economy of Overkill." In *The Political Economy of Development and Underdevelopment*, edited by Charles K. Wilber, 146–68. New York: Random House.

Drakakis-Smith, David. 1992. *Pacific Asia*. London: Routledge.

Galli, Rosemary E., ed. 1991a. *Rethinking the Third World: Contributions toward a New Conceptualization*. New York: Crane, Russak.

Galli, Rosemary E. 1991b. "Winners and Losers in Development and Antidevelopment Theory." In *Rethinking the Third World: Contributions toward a New Conceptualization*, edited by Rosemary E. Galli, 1–27. New York: Crane, Russak.

Girvan, Norman. 1984. "Swallowing the IMF Medicine in the Seventies." In *The Political Economy of Development and Underdevelopment*, edited by Charles K. Wilber, 169–81. New York: Random House.

Harris, Nigel. 1976. *The End of the Third World*. Harmondsworth, Middx., England: Penguin.

Hintzen, Percy C. 1989a. *The Costs of Regime Survival: Racial Mobilization, Elite Domination and Control of the State in Guyana and Trinidad*. Cambridge: Cambridge University Press.

Hintzen, Percy C. 1989b. "Pluralism and Power: Racial Politics and Middle-Class Domination in LDCs." Paper presented at the Conference on Pluralism in the Late Twentieth Century, Institute of Social and Economic Research, Port of Spain, Trinidad, December 7–9.

Hintzen, Percy C. 1993. "Democracy and Middle-Class Domination in the West Indies." In *Democracy in the West Indies: Myths and Realities*, edited by Carlene J. Edie, 9–24. Boulder, CO: Westview Press.

Hinzten, Percy C., and Ralph Premdas. 1983. "Race, Ideology, and Power in Guyana." *Journal of Commonwealth and Comparative Politics* 21, no. 2: 175–94.

Kothari, Rajni. 1970. *Politics in India*. Boston: Little, Brown.

Manley, Michael. 1982. *Jamaica: Struggle in the Periphery*. London: Third World Media.

McAfee, Kathy. 1991. *Storm Signals: Structural Adjustment and Development Alternatives in the Caribbean*. London: Zed Books.

Pryor, Frederic L. 1986. *Revolutionary Grenada: A Study in Political Economy*. New York: Praeger.

Rudebeck, Lars. 1991. "Conditions of People's Development in Postcolonial Africa." In *Rethinking the Third World: Contributions toward a New Conceptualization*, edited by Rosemary E. Galli, 29–88. New York: Crane, Russack.

Segal, Daniel. 1992. "'Race' and 'Colour' in Pre-Independence Trinidad and Tobago." In *Trinidad Ethnicity*, edited by Kevin A. Yelvington, 81–115. London: Macmillan Caribbean.

Standing, Guy. 1992. "Global Feminization through Flexible Labor." In *The Political Economy of Development and Underdevelopment*, 5th ed., edited by Charles K. Wilber and Kenneth Jameson, 346–75. New York: McGraw Hill.

Weaver, Frederick Stirton. 1991. "Toward an Historical Understanding of Industrial Development." In *Rethinking the Third World: Contributions toward a New Conceptualization*, edited by Rosemary E. Galli, 107–52. New York: Crane, Russak.

Chapter 4

RETHINKING DEMOCRACY
IN THE POSTNATIONALIST STATE

PERCY C. HINTZEN

INTRODUCTION

While teaching a course on development during a sabbatical year at the University of Guyana in 1993, I was struck by the unquestioned and uncritical support expressed by my students for the program of economic recovery fashioned by the Guyanese government to satisfy the terms of "stabilization" and "structural adjustment" imposed by multilateral and bilateral lending institutions, particularly the International Monetary Fund (IMF) and the World Bank. This was during a period of endemic economic crisis that had lasted at least one and a half decades and had intensified considerably to the point where the country was ranked as the second poorest in the Western Hemisphere after Haiti. The support and optimism of the students came at a time when the Institute of Development Studies at the university was documenting dramatic drops in income over the previous decade and poverty rates that were estimated as high as 86 percent by some international agencies (Institute of Development Studies 1993, 5–17). An economic recovery program, begun in 1985 to satisfy conditions stipulated by the IMF and World Bank, had become fully operational by 1986. Its implementation was accompanied by the intensification of poverty, economic insecurity, and economic crisis. It seemed contrary to my own logic that university students familiar with the critical literature on development and experiencing the throes of economic crisis would accept, unquestionably, an economic program that had little to show in terms of actual results in the improvement of *their own* lives and opportunities. I came to the conclusion that an analysis of the real "objective" conditions of these students and of the population at large offered very little by way of explanation for their support of policies that were arguably detrimental to their own economic well-being.

Clearly, this uncritical support for structural adjustment by students at the University of Guyana could hardly be explained with reference to "objective social facts." Unquestionably, the students in my class viewed structural adjustment from the perspective of understandings that had little to do with extant economic consequences. Structural adjustment is not merely a complex of policies whose implementation comes with consequences that can be analyzed. It must be analyzed in terms of its meaning for those who participate in what sociologists call social action.

The attitudes I observed toward the complex of development policy known as structural adjustment were at the heart of the problem that has taken center stage in my intellectual inquiry: Why are relations of domination and conditions of economic exploitation that are little different, and sometimes more severe, than those suffered under colonialism understood and interpreted differently in the postcolonial era? What explains the universal predisposition of those who engaged in and supported anticolonial struggles to accept the conditions of postcolonial repression and exploitation? The answer seemed to rest in the idea and meaning of nationalism, which has acted to transform understandings of conditions that are, in the eyes of the objective social scientist, identical. Nationalism, it seems, has acted to change understandings of who one is and of what is normal and desirable.

Nationalism in the West Indies, as elsewhere, has a specific meaning. It was an assertion of the right to self-determination manifested in the replacement of the colonial elite in positions of power and authority by their former colonialized subjects. The right to self-determination was not asserted in a vacuum. It had, as its objective, the need for the assertion of equality. Implicit was the claim that the colonial condition of inequality and white superiority was artificial and imposed. Once removed, a "natural state" of equality would assert itself. The task in the postcolonial era was to remove the legacies of colonialism that act as impediments to equality. The goal was to replicate the conditions of the colonizers in postcolonial reality. I will make the argument that anticolonial nationalism contains an inherent dialectical logic that leads not to less inequality but to more, not to more self-determination but to less. At the same time, the conditions of inequality and dependency become subject to different interpretations. This is precisely what I was observing among the students in Guyana.

In this manner, nationalism becomes transformative. Once the condition of equality is asserted in the postcolonial context, everything associated with colonial inequality is rendered irrelevant and subject to different interpretations, irrespective of the objective conditions. What once was exploitation becomes sacrifice. What was privilege becomes reward. What was discrimination becomes strategic allocation. These transformations are explained by the logic of equality embedded in the meaning of nationalism. Presuppositions of postcolonial equality become the force driving predispositions toward the acceptance of conditions of extreme inequality.

This is not to say that conditions of inequality become irrelevant and unrecognized. Rather, the context within which inequality becomes relevant is shifted from the national to the international. While anticolonial nationalism is directed at the elimination of colonial inequality, the quest of postcolonial nationalism is for equal status among the international community of national states. Postcolonial elites are able to employ this national quest to explain their privilege. It is a privilege accorded to them as a "modernizing elite."

Once the privilege of the modernizing elites is normalized and legitimized, it can be employed to break out of nationalist constraints and become ensconced in a metropolitan reality. This is one way in which nationalist interests are replaced by global and metropolitan interests. Another way pertains to the international level. International public policy, under the guise of promoting national economic and political development, employs the nationalist quest for equality to eviscerate any objective claim to self-determination. The quest for national "development" is at the heart of international public policies of structural adjustment. Development, in turn, comes to be considered as the sole basis of equality with the formerly colonial metropole.

If what is outlined above is true, then why do these conditions come to be accepted as desirable? The question is pertinent because the undermining of national self-determination and sovereignty and the growth of inequality as external exploitation are the very conditions that sparked and sustained anticolonial nationalism. The explanation lies in differences in conceptual understandings brought about by nationalist discourse. Understandings are shaped by idea complexes that can change over time and that can produce profoundly different and even conflicting interpretations of social realities that may appear, objectively, to be identical. This, I will argue, was the case when colonialism was replaced by nationalism as the driving force in the understandings of formerly colonialized populations. Second, understandings are shaped by the participatory experiences of social actors. The two are integrally linked.

My intention is to examine constructs of identity pertaining to understandings of who one is and where one belongs in relation to others. Constructs of legitimacy pertain to what the normative ideal in social organization is. My analysis will focus on nationalism and its implications for identity and legitimacy in the postcolonial reality of the English-speaking West Indies.

THE CONTOURS OF POSTIMPERIALISM

"Postimperialism," writes David Becker, "signifies *transnational* class domination on a global scale," exemplified by the production and reproduction of "an international bourgeois class." The latter comprises "members of [a] 'corporate international bourgeoisie' . . . united by mutual interests transcending those expressed through the states whose passports they happen to carry" (1987, 51; emphasis mine). If we accept this postimperialist reality of the modern world, then the possibility for democracy must be fully rejected, barring a fundamental social transformation. Yet, the *illusion* of democratic participation permeates the consciousness of those in the very regions of the world where domination and exploitation by an international bourgeois class is most embedded and most pervasive.

The English-speaking West Indies ranks consistently among the very top in conventional indices of democracy. Yet its territories constitute, arguably, the most penetrated and exploited by global capital. Indeed, as creations of Europe's colonial enterprise, they enjoy an ontogenetic link to global capital that is integral and inseparable. If we accept the Marxist notion of the state in whose institutional form the social power of the bourgeois class is instituted and exercised and its interests expressed (albeit as universal or general interests), then the sheer impossibility of a democratic postcolonial transformation becomes evident.

What accounts, therefore, for this collective and almost universal consensus of "democracy" in the postcolonial practice of the English-speaking West Indies? The explanation rests in the centrality of notions of territoriality in West Indian self-conceptualizations. Such notions serve to camouflage the deep embeddedness of each of the territories in the global reality outside of which they would cease to exist, at least in their present constitution. These conceptions of territory make sense for a number of reasons, not least of which is their reflection in the geomorphology of the region and in the almost unique history of each of the small islands and the few mainland countries.

Discussion here is confined to the eleven island territories and the two small mainland countries that have, together, organized themselves into the Caribbean Community and Common Market (CARICOM). Guyana, the largest in land area, is a mere 83,044 square miles with a population of less than 760,000. It is the only English-speaking country in South America. Belize, the second of the mainland territories, enjoys a similar official linguistic distinction in Central America, even though half of its population is Spanish speaking. Its history is unique, even for Latin America. Anything resembling an institutionalized colonial administration in Belize emerged only in the late eighteenth century.

The island territories are similarly diverse in size and history. While Barbados enjoyed untrammeled and uninterrupted British sovereignty from its beginnings in the seventeenth century, most of the other islands changed hands (some more frequently than others) with the winds of historical fortune of the various European contenders for colonial possession. Jamaica, with nearly

2.5 million people, is the largest and most populous of the islands, at 4,244 square miles. It passed from Spanish to British colonial control in the mid-seventeenth century, remaining a British colony for more than three hundred years. It is the only CARICOM member of the Greater Antilles group, separated from the rest by distances of several hundred miles. The twin-island republic of Trinidad and Tobago, the second-largest of the island nations, came under British colonial rule after being captured from Spain in 1797. Its history as a slave economy began only in the mid-eighteenth century. The rest of the group are single- and multi-island territories with only two (Dominica and Saint Lucia) exceeding 200 square miles in size. Apart from Barbados, with a population of 250,000, only Saint Lucia (136,000 people) and Saint Vincent (115,000 people) have populations that exceed 100,000. The people of Saint Lucia and Dominica speak, for the most part, a variant of French creole, reflecting the influence of their colonial past. In Trinidad and Tobago, on the other hand, the influence of the country's Spanish colonial heritage is everywhere. This influence is tempered by the pervasive presence of French planters and the relative recency of its history of African slavery. Moreover, the largest segment of the populations of Trinidad and Guyana are Hindu and Muslim descendants of indentured labor from South Asia (India and Pakistan). CARICOM countries have also enjoyed a great degree of economic diversity since they became independent from Britain, with Trinidad (oil and gas), and Guyana and Jamaica (bauxite), being significant producers of minerals. There are differences in agricultural production, with the cultivation of sugar, bananas, citrus, rice, and spices spread among the various territories, as well as differential emphases on tourism in their economies. Manufacturing enjoys varied degrees of importance in the gross domestic products of the territories.

In other words, there is not much to cement a sense of "oneness" among the CARICOM territories. Their economic, cultural, and historical differences reinforce their natural physical insular isolation and their separation by vast stretches of water. The sense of territoriality that all these factors have engendered has acted to hide the rooting of these political economies in a globalized reality. It has provided meaning to the nationalist struggle and has laid the foundation for the illusion of postcolonial democracy. With the image of national community confined to territorial and insular space, global actors have come to be understood as being outside the realm of democratic discourse. Their actions and behavior are not accountable to the will of the people. At the same time, it is these very global actors, more than anyone else, whose social power is constituted in the state, whose interests are represented as universal, and whose class privilege is protected by law. Thus, the image of democracy is preserved, supported by a governing elite playing musical chairs in the occupancy of elective office. This gives substance to their claims of democratic governance.

SOVEREIGNTY, DEVELOPMENT, AND HEGEMONY

At the core of the nationalist project was the quest for equality. From the inception, it was the project of a nascent elite. Equality, for the latter, was unrealizable under a colonial condition that depended upon the discourse of actual difference for its legitimation. This discourse necessitated a challenge to the ideology of white supremacy as the linchpin of colonial order. Thus, the struggle for racial equality had to be represented as the *universal* or *general* will. This is not to argue that racial equality is unimportant. However, the challenge to racial inequality cannot be separated from its social ontology (in this case, the construct of colonial plantation exploitation). When it is separated, the quest for equality, *qua racial equality*, cannot but serve to hide the manner in which social power is actually constituted. Indeed, and this is true for West Indian nationalism, it can act to legitimize the constitution of social power, however exploitative and repressive. Unlike those of colonialism, conditions of postcolonial exploitation and repression need not depend upon a discourse of racial inequality. When colonization is challenged exclusively on the grounds of white supremacy, the fundamentals of exploitation and repression remain and become legitimized.

Anticolonial nationalism had to be represented as the "general will." Thus, the terrain of colonialism had to be contested not merely or exclusively from the position in which the constellation of interests of the nascent elite was located. Colonialism was a "field of contestation" in which all social actors participated. In other words, it was a "set of objective historical relations between positions anchored in certain forms of power" that were the object of perpetual contestation (Bourdieu and Wacquant 1992, 16). Thus, any challenge to colonialism, when directed against the colonial elite, could easily have been constructed as a universal challenge. With anticolonial nationalism, it was the interests of an emergent elite from the middle strata of colonial society that came to be represented as the universal will. This nascent elite, objectively constrained by colonialism, came to "hegemonize" mass support and bring such support into equilibrium under its "party leadership" (Chatterjee 1986). Antonio Gramsci's conceptualization of hegemony applies particularly to this nationalist project. In a field of contestation, such as colonialism, various social groups

> come into confrontation and conflict, until only one of them, or at least a
> single combination of them, tends to prevail, to gain the upper hand, to
> propagate itself throughout society—bringing about not only a unison of
> economic and political aims, but also intellectual and moral unity, pos-
> ing all the questions around which struggle rages not on a corporate but
> "universal" plane, and thus creating the hegemony of the fundamental

social group over a series of subordinate groups. . . . The development and expansion of the particular group are conceived of, and presented, as being the motor force of a universal expansion, of a development of all the "national" energies. In other words, the dominant group is coordinated concretely with the general interests of the subordinate groups. (Gramsci 1971, 181–82)

Under the nationalist project, the interests of the subordinate groups came to be coordinated with those of the nascent elite through a discourse of equality. The institutions organized and controlled by the nascent elite became, in the nationalist transformation, the instruments of such equality.

Nationalist discourse had, at its core, ideas of sovereignty and development. The latter spoke to the objective conditions of colonial exploitation—that is, the expropriation of surpluses by the colonial metropole to support colonial privilege. The trust of nationalism was the national appropriation of these surpluses. It was a discourse of modernity that effectively precluded any attempt to explain conditions of poverty and immiseration by demystifying capital. According to this logic of developmentalism, explanations for these conditions lie in the fact that control of capital is not located in the "national" arena where it can be allocated in the "national" interest. Sovereignty thus becomes, in part, the "sovereign" right to exercise control (as opposed to ownership) over the conditions that govern capital accumulation. Sovereignty, in this nationalist construction, becomes the claimed right to dictate and determine the laws and policies of capital accumulation *in the sovereign territory.* In this manner, development can be represented as a resolution of the economic crisis of colonialism. To the extent that this crisis was universal, nationalist development can make legitimate claims as representing the universal will. In the West Indies, the crisis of colonial capitalism was particularly evident in the 1930s. It stemmed partly from a generalized crisis of capitalism and partly from increasingly successful contestations of white supremacy upon which colonial legitimacy rested. The crisis sparked mass working-class mobilization and rioting. The nationalist movement was built on the backs of such mobilization.

The objective conditions for the nationalist challenge were laid in the changing technical and social conditions of colonial capitalist production. They emerged in the shift to the Crown Colony system and the replacement of the local merchant plantocracy by absentee owners and corporations based in the colonial metropole. This shift severed many of the organic links between those who owned capital and officially engaged in the exercise of power on the one hand, and groups with legitimate "national" credentials on the other. The introduction of more capital-intensive forms of plantation production, urbanization, the growth of an urban working class, and the increasing bureaucratization of economic and political organization acted, inter alia, to erode the objective conditions that sustained and supported colonial discourses of difference. With a growing expatriate ownership, claims that economic production benefited territorial interests could no longer be sustained because of the association of the "general will" with the will of those with organic links to the geographically defined territory. Without organic links to the territory, those who exercised economic and political power lost their ability to represent themselves legitimately as the embodiment of universal or general will. In this manner, colonialism began to suffer a crisis of legitimacy.

Sovereignty, realized through constitutional independence, resolves this crisis by transferring authorial power to a group with organic links to the territory. For the former colonial territories, sovereignty became a symbolic manifestation of equality as the newly independent state began to participate in the international system of nations. Sovereignty came to represent the general will to be free and equal with the state as agent. It allows the exercise of free choice by the state in new relations established between the former colonial territories and extraterritorial actors.

It was mass support that allowed the aspiring elite to ascend to political power, breaking the barriers of colonial exclusivity—both political and social. Hegemonization of the subordinate groupings, under the terms suggested earlier by Gramsci, was the precondition for the generalization of elite interests as the universal will. This was accomplished through the incorporation of diverse movements of protests, including trade unions, ethnic and cultural organizations, and other politicized voluntary organizations into the nationalist political parties. These movements were the organizational expressions of groups with the most legitimate claims to the "territory." They were, at the same time, the expressions of the will of those whom they represented and for whom they spoke. With the adoption of variants of the Westminster model of parliamentary democracy, nationalist political parties became incorporated into the state. As a result, mass organization, representing the national will, became integrally, though symbolically, identified with the postcolonial state. With nationalist transformation, the latter came to be understood, universally, as the "motor force of a universal expansion, of a development of all the national energies" (Gramsci 1971, 181). As such, the interests of the now emergent elite came to be understood as national interests.

Almost universally, the emergent elite leadership rose from educated factions of the middle strata. As actors in the colonial "field of struggle," their goal was the transformation of the "structure of objective relations" (that is, of power) in efforts to "improve their position and to impose a new principle of hierarchization" most favorable to their own interests (Bourdieu and Wacquant 1992, 101). In the process, they employed their social, cultural, and symbolic capital to impose their own organizational rationality on the institutional expressions of the collective will. Their "leadership" was legitimized as the sole means for contestation of colonial authority rooted, as it was, in a discourse of white supremacy. In other words, the nationalist political organizations, headed by middle-strata elites, came to be represented as the only legitimate challenge to the organizational rationality of the colonial state and to white supremacy, and as incorporating the universal will. The organizational rationality of the middle class brought with it the promise of a sovereign state and the guarantee of "development."

The formal organization of the proletarian and peasant groupings established and cemented relations of affinity among professionals, intellectuals, and nonproletarian wage and salaried workers on the one hand, and the proletarian and peasant lower classes on the other. The process was uneven both within and across territories. It fed upon proletarian mobilization, with intellectuals and professionals successfully incorporating lower-class movements of protest into organized trade unions and, later, into protonationalist political parties. To lower-strata demands for racial and economic justice were added the demands of the middle strata for national sovereignty and power.

Thus, with the introduction of self-government and, later, the granting of independence, popular organizations of nationalist struggle came to be symbolically included in the governing structures of the state. In this manner, the state became synonymous with the national will in popular consciousness. Its area of jurisdiction came to be firmly linked with the specific territories of the region. It is important to emphasize the purely symbolic nature of this incorporation. The state is nothing more than a "set of objective, historical relations between positions anchored in certain forms of power" (Bourdieu and Wacquant 1992, 16). It is differentiated by its ultimate relationship to *political power*, by its claim to authoritative decision-making over all activities in all other fields and over the rules that regulate such activities, by its claim to jurisdictional authority over a specified territory and over all its inhabitants, and by the use of the rule of law as a mechanism to protect the social power of the interests embodied in its constitution (Bourdieu and Wacquant 1992, 100). The interests represented and protected by the state stem from the relative positions of power and principles of hierarchization evident in the objective relations among occupants of "positions of force" (Bourdieu and Wacquant 1992, 101). As a field of struggle, the principles of hierarchization are in constant flux as occupants seek to safeguard or improve their positions. This is precisely what occurred in the transformation from the colonial to the postcolonial state, and in the "neoconservative transformation" that occurred beginning in the 1980s.

The definition of the state as a field of contestation allows for the incorporation in analysis of "extraterritorial" actors. The criterion of inclusion becomes participation in the objective, historical relations that constitute the "field" of state behavior as earlier defined. Determining the hierarchy of authoritative decision-making, the hierarchy of jurisdictional authority, and how the rule of law is fashioned and implemented are the methodological prerequisites in any attempt to map the field of the state. Naturally, the field is in constant flux. At the same time, certain overall historical patterns might be observed in the West Indies.

It is evident that, under colonialism, the most powerful social actors in the field of the state were extraterritorial representatives of the colonial power. This was particularly true of the era of Crown Colony government and less so when local merchant-plantocracies employed their control of the purse and local assemblies in order to gain and maintain hierarchical power. The situation after the postcolonial transformation became much more complicated within the context of contemporary forms of globalization.

As extensively discussed in chapter 3, there was a fundamental change in the field of the state that accompanied changes in the technical and social conditions of global capital beginning in the early 1970s. It came in the wake of an inflationary explosion that followed the first oil shock of 1973–1974. This had profound effects on the economies of the Global South as a result of the doubling of import commodity prices and the quadrupling of oil prices. An international recession that followed in their wake placed downward pressure on the volume of exports and their prices (Girvan 1984, 169). A second oil shock in 1979–1980 had even more devastating consequences. It engendered a severe contraction in access to foreign exchange by these countries. The inability of many countries to honor the terms of debt servicing coupled with fears of default on their debt resulted in the shutting down of credit windows by commercial lenders. This forced many countries in the Global South to turn to the IMF as the agency of first resort for balance-of-payments support. These were the conditions under which the stabilization programs and structural adjustments, elaborated in chapter 3, were imposed on beleaguered countries. New conditionalities of access to international economic resources imposed by the IMF, the World Bank, and other bilateral and multilateral financial institutions became the linchpins for insertion of agents of the new globalized capital into the field of the state. The conditions of access to what they imposed were shaped and determined by the need to transform the character of peripheral capitalist production to ensure the effective functioning of the new neoconservative form of globalization. In the West Indies, the transformation was facilitated by a change in the dynamic structure of the state with the help of direct intervention by the United States through the provision of direct support to political leaders with neoconservative agendas, and through US efforts to demobilize groups, neutralize political leaders, and destabilize governments opposed to the emergent neoconservative agenda.

Structural adjustment and international interventionism led to the respectification of "national interests" in ways that were consistent with the changing demands of international manufacturing and international finance capital. The consequences of these, discussed in detail in chapter 3, are worthy of a brief summary. They resulted (1) in the weakening of the power of those in the field of state struggle who were engaged in challenging and contesting the interests of global capital; (2) in the positioning of transnational agents of global capital in the upper echelons of the power hierarchy of national authority and decision-making, where they were able to embed the interests of international capital even more deeply into the national apparatus of governance; (3) in the enhancement of the power and influence of domestic groups whose interests coincided with international capital; (4) in severe reductions in fiscal revenues, leading to a drastic contraction of public sector employment and reductions in the wages and salaries of those who remained (which had a particularly deleterious effect on the influence exercised by government workers and those in the non-capitalist-owning sectors who formerly exchanged support for the regime for the benefits of transfers from the state); and (5) in cuts in consumer subsidies and state-provided services such as health, education, welfare, and social security upon which the population depended, and which provided income and employment opportunities for many in the public and private sectors. During the era of early nationalism, these services became the bases of elite reproduction and the foundation for a system of patron-clientelism upon which regime support and legitimacy rested (Bienen and Waterbury 1992, 382–86).

What remained in the new formulation was a political executive that became highly dependent upon international intervention (including military intervention) for its power. It was joined by a group of technical experts engaged in international negotiations with private and public sector international financial institutions (bilateral and multilateral) that were involved in setting and enforcing the terms of structural adjustment, a group of technocrats managing the neoconservative transformation, and a group of domestic and international entrepreneurs along with an emergent group of local and foreign industrialists engaged in trade and export processing. (Crow, Thorpe, et al., 1988).

Neoconservative transformation forces groups with little or no influence on government policy and practice to seek out extraterritorial opportunities as survival strategies. Many resorted to legal and illegal emigration, providing necessary support in cash and kind through remittance transfers to their families at home. Such transfers played a central role in the general sustenance of a large segment of the population. Others chose engagement in small-scale, semilegal or illegal activities in the informal sector, including petty trade, smuggling, gambling, thieving, outworking, personal services, drug dealing and the international drug trade, and prostitution. Some of these activities are tied directly to the tourist industry, and replaced the traditional sources of foreign exchange earnings and employment mentioned earlier. There was also an intensification of women's participation in the formal sector in efforts to lower wages and salaries.

Increasingly, the power hierarchy in the field of state contestations becomes dominated by national and global actors engaged, directly or indirectly, in the management of the international system of manufacturing and finance because of their technical and professional training and qualifications. They join an international elite who enjoy unrestricted means of geographic and even sectoral mobility.[1] This reduces, significantly, the commitment of those at the apex of power to national interests as they become firmly imbricated in the global political economy. National interests and the domestic agenda of national development are increasingly neglected in this new constellation of state power. To fill the gap, there is a growing reliance on nongovernmental organizations, which increasingly undertake the task of reproducing labor and the functions of its control and regimentation. Their presence allows governments "pressed by economic constraints and structural adjustment conditionalities" to reduce spending on health, education, welfare, and social security (McAfee 1991, 217).

I would like to address what the crisis that ensued as a product of the neoconservative transition reveals about the entanglements of the state, capitalism, and national governance. Michel-Rolph Trouillot has forced us to rethink the fallacy of the "state-nation homology," by which he means the practice of collapsing the state and the nation into one entity. Instead, he argues for an understanding of the state as "a set of practices and processes and their effects . . . whether or not they coalesce around central sites of governments" (Trouillot 2001, 137). What the neoconservative transformation exposed is a need for the analytic separation of the exercise of authority over nationally specified territory by apparatuses of governance and for a focus on the "state-effects" of the processes and practices of capitalism and its precapitalist forms of accumulation. These have always been transnational in scope in what William Robinson calls a "*world economy*, in which countries and regions were linked to each other via trade and financial flows in an integrated international market" (2014, 2). These processes and practices of the state produce their "effects" through the "institutional politics" of national formation and their impact on social formation. They are directed at populations located in the national territory where accumulation is concentrated by powerful global actors linked to these territories through forms of colonialism, neocolonialism, and/or imperialism. This is the necessary condition of accumulation for the system of global capitalism. In the postcolonial phase of the world economy prior to the neoconservative transformation, capitalists depended on state power, exercised through sovereign national authorities directly and in their international relations, to protect their accumulative interests against threats and challenges locally, nationally, and in territories under imperial control. They also depended on national governments to open new areas for capitalist exploitation, both domestically and globally. This dependence was transformed significantly in the neoconservative phase. And it undermined the relationship between domestic interests that were organized into localized social formations in the form of political parties, trade unions, and civic organizations on the one hand, and the national apparatus of governance and authority that depended upon them for regime survival on the other. Once this relationship was severed, it provided global capital with unfettered access to what was "useable" to its processes and practices, in terms of people and things. Those that were not "useable" were "sloughed off" to fend for themselves by devising survival strategies either within or outside the zones of global market capitalism (Hintzen 2018).

DEVELOPMENT, EQUALITY, AND LEGITIMACY

How, in this neoconservative transformation, do the interests of this new form of global capital come to be represented as the general will, despite new evidence of intense and growing immiseration? The answer lies in the embeddedness of discourses of equality in nationalist ideology. Anticolonial nationalism was, first and foremost, an expression of the general will for equality. This expression was transformed by petit bourgeois ideology into demands for sovereignty, which was then acquired when those with claims to an organic connection to the territory gained control of the governing institutions of the state. Full equality cannot be successfully realized, however, until the material conditions of the metropole come to be replicated in the territories under the jurisdiction of the newly independent states. Industry and the consumptive styles of Europe and North America were the pervasive symbols of white supremacy. Equality in the postindependence era demands a developmental transformation to forms of industrial production and consumption typical of the metropolitan North.

The ideology of development, embedded in nationalist discourse, came with the promise of the power to transform "underdeveloped" political economies into developed (that is, metropolitanized) ones. As agents of modernization, the emergent national elite has been able to assert its exclusive and paramount role in "developmental transformation." In the West Indies, development gained additional legitimizing force because the nationalist movement was rooted in the economic crisis of the 1930s. Nationalism came with the promise of an end to this crisis.

Thus, as an ideology, development contributed to the legitimization of the authorial power of the new elite by transforming this elite into its agents. The claims of these elites to power are enhanced by their possession of the technical, managerial, and bureaucratic skills considered to be the prerequisites for developmental transformation. As general will, development has come to be firmly identified with the state. It is to be effected through the incorporation of developmental function into state function (Hintzen 1995; Lewis 1949). The symbolic power of such incorporation rests in its significance for the realization of true and full equality by the territorial population. Such equality comes with the material life conditions and productive technology of western Europe and North America that development brings in its wake. It is in this manner that the ideology of development comes to constitute a legitimacy construct. It justifies the authorial power of managers, professionals, technicians, and bureaucrats who possess the skills, capacities, credentials, and education needed for developmental planning and for its implementation (Hintzen 1993). International global capital brings in its wake these trappings of development. Those participating in its field of activity begin to resemble the white population of the metropole. It is left for those located outside of its realm to devise strategies to secure their incorporation. Equality, it appears, is within reach to them, only for the want of trying. With its promise, the illusion of consensual democracy is maintained.

NOTE

1. Frederick Stirton Weaver (1991) identifies these elements in the social and cultural order as characteristics and conditions of the "monopoly capitalist" phase of industrial development. This phase corresponds to the process of internationalization of manufacturing and finance capital here identified.

BIBLIOGRAPHY

Althusser, Louis. 1971. *Lenin and Philosophy and Other Essays*. Translated by Ben Brewster. New York: Monthly Review Press.

Amin, Samir. 1976. *Unequal Development: An Essay on the Social Formations of Peripheral Capitalism*. Translated by Brian Pearce. New York: Monthly Review Press.

Ashley, Richard K. 1984. "The Poverty of Neorealism." *International Organization* 38, no. 2 (Spring): 225–86.

Becker, David. 1987. "Development, Democracy, and Dependency in Latin America: A Postimperialist View." In *Postimperialism: International Capitalism and Development in the Late Twentieth Century*, by David Becker, Jeff Frieden, Sayre P. Schatz, and Richard L. Sklar, 41–62. Boulder, CO: Lynne Rienner.

Best, Lloyd. 1968. "The Mechanism of Plantation-Type Economies: Outlines of a Model of Pure Plantation Economy." *Social and Economic Studies* 17, no. 3 (September): 283–326.

Bienen, Henry, and John Waterbury. 1992. "The Political Economy of Privatization in Developing Countries." In *The Political Economy of Development and Underdevelopment*, 5th ed., edited by Charles Wilber and Kenneth Jameson, 376–402. New York: McGraw Hill.

Bourdieu, Pierre, and Loïc J. D. Wacquant. 1992. *An Invitation to Reflexive Sociology*. Chicago: University of Chicago Press.

Chatterjee, Partha. 1986. *Nationalist Thought and the Colonial World: A Derivative Discourse*. London: Zed Books.

Crow, Ben, Mary Thorpe, et al. 1988. *Survival and Change in the Third World*. New York: Oxford University Press.

Dell, Sidney. 1984. "Stabilization: The Political Economy of Overkill." In *The Political Economy of Development and Underdevelopment*, edited by Charles K. Wilber, 146–68. New York: Random House.

Drakakis-Smith, David. 1992. *Pacific Asia*. London: Routledge.

Galli, Rosemary E., ed. 1991a. *Rethinking the Third World: Contributions toward a New Conceptualization*. New York: Crane, Russak.

Galli, Rosemary E. 1991b. "Winners and Losers in Development and Antidevelopment Theory." In *Rethinking the Third World: Contributions toward a New Conceptualization*, edited by Rosemary E. Galli, 1–27. New York: Crane, Russak.

Girvan, Norman. 1984. "Swallowing the IMF Medicine in the Seventies." In *The Political Economy of Development and Underdevelopment*, edited by Charles K. Wilber, 169–81. New York: Random House.

Gramsci, Antonio. 1971. *Selections from the Prison Notebooks*. Translated by Quintin Hoare and Geoffrey Nowell Smith. New York: International Publishers.

Harris, Nigel. 1976. *The End of the Third World*. Harmondsworth, Middx., England: Penguin.

Hintzen, Percy C. 1989a. *The Costs of Regime Survival: Racial Mobilization, Elite Domination and Control of the State in Guyana and Trinidad*. Cambridge: Cambridge University Press.

Hintzen, Percy C. 1989b. "Pluralism and Power: Racial Politics and Middle-Class Domination in LDCs." Paper presented at the Conference on Pluralism in the Late Twentieth Century, Institute of Social and Economic Research, Port of Spain, Trinidad, December 7–9.

Hintzen, Percy C. 1993. "Democracy and Middle-Class Domination in the West Indies." In *Democracy in the West Indies: Myths and Realities*, edited by Carlene J. Edie, 9–24. Boulder, CO: Westview Press.

Hintzen, Percy C. 1995. "Structural Adjustment and the New International Middle Class." *Transition*, no. 24 (February): 52–74. University of Guyana Press.

Hintzen, Percy C. 2018. "Rethinking Identity, National Sovereignty, and the State: Reviewing Some Critical Contributions." *Social Identities* 24, no. 1: 39–47.

Hintzen, Percy C., and Ralph Premdas. 1983. "Race, Ideology, and Power in Guyana." *Journal of Commonwealth and Comparative Politics* 21, no. 2: 175–94.

Institute of Development Studies. 1993. "Poverty in Guyana: Finding Solutions." *Transition*, nos. 20–21.

Kothari, Rajni. 1970. *Politics in India*. Boston: Little, Brown.

Lewis, Arthur. 1949. "The Industrialization of the British West Indies." *Caribbean Economic Review* 11, no. 1: 1–53.

Manley, Michael. 1982. *Jamaica: Struggle in the Periphery*. London: Third World Media.

McAfee, Kathy. 1991. *Storm Signals: Structural Adjustment and Development Alternatives in the Caribbean*. London: Zed Books.

Pryor, Frederic L. 1986. *Revolutionary Grenada: A Study in Political Economy*. New York: Praeger.

Robinson, William I. 2014. *Global Capitalism and the Crisis of Humanity*. New York: Cambridge University Press.

Rudebeck, Lars. 1991. "Conditions of People's Development in Postcolonial Africa." In *Rethinking the Third World: Contributions toward a New Conceptualization*, edited by Rosemary E. Galli, 29–88. New York: Crane, Russak.

Segal, Ronald. 1992. "'Race' and 'Color' in Pre-Independence Trinidad and Tobago." In *Trinidad Ethnicity*, edited by Kevin A. Yelvington, 81–115. London: Macmillan Caribbean.

Standing, Guy. 1992. "Global Feminization through Flexible Labor." In *The Political Economy of Development and Underdevelopment*, 5th ed., edited by Charles K. Wilber and Kenneth Jameson, 346–75. New York: McGraw Hill.

Trouillot, Michel-Rolph. 2001. "The Anthropology of the State in the Age of Globalization: Close Encounters of the Deceptive Kind." *Current Anthropology* 42, no. 1 (February): 125–38.

Weaver, Frederick Stirton. 1991. "Toward an Historical Understanding of Industrial Development." In *Rethinking the Third World: Contributions toward a New Conceptualization*, edited by Rosemary E. Galli, 107–52. New York: Crane, Russak.

Chapter 5

RACE AND CREOLE ETHNICITY
IN THE CARIBBEAN

PERCY C. HINTZEN

CARIBBEAN IDENTITY

Caribbean identity occurs within the discursive space of the "creole." To be "Caribbean" is to be "creolized," and within this space is accommodated all who, at any one time, constitute a (semi)permanent core of Caribbean society. Creolization brought with it notions of organic connections across boundaries of ethnicized and racialized difference. It was the mechanism through which colonial discourses of difference, necessary for its legitimation, were accommodated. Everyone located in its discursive space, whatever her or his diasporic origin, becomes transformed in a regime of identific solidarity. At the same time, the creole construct is integrally inserted into a discourse of exclusion as a boundary-maintaining mechanism. Maintaining a strict and rigid boundary between "Caribbean" and "non-Caribbean" (local versus foreign) has functioned strategically as a mechanism for manipulation in the maintenance of order and control.[1]

From this perspective, Caribbean ethnicity is constituted by its hybridized creole formation. In their panoptic gaze, white colonizers imposed this hybridized narrative to render invisible the racialized division of labor and the racial allocation of power and privilege. Historically, the discourse of racial difference has been shifted to distinctions between the creole and non-creole. The result has been a valorization of white purity, located outside creole space. This valorization, at the root of white supremacy, became the foundational principle of colonial power, privilege, honor, and prestige. Creoleness went hand in hand with the symbolic capital of whiteness.[2] It offered the possibility of "whitening" while demonstrating the consequences of descent into the world of savagery represented, in European discursive construction, by the colonized.

Nationalism, according to Benedict Anderson, is to be understood in terms of "the large cultural system that preceded it, out of which—as well as against which—it came into being" (1983, 19). And culture constitutes the representations and practices of ethnicity. As its precedent, a creole imaginary has imposed upon Caribbean nationalism European aspirations that have become hidden behind the veil of anticolonialism. It has served to hide commonalties in social practice that could have formed the basis of counterdiscursive challenges to North Atlantic power. The visualization of similarities located outside of European constructs could have come with "new possibilities for struggle and resistance, for advancing alternative cultural possibilities" (Escobar 1995, 155).

Creole discourse has been the bonding agent of Caribbean society. It has functioned in the interest of the powerful, whether represented by a colonialist or nationalist elite. It is the identific glue that bonds the different, competing, and otherwise mutually exclusive interests contained within Caribbean society. It paved the way for the accommodation of racialized discourses of difference upon which rested the legitimacy of colonial power and exploitation. Difference was rendered invisible in a cognitive merger created and sustained by its impositions. Competing interests and relations of exploitation and privilege became socially organized in a fluid clinal system of racial and cultural hierarchy. This was the observation of Caribbean sociologist Lloyd Braithwaite in what has been termed a "reticulated" color/class pattern of social stratification by anthropologist Leo Despres (Despres 1967; Braithwaite 1953).

To be Caribbean, then, is to occupy the hierarchical, hybridized "creole" space between two racial poles that serve as markers for civilization and savagery. It is to be constituted of various degrees of cultural and racial mixing. At the apex is the white creole as the historical product of cultural hybridization. The Afro-creole is located at the other end of the creole continuum. The "creolization" of the latter derives from transformative contact with Europe's civilizing influences and from physical separation from Africa. Valorized forms of European racial and cultural purity become unattainable ideals in creole representation and practice. Distance from the ideal European phenotype and from Europe's cultural practices determines and defines the creole's position in the social hierarchy.

Thus, the principles of hierarchization of West Indian creole society are intimately tied to notions of European civilization and African savagery. When applied to Europeans, creolization implies the taint of savagery. When applied to Africans, it implies a brush with civilization. The Caribbean is the location where civilization and savagery meet and where both become transformed. In this regard, creole nationalism becomes a quest to be fully European.

The discourse of purity is one of the means through which disciplinary power is imposed upon Caribbean society. Under colonialism, white purity came to be represented as symbolic capital in the practices of the colonial administrators. This was contrasted with the hybridized practices of the white creole. In the English colonies, these different regimes of representation were concretized in colonial institutional practices of the nineteenth century. In the administration of governance, white creole practices were represented in the merchant-planter-dominated Financial College, which became the representative arm of the local white population. British colonial interests came to be signified and represented in the practices of the Court of Policy, which served, in effect, as the legislative arm of government. Executive power was exercised through a colonial administration centered on the governor and comprising civil servants appointed by the Crown (Daly 1966, 214). This development in political representation and practice contributed significantly to the process of white creolization. It paralleled the development of divergent material interests between local and metropolitan capitalists. It differed across territory, irrespective of colonial jurisdiction, and presaged differences in the presence and significance of white creoles in the development of creole identity across the region.

THE DISCOURSE OF PURITY

The hybridized reality of creole society left little room for the accommodation of claims to cultural and racial purity. It is important to emphasize here that purity, like race, is socially constructed. It emerges out of discursive regimes of representation and practice. In Dominica, for example, despite a long history of racial intermixing with Blacks, cultural conversion, and the practice of creole forms of social organization, discourses of purity still exclude the putative descendants of the indigenous Caribs from creole society. Purity emerged as a boundary that defined and maintained the principle separating creole society from the external world. It is a central principle in the discourse of difference that separates the "local" creole white from the foreign "pure" European. This distinction is quite important in the assertions by national elites of cultural claims to the new global order of North Atlantic universalism. These assertions have been made possible by the nationalist rejection of white supremacy. As symbolic and cultural capital (acquired knowledge, skill, and capabilities), such assertions have come to embody the European aspirations of the new nationalist elite.

To be "genuinely" white in the Caribbean is to be culturally and racially pure, untainted by absorption into the society of the Black former slaves. This taint of impurity, forged out of cultural and sexual contact with the African, became the basis for the exclusion of white creoles from colonial power and privilege. Paradoxically, the organic connection to the "territory," which was at the root of such exclusion, ensured the white creole a position of privilege in nationalist construction. White inclusion in the nationalist space suggests the need for a much more nuanced view of the nationalist movement. The embrace of representations and practices of the racialized European mirrors precisely the position of the nationalist movement toward European institutional and cultural forms. Many of the latter were adopted wholeheartedly after independence.[3] Whiteness, however tainted, retains its valorized position in creole nationalist construction. The rights of white creoles to social and economic privilege and preference in the territorial space were retained, and even enhanced, with the departure of the colonial power. In many instances, white creoles are used as international brokers in the new regimes of sovereignty. At the same time, their representation as cultural and racial hybrids and their organic claims to the territory served to protect their social and economic privilege in the crucible of anticolonial nationalism with its anti-European and antiwhite implications. Such representations rendered their "whiteness" invisible in the face of a nationalist rejection of white supremacy. In this way, white creolization became the mechanism for the nonproblematization of whiteness. It legitimized a postcolonial version of racial capitalism and explains the continued domination of whites in the private sector of the postcolonial Caribbean.

Thus, the nationalist movement was neither antiwhite nor anti-European. Rather, it was a contestation of the claims of whites and Europeans to supremacy and superiority. Its various assertions of Africanity in national expression must be understood in these terms. The meaning of such assertions continues to be subject to debate among scholars and writers in the Francophone Caribbean under conditions in which nationalist ambitions have been frustrated. Rather than shifting to sovereign independent status like their Anglophone counterparts, the two largest French Antilles have become incorporated into the administrative and jurisdictional structure of the French state as *départements*. Frustrated nationalist ambitions have fueled the development of a *créoliste* movement "agitating for the local culture and language of the French West Indies" (Taylor 1997, 124). This has supplanted earlier nationalist expressions framed around notions of negritude. Leading members of the movement have rejected negritude's notions of Africanity that were integral to West Indian nationalism. They consider claims to an African past to be an "illusion of Europe with that of Africa" (Taylor 1997, 128). They have painstakingly pointed out the contradictions in the negritude movement in the support provided by its leadership, headed by Aimé Césaire of Martinique, for *département* status and in Césaire's firm embrace of the party politics of France. In all of this, what clearly emerges is the rejection of Africa. It is replaced by an embrace of Europe. It is an embrace that is firmly implanted in Caribbean nationalist representations and practices. Its themes are more convincingly evident in the competing versions of nationalist expression in the French West Indies. They are not so obvious in its Anglophone versions. The necessity of challenging the authorial power of Britain rendered invisible the latter's fundamentally European character.

Creole discourse locates all with claims to purity outside of the territorial community of the Caribbean. This is the point of the *créolistes'* charge of African and European illusion. Indeed, they go a step further by valorizing hybridity as "the vanguard of a world-wide movement" (Taylor 1997, 141). In other words, *créolité* portends the racial and cultural hybridity of a new North Atlantic that is at the forefront of neoglobalization. Such hybridity is essential to the notions of creole nationalism and to the European aspirations contained within them. It substantiates the self-location of the creole at the center of a new globalization of the Europeanized North Atlantic. Thus, Patrick Chamoiseau, one of the movement's leading ideologues, describes creolization as a "great poetics of relation, which allows people to express their newfound diversity, to live it fluidly. In creolization, there never comes a time of general synthesis, with everyone beatifically at one with one another" (Taylor 1997, 136).

Thus, claims to purity, essentialized around geographic discourses of origin, cannot be accommodated in creole discourse. This is the basis of the *créolistes'* discomfort with "illusions of Africa and Europe." It is why the North must first undergo a *métissage* transformation to accommodate the European aspirations of creole nationalism. Thus, firmly embedded in nationalist aspirations is the goal of the conversion of Europe into the pregnable, transitory, and open space that is the Caribbean. This is very much what has occurred in the French Antilles. The assertion of *créolité* is very much a declaration of the hybridization of European space occupied exclusively by whites. Indeed, the term "creole," before its hybridization, signified the representations and practices of white French West Indians known as *békés*, referring specifically to "a white person of pure race born in the Antilles" (Taylor 1997, 132).

Postemancipation indentureship imposed its own legitimating regime of exclusion. Its legitimacy rested upon the "racial" and cultural location of the new indentures outside of the European-African continuum of creole society. But the new rationality of exclusion applied also to European and African postslavery indentures. Portuguese indentures, imported from Madeira, were unable to make immediate claims of racial affinity with the white creoles in Trinidad and British Guiana. They remained for a time outside of creole society. For postemancipation African indentures, the boundary maintaining the distinction between African and Afro-creole, typical of slave society, prevailed. Once inserted into plantation society, however, Portuguese and Africans became quickly amalgamated. For the African, creolization came with location at the lowest rung in the color/class hierarchy (Warner-Lewis 1990). The Portuguese took over from coloreds in small-scale retailing. They followed a trajectory of incorporation into creole society by whites and near-whites as "trading minorities" (Nicholls 1981, 422–26). This was also the path followed by the small migrant population of Lebanese, Syrians, Jews, and postindenture Chinese who, with the Portuguese, were able to establish themselves in the retail sector, particularly in Trinidad and Jamaica.

Amalgamation has become integral to the historical reproduction of creole identity. It calls for an abnegation of purity through sexual and cultural immersion. The creole space "swallows everything up . . . remaining permanently in motion, pushing us headlong in a movement of diversity, of change and exchange" (Taylor 1997, 142). "Blending and impurity" stand as its fundamental values (Taylor 1997, 137). With the exception of the Syrians and Lebanese, whose cultural forms disappeared with their creolization, immersion has acted historically to modify the African-European continuum in the Anglophone Caribbean. Rituals and practices of creole transformation can include racial immersion through miscegenation. Cultural immersion can occur through marriage, religious conversion, association, and adoption of the tastes and style of creole society. Cohabitation has become quite important in individual practices of creolization. For the offspring of the ensuing unions, creole parentage negates any claim to purity. It brings with it automatic location within the white-Black continuum. To some degree, cohabitation with white creoles has offered the most acceptable means of immersion into creole society for those located outside of the European-African space. Cohabitation with whites, the most "desirable" of the creoles, serves to lessen the social opprobrium of creolization with its implications of impurity. Thus, with the exception of the whites who were pushed "downward" into creole space, the thrust of creolization has always been upward to the European end of the racial and cultural spectrum. The quest of the nationalist movement was to penetrate the barrier of racial purity by hybridizing European space.

EXCLUSION AND INCORPORATION

Symbolic exclusion is the instrument of disciplinary power wielded historically against diasporic communities functionally integrated into Caribbean political economy. It rendered legitimate the systematic denial of any claims non-creoles might make upon the resources of creole society. This became the basis for exclusion from opportunities provided through access to these resources. While historically pervasive, the discriminatory and exploitative consequences of symbolic exclusion were not always universal. With exclusion came also the benefits of freedom from the normative strictures of creole society. It created

opportunities unavailable to those located in the color/class hierarchy of creole social space. The discourse of purity served historically, until well into the
twentieth century, to confine East Indians to rural agriculture and to justify
their semiservile status. At the same time, however, East Indians have managed to use peasant agriculture as a springboard for upward mobility through
business and the professions. In the process, they have been able to eviscerate
the social stigma of agricultural labor. Their agricultural background did not
prefigure in social evaluations of their fitness for business and higher education, as it would have for creole subjects. Because they are "outsiders," these
standards of evaluation were rendered irrelevant.

The benefits of exclusion were evident also in the ability of Chinese and
Portuguese (coming in as nineteenth-century indentures), Syrians, Lebanese,
and the small number of Jews (all arriving after World War I) to exploit economic opportunity. Their exclusion from creole society freed them from the
strictures of color imposed by their light complexion. As such, they were able
to ignore the principles of behavior and association implicated in the color/
class hierarchy of creole society. They established themselves in petty trade by
developing highly personalized relationships with customers lower down in the
color/class hierarchy. From here, they created niches in small-scale retailing,
particularly in Trinidad, Jamaica, and British Guiana. Their activities, and the
pattern of associations and practices engendered by them, became springboards for their structural and social insertion into colonial creole society. Once
located in creole space, they were able to combine symbolic capital (derived
from their color) with economic capital to move up in the social hierarchy.
Many came to occupy positions identical to or just below those of creole whites.
What became most evident in their upward mobility was the importance of
the symbolic capital of whiteness. This pattern of amalgamation and upward
mobility was not available to the more than forty thousand postemancipation
Africans brought to the West Indies between 1834 and 1867 for plantation labor
(Asiegbu 1969, 189–90). Their amalgamation occurred at the lowest rung of
the color/class continuum of creole society.

It is through racial and cultural incorporation that the transitory nature of
creole society is preserved. Incorporation allows Caribbean society to respond
to the constantly changing pressures and demands from outside its borders.
These must be accommodated for the very economic survival of the territories
of the region. Practices of amalgamation have changed the racial and cultural
character of creole society. They have produced new forms of racial hybridity involving, particularly, East Indian and Chinese postslavery additions to
plantation society. Similarly, newly emergent forms of cultural hybridity have
become integrated into creole practice. Thus, cultural and racial insertion has
contributed to a historical reformulation of creole identity. It has produced,

over time, a modification of its racialized construction. Dark skin continues to retain the signifying power of inferiority. However, its exclusive association with African diasporic origin is no longer a firmly entrenched principle. Thus, a white-Black polarity based on color has replaced Europe and Africa at opposite ends of the creole continuum. This has been particularly the case as new diasporic communities with origins in Asia, the Middle East, and the indigenous population of the region have become immersed into Caribbean reality. "Blackness," however, continues by and large to retain its association with Africa in an ongoing counterdiscourse to creole construction. This is quite evident in the regional spread of the Rastafarian movement, which originated in Jamaica (Chevannes 1995), and in the Orisha religious movement in Trinidad (Houk 1993, 161–79).

For the most part, the indigenous and diasporic communities with cultural and racial origins outside Africa and Europe remain, in representation and practice, outside of creole reality. For members of these communities, amalgamation is available through individual practices of cultural and sexual immersion. For East Indians, individual practices of racial miscegenation with Afro-creoles have been significant enough to produce a distinct creole variant identified as "douglas" in the local lexicon. As the products of Afro-Indian unions, douglas have become integral to the construction of creole identity in Guyana and Trinidad. They have also come to symbolize the threat posed by creolization to East Indian purity. The theme of "douglarization" emerges persistently in East Indian narratives of purity. It has become emblematic of the polluting consequences of sexual contact with Africans. Douglarization, therefore, is the process of transformation of East Indians into racial creoles through miscegenation. Another route to East Indian creolization is through cultural amalgamation. East Indians may enter the social space of creole organization through practices of intermarriage, religious conversion, creole association (including location of residence), and the adoption of creole style and tastes.

The representations and practices of creoleness are responses to the deployment of symbolic power at the disposal of the constituents of its various segments and of those located outside its symbolic space. Each is engaged in a constant struggle to define creole reality. Creoles activate honor and prestige as symbolic power, they activate the resources of economic, social, and cultural power available to them, and they activate the privilege of belonging to maintain the existing integrity of creoleness. Those excluded from the creole space are perpetually engaged in efforts to redefine its character or to challenge its centrality in national conceptions of belonging. These struggles produce constant reformulations over time of the cognitive schemata that inform creole identity and out of which its representations and practices are fashioned. They have also produced territorially specific manifestations of creole constructs.

Trinidad provides an example of the complexities and idiosyncrasies of creole construction and its implications for nationalist discursive formation. The

European cultural component of Trinidadian society has been shaped significantly by Spanish colonialism (the former colonial power) and by the presence of a French merchant plantocracy (via Haiti after the Haitian revolution). As "local whites," French and Spanish creoles were historically differentiated from the administrative class of the British in colonial representation and practice. As a result, creole identity in Trinidad became heavily infused with French and Spanish representations and with Roman Catholicism. It has also been influenced by the presence of East Indian, Chinese, Portuguese, Syrian, and Lebanese diasporic populations and by the various racial and cultural hybridities produced in social interaction among all these groupings. In particular, hybridized rituals and symbols of East Indian representations and practices are gaining considerable visibility in creole construction. This is despite the latter's historical exclusion from the creolized space of Trinidadian identific discourse. At the same time, Trinidadian creole formation has amalgamated the representations and practices of douglas, Portuguese (by giving up their claims to whiteness), and Chinese, Syrians, and Lebanese (through cultural amalgamation and miscegenation).

At over 40 percent of the population, the size and functional integration of East Indians in Trinidad have had profound consequences for the reproduction of creole society. This has produced considerable challenges to the central role that creoleness has played in nationalist construction. The fundamental contradiction between the structural integration of East Indians in Trinidad's political economy and their symbolic exclusion from nationalist space has generated an increasing crescendo of national conflict as well as persistent contestation of nationalist discourse. Access to creole society has been available only to those members of the East Indian community prepared to reject representations and practices of purity on cultural grounds or to those who are prepared to reject patterns of racial solidarity and marriage endogamy. One avenue for rejection is through conversion to Christianity. For the smaller population of Muslim East Indians (less than 25 percent of the total East Indian population), religion poses less of a barrier to creolization, given their monotheism and the common foundation of beliefs that they share with Christianity. As a result, Muslims have been much more visibly included in the representation and practices of creole nationalist expression. However, discourses of purity continue to locate the large majority of East Indians, as Hindus, outside of the national space. Members of the East Indian middle class, particularly its economic, social, and political elite, experience the most profound pressures for creolization. This derives from their high degree of functional integration into the "creole" segments of Trinidad's political economy. To this is added their own predispositions toward creolization as they seek to realize the benefits of nationalism that have accrued to their creole counterparts in the postcolonial era. The pressures and predispositions have resulted in the incorporation by many Hindus of more universal Western forms into their religious practices and the opening of their religion to creole practitioners. It has produced a form of creolization that comes with little sacrifice to Hindu identity (Klass 1991).

Notwithstanding the pressures placed upon the Hindu middle classes and their own predispositions toward creole incorporation, there is mounting resistance to creolization among the Hindu cultural elite. In their campaign, they activate the symbolic power of purity to petition for inclusion in the nationalist space *as East Indians*. Hindu purity is deployed as a symbolic resource by these leaders to delegitimize "polluted" creole discourse. The leaders reject the central role that creole representations occupy in notions of national belonging. Such rejection is organized around narratives of cultural degradation directed particularly at the cultural ascendance of Afro-creole forms in nationalist discourse. There is mounting contestation of the claim made by Afro-creoles of their own central role in nation building. East Indians are beginning to present themselves as the true builders of the nation. Their cultural elite has constructed a historical narrative of East Indians as redeemers who have, time and again, delivered the country from the abyss of Afro-creole degradation (Yelvington 1995, 77). The East Indian challenge to creole nationalism is not merely a quest for nationalist inclusion. Rather, it is an attempt to retain representations and practices of cultural purity while resisting "douglarization." It represents a redemptive counterdiscourse to Afro-creole nationalism and presents a fundamental challenge to the Trinidadian creole imaginary. It remains a rejection of the "blending and impurity" of the form of hybridity that occupies the critical center in the value framework of creole's discourse.

Notwithstanding Hindu challenges, the fundamental thrust of creolization is deeply embedded in the historical development of Trinidadian national identity. Creoleness occupies the critical core of the country's national psyche. This is evident in the mythic representation of the "Spanish." As a social construction of the ideal-typical Trinidadian, it has emerged as a means of managing the complexities and conflicting pulls of diasporic identity. But "Spanish" identity is instructive in another important way. It exposes and externalizes the European aspirations that exist at the root of creole discourse and that are integral to the country's nationalist expression. It is a narrative of a simpler time in Trinidad colonial history before the introduction of plantation slavery (and hence of the complexity of the African presence). The "Spanish" construct embodies all the positive elements of the various ethnic groupings that occupy the country's territorial space (creolized or otherwise). As such, it is a trope of hybridized harmony in the face of multiple and competing representations and practices of difference (Khan 1993). But it is a harmony forged out of idealized "European" qualities, devoid of notions of ethnic, cultural, and social exclusivity.

In Trinidad, the struggle for the nation occurs in the field of symbolic production and reproduction. Representations and practices of purity are raised as challenges to creole nationalism. In Guyana, symbolic representations of nationhood that valorize creole cultural forms are less important than practices of institutional solidarity. This is related partly to a historical absence of white creoles in the color/class order of Guyanese social construction. Nationalist discourse did not have to accommodate a white creole presence through the activation of colonial notions of cultural and biogenetic hybridity. The absence of creole discourse left a cultural vacuum in the nationalist movement, which was filled by competing racial claims to the state. Competing political elites activated such claims after 1955 by deploying institutional resources under exclusive racial control. This occurred in the wake of a breakdown in the multiracial nationalist movement. It set the stage for the development of an integral association between nationalist organization and existing racialized practices of institutional inclusion and exclusion.

Between 1957 and 1964, racial claims to British Guiana by East Indians were held in check by colonial overlordship and colonial predispositions to countenance the demands of the creole elite for control of national power and privilege. But the efforts of the British Colonial Office to place this elite in power through fiat collapsed after an uncertain tenure between 1964 and 1967. Creole elite ascendance was stymied in the face of a successful effort to press a more Africa-centered stamp on Guyanese nationalist expression. During the 1960s, the African Society for Cultural Relations with Independent Africa (ASCRIA) became highly integrated into the structure and organization of the Black nationalist People's National Congress (PNC) that had run the country since 1964. ASCRIA's leaders enjoyed powerful positions in the government and saw their role as ensuring the location of the Black lower class at the center of the country's nationalist agenda. In the color/class hierarchy of creole society, this grouping's historical location at the bottom of the sociocultural ladder facilitated and reinforced identific notions of its own African origin. The Black lower class comprised Afro-Guyanese rural own-account peasantry and urban proletariat, many of whom were migrants from rural villages. They were able to organize as members of ASCRIA. The association's leadership mounted challenges to creole discourse with narratives of African belonging. Under its influence, the country's foreign relations shifted to an emphasis on the development of close relations with the African continent. At ASCRIA's insistence, elements of the state's national policies were adopted, almost wholeheartedly, from Tanzania's version of cooperative socialism.

The emphasis on Africa conflicted with the culturally rooted aspirations and practices of the country's creole middle classes, a significant proportion of whom were colored. By 1971, middle-class opposition forced the ruling party to abandon its ideology of Africa-centered nationalism. In response, ASCRIA's leaders resigned from their government posts and began a scathing campaign against the ruling PNC. Added to the rejection of African-centered nationalism by the Black and colored middle classes was strong and organized opposition from the East Indian population, which exceeded 50 percent of the country's total. As a means of neutralizing East Indian challenges to its nationalist agenda, the PNC was forced to embark on a strategy of co-optation of the most strategic sectors of the East Indian political economy, particularly its businesspeople, professionals, and educated elite. This received added impetus from the ruling party's quest for institutional control of the public space. In turn, the East Indian elite came to rely upon the protection and patronage of a ruling party in control of the overdeveloped Guyanese state.

The absence of a legitimate historical cultural claim to nationhood rendered Afro-creole assertions of nationalism in Guyana problematic. East Indian opposition produced a need for co-optation of the East Indian elite. Co-optation combined with middle-class opposition to dilute Afro-creole nationalist expression.

Through its strategy of co-optation, the ruling party exercised considerable control over the public activities of strategic sectors of the East Indian population. It was able, also, to neutralize the effects of East Indian opposition. East Indians are strategically located in all the major institutional sectors of the political economy, much more so, in most cases, than the creole population. This is particularly true of the local private sector, where ownership and control is almost exclusively East Indian and is reinforced by the type of racially endogamous patterns of recruitment and hiring that typifies every sector of the Guyanese political economy. There is also a significant presence of East Indians in the professional sector. They enjoy an almost exclusive racial presence in the country's agroproductive sector as cash crop producers and plantation labor.

By 1975, the international relations of Guyana's ruling party shifted to a close alliance with Eastern Europe. This occurred in the wake of state takeover of the foreign private sector and many large local merchant and trading enterprises. In the process, the "nation" came to be constituted by the institutions of the state. The latter began to play a pervasive role in almost every aspect of public behavior. The justifying ideology of socialism displaced cultural notions of creole national belonging from the center of nationalist discourse.

Socialism, a Eurocommunist orientation in foreign policy, and co-optation of the East Indian institutional elite all combined to produce a form of nationalist expression that was less integrally tied to creole representation than was the case in Trinidad. Guyanese nationalism began to take the form of state-centered institutional cooperativism. It became identified with the institutions of governance and the domestic institutional interests represented by and identified with the governing elite and its allies (Hintzen 1989, 169–71). In Trinidad, competition for the national space occurs over issues of its ethnocultural character. In Guyana, competition for the national space occurs over access to the institutional resources of power. In both cases, however, challenges to nationalist construction emerged from within the East Indian population. In Guyana, they were mounted by representatives of East Indian working-class interests.

Nationalist expression in Guyana has come to incorporate the symbolic capital of the governing elite and the interests it represents. In popular consciousness, these continue to be understood in racial terms despite efforts at cross-racial co-optation. The result is a racialized struggle over control of the national space that takes place in the political arena. The struggle is objectified in political competition for control of the governing institutions of the state. It takes place among competing racialized political organizations. These include political parties and trade unions. It is a struggle for the institutional domination of the national political space. In 1992, the East Indian political elite organized in the People's Progressive Party (PPP) and regained the executive and legislative power it had lost in 1964. It proceeded to redefine the national space using the control it exercises over the executive and legislative branches of the state. In response, the campaign for control of the nation has shifted to the bureaucratic apparatus of government (including the country's police and security forces) and to the judiciary. Both remain largely under the control of a Black and colored bureaucratic elite (Hintzen 1998, 13–16). These have become the locomotive centers of Afro-Guyanese challenges to the East Indian takeover of the institutionalized national space.

East Indians in Trinidad and Guyana have employed different strategies to challenge nationalist constructs and redefine national identity. In Guyana, challenges have been mounted also by the Black lower classes. Each challenge represents a specific instance of the incorporation over time of multiple and competing claims to the national space. Each is a particular response to colonial and postcolonial discourses of exclusion, legitimized in the historical production and reproduction of creole reality. Each challenge presents itself as an assault against the rituals, symbols, and institutions of Caribbean self-representation. In the final analysis, each represents a counterdiscourse to the complexity of cultural and racial representations and practices constitutive of creole identity and to the honor and prestige that underlie creole claims to privilege and power. In Trinidad, the creole imaginary remains visible as the critical component of nationalist expression. In Guyana, it is rendered invisible by the institutional construction of national space. At the same time, it continues to be pervasive in the representations and practices of all the racialized groupings of elite. Its nonproblematization in Guyana has intensified the process of East Indian creolization, producing a creole elite distinguished from its Afro-European counterparts only by the racialized sources of its institutional power.

Creole discourse is so integral to national identity in the West Indies that nation-state contestation seems to lead, inevitably, to the intensification of the process of creolization for those located outside the creole space. Efforts aimed at dislocation from the state seem to be capable of producing a more successful result. In Dominica, the Karifuna descendants of the indigenous Caribs are engaged in a struggle for autonomy against the creole nation-state. The struggle is a manifestation of the developing organization of indigenous peoples in Latin America and the Caribbean. It has emerged in response to colonial and postcolonial practices of exclusion and displacement organized through the historical containment of the Karifuna in a Carib reserve. Ironically, these very practices have become bases for the rejection of creole nationalism. During colonialism, they facilitated the superexploitation of the Karifuna as they became structurally integrated into the Dominican political economy.

Karifuna contestation of nationalist authority occurs through rejection of the historical practices of marginalization and displacement. They have engaged the legal system to make a claim for exclusive right of occupation of the very "Carib Territory" developed for their exploitation. In the process, the "Territory" has been transformed into the symbolic objectified center of Karifuna identity. The demand for autonomy is accompanied, periodically, by ritual acts of purification. These include expulsions of non-Caribs, particularly Afro-creole males and their Karifuna female partners, from Carib territory (Gregoire, Henderson, and Kanem 1996, 107–71). What is significant here is that Karifuna claims to territory are based on notions of prior occupation. The contestation of creole nationalist practice is organized by groups with putative claims to indigenous identity. This provides them with considerable moral legitimacy, which is transformed into symbolic power in the deployment of the honor and prestige that attaches to the rights of prior occupation. As such, Dominica provides an example of the strategic deployment of symbolic power in the contestation of creole domination. This form of contestation is not confined to Dominica. Parallel movements have emerged among Carib populations in Saint Vincent and the Grenadines.

Creole nationalism has been negotiated differently by the much larger indigenous population of Guyana. Amerindians occupy a much more ambiguous position in Guyanese nationalist space when compared with the Karifuna in Dominica. They do not have at their disposal a single territorial location that can be converted into a symbol of identific separation from creole society. Rather, they are scattered throughout the hinterland of the country in numerous small communities under the disciplinary authority of creole administrators and functionaries. Their integration into creole society and national institutions varies with geographic location and is not uniform. This is accompanied by an uneven pattern of economic integration into the Guyanese political economy. Amerindian communities display varying degrees of cultural hybridity. Most of their members have been converted to Christianity, and miscegenation has occurred unevenly across the several geographic communities. Amerindians experience differing degrees of co-optation in the institutional arena of politics, and of access to the institutionalized national space.

The absence of a definitive identific boundary between Amerindian and creole societies in Guyana has diluted Amerindian demands for autonomy from nationalist representations and practices. Their indeterminate relationship to creole practice and to nationalist expression has produced less of a predisposition to nationalist rejection than among their counterparts in Dominica. This is despite their participation in international and local organizations of indigenous peoples (Fox and Danns 1993).

CONCLUSION

The representations and practices of creole nationalism differ significantly across the territories of the English-speaking Caribbean. Such differences reflect the diverse compositions of colonial and postcolonial societies and the different ways that the various diasporic communities have become inserted into the political economy. Ultimately, they reflect, in all the manifestations of creole, differences in the technical and social conditions of capitalist production over time and space. Conceptualizations of white purity continue to reinforce and legitimize a system of globalized dependency. Domestically, creole nationalism continues to hide the reality of racial capitalism. Aspirations to cultural purity have prevailed in the face of hybridity. They have been at the root of an endemic conflict over identity and nationalism in the region. And they have foreclosed opportunities for regional integration. Creole nationalism in the postindependence era has prevented the development of a social construction that can serve as an alternative to the cultural and social legacy of Europe. It has wedded the former colonies to patterns of international relations characterized by an uncritical acceptance of the North Atlantic as the center of the social, cultural, political, and economic universe. This has been the tragedy of the current colonial construction of creole discourse in the West Indies.

NOTES

1. For an elaboration of the ideas discussed in this chapter and their application to race and ethnicity in the Caribbean, see Hintzen 2002.

2. The term "symbolic capital" is taken from Pierre Bourdieu and pertains to the accumulation and display of symbols of honor and prestige that render "unrecognizable" the true exploitative nature of relationships of economic exchange. It is "denied capital recognized as legitimate" (Bourdieu 1990, 118, 112–21).

3. The point here is not that white creoles should not be included in the nationalist definition. Rather, it is to point out the paradox of this embrace by a nationalist movement rooted in challenges to white supremacy.

BIBLIOGRAPHY

Anderson, Benedict. 1983. *Imagined Communites: Reflections on the Origin and Spread of Nationalism*. London: Verso Books.

Asiegbu, Johnson U. J. 1969. *Slavery and the Politics of Liberation, 1787–1861: A Study of Liberated African Emigration and British Anti-Slavery Policy*. London: Longmans, Green and Company.

Bourdieu, Pierre. 1990. *The Logic of Practice*. Stanford, CA: Stanford University Press.

Braithwaite, Lloyd. 1953. "Social Stratification in Trinidad: A Preliminary Analysis." *Social and Economic Studies* 2, no. 2: 5–175.

Chevannes, Barry. 1995. *Rastafari: Roots and Ideology*. Syracuse, NY: Syracuse University Press.

Chude-Sokei, Louis. 1995. "The Incomprehensible Rain of Stars: Black Modernism, Black Diaspora." PhD diss., University of California, Los Angeles.

Daly, Vere T. 1966. *A Short History of the Guyanese People*. Georgetown, Guyana: Daily Chronicle.

Despres, Leo A. 1967. *Cultural Pluralism and Nationalist Politics in British Guiana*. Chicago: Rand McNally.

Despres, Leo A. 1968. "The Implications of Nationalist Politics in British Guiana for the Development of Cultural Theory." In *State and Society: A Reader in Comparative Political Sociology*, edited by Reinhard Bendix, 502–28. Berkeley: University of California Press.

Escobar, Arturo. 1995. *Encountering Development: The Making and Unmaking of the Third World*. Princeton, NJ: Princeton University Press.

Fox, Desrey, and George K. Danns. 1993. *The Indigenous Condition in Guyana*. Georgetown, Guyana: University of Guyana.

Gilroy, Paul. 1993. *The Black Atlantic: Modernity and Double-Consciousness*. Cambridge, MA: Harvard University Press.

Gregoire, Crispin, Patrick Henderson, and Natalia Kanem. 1996. "Karifuna: The Caribs of Dominica." In *Ethnic Minorities in Caribbean Society*, edited by Rhoda E. Reddock, 107–71. Saint Augustine, Trinidad: Institute of Social and Economic Research, University of the West Indies.

Hanoomansingh, Peter. 1996. "Beyond Profit and Capital: A Study of the Sindhis and Gujaratis of Barbados." In *Ethnic Minorities in Caribbean Society*, edited by Rhoda E. Reddock, 273–342. Saint Augustine, Trinidad: Institute of Social and Economic Research, University of the West Indies.

Hintzen, Percy C. 1989. *The Costs of Regime Survival: Racial Mobilization, Elite Domination and Control of the State in Guyana and Trinidad*. Cambridge: Cambridge University Press.

Hintzen, Percy C. 1997. "Reproducing Domination: Identity and Legitimacy Constructs in the West Indies." *Social Identities* 3, no. 1: 47–75.

Hintzen, Percy C. 1998. "Democracy on Trial: The December 1997 Elections in Guyana and Its Aftermath." *Caribbean Studies Newsletter* 25, no. 3 (September–October): 13–16.

Hintzen, Percy C. 2002. "The Caribbean: Race and Creole Ethnicity." In *A Companion to Racial and Ethnic Studies*, edited by David Theo Goldberg and John Solomos, 475–94. Malden, MA: Blackwell.

Houk, James. 1993. "Afro-Trinidadian Identity and the Africanisation of the Orisha Religion." In *Trinidad Ethnicity*, edited by Kevin A. Yelvington, 161–79. Knoxville: University of Tennessee Press.

Khan, Aisha. 1993. "What Is 'a Spanish'? Ambiguity and 'Mixed' Ethnicity in Trinidad." In *Trinidad Ethnicity*, edited by Kevin A. Yelvington, 180–207. Knoxville: University of Tennessee Press.

Klass, Morton. 1991. *Singing with Sai Baba: The Politics of Revitalization in Trinidad*. Boulder, CO: Westview Press.

Lewis, Gordon K. 1968. *The Growth of the Modern West Indies*. New York: Monthly Review Press.

Mitchell, Timothy. 1988. *Colonising Egypt*. Cambridge: Cambridge University Press.

Nicholls, David. 1981. "No Hawkers and Pedlars: Levantines in the Caribbean." *Ethnic and Racial Studies* 4, no. 4 (October): 415–31.

Rabinow, Paul. 1986. "Representations Are Social Facts: Modernity and Post-Modernity in Anthropology." In *Writing Culture: The Poetics and Politics of Ethnography*, edited by James Clifford and George E. Marcus, 234–61. Berkeley: University of California Press.

Ryan, Selwyn. 1972. *Race and Nationalism in Trinidad and Tobago*. Toronto: University of Toronto Press.

Stavans, Ilan. 1995. *The Hispanic Condition: The Future Power of a People*. New York: HarperCollins.

Taylor, Lucien. 1997. "Créolité Bites: A Conversation with Patrick Chamoiseau, Raphaël Confiant, and Jean Bernabé." *Transition*, no. 74: 136.

Trouillot, Michel-Rolph. 1990. *Haiti: State against Nation; The Origins and Legacy of Duvalierism*. New York: Monthly Review Press.

Warner-Lewis, Maureen. 1990. *Guinea's Other Suns: The African Dynamic in Trinidad Culture*. Dover, MA: Majority Press.

Yelvington, Kevin A. 1995. *Producing Power: Ethnicity, Gender, and Class in a Caribbean Workplace*. Philadelphia: Temple University Press.

Zavala, Iris M., and Rafael Rodriguez, eds. 1980. *The Intellectual Roots of Independence: An Anthology of Puerto Rican Political Essays*. New York: Monthly Review Press.

Chapter 6

CREOLENESS AND NATIONALISM IN GUYANESE ANTICOLONIALISM AND POSTCOLONIAL FORMATION

PERCY C. HINTZEN

An analysis of the postcolonial formation of Guyana (formerly the colony of British Guiana) and its relationship to belonging (peoplehood) raises profound questions for the analytics of nationalism. These relate to the state's "power of delimitation through exclusion and of empowerment through inclusion" (Goldberg 2002, 10). The inscription of race into Guyana's politics may very well challenge propositions about the homogenizing agenda of the state through the discursive deployment of ideology. This refers to the historical production and reproduction of the "nation" as a "coherent populace." From the analytics of critical theory, we have come to understand the racial state as the antithesis of heterogeneity. But a coherent peoplehood may be troubled by the politics of race, especially when claims to belonging by each of the instrumentally organized racialized groupings are universally recognized and uncontested (Goldberg 2002, 7–11; Winant 2001; Marx 1998). This, I argue, was precisely the case in Guyana. Such *racially* heterogeneous but nonetheless legitimate claims to national belonging emerged at the conjunctures of economic, ideological, political, social, and cultural forces that need to be historicized. They were forged in the crucible of the anticipated and the actual relinquishing of control of the bureaucratic and legal apparatuses of the colonial state by Great Britain. But with relinquishment, the logic of colonialism reasserted itself in the form of competition for control of the instrumentalities of the state, and of policy- and lawmaking. What emerged were imageries of heterogeneity that contradict the "natural" condition of national (racial) unity ideologically inscribed in the idea of the nation-state.

The existence of heterogeneous claims to national belonging, made particularly by racially mobilized segments at the end of formal colonial rule, may be a necessary condition for the maintenance of the racial state if the latter is understood to be the exclusive preserve of whiteness. Such an understanding can be unsettled under conditions in which the apparatuses of the colonial state are transferred to inferiorized former colonial subjects without a subsequent disruption of order. The issue turns, at this juncture, to the means whereby the interests of the Global North reassert themselves in a statist organization. The emergence of heterogeneous claims, therefore, functions as a signifier of the unsuitability of the colonized subject to participate in the modernist project of state formation. It demonstrates the "historical immaturity" of the colonial subject and the pervasive and continuing necessity for white supremacy. Chaos and crisis become the instrumentality for the latter's reassertion. One may anticipate, therefore, that when forms of coloniality, modified in keeping with the changing technical and social conditions of international capital, go unchallenged in the quest for independence, heterogeneous political claims for control of the state apparatuses would be limited or nonexistent. Independence movements seeking control of these apparatuses and of policy- and lawmaking would retain what David Theo Goldberg identifies as the "governmental technologies" of colonialism (2002, 9). The latter include "census categories," "invented histories and traditions," "ceremonies," and "cultural imaginings." These retentions serve as iterations of a *naturalized* racial ordering that, with "independence," becomes transferred from colonial to international relations. In the Caribbean and Latin America, such naturalization derives from the discursive deployment of hybridity as ideology. It is important to distinguish the latter from the hybridized practices identified through critical analytics or that emerge in intellectual and cultural production proposed as possibilities for an alternative future (Puri 2004). In this sense, hybridity as a "governmental technology" needs to be separated from hybridized practices that emerge in the unfolding of the material processes of life. There is, of course, an integral relationship between the two. Ideology both produces and is a product of such materialities. At the same time, however, ideology functions to render invisible and to distort when articulation and publicization are fraught with counterhegemonic possibilities (Steger 2009, 5–7).

As governmental technology in the English-speaking Caribbean, creole discourse served the ideological function of integration (Hintzen 2001). It was the identific glue that bonded the different and competing interests of the colonizer and the colonized constitutive of Caribbean society. It was framed by the idea of a hybridized and hierarchically organized European-African continuum. At its root were "naturalist" ideologies of a racial order typified by the savage statelessness of Africans and the civilized Europeans governed by reason and rationality. In the ideological memory of the colonial encounter, the two are brought together, producing civilizing possibilities for the African, realized in the acquisition of the attributes of the European. This paved the way for the legitimization of colonial power and its instrumental deployment. In its materialities, colonialism emerged in the Caribbean as a "reticulated" color/class social formation hierarchically organized in a seamless incline of race and culture for the racial distribution of power, privilege, status, and wealth. At its apex was the white European colonizer (Braithwaite 1953; Despres 1967). Its creolist discourse formed the ideological underpinnings of nationalist imaginings, producing the notions of a coherent peoplehood that fueled independence movements in the insular Caribbean.

This color/class pattern of social stratification had its own particular manifestation in the colony of British Guiana. There was no significant "local" white creole presence in the colony. At the beginning of twentieth century, small groups of Portuguese and near-whites were positioned at the apex of the creole hierarchy. Because of the introduction of the Portuguese as indentures, they could make no claim to whiteness, which was reserved for the British colonizer. Nonetheless, their upward mobility was guaranteed in the color/class hierarchy of colonial social formation. Chinese and coloreds were socially located just below this group. Afro-creole Blacks and Asian Indians predominated on the lowest strata of colonial society, the former as an urban proletariat and the latter as plantation workers and small own-account farmers. Asian Indians also worked in unskilled service jobs in the private urban sector or as urban professionals and business owners. In the country's interior regions, Amerindian descendants of the country's indigenous population lived a very marginal existence, separated from the mainstream of colonial and creole society.

Thus, class and race were highly imbricated in British Guianese colonial society, tempered by a color-based clinal hierarchy. The educated, professional, and skilled spanned the spectrum from lower middle class to the apex of creole society according to qualifications and economic status. There was an entanglement of color and cultural and economic capital.[1] Each facilitated the acquisition of the other.[2] In colonial British Guiana, class differences and racialized patterns of distribution of privilege were managed under a rubric of creoleness that incorporated the various groupings of Blacks, mixed, Portuguese, Chinese, and a few whites. As an ideology, creoleness explained colonial society, determined its standards of normative evaluation, served as a guide and compass for action, and was the basis for simplification of the colonial complex.[3] These became bases for the distortion of colonial society and for rendering invisible its "plane of material reality." The cognitively inscribed imageries of creoleness contrasted sharply with this reality, rooted in relations of domination and exploitation. Creoleness served as a basis for the legitimation of the colonial project and for the integration of colonial society.[4] It was the instrumentality by which technologies of discipline and control were deployed against the colonized population.

THE DISCOURSE OF PURITY:
EXCLUSION AND INCORPORATION

The hybridized reality of creole society left little room for the accommodation of claims to cultural and racial purity. It is important to emphasize here that purity, like race, is socially constructed. It emerges out of discursive regimes of representation and practice. Under creole colonialism, purity was transformed into a boundary-defining and boundary-maintaining principle separating creole society from the external world. It legitimized and normalized the imperialist privileges of the white colonizer while at the same time privileging the group of "local" whites and "near-whites" just subordinate to the white colonial class.

Symbolic exclusion is the instrument of disciplinary power wielded historically against diasporic communities functionally integrated into the Caribbean political economy. It renders legitimate the systematic denial of any claims non-creoles might make upon the resources of creole society. Exclusion was not universally negative. It came also with the benefits of freedom from the normative strictures of creole society, creating opportunities that were unavailable to those located in the color/class hierarchy of creole social space. In British Guiana, the discourse of purity served historically, until well into the twentieth century, to confine Asian Indians to rural agriculture and to justify their semiservile status. At the same time, however, Asian Indians managed to use peasant agriculture as a springboard for upward mobility through business and the professions. In the process, they were able to eviscerate the social stigma of agricultural labor. Their agricultural background did not prefigure in social evaluations of their fitness for business and higher education, as would have been the case for creole subjects. Because they were "outsiders," these standards of evaluation were rendered irrelevant.

NATIONALISM AS COUNTERDISCOURSE

There were considerable differences between British Guiana and the remainder of Britain's West Indian colonies in the way these idealizations became constitutive of nationalist discourse.

The nationalist movement in British Guiana represented a counterdiscursive challenge to the idea of white supremacy. It was directed at the externalization and exposure of white immorality and banality. Because white colonial power was so integrally tied to the organization of the colonial capitalist economy, the movement took an anticapitalist turn. The small size and strategic weakness of the grouping of national capitalists, and its racial exclusivity in the hands of a few Portuguese and a scattering of Lebanese and Syrian families, significantly curtailed its influence on the nationalist movement. These national capitalists became dependent on colonial protection at a time when colonialism was under siege. This explains the fundamentally different trajectory taken by the nationalist movement in British Guiana compared with its counterparts in Britain's West Indian island colonies. There, anticolonialism was, from the inception, converted into a mechanism facilitating the penetration of neocolonial forms of global capital. Challenges to relations of empire were employed to accommodate the new system of international relations centered around the United States. The discourse of sovereignty freed the new postcolonial leadership from obligations imposed and maintained by colonial power. It facilitated a reorientation of economic relations toward the United States. This came with the tremendous benefits derived from closer relations with the world's newly dominant economic, financial, and military power (Hintzen 2001).

Thus, in the 1950s, West Indian nationalist leaders began to employ their increasing autonomy, derived from the reform of colonial political organization, to effect a gradual shift in their economic and political relations toward the United States. A potent signal of the shift was the development of plans to introduce a "Puerto Rican"–type economic model into the region. This was patterned after forms of "industrialization by invitation" through which the bootstrap policies of the United States were being implemented in Puerto Rico (Mandle 1996, 57–71). This development was consistent with the interests of a strong and politically powerful national capitalist class, particularly in Jamaica, Barbados, and Trinidad, and of US mining investment capital significantly present in Trinidad (oil) and Jamaica (bauxite). The predictable outcome for the region was the deepening of ties of dependence on the United States. These were intensified even further by a developing tourist industry based on North American visitors that was becoming indispensable to the economic well-being of islands such as Barbados and Jamaica. Additionally, the United States was beginning to absorb a growing number of West Indian immigrants under conditions of escalating unemployment and underemployment in the region. North American migration was becoming critical to the region's efforts at poverty alleviation. Remittances from these migrants were proving important as additional sources of income, revenue, and economic support (Fraser 1994). Creole nationalism allowed the accommodation of the white elite into the national space even while rejecting British colonial domination. The idealization of whiteness that was at the core of colonial historical construction became the basis for postindependence neocolonial accommodation (Hintzen 2002). Creole nationalism retained this idealization with all its economic and political implications.

The material conditions of British Guiana's political economy during the period of nationalist mobilization were significantly different from those of the rest of Great Britain's West Indian colonies. Sugar and bauxite, the colony's major colonial industries, were owned and controlled primarily by British and Canadian companies. So were its commercial and financial enterprises. British Guiana did not have the pristine beaches that proved attractive to North American tourists, and it lacked the infrastructure to support a tourist industry geared to its interior. Its population was small relative to its geographic size, and it had a vibrant domestic and export agricultural sector that served a regional market. Moreover, its bauxite exports (both metal grade and calcined) occupied a strategic niche in the world market. There was little reason to see relations with the United States in panacean terms. Unrestrained by domestic capital, the nationalist movement in the colony took on a decidedly anticapitalist, radical turn. Unlike the rest of the region, the class dynamics of British Guiana dictated an alternative path that challenged the tenets not only of colonialism but also of neocolonial dependence on the United States. By 1950, the colony's anticolonial movement had formalized itself into a radical class-based nationalist party called the People's Progressive Party (PPP). It was organized and led by a group of anticapitalist radicals who were strongly supported by the colony's Black and Asian Indian working class, the two ethnoracial groups that together constituted over 90 percent of the country's population. From the very beginning, the stated goal of the party, contained in its manifesto, was the establishment of an independent socialist state:

> Recognizing that the final abolition of exploitation and oppression, of economic crises and unemployment and war will be achieved only by the socialist reorganisation of society, [the party] pledges itself to the task of winning a free and independent Guiana, of building a just socialist society, in which the industries of the country shall be socially and democratically owned and managed for the common good, a society in which security, plenty, peace and freedom shall be the heritage of all. (People's Progressive Party 1971, 5)

The socialist populism of the party generated tremendous support among the colony's working classes. This propelled the PPP to victory in 1953 in the first national elections to be held under universal suffrage.

Thus, Guyanese nationalist ideology emerged from the entanglements and contestations of class. It represented a working-class challenge to capitalism, formed and fashioned within the context of coloniality. Guyanese nationalism became synonymous with anti-imperialism. The possibilities for accommodation of this nationalist imaginary were framed by the absence of a white-creole grouping that would have had to be included in the production of a "coherent" postcolonial peoplehood. An anticapitalist nationalism would have been fraught with conflict, given the interests and power of this group with its legitimate claims of belonging. Creole nationalism left intact the racial order underpinning colonialism while providing the ideological basis for national "coherence." It left unchallenged notions of a "natural" racial hierarchy. In Guyana, this hierarchy was implicitly challenged, but on the explicit and publicized grounds of class. The coincidence of race and class transformed the white colonizer and the white expatriate into the local face of colonial capitalism. For the working classes, capitalist exploitation was universally experienced, in its everyday reality, in relations with this group of white functionaries. Nationalism was forged in the crucible of the cross-racial uniformity of this everyday experience of white capitalist exploitation and repression. But as a *political* phenomenon, Guyanese nationalism left intact and uncontested the social, cultural, and even economic entanglements of difference with race. Guyanese nationalism brought the Asian Indians into the coherent peoplehood of an independent nation. Their insertion into the national space laid the foundation for heterogeneous claims to national belonging and for the shift from deployment of "naturalist" knowledge rooted in notions of a racial hierarchy to a "historicist" interpretation of the Guyanese nation-state. The latter is founded in notions of premodernity and its ineluctable relationship to chaos (Goldberg 2002, 11). Thus, the assumption of control of the state apparatus by "nationals" came to presage a reversion to the premodern condition of nondevelopment.

Chaos was inevitable, whether or not it was orchestrated by British colonial machinations. In the final analysis, the entire creole order coalesced against the Asian Indian political organization that had come to understand itself in these terms (Hintzen 1989, 48–49; Spinner 1984, 53–55). Creole nationalist accommodation of pro-Western neocolonialism was starkly evident in the willingness of the Portuguese creole elite to employ anticommunism to demobilize the class-based radical nationalist movement. Cold War definitions, coincident with creole nationalist interests, were deployed to solicit and support colonial and neocolonial interventionism. Like their West Indian counterparts, the creole elites in British Guiana saw their future tied to the United States. Thus, a form of creole nationalism entered into nationalist politics through the instrumentality of anticommunism. It bifurcated popular interpretations of political and labor organization along the Cold War divide. Even before the elections that successfully catapulted the nationalist movement into office in 1953, Cold War slogans and images were deployed in a vicious assault against the PPP, which was the movement's political arm. This shift to Cold War terminology was important because it brought the United States into the picture. Concerns were raised that events in British Guiana foretold the direction of the emerging nationalist anticolonial movements in the region (Fraser 1994).

The split in the class-based nationalist movement, which occurred in 1955, was therefore inevitable, and inevitably racial. It presaged the development of a creole nationalist alliance against what came to be perceived as an Asian Indian takeover of the state (Fraser 1994). Soon, the entirety of the creole social order was arrayed against Asian Indian nationalist claims.

Britain agreed to new elections in 1957 with the hope that creole nationalist sentiment would coalesce in opposition to the now Indianized segment of the nationalist movement. The enormous support base of the latter propelled its leadership to office, which it held until 1964 after winning elections once again in 1961. Colonialism rendered meaningful the creole challenge to the nationalist movement. The latter's accommodation of Asian Indian claims to belonging was anathema to nationalist discourse in the insular Caribbean. Regional governments refused to acknowledge the right of the nationalist PPP to govern. In 1953, British intervention to oust the Guyanese nationalist movement was strongly supported by West Indian leaders. Alexander Bustamante, chief minister of Jamaica; Norman Manley, Jamaica's opposition leader; and Grantley Adams, chief minister of Barbados, all wrote strong letters supporting the intervention. The three were the foremost leaders of the West Indian nationalist movement (Jagan 1980). In making their decision, they chose to eschew defense of the very principles of self-determination for which they themselves were fighting. This challenges notions of creoleness as inevitably transformative and liberatory. Shalini Puri makes a convincing argument for the centrality of hybridity in the theoretics and intellectual and cultural production of the Caribbean region (Puri 2004). While unveiling the theoretics, poetics, and aesthetics of the region's hybridized reality (expressive and practical), she exposes the limitations of the almost universalistic argument for its inevitable contestation of nationalism's discourses of difference. In the process, she manages to challenge the profound fallacy that hybridity is essentially transformative and universally pitted against a racialized heteronormative capitalist nationalism. Hybridity is exposed for its polysemous and multivalent possibilities. Its deployment is fraught with ambiguous and contradictory consequences. In the Guyanese case, creoleness was an instantiation and iteration of a coloniality that was being transformed with the emergence of North America as the new center of metropolitan capitalism. Hence, the United States was an active agent in its deployment. West Indian leaders committed themselves firmly to support the creole antinationalist alliance. They justified this support on the ideological grounds of anticommunism and on the need for the region to enter into an unequivocal political, economic, and ideological alliance with North America.

In Guyana, the creole alliance was organized around two political parties. The Portuguese and Chinese national capitalist elite joined with the colored and near-white professional and managerial elite to form the United Force (UF) under the leadership of a Portuguese industrialist. It entered into an alliance with the Black and colored middle and lower strata organized in the People's

National Congress (PNC). These, together, became the instrumentalities of
creole antinationalist interests. In 1964, the British Colonial Office employed
international interventionism and manipulative fiat to place this coalition in
power. This positioned the Portuguese, near-white, colored, and Black elite to
protect national and international capital and Western political interests. With
this creole elite firmly in control, the country was granted independence in
1966. The coalition lasted through an uncertain tenure between 1964 and 1968
(Hintzen 1989, 65–68).

The fashioning of the nationalist movement out of working-class, anticapitalist sentiments conflicted with the pro-capitalist, pro-American thrust of
creole discourse. Two distinct national imaginations competed with each other
in the construction of a postcolonial order. Conflicts between the two coalition
partners began to emerge soon after independence was granted in 1966. In 1967,
the PNC shed itself of its UF coalition partner by encouraging a few of the
latter's elected legislators to "cross the floor" (Hintzen and Premdas 1982). The
impetus for the split was precisely the thrust of the United Force toward unfettered accommodation of Western capitalist interests. The faction within the
PNC comprising the former middle-class supporters of the United Democratic
Party (UDP) did not necessarily oppose this thrust. However, the support base
of the party rested firmly in the Black urban proletariat and the rural Black
communities that were integral to the formulation of Guyanese nationalism.
They remained suspicious of notions of racial and cultural hybridity, which
were the central tenets of creole discourse. But their rejection of creolism was
ideologically framed in racially exclusivist terms. They launched a successful
bid to place a more Africa-centered stamp on Guyanese nationalist expression and to define themselves, counterdiscursively, in terms of African purity.
By 1960, the African Society for Cultural Relations with Independent Africa
(ASCRIA) managed to position itself strategically in the power structure and
hierarchy of the ruling PNC (Hintzen 1989, 170–72). It appealed to the Black
rural own-account peasantry and to Black urban proletarian migrants from
rural villages, who were the least integrated into creole society (ASCRIA 1973,
1974). They came from the historically marginalized, positioned at the bottom
of the color/class hierarchy and separated from the urban arenas where creole
nationalist discourse was produced and reproduced (Moore 1998, 235–48).
Through their early involvement in anticapitalist nationalism, they became
unfettered from colonial creole constructs. At the same time, however, they
retained the anti-Indianism of creole discourse that became the basis for the
successful challenge to Guyanese nationalism. They attached themselves to the
new ideologies of African belonging and notions of universal African intimacy
that were gaining strength in anticolonial nationalist struggles in Africa and the
civil rights struggles in the United States. These ideologies offered them the

possibility of rejecting capitalism while, at the same time, resisting efforts of the East Indian nationalists to regain control of the apparatuses of the state. This signaled the racial bifurcation of the anticapitalist class-based nationalist movement. ASCRIA's ideology centered on narratives of African belonging deployed against creole nationalist discourse. The group's leaders saw their role as ensuring the location of the Black lower class at the center of the country's nationalist agenda. They used their powerful positions to impose that agenda on the post-1967 government. Under the influence of their leadership, the country's foreign relations shifted to an emphasis on the development of close relations with the African continent. Elements of the state's national policies came to mirror, almost wholeheartedly, Tanzania's version of cooperative socialism (Thomas 1983). In 1971, the country severed the remaining formal ties with Great Britain by declaring itself the Co-operative Socialist Republic of Guyana in keeping with its new African-centered nationalism.

The new thrust did not go uncontested. It conflicted with the culturally rooted aspirations and practices of the country's creole middle classes. In 1971, creole opposition forced the ruling party to abandon its ideology of Africa-centered nationalism. In response, ASCRIA leaders resigned from their government posts and began a scathing campaign against the ruling PNC (ASCRIA 1973; Hintzen 1989, 171). Faced with anti-creole opposition from both the Black and East Indian lower classes, the ruling party began to resuscitate the anticapitalism and anti-Westernism of the early nationalist movement. It embarked on a campaign of national economic self-sufficiency with the Feed, Clothe, and House Ourselves (FCH) program aimed at weaning the country's economy away from dependence on foreign imports (Hintzen 1989, 184). It attempted to mobilize the working classes for ownership of small-scale and midscale productive and commercial enterprises through cooperative organization. The intention was to "make the small man a real man." Funds were diverted into cooperative development to catapult the urban population into agricultural and fishing enterprises and the lower classes into small- and midscale productive and commercial activity. Most significantly, the ruling party began efforts to acquire equity participation in the foreign-owned extractive sectors of the economy. By 1976, most of the major holdings of foreign capital were nationalized, placing the state in control of over 80 percent of the productive assets of the national economy. This radical turn was accompanied by efforts to recruit East Indians into the ranks of the ruling party. In 1975, the PNC made an unambiguous commitment to socialism, prompting the PPP to provide the regime with "critical support" (Hintzen 1989, 170).

Thus, Guyanese nationalism asserted itself on statist organization, notwithstanding the challenges mounted by creole antinationalists. But it remained racially bifurcated. None of its racialized segments were able to break out of the colonial straightjacket. An effort to re-create the working-class nonracial anticapitalist mobilization of the early 1950s was stymied by the new racial imageries that had come to inform nationalist discourse. Even though successfully repelled, antinationalist creolism left in its wake a nationalism that was organized around competing racial claims to the state. And, despite efforts to reconstitute the ruling PNC, the division between creole antinationalist and African nationalist expression persisted within its ranks. These, together, militated against cross-racial recruitment. Asian Indians, more than 50 percent of the population, were solidly in support of the PPP. This made it highly improbable that the PNC could win free and fair elections. After efforts to recruit Asian Indian supporters were rejected by party rank and file, party leaders returned to racial exclusivity. But in keeping with its anticapitalist ideology, the regime became increasingly allied with the communist group of nations. By 1975, the international relations of Guyana's ruling party shifted to a close alliance with Eastern Europe, China, and Cuba. The state began to play a pervasive role in almost every aspect of life using the justifying ideology of socialism. This displaced cultural notions of creole national belonging from the center of nationalist discourse. Governance was organized around a racialized form of African socialism.

A nationalism that was fractured by racially rooted heterogeneous claims to control of the apparatuses of the state led, inevitably, to socioeconomic and political crisis. This, of course, fit well with historicist claims of the immaturity of the colonized subject to rule and the inevitability of a reversion to nondevelopment if such were the case. To retain power, the party was forced to rig elections in 1973, 1980, and 1985. It also rigged a referendum in 1978 to gain exclusive control over constitutional changes. This paved the way for an executive presidency in 1980. The suspension of democratic practice was one indicator of immaturity. The other was the country's descent into economic crisis. The PNC's racially rooted anticapitalist nationalism left it with little support from major strategic sectors both nationally and in its international relations. The country's economic dependency and its inextricable ties to Western capital opened the way to punitive retaliation. This came with a vengeance in the wake of anticapitalist policy assertions by the PNC and the forging of ties with the communist international bloc. Spiraling oil prices and an international recession spurred on by the 1973 Arab-Israeli War magnified the effect. By 1978, the country was in the throes of an escalating economic crisis. During the 1980s, Guyana's economy teetered on the brink of economic collapse. The unemployment rate reached 30 percent, and the country struggled with a severe health crisis. Its foreign debt ballooned dramatically (Hintzen 1989, 183–92). Crisis became the instrumentality deployed to discipline nationalist aspirations. It led to antiregime mobilization by the Black and colored middle class, supported by some Black lower-class beneficiaries of racial nationalism. This swelled the ranks of the creole antinationalists.

During the 1980s, the disciplinary technology of race was deployed against Guyanese anticapitalist nationalism. The regime's racial opponents among the vast majority of the country's Asian Indian population joined a growing group of radicals to form a movement that challenged the ruling party's racial exclusivity. These groups were organized around the most radical expressions of the country's anticapitalist nationalism. They were not hamstrung by the need to accommodate or placate creole interests. In response, the ruling party came to rely increasingly on creole antinationalists who were firmly in control of the apparatuses of the state to contain growing opposition to its rule. A combination of repression, coercion, institutional control, and patronage became the hallmarks of this phase of Guyanese statist practice (Hintzen and Premdas 1983; Thomas 1983). Regimented discipline organized through semimilitarized institutions such as the National Service became compulsory for most state-sector employees and for access to higher education. This was accompanied by a strict regime of surveillance in the public sector and the parastatals (Hintzen 1989, 159–60; Thomas 1983). All this created conditions for the reinscription of a creolist discourse into postcolonial formation. Its agenda was organized both within the ruling party and among the country's middle and upper strata. An anti-PNC mobilization campaign by a new movement calling itself the Patriotic Coalition for Democracy (PCD) emerged from the conjoining of forces of the Asian Indian PPP, the creole elite United Force, and the radical antiracist opposition organized in the Working People's Alliance that combined radical ideology with multiracial representation. The effectiveness of the campaign was guaranteed because of the institutional rooting of the various opposition parties in the organized trade unions, in the Asian Indian populace, in Black institutional opposition to the ruling party, and in the national capitalist elite.

The aspirations of the creole elite are to replace the white colonizer. In Guyana, they were stymied by the anticapitalist nationalism of the independence movement. The political and economic crisis of the 1970s and 1980s presented the opportunity to contest this ideology both within the ruling party and within the growing opposition despite the latter's ideological roots in anticapitalism. In 1986, the unexpected death of Forbes Burnham, the leader of the PNC and its executive president, paved the way for a creolist reassertion of power within the ruling party. Under the executive presidency of Desmond Hoyte, Burnham's successor and the former minister of economic development, the government entered into negotiations with the International Monetary Fund and World Bank. It signed a policy framework for economic stabilization with the two multilateral agencies, agreeing to reorganize the country's economy and dismantle most of the institutions of state socialism. This was the harbinger of the end of the era of anticapitalist nationalism. The challenge to the ruling party intensified, notwithstanding this policy reversal. The issue for nationalists was the party's racial exclusivity, which compromised its nationalist credentials. Capitulation to the terms of global capital only served to confirm their assessment that the party had been "capitalist" all along (Thomas 1983). The creole elite remained wary of the PNC's radical past. For both, the removal of the party from office was the only acceptable alternative. Seeing its opportunity, the creole elite forged a new alliance of businesspeople, religious leaders, public officials, professionals, and trade union leaders. This alliance, Guyanese Action for Reform and Democracy (GUARD), cultivated international ties with the Guyanese diasporic community overseas to gather support for its petitions in support of international intervention to oust the ruling party. The World Union of Guyanese was formed to lobby the United Nations, the Organization of American States, and Caribbean, North American, and western European governments (*Miami Herald*, March 26, 1990).

Internationally, the justifying mantra for intervention had shifted from anticommunism to the restoration of democracy and human rights. This crystallized around protest movements in Eastern Europe that were succeeding in bringing a swift and abrupt end to Eurocommunism. To exploit these new justifying legitimations, the radical, racial, and creole opposition in Guyana combined to demand foreign intervention against the PNC in the face of the violations of these two principles of governance. It proposed a "national front" government of opposition parties to succeed the ruling party. As international pressure began to mount, the Hoyte regime was finally forced to commit itself to fair and free elections. In a position to win elections outright, the PPP made the decision to abandon the coalition. It made a concession to creole elite interests by joining with the Civic political group, formed by a multiracial collective of mainly professionals. The leader of the group was promised the prime ministership under terms of governance inherited from the 1980 constitution, which gave the executive presidency "almost dictatorial power" (*Nation*, November 15, 1980).

Under heavy scrutiny by Caribbean, Commonwealth, European, Canadian, and US observers, elections were held in 1992, and the PPP was returned to power. By then, the ideology of neoliberalism imposed by international financial institutions had rendered nationalist aspirations irrelevant in the organization of governance and in policy making. Multilateral agencies such as the IMF and the World Bank were imposing economic liberalism on governments through the disciplining regimes of international public policy. Democracy and human rights posed little threat to international capital in Guyana even though its imposition came with the certainty of an even more radical nationalist party coming to power. Even before the PPP's electoral victory, Cheddi Jagan, the party's leader, made several pilgrimages to the United States to repudiate past attempts at socialism and sing the praises of foreign private investments (Bohning 1990; *Miami Herald*, March 26, 1990). Once in power, the PPP did not deviate from the policies of the Hoyte government presented in the earlier policy framework prepared for the IMF and World Bank (Hintzen 2001).

When the PPP withdrew from efforts to establish a national front government, the creole elite and radical antiracists were left without a significant popular base. What remained were two parties organized under terms of competing racial nationalisms that commanded the support of close to 96 percent of the voting electorate. The anticapitalist nationalism of both parties was neutralized by a new international governmentality that disciplined nationalist aspirations through the deployment of international public policy. A diffuse cosmopolitanism in global reorganization acted to eviscerate much of the authority of the nation-state.[5] Ideologies formally organized for capturing governance have become irrelevant. The outcome in Guyana has proven disastrous while serving to confirm the "immaturity" of the former colonized subjects to run the affairs of the modern state. The ensuing crisis has legitimized the need for a continuation of metropolitan tutelage from the North Atlantic. This is the crux of globalization.

On March 19, 2001, the electorate of the Co-operative Republic of Guyana went to the polls. By the unanimous account of all neutral observers, including official foreign delegations, the elections could have served as a poster child for fairness and transparency. Former US president Jimmy Carter, who led an observer mission for the Carter Center in Atlanta, declared the elections to be "almost perfect." With a full 88 percent of the electorate voting, the PPP and PNC received 54 and 42 percent of the votes, respectively. With thirty-four seats in the country's National Assembly, the leader of the PPP became, once again, the country's executive president.

It was the third electoral victory for the PPP since 1992. In elections held in December 1997, the party won with 55.3 percent of the votes, and with 53.4 percent in 1992. Yet despite the unanimous opinion of all electoral observers that the 2001 elections were fair, free, and devoid of fraud, the results were immediately contested by the People's National Congress. This was despite the strong endorsement by its own appointed members to the Guyana Elections Commission as to their fairness and transparency. The commission was charged with running the election under a chairman who was considered, universally, to be neutral and impartial. Charges by the PNC that the elections were fraudulent were accompanied by an orchestrated campaign of violence. The campaign began even before the elections were contested, and it escalated into mass mobilization in Georgetown, accompanied by politically motivated beatings and murder. On April 9, 2001, an area of the city was torched. Persons racially marked as supporters of the governing party owned many of the businesses that were burned.

The country descended into a political "state of nature," with activists within the solidary bloc of Afro-Guyanese employing violence, intimidation, and disruption in attempts to oust the PPP from power. The Asian Indian ruling party responded with escalating brutality from the country's security forces. While this occurred, the operations of the new industries of global capital, organized around the export of gold and timber, remained unaffected under conditions in which, in 1995, 43.2 percent of the Guyanese population lived below the poverty line and 27.7 percent were unable to secure enough food for survival (Thomas 1983). This is the state of democracy and of civil and human rights that undergirds the new liberalism while chaos and crisis pervade the society. It speaks to a new governmentality that protects capital against social and political disruptions. And democracy gives it the blessing of "popular will."

NOTES

1. I use these dimensions of capital following Pierre Bourdieu (1977, 1984). See also Turner 1991, 512–18. In Bourdieu's formulation, economic capital refers to the ownership and control of productive resources. Social capital refers to those prerequisites that determine location in the hierarchically organized social groups, aggregates, and categories, and the social networks associated with them. Cultural capital refers to those "interpersonal skills, habits, manners, linguistic styles, educational credentials, tastes, and lifestyles" acquired by persons in their lifetime (Turner 1991, 512). Symbolic capital has to do with the recognized forms of deployment of social, cultural, and economic capital through ritualized and symbolic displays.

2. This is not so obvious in the case of the acquisition of "color." Wealth, education, style, tastes, and so on facilitated the intergenerational process of whitening by allowing those who possessed them to marry persons higher up in the color hierarchy.

3. The terms "explanation," "standards of normative evaluation," "guide and compass for action," and "simplification" are taken from Steger 2009, 5–7, following propositions about the nature of ideology by Terrell Carver (2020) and Paul Ricoeur (1986).

4. For a discussion of "distortion," "legitimation," and "integration" in their relationship to ideology, see Manfred Steger (2009, 7), in his reference to Paul Ricoeur (1986).

5. The notion of governmentality is taken from Foucault 1979. It proposes the reassertion of sovereign rule through the disciplining of governance. The argument here is that this occurs on an international scale. For arguments related to the weakening of the nation-state, see Rivero 2001 and Abrahamsen 2001.

BIBLIOGRAPHY

Abrahamsen, Rita. 2001. *Disciplining Democracy: Development Discourse and Good Governance in Africa*. London: Zed Books.

African Society for Cultural Relations with Independent Africa (ASCRIA). 1973. "Statement on the Negative Direction in Guyana, the Race Question and the Suffering of the People." Pamphlet, April 1.

African Society for Cultural Relations with Independent Africa (ASCRIA). 1974. "The Race Question and the Suffering of the People." Pamphlet, January 11.

Bohning, Don. 1990. "Ex-Enemy Seeks U.S. Help to Gain Fair Guyana Vote." *Miami Herald,* December 8.

Bourdieu, Pierre. 1977. *Outline of a Theory of Practice.* Translated by Richard Nice. Cambridge: Cambridge University Press.

Bourdieu, Pierre. 1984. *Distinction: A Social Critique of the Judgement of Taste.* Translated by Richard Nice. Cambridge, MA: Harvard University Press.

Braithwaite, Lloyd. 1953. "Social Stratification in Trinidad: A Preliminary Analysis." *Social and Economic Studies* 2, no. 2: 5–175.

Carver, Terrell. 2020. "Ideology: The Career of a Concept." In *Ideals and Ideology: A Reader,* edited by Terence Ball, Richard Dagger, and Daniel I. O'Neill, 11th ed., 3–10. New York: Routledge.

Despres, Leo A. 1967. *Cultural Pluralism and Nationalist Politics in British Guiana.* Chicago: Rand McNally.

Foucault, Michel. 1979. "On Governmentality." *Ideology and Consciousness,* no. 6: 5–22.

Fraser, Cary. 1994. *Ambivalent Anti-Colonialism: The United States and the Genesis of West Indian Independence, 1940–1964.* Westport, CT: Greenwood Press.

Goldberg, David Theo. 2002. *The Racial State.* Malden, MA: Blackwell.

Hintzen, Percy C. 1989. *The Costs of Regime Survival: Racial Mobilization, Elite Domination and Control of the State in Guyana and Trinidad.* Cambridge: Cambridge University Press.

Hintzen, Percy C. 2001. "Cheddi Jagan (1918–97): Charisma and Guyana's Response to Western Capitalism." In *Caribbean Charisma: Reflections on Leadership, Legitimacy, and Populist Politics,* edited by Anton Allahar, 121–54. Boulder, CO: Lynne Rienner.

Hintzen, Percy C. 2002. "The Caribbean: Race and Creole Ethnicity." In *A Companion to Racial and Ethnic Studies,* edited by David Theo Goldberg and John Solomos, 475–94. Malden, MA: Blackwell.

Hintzen, Percy C., and Ralph Premdas. 1982. "Coercion and Control in Political Change." *Journal of Interamerican Studies and World Affairs* 24, no. 3 (August): 337–54.

Hintzen, Percy C., and Ralph Premdas. 1983. "Race, Ideology, and Power in Guyana." *Journal of Commonwealth and Comparative Politics* 21, no. 2: 175–94.

Jagan, Cheddi. 1980. *The West on Trial: My Fight for Guyana's Freedom.* East Berlin: Seven Seas.

Mandle, Jay R. 1996. *Persistent Underdevelopment: Change and Economic Modernization in the West Indies.* Amsterdam: Gordon and Breach.

Marx, Anthony W. 1998. *Making Race and Nation: A Comparison of the United States, South Africa, and Brazil.* Cambridge: Cambridge University Press.

Moore, Brian. 2009. "The Social and Economic Subordination of the Guyanese Creoles after Emancipation." In *Themes in African-Guyanese History,* edited by Winston F. McGowan, James G. Rose, and David A. Granger, 141–58. London: Hansib Publications.

People's Progressive Party. 1971. "People's Progressive Party: 21 Years." Georgetown, British Guiana: New Guiana.

Puri, Shalini. 2004. *The Caribbean Postcolonial: Social Equality, Post-Nationalism, and Cultural Hybridity.* New York: Palgrave Macmillan.

Ricoeur, Paul. 1986. *Lectures on Ideology and Utopia*. Edited by George H. Taylor. New York: Columbia University Press.

Rivero, Oswaldo de. 2001. *The Myth of Development: Non-Viable Economies and the Crisis of Civilization*. London: Zed Books.

Spinner, Thomas J. 1984. *A Political and Social History of Guyana, 1945–1983*. Boulder, CO: Westview Press.

Steger, Manfred B. 2009. *Globalisms: The Great Ideological Struggle of the Twenty-First Century*. 3rd ed. Lanham, MD: Rowman and Littlefield.

Thomas, Clive Y. 1983. "State Capitalism in Guyana: An Assessment of Burnham's Co-Operative Socialist Republic." In *Crisis in the Caribbean: Internal Transformation and External Constraints*, edited by Fitzroy Ambursley and Robin Cohen, 27–48. New York: Monthly Review Press.

Turner, Jonathan H. 1991. *The Structure of Sociological Theory*. Belmont, CA: Wadsworth.

Winant, Howard. 2001. *The World Is a Ghetto: Race and Democracy since World War II*. New York: Basic Books.

RETHINKING DEMOCRACY IN THE POSTNATIONALIST STATE

The Case of Trinidad and Tobago

PERCY C. HINTZEN

In Africa and throughout the African diaspora, a Black elite has employed notions of Black diasporic intimacy as a basis of political mobilization. It has done so in pursuit of aspirations for inclusion in national and international arenas of power. Since the advent of colonialism, these arenas were exclusive preserves of a white elite organized internationally in support of racialized forms of national domination. The Black elite exploited popular sentiments of diasporic intimacy to organize racial challenges to white supremacy within and across national borders. In the process, it rendered invisible its own aspirations to whiteness. Its challenge to the racial exclusivity of white power was based on its own claims, as an elite, to white status and privilege. The argument, implicit in such claims, was that its acquisition of the cultural capital of Europe justified a status of equality with the European colonizer and the white colonizing elite.

In making their claims to white elite status, the elites of colonial Africa and their colonized diaspora have managed to reproduce, in the postcolonial political economy, forms of domination identical to those that existed under colonialism. These forms are rooted in racial exclusivity and racial privilege. In their quest for power, these political leaders employ identical tactics of divide and rule across identific divisions of belonging to make exclusive claims to governance. Race, tribe, religion, region, and ethnicity have become tools in the competition for power among this Europeanized elite.

Trinidad and Tobago is presented as a case study in the organization of Black communal intimacy. The result has been the institutionalization of a system of racialized politics organized for elite domination. Popular understandings of Blackness and a collective sense of Black intimacy were exploited in the fashioning of a nationalist agenda to serve the exclusive interests of a European-ized elite. Racial politics, in turn, has jeopardized and undermined the collective interests of the Black population in whose name nationalism was represented. By the end of the twentieth century, this very population found itself and its interests excluded in the power dynamics of elite control of governance. The social and economic conditions of a new globalized political economy rendered its support less important in a new constitution of elite interests.

BACKGROUND

The Republic of Trinidad and Tobago is a twin-island former West Indian colony of Great Britain. After Jamaica, it is the second-largest of the English-speaking territories of the West Indies, coming under British colonial rule after capture from Spain in 1797. At the time, Trinidad's history of slavery was less than fifty years old. The British colonizers joined a white Spanish colonizing elite and a French elite of merchants and planters, many of whom had fled the Haitian slave revolt in the organization and support of a system of racial capital. As Britain solidified its political and economic domination, the Spanish and French creoles were quickly differentiated from the white colonizing class in colonial reproduction.

Trinidad's unique history distinguishes it from the rest of the English-speaking Caribbean in many respects. The country's Spanish colonial heritage has had a significant influence on national cultural expression. Its French planter class has become historically reproduced into a "local white" elite that has domi-nated the private economic sector. The continued importation of Africans as indentures after the abolition of slavery in 1833 has left the country with much more of an "African" heritage than is evident in most other English-speaking countries of the region. And the largest segment of its population comprises Hindu and Muslim descendants of indentured laborers shipped from South Asia after slavery's abolition. These indentures were brought to the island in the nineteenth and early twentieth centuries along with indentures from Portugal and China. They replaced African plantation labor.

The colonial project sustained and supported a group of domestic busi-nesspeople, almost exclusively from the population of "local" whites who were joined later by a small but influential number of Lebanese and Syrian immi-grants. In the face of a colonial strategy of exclusion from the public sector aimed at sustaining agricultural labor, successful middle-strata East Indians sought out opportunities opening up in manufacturing and commerce. By the latter half of the twentieth century, rich and powerful East Indian busi-nesspeople had managed to break the stranglehold of whites at the apex of domestic capital. By 1996, East Indians owned and controlled 54.2 percent of all businesses employing five or more persons, 60 percent of businesses in the distribution sector, and 51 percent of manufacturing establishments (Ryan 1996, 254). Close to two-thirds of large businesses and 78 percent of small businesses owned by East Indians in 1993 were established after 1980 (Ramsaran 1994, 131–53).

In the middle strata, the color/class hierarchy of colonial construction gave privileged access to the mixed "colored" and "near-white" (light-complexioned colored) population to professional training and professional occupations, and to small- and midscale private sector business. In the wake of postwar upward mobility, members of the Black population soon began to carve out a significant presence in the professions. Blacks and coloreds also predominated as teachers, civil servants, and, later on, managers in the country's state-owned business ventures. These occupations became the mainstays of their middle-class status.

The majority of Trinidad's population is dependent on earnings from urban and rural working-class occupations and from the cultivation and sale of cash crops. From the beginning of the twentieth century, this majority has been bifurcated along racial lines. Traditionally, members of the East Indian lower and working classes have made their living in agricultural or agriculture-related occupations. Some have used these earnings to branch out into small service-type businesses. Their Black counterparts depend upon nonagricultural labor, with a few engaged in subsistence agriculture. Increasingly, however, the East Indian population has become much more urbanized. Many are joining Blacks in public and private sector nonagricultural occupations.

In 1990, the estimated population of Trinidad and Tobago was 1,272,000. Census figures showed the Afro-Trinidadians to be 39.6 percent of the population. Combined, the descendants of interracial unions of Blacks and whites (coloreds) and Blacks and East Indians (douglas) were counted at 18.4 percent of the population. East Indians were 40.3 percent of the population. Whites, including "Portuguese," "French Creole," "Spanish Creole," and the descendants of the English colonizers made up 0.6 percent. A distinctive identity of "local white" has emerged in the racial lexicon of Trinidad, allowing the accommodation and inclusion within the white social category of many with mixed "racial" backgrounds. The 1990 census also showed a small number of persons collectively classified as Chinese (0.4 percent).[1]

THE RACIAL ORGANIZATION
OF TRINIDAD'S POLITICAL ECONOMY

There has been a historical development of contingent differences related to religion in the organization of social relations among East Indians in Trinidad. Hindus (who are exclusively East Indian) constitute 23.8 percent of the country's population. Muslims (predominantly East Indian, with a very small number of Blacks) constitute 5.8 percent. East Indians make up 9.7 percent of the grouping of Christians; Christians altogether make up 43.7 percent of the total population of the country. Whites are almost exclusively Christian.

Racial and ethnic categories occupy center stage in almost all aspects of Trinidadian society. This is no less true for the country's political organization. Historically, the social system of colonial organization and regulation has produced and sustained contingent social groupings defined, perceived, and identified idiomatically in racial terms. The particular circumstances of a group's first entry into and continued presence in colonial Trinidad, the history of its collective participation in Trinidadian society, and the nature and type of resources and interests to be protected and enhanced have placed racial groups in competition with each other. The acquisition and protection of political power and economic resources are at the root of such competition.

Colonial political economy was organized around the exercise of centralized control by a powerful colonial bureaucracy. With the granting of independence, these governing institutions were inherited by an educated grouping of Black and colored bureaucrats and professionals who assumed functional control over them. The politicization of Black identity created the conditions for their assumption of power.

There was a developing relationship between the process of elite reconstruction, the politicization of Black identity, and the practice of parliamentary democracy. The Westminster model of parliamentary democracy, inherited from Britain, and the institutionalization of racial voting combined into an instrument of regulation for the country's elite. At the time independence was granted, these conditions provided the political representatives of the Black and mixed elite with a guaranteed electoral majority employed to secure control of the governing institutions of the state. Racial regulation was particularly suited to the Black elite contenders for power. Despite its large numbers, the East Indian population was at an electoral disadvantage because of its concentration in the sugar-growing areas of the country. The political regulation of the population along racial lines left the East Indian political elite with victories in fewer constituencies than their Black and colored counterparts. The numbers of whites and Chinese were too small to support the power contentions of their leadership in the developing racialized politics in the country.

NATIONALISM AND ANTICOLONIALISM

Nationalism was the instrument of Black regulation. The anticolonial nationalist movement was born and nurtured in a twentieth-century tide of rising expectations among urban wage laborers frustrated by the organization of the colonial political economy. In the second decade of the century, these frustrations fueled sporadic episodes of labor unrest. They led to the formation of a unified labor movement demanding better wages, improved work conditions, and the establishment of formal collective bargaining procedures (Ryan 1972, 28–45; Oxaal 1968, 80–95).

Quickly, educated and professional members of the colonized population assumed positions as leaders in the new trade union movement. They formalized union organization and changed their demands to reflect their own interests in political reform. By the 1930s, they were using labor mobilization to back demands for more representative government, for the sharing of political power between colonial and local leaders, and for a shift of political control away from the British Colonial Office and its colonial functionaries to "representative" institutions. In other words, the educated and professional elite used its leadership position to transform labor mobilization into a protonationalist political movement aimed at inserting its members into the colonial domains of power (Ryan 1972, 28–45; Oxaal 1968, 80–95).

Widespread labor riots during the latter part of the 1930s forced Britain to concede to demands for more "representative" government. By 1946, the British Colonial Office had initiated a process of gradual devolution of power. For the first time, universal adult suffrage was introduced, and elected local officials were allowed significant participation in the political affairs of the colony (Hintzen 1989, 30–31). This paved the way for the development of political parties in the 1950s under the leadership of a Black and colored intellectual and professional elite, and by East Indian and white businesspeople and professionals. In their appeals for political support, the emergent political leaders exploited the racial affinities and sentiments of the voting population. As the appeal to race took root, the role of labor, with its class implications for political organization, began to diminish. This became immediately evident with introduction of adult suffrage in 1946. The People's Democratic Party (PDP) was formed in the early 1950s by a group of East Indian businessmen who controlled a predominantly East Indian sugar workers' union and the major Hindu religious organizations. Their appeal for votes was pitched exclusively to East Indian workers and agricultural peasants. In the process, East Indian identity, and more purposefully "Hindu" identity, became politically salient.

The politicization of Black identity was much more profound. Black and colored intellectuals and professionals began to fashion an ideology of creole nationalism that was directly linked to Afro-Trinidadian culture (Yelvington 1992, 13). In 1956, they formed the People's National Movement. From its inception, the PNM leadership reflected the multiethnic composition of the country's elite. East Indians were included among the party's leaders. But the appeal of the party was organized around the regulating idiom of race, and this was high-lighted in the creole nationalism preached by its Black and colored intellectual and professional leaders. The cultural symbols of the Black population were appropriated and used in mobilization campaigns directed at the Black lower strata. The rejection of "white" domination of the economy was accompanied by references to East Indians as "a recalcitrant and hostile minority" (Yelvington 1992, 13, citing Ryan 1972; see also Oxaal 1968).

The nationalist movement was neither "nationalist" nor "Black." Rather, it was the embodiment of a strategic reorganization of the noncapitalist and non-farming educated, bureaucratic, and professional elite. This elite constituted itself into a single aggregated interest group. Its goal was to capture control of the exec-utive, legislative, and bureaucratic branches of the postcolonial state. Its agenda had little to do with the social, cultural, or economic interests of its Black lower-strata supporters except through the delivery of politically strategic patronage.

Whites and near-whites had seen their own opportunity for political power dashed in the throes of majoritarian politics. With the introduction of repre-sentative government, white creole politicians, representing the interests of the business and planter elite, saw their chances for control of a postcolonial state rapidly diminishing (Hintzen 1989, 39–41; Ryan 1972, 86–96). They organized around the newly formed Political Progress Group (PPG), which also received support from the near-white social grouping of fair-complexioned coloreds. Many members of this near-white grouping soon became incorporated into the population of creole whites in a reformulated category of "Trinidad white" (D. Segal 1992, 87–89). By 1950, the relationship between this all-inclusive creole white population and the colonizers had become quite strong; they collectively benefited from the discretionary power of the governor, who assured them of almost exclusive access to executive authority reserved for locals.

The elite interests that were served by the newly formed racialized political parties became immediately obvious. The PPG and PDP initially opposed inde-pendence, fearing that the interests of the business and planter classes would be jeopardized if the PNM came to power. The PDP also mounted a campaign of opposition to a proposed federation with the rest of the overwhelmingly Black British West Indies.

The issue of federation was critical in the racialization of politics. The Butler Home Rule Party had become by 1950 the single largest political organization in Trinidad. It achieved its prominence by relying on the votes of Black and East Indian wage laborers and small cultivators. Despite its multiracial composition, the party was influenced somewhat by the philosophy of Marcus Garvey. Its lower-class leadership successfully employed an antiwhite and anticolonial agenda in a campaign of mobilization. But in the developing racial terrain of nationalist politics, the federation issue proved the death knell for the party. It was deserted by most of its East Indian supporters, propelled by fears of Black domination in a federation with the rest of the British West Indies. The theme of Black domination was pivotal in the opposition to federation mounted by the PDP. And this is the party to which the erstwhile East Indian Butlerites turned (Albert Gomes, cited in Ryan 1972, 100).

The PNM won the general elections held in 1956 by taking thirteen of twenty-four electoral constituencies. The PDP managed to capture only five seats, all in rural constituencies with overwhelmingly East Indian voting majorities. In the wake of this defeat, the PDP merged with the political representatives of the white business and planter elite to form the Democratic Labour Party (DLP). This was a strategic reorganization aimed at ousting the PNM from power. The conjoining of the two parties was quite natural given the rooting of their political interests in a common socioeconomic base. As businesspeople, professionals, and planters, the East Indian and white leaders of the new party were opposed to any form of statist expansion. This placed them on a collision course with the Black and colored educated, salaried, and professional elite. The interests of the latter, concentrated in the public sector, were best served by the very statist agenda that the former perceived as anathema.

An almost universal feature of the post–World War II era in underdeveloped countries is the historical emergence of an ascendant grouping of white-collar clerical, bureaucratic, professional, and intellectual elites. They own neither capital nor land; they are distinguished by their Western education, upward mobility, and ascending social status, all derived from colonial privilege.[2] Political leaders coming from and representing this social grouping have managed to erect and institutionalize systems of organization that serve its members' vested interests in economic accumulation and control of the state. They have done so by regulating the relations of politically strategic social groupings. In Trinidad, this was accomplished through the development of the ideology of nationalism.

NATIONALISM AS NEOCOLONIAL CONSTRUCTION

The ideas that have had the most significant and profound impact on twentieth-century West Indian political economy are those contained in the ideology of anticolonial nationalism. This form of nationalism became the basis for the rejection of colonialism and the development of a political strategy for overthrowing colonial domination. It has also served as the basis for legitimizing the transformation of the political economy in the postcolonial era. The blueprint for such transformation was fashioned and formulated by an ascendant anticolonial elite. It was justified on the grounds of self-determination, racial equality, and developmental transformation.

Embedded in nationalist discourse were two distinct sets of constructs. One was directed at the intensification, clarification, and crystallization of identity. These are what I term "identity constructs." The other was directed at the legitimization of forms and structures of postcolonial political authority. These I choose to call "legitimacy constructs." Idioms of identity encoded in nationalist constructs were integrally linked to notions of "self-determination." They became bases for organizing and channeling the participatory experiences of those engaged in contesting the colonial order and for the "invention" of the "imagined political communities" (Anderson 1983, 15) that were to be the independent nations of the British West Indies.

Political parties in the Caribbean have become the organizational (power) instruments through which the "images" of the new nations are hegemonically imposed. Democratic participation and developmental transformation were organized as legitimizing constructs authenticating the authorial power of an educated elite. These elites managed to secure the legitimate right to organize and fashion postcolonial society. Their right to do so was justified by what French philosopher Michel Foucault calls a regime of "political rationality" (Foucault 1979; Dreyfus and Rabinow 1983, 128–42), exercised in the postcolonial state as the "proper subject matter of [a] new technical and administrative knowledge" (Dreyfus and Rabinow 1983, 137). In other words, the technical and administrative knowledge possessed by this new elite was employed, through the mechanisms of the state, in the exercise of "disciplinary power" (Foucault 1979, chap. 7). This power to discipline the masses through political organization characterizes the exercise of postcolonial democratic practice and its nationalist precursor. The argument of this chapter is that it is exercised in the service of the different and changing constellations of interests of the most strategic segments of the elite populations. The interests of this strategic elite are rendered invisible by the formal practice of democracy.

The language of liberation is central to the ideology of anticolonial nationalism. Explicit in its formulation is liberation from colonial domination. Colonialism becomes translated into *the* universal metaphor for all forms of domination (both external and internal), and into a symbolic allegory for poverty and want. Domestically, it came to signify the repressive and exploitative conditions of domination of the colonized by the colonizer. Internationally, it came to signify the imperialist exploitation of the peripheral economies by the European metropole. Anticolonialism signifies the quest for liberation from domination, poverty, and want. But in its formulation, nationalist discourse is devoid of any possibilities for liberation. Historically, postcolonial political economies have failed to reflect the ideological promise of self-determination, development, and de facto democratic participation. The promise of liberation has failed to materialize in postcolonial social constructions. Instead, colonialism has been replaced by even more egregious forms of domination, superexploitation, and dependency.

Embedded in notions of self-determination were the ideas of sovereignty and autonomy of the state. These were central to efforts by the nationalist elites to capture control of their governing institution. Once state authority was transferred, however, self-determination was used as justification to intensify, deepen, and widen elite access to economic, social, and cultural capital. It supported the accumulation of wealth, income, status, and prestige by this elite.

Nationalism as an ideology has shown itself to be quite amenable to those whose interests rest in the ownership and control of economic capital. As a construct, it has accommodated the changing technical and social conditions of economic capital without losing its symbolic power. These changes have occurred at the same time that colonialism was giving way to the new nationalist movements. They are central elements in newly emergent postindependence neocolonial formations. And they have been responsible for a reconstitution of the power elite whereby businesspeople, professionals, and managers have displaced salaried bureaucratic functionaries at the apex of domestic power.

Nationalism has supported the maintenance and expansion of relations of affinity with dominant class actors internationally, particularly those in the northern industrial countries. It has supported an intensification of relations with the elite in the very colonial metropole against which it was directed. The focus of new relations of affinity among Britain's former colonies in the West Indies has been the United States. The anticolonial agenda of the West Indian nationalists demanded the establishment of closer relations with the United States for pragmatic as well as symbolic reasons. As economies that were dependent upon commodity exports, the West Indies had to seek alternatives to economic relationships with the British colonial metropole. There was an inherent contradiction between the quest for sovereignty and continuation of the exclusive pattern of economic relations with Britain. Absolute dependence upon the former colonial power was inconsistent with ideas of national self-determination as a critical component of sovereignty. The emergence of the United States as the dominant global economic power led the way out of this dilemma. A symbolic shift in the focus of economic and political relations from Britain to the United States became one of the central elements in nationalist assertions of sovereignty. It allowed the newly independent countries to retain relations of economic dependency in the global capitalist economy while freeing such relations from the taint of colonial domination. The establishment and intensification of economic and political ties with North America were justified also in terms of developmental transformation. As the dominant, richest, and most technologically advanced economic power, the United States offered ideal opportunities for such transformation.

There is a contradiction inherent in an anticolonial agenda that advocates the intensification of economic and political relations with the uncontested hegemon of international capitalism. But this did not deter the leadership of the Trinidadian ruling party, like their West Indian nationalist counterparts, from doing so. Eric Williams, the leader of the PNM, was ranked among the most strident of these anticolonial leaders. His quest to intensify ties with the United States was also the most vigorous. Williams saw domestic industrialization as the means of escaping from the economic strictures of the colonial political economy, and he expressed strong interest in the "Puerto Rican model" of industrialization by invitation (Fraser 1994, 139). The contradiction inherent in neocolonial insertion as a strategy for self-determination quickly erupted into confrontation with the United States. It forced Williams to make a choice that set the stage for US-imposed limits on nationalist self-assertions for the entire region. The conflict erupted in 1957 during negotiations over the location of a site for the capital of the West Indies Federation, which was to be the framework for the region's postcolonial political organization. West Indian nationalist leaders had voted in favor of locating the capital in Trinidad on land leased to the United States during World War II. The land was the home of a functioning US naval base. The US administration rejected the proposal on grounds of the base's strategic military importance. Williams, insisting on his country's sovereign right, demanded release from the agreement made between Britain and the United States in 1940 for the base's establishment. The United States refused to concede to the demand.

The confrontation served to highlight the ambiguities and contradictions of West Indian nationalist representation and practice. It exposed the limits inherent in a nationalist discourse shaped by a colonial legacy of racial and ethnic division. In effect, the impossibility of sovereignty was conceded by the nationalist leadership in the fashioning of a new dependency centered around the United States. Rather than an assertion of the right of self-determination, sovereignty was employed symbolically to establish the racial boundaries of nationalist construction. The organized East Indian and white opposition strongly supported the United States in an effort to undermine the bid by the Black and colored leadership for control of the postcolonial state. This allowed the Black political leaders of the PNM to question East Indian and white allegiance to the "nation" and to impugn the nationalist credentials of their political leaders. They were able to shore up their support base in the Black and colored segments of the population by exposing the "antinationalist" predispositions of the racial opposition. In the process, sovereignty fell victim to the racial strategies of elite contenders for power. In defense of the nationalist agenda and of Trinidadian sovereignty, members of the Black and colored population threw the full weight of their support behind the PNM (Ryan 1972, 132). In the process, the boundaries of the nation-state became firmly identified with the country's Black and colored population, and the PNM's role as the sole promoter and defender of nationalist interests was concretized and legitimized in the popular consciousness.

The power of the PNM leadership was undergirded by the political solidarity of its racial supporters cemented through the party's nationalist credentials. In the popular imagination, the national will came to be firmly associated with the interests of the party's natural constituency of middle-strata possessors of cultural capital. This "nascent" elite, objectively constrained by colonialism particularly during the period before World War II, came to "hegemonize" mass support under the discipline of its political representatives (Chatterjee 1986) as the technical and social conditions of racial capitalism began to shift in favor of the twentieth-century anticolonial movements that they organized and fashioned. The racial idiom, deployed as a means of discipline, was sustained through an intensification of the association between the DLP opposition and its exclusive Hindu support base.

In the final analysis, nationalism and sovereignty were deployed in the confrontation over the naval base as instruments in service of the ideological and power interests of the middle-strata elite. The constellation of middle-class power was reflected in developing political alliances established around the ideological agenda of the political leadership of the ruling party. It developed strong ties with the local business elite and with multiracial groups of professionals, managers, and skilled and technical labor. It recruited white business-people to advisory positions in the government, giving them considerable influence over economic policy. All these became linked to the party's middle strata of Black and colored workers in the public sector, in a new constellation of elite interests.

PNM leaders used the new alliances to isolate the Hindu-dominated East Indian DLP, highlighting its racial exclusivity. This ensured the party's hold on political power by sustaining solidary support from the Black masses. The use of the racial idiom freed the political executive to pursue a policy of "mixed-economy capitalism" that catered to the diverse interests of the country's elite, now organized around the PNM. The policy allowed for growth in the public sector, the development and expansion of state enterprises, and state-generated and state-supported private sector expansion. To succeed, the policy demanded an intensification of ties with international capital, and especially with the United States as the world's leading capitalist power. In the Cold War environment of the time, this required unquestioned allegiance to the superpower. The party expelled its radical leaders, among whom were the leading ideologues of its successful anticolonial campaign. In justification, Eric Williams, the party's leader, denounced communism as one of the five "dangers" facing his party. He compromised with the United States over the issue of the naval base, allowing a continuation of the US presence for a negotiated period. And he declared the country unequivocally pro-capitalist and allied with the West in the Cold War geopolitical divide (*Trinidad Guardian*, October 1, 1961).

The exclusive identification of the nation with its Afro-creole population produced anticipation among the PNM's Black and colored supporters that their interests alone would be represented and protected at the apex of state power. Excluded from the national space, the East Indian rural population rallied around its Hindu political leadership, who began to challenge the legitimacy of the claims by the Afro-creole population upon the nation-state. The racialization of national discourse camouflaged the use by a multiracial elite alliance of moderates and conservatives of racial support from a progressive working class in the service of its interests in the accumulation of social and economic capital. The Black urban and rural working-class supporters of the PNM were politically organized under the disciplinary power of a governing and state-controlling elite pursuing policies that were anathema to their own objective interests. The contradiction erupted during an economic crisis in 1965, just three years after the country received its independence. An economic downturn during that year led to significant increases in Black unemployment and underemployment, particularly in the oil industry with its predominance of Black workers. The crisis came at a time when PNM antipathy toward the agricultural sector was contributing to an intensification of the economic marginalization of its overwhelmingly East Indian rural workers and peasantry. As the crisis deepened, Black and East Indian workers joined together in a campaign of strikes and violence against the government that potentially threatened the racial appeal of the ruling party. In the face of an erosion of its racial support base, the party responded with coercive legislation directed against worker mobilization (Government of Trinidad and Tobago 1965). It was the first of a number of challenges by the Black lower classes to their racial representatives in government, sometimes in alliance with East Indian rural laborers and peasants. It also set the stage for use of the state's coercive mechanism in retaliation.

The PNM's response to the crisis served to define the limits of democratic practice in the political economy of Trinidad and Tobago. It exposed the true grounding of elite power in coercion and executive fiat. The formalities of democratic practice are tolerated and maintained only when mass mobilization coincides with the interests of the country's middle and upper classes. They serve to give legitimacy to elite power. When the latter is threatened, the coercive authoritarian base of governance is exposed. The PNM's response to lower-class mobilization established the organized practice of governance that came to typify the Trinidadian political economy.

In sum, anticolonial nationalism was constructed as the embodiment of Afro-creole interests. While East Indians contested the legitimacy of this formulation, Blacks and coloreds became intent on imposing this understanding on state organization. It became the basis for legitimate claims of preferential access to state resources. The middle-strata interests of the PNM conflicted sharply with Black working- and lower-class expectations, and the contradiction was exposed under conditions of economic downturn. In the immediate postindependence period, it produced a cross-racial working-class alliance between Blacks and East Indians, forcing the regime to rely on its arsenal of coercion to stay in power.

The use of coercion and control against Black mass mobilization has made visible the role of the state as an instrument of oppression. The strategic use of violence and executive fiat has become a central pillar in the maintenance of political power by Trinidad's governing elite. It emerges directly from the construction of nationalist discourse around notions of racial exclusivity in the service of elite interests. This has placed severe limits on democratic practice. The reliance on violence and executive fiat underscores the class basis of power in Trinidadian postcolonial statist construction, which is rooted in the systematic oppression of the working and lower classes by an international and national capitalist elite, along with its functionaries and allies. The majoritarian demands of a fictive claim to democracy was supported and sustained at independence by the mobilization of the ruling party's Black support base. In power, the party maintained support by resorting to racial patronage. In times of economic crisis, such patronage cannot be maintained.

In 1970, the PNM was again the target of a campaign of mass revolt by the country's urban Black workers and students, and of a rebellion by the predominantly Black army. Borrowing from the struggle for civil rights in the United States, workers, students, and soldiers began to rally in support of a demand for "Black power." The legitimacy of the claim by the ruling party to be the protector of Afro-creole interests was being challenged. The rebellion was crushed, and the ruling party maintained its hold on executive power through a campaign of coercive retaliation. This forced many of the dissident activists to go underground in a prolonged campaign organized by a Black guerrilla movement. The guerrillas enjoyed considerable sympathy from within the Black lower-class population until economic good fortune returned to the country. The campaign ended only when an unanticipated tripling of oil prices in 1973 swelled the state coffers and restored racial patronage to unprecedented heights.

Notwithstanding the restoration of racial patronage, the legitimacy of the PNM as the political arm of the Black lower class was severely undermined by events of the early 1970s. The 1970 Black power rebellion and the guerrilla campaign that followed succeeded in inserting the language of class oppression into political discourse. This produced sustained and enduring Black lower-class ambivalence toward, and often rejection of, the PNM. It opened the door to an acceptance by the country's Black and colored population of an alternative to the ruling party, whatever its racial designation. It also resuscitated a willingness to enter into cross-racial coalitions.

In 1975, a Black radical challenge to state legitimacy combined with East Indian contestation of Afro-creole nationalism to produce a mobilization campaign against PNM rule. Radical Black intellectuals and union leaders established formal ties with Hindu sociopolitical organizations. Many had participated in the anti-PNM campaigns of the early 1970s. They were buoyed by the exhibited weakness of the PNM during the disturbances. The United Labour Front (ULF) was formed in 1976 as an alliance between Black labor and East Indian rural agriculture. This was to signal a new chapter in party political organization and presaged a shift in the dynamics of power. The strategic significance of the East Indian population was increasing rapidly, both from growth in relative numbers and from a pattern of rural-to-urban migration that was changing the population dynamics of constituency politics. The mobilization of the East Indian population in a multiracial alliance presented an opportunity for representatives of the middle-strata elite to challenge the domination of the PNM. They opposed what they considered to be policy excesses in the development of a system of racial patronage targeted at the Black urban population. The lessons of the early 1970s forced the PNM into the dilemma of maintaining its mass support base while continuing to cater to its natural constituency of elite interests. Faced with the experience of a mass rebellion that left the party barely clinging to power, it chose a program of progressive redistribution that taxed the economic surpluses of the middle and upper classes. Since the redistributive efforts were directed at the Black urban working class, the elite found a natural ally in the East Indian population. Added to this was lingering Black animosity to the ruling party.

The problem for the ULF was that it was spawned in radical mobilization. Its campaign of class warfare alienated the country's middle and upper classes. Without significant support from the country's elite, it quickly collapsed, falling victim to the antiradical bias in national discourse. In 1977, however, the ULF was reestablished, purged of its more radical members. This was a telling replay of the PNM's decision to reject radical politics in its successful campaign to gain control of the postcolonial state. It underscored the strategic power of the elite in the power dynamics of governance. The new party entered into a loose arrangement with two other opposition parties. One, the Democratic Action Congress (DAC), organized its support within the predominantly Black population of Tobago. Its leader, A. N. R. Robinson, was a former heir apparent to Eric Williams in the PNM who had resigned from his cabinet portfolio during the Black power revolt. He came with considerable Black working-class legitimacy. The second party in the loose alliance was the Tapia House Movement, headed by a Black moderate intellectual, Lloyd Best, who had begun to articulate concerns over the policies of the ruling party. This, in essence, represented a new elite alliance that relied upon the support of the surging East Indian population for its claim to power.

The anti-PNM alliance presaged a reconstruction of forces within the power relations of statist organization. It had profound implications for the future and anticipated the demise of Afro-creole nationalism. In relative terms, the strategic position of Hindus in the power equation of governance was on the ascent as their leaders began developing politically strategic alliances across racial boundaries. The emergence of Tapia was a distinct indication of the onset of Black middle-class alienation from the governing party. Opposition to the PNM intensified after 1978 as the country began to experience a significant decline in export earnings from petroleum production, the mainstay of the Trinidadian economy. In 1982, government revenues went into deficit for the first time since 1973, and public debt began to escalate (Hintzen 1989, 179–81; Bobb 1983, 94; *Trinidad Guardian*, June 30, 1983, 3). Economic decline provided the catalyst cementing a new political realignment. Business and professional elites began to oppose the continued distribution of racial patronage by the PNM. They began to place the blame for the country's economic woes squarely on the appropriation of state funds for such patronage. With challenges mounting against the governing elite, the strategic importance of the Hindu opposition increased dramatically.

In national elections held in 1981, two new political parties, the National Alliance and the Organisation for National Reconstruction (ONR), mounted significant challenges to the PNM. This was the first clear and unambiguous indication of erosion of PNM support among the middle and upper strata. The National Alliance was an amalgamation of the ULF, DAC, and Tapia, formalized into a grouping in 1976. The ONR was a political organization of the country's business and professional elites that enjoyed significant support among the country's upper and upper-middle classes. While significant in absolute terms, support for the two parties was not enough, separately, to defeat the PNM in national elections held in 1981. Nonetheless, the indications were clear. There was a fundamental reformulation of political relations that was threatening the PNM's continued ability to hold onto power. In attempts to cater to the interests of the Black lower strata by developing an elaborate system of patronage, the PNM found itself in confrontation with a highly politicized middle and upper strata.

The new constellation of elite interests and upper- and middle-class desertion of the PNM was aimed at preserving the position of these class groupings at the apex of governance. This reformulation of elite power was, in part, directed against the influence of the Black working class and limiting its access to the distributive resources of the state. In other words, it was an attempt to reduce its power. The middle and upper strata developed new political alliances with the rural Hindu social grouping and with the Black population in Tobago in an effort to negate the role of Black mobilization. The need for such alliances was dictated by the majoritarian impositions of Westminster democracy, which demanded the cultivation of a popular support base to legitimize elite domination. And the conditions of Black popular support began to conflict sharply with elite accumulative and power interests. Rural East Indians were less disposed to make demands upon the distributive resources of the government under conditions of national marginalization. The representation of Tobago in the popular imagination as a national backwater and of Trinidad as the engine of development combined with the former island's small population to render insignificant any demands its population might make on state resources in exchange for political support. In other words, the redistributive claims by the elite's new mass base of supporters would be significantly reduced when compared with the substantial demands made upon state resources by the Black working and lower classes.

By 1983, a loose coalition, calling itself the Accommodation, was formalized between the National Alliance and the ONR. Its effectiveness was tested in local government elections held that very year. The result was a resounding defeat for the PNM, with the Accommodation capturing 54.07 percent of the popular vote to the PNM's 39.11 (Ryan 1989, 43–45). The ruling party lost control of all but three urban municipalities and one county council, winning only fifty-four local government seats to the Accommodation's sixty-six. With its demonstrated success, the leaders of the two political parties making up the Accommodation entered into a formal coalition called the National Alliance for Reconstruction (NAR). The new party contested the general elections in 1986 in a campaign that mounted a frontal assault on "racial politics" that symbolized a rejection of the PNM's appeal to the country's Black population. The party won a landslide victory, capturing thirty-three of the thirty-six parliamentary seats and 67 percent of the popular vote. This ended the thirty-year rule of the PNM despite continued strong support in Black working-class constituencies (Ryan 1989, 85). The defeat signaled the decline in the strategic influence of the Black working and lower classes in electoral politics.

In its defeat, the PNM fell victim to its own successful strategy of creating opportunities for upward mobility for members of the Black working class through its policies of redistribution and patronage. Many of its Black supporters had become absorbed into a reconstituted middle strata. Their upward mobility was facilitated by massive earnings accruing to the state from oil-generated wealth between 1973 and 1981. These earnings supported policies of state expansion, allowing increased employment of Blacks in government services. The earnings also supported, through massive liquidity transfers of state surpluses, the expansion of private sector business and professional activity. There was also considerable expansion in postsecondary education. Finally, state revenues supported an extensive system of racial patronage directed at the Black urban and semiurban population. When the economy collapsed, the response of the Black and colored middle-class beneficiaries was to protect their newly acquired socioeconomic status by supporting the NAR opposition. This stemmed as much from a desire by these parvenus to maintain their newfound socioeconomic status, as it was a reflection of Black ambivalence to the PNM spawned in the rebellion of 1970.

In effect, the NAR was nothing more than a reconstituted PNM. Its unabashed purpose as a governing party was to defend the relative position of the middle and upper strata against claims by the lower strata. Affinity with the Black working class was jettisoned in favor of an alliance with the representatives of rural Hindus. When the Hindus began to make distributive claims on state resources, their political leaders were systematically marginalized. This caused the coalition to collapse in 1988 after five members of parliament, all former members of the Hindu-based ULF, were suspended from the ruling party. The departure of the ULF membership left an elite representing the urban middle and upper classes and the predominantly Afro-Trinidadian Tobago constituency in control of the governing institutions of the state.

All this was occurring during a period of rapid economic decline that compelled the government to seek relief from international financial institutions. In 1988, foreign exchange assistance was sought from the International Monetary Fund (IMF). A regimen of structural adjustment was negotiated and implemented to ensure agreement by the country's international creditors to a program of debt rescheduling organized with the Fund's blessing. With the intervention of the IMF, the newly reconstituted government gave up much of its control of the economy to international financial institutions. IMF intervention paralleled the development of new technical and social conditions of international capital that favored the interests of the domestic entrepreneurial, managerial, and professional elite. Policies of structural adjustment undermined the economic and social interests of the salaried middle classes, particularly those dependent upon the state for employment, education, health, welfare, and subsidies. The regime lost the ability to cater to the interests of this segment of its middle-strata supporters. The government was forced, inter alia, to embark on two rounds of devaluation, to cut back significantly on public spending, to divest itself of public assets, to abandon state-funded projects (particularly those in the energy-intensive sector), to cut public sector salaries, to retrench public sector workers, to curtail financial support for the private sector, to cut back significantly on patronage, to eliminate subsidies, and to increase utility rates. As a result, real incomes plummeted, unemployment increased phenomenally, and the level of poverty increased. The economy moved into severe recession (Ryan 1989, 318–42). This compounded the problem caused by the departure of the coalition's rural Hindu supporters.

By 1990, the government was facing an absolute crisis of legitimacy compounded by the loss of its Hindu mass support base and by the economic crisis. On July 27, 1990, a group of Afro-Muslims, known as the Muslimeen, numbering fewer than three hundred and without any discernable support from any segment of the population, exploited widespread disenchantment stemming from the crisis of legitimacy to organize a bid to oust the government from power. Members of the group exploded a bomb in the national police headquarters, invaded parliament, and took the prime minister, seven cabinet ministers, and a number of parliamentarians hostage. They almost succeeded, helped by an initial reluctance on the part of the military and police to intervene in support of the government. At the time of the attempted coup, the police had been engaged in acrimonious labor negotiations; they had suffered significant cutbacks in wages, while work conditions were deteriorating badly. The force had lost much of its prestige. This reflected the general condition of the salaried middle class, particularly state employees and those in the private sector vulnerable to a decline in the relative wage rate. The desire by this segment of the population to see the regime out of office was matched only by its unwillingness to allow the Muslimeen to capture control of governance. The Muslimeen's anti-Western ideology rooted in notions of Black liberation was anathema to middle- and upper-class interests. The attempted coup precipitated a total breakdown of law and order in the capital city and its environs, and a near demobilization of the police force. The weakened regime was forced into negotiations with the rebels.

The response to the attempted takeover of the government signaled a new divide in the country's political economy and the loss of the ruling party's ability to sustain the strategic support that had brought it to power. To the loss of its Hindu supporters, necessary to ensure the party's democratic majority, was now added the loss of a significant segment of its middle-class support base. The general attitude of most was to support neither the rebels nor the ruling party. Indeed, a majority (60 percent) supported the social agenda of the rebels while condemning their assault on democracy (Ryan 1991, 218). Some felt that the ruling party's insensitivity to the poor, its vindictiveness, and its alliance with the white and near-white elite were principal causes of the rebellion (Ryan 1991, 200–201). After the attempted coup, a full 73 percent of the public held negative views of the prime minister, and 32 percent claimed that they had become less sympathetic to him after the rebellion. Seventy-one percent of the population held negative views of the ruling party as a whole (Ryan 1991, 220). This left the governing executive politically isolated, apart from the support it continued to enjoy from the upper and upper-middle classes and from the Tobago constituency. The NAR government was transformed into an arm of the international financial institutions. In doing so, it was forced to desert those of its strategic supporters whose interests were jeopardized by the dictates of the new forms of capitalist globalization. The entrepreneurial, professional, and managerial elite had every reason to support the new conditions of economic globalization imposed by international public policy. They were its beneficiaries. Apart from personal allegiance to the NAR leadership, there was every reason why the Black lower-class population of Tobago would support international capitalist penetration. A history of economic neglect by the central government was forcing the smaller island to fall back on its reputation as a tropical paradise to develop a tourist industry. Moreover, there was tremendous potential for the development of offshore oil and gas reserves. Both initiatives depended upon massive amounts of foreign investment as well as foreign assistance for infrastructure development. The problem for the NAR was its loss of the majoritarian base needed to preserve the legitimizing fiction of democratic governance.

Elections were held in 1992, and the NAR was defeated in every constituency in Trinidad. It won only in the two Tobago constituencies, in the island stronghold of the prime minister and party leader. With some exceptions, the middle and upper classes returned to the fold of the PNM, adding their strategic power to the party's racial support among the Black working class. Once again, rural Hindus were left out of the governing equation, returning to their former exclusivity and isolation. The Hindu elite organized itself into a new party, the United National Congress (UNC), which won in all of the rural East Indian constituencies. While the new party lost the election, its support base presaged a new constellation of power interests that had all the ingredients necessary for capturing control of state governance. The new social and technical conditions of global capital had catapulted the East Indian elite into the most strategic sectors of the domestic political economy. The East Indian domestic business class owns and controls a significant share of the country's economic capital, and East Indian professionals and intellectuals are heavily represented in the technical and managerial professions and disciplines. Significant numbers of East Indian salaried and wage workers are migrating to the urbanized areas of the country, formerly the exclusive preserve of the creole segments of the population (Blacks, coloreds, whites, etc.). They have changed the voting dynamics in a number of urbanized constituencies. And the UNC can count on the solidary support of East Indians in Hindu rural constituencies.

The increasing urbanization and urbanism of East Indians has been accompanied by the cultural creolization of the population. In the past, such creolization lessened the racial and ethnoreligious appeal of its political elite. As a result, in its heyday, the PNM enjoyed substantial support from urban Muslim and Christian East Indians. But, with the growing prominence of the East Indian elite, creolization has gone hand in hand with the growth and retention of Hindu religiosity. Pressures for creolization have been most evident on the East Indian middle class. These derive from their functional insertion into Trinidad's political economy and the postcolonial benefits of nationalism that have accrued to their creole counterparts. Such benefits have propelled many Hindus to incorporate more universal Western forms into their religious practice, signaling some measure of creolization without sacrifice of their Hindu identity (Klass 1991). The middle and upper classes have managed an accommodation of the two, particularly through the practice of new forms of Hinduism that are distinguished from its more traditional forms practiced by rural agriculturalists (Klass 1991). At the same time, there is mounting resistance to creolization among the Hindu cultural elite. In their campaign, they are employing resources of symbolic power to petition for inclusion in the nationalist space *as East Indians*. The theme of "douglarization" emerges persistently in East Indian narratives of purity. It has become emblematic of the polluting consequences of sexual contact with Africans. Douglarization, therefore, is the process of transformation of East Indians into racial creoles through miscegenation. Hindu purity is being deployed as a symbolic resource by these leaders to delegitimize the representations and practices of what they present as a "polluted" creole discourse. Their challenge is organized around narratives of creole cultural degradation directed particularly at the cultural ascendance of Afro-creole forms in nationalist discourse. The campaign is accompanied by mounting contestation of the claims made by Afro-creoles of a central role in nation building. In their self-representations, East Indians are beginning to present themselves as the true builders of the nation and as the nation's saviors from Afro-creole degradation (Yelvington 1995, 77). Theirs is not merely a quest for nationalist inclusion. It represents a claim to the nationalist space that is legitimized through a redemptive counterdiscourse to Afro-creole nationalism. In this regard, it presents a fundamental challenge to Trinidad's creole formation through a rejection of notions of hybridity and of "blending and impurity" as its fundamental values. While the Hindu elite is at the forefront of the challenges to Afro-creole nationalism, what has emerged is a growth of a sense of East Indianness, independent of religion, in which both Christians and Muslims participate. This process of "re-Indianization" of the creolized Indo-Trinidadian has been attributed to the upward mobility of Hindus, which has produced a leveling effect on the population, and to a growing sense of Afro-creole domination of the national social, cultural, and political arena (Premdas and Sitahal 1991, 347–49). The twin themes of Hinduism and purity have become new bases for East Indian solidarity upon which disciplinary power is exercised on the East Indian electorate. Each, by itself, guarantees the support of the urbanized and socially creolized East Indian population, which otherwise may have been resistant to racial and ethnoreligious appeals.

In 1995, support by these strategic segments of the population combined to produce a victory by political representatives of the Hindu elite, organized in the UNC under Basdeo Panday, in national elections. For the first time, a party identified with rural East Indians was able to take exclusive control of the governing institutions of the state. Like the PNM before them, leaders of the party employed the idioms of race and ethnicity to assure themselves of majoritarian support. And, like the PNM before them, the leaders quickly accommodated the reconstituted interests of a new elite, organized around business, the professions, and a managerial class in their exercise of governance. This assures the ruling party of the strategic support necessary to remain in power. The willingness of the Black population to accept an "East Indian" government, and of many of the Black elites to serve in its executive and legislative branches, underscores both the weakening association of the nation with its Afro-creole population and the loss of racial legitimacy by the PNM.

But changing social and economic conditions of capitalist production are creating a new role for the PNM. The conditions of globalization, favoring a new managerial, professional, and business elite, has provided opportunity for the party to attract segments of the Black and colored salaried middle class away from the coalition of elite interests that catapulted the NAR into power during the 1980s. The social and economic capital of the latter has been significantly devalued in the new political economy. By combining its version of populist welfarism with a resuscitated racial appeal, the PNM has been able to rebuild a strong support base to challenge the UNC. In elections held in December 2000, the UNC barely managed to hold onto power against a strong electoral challenge mounted by the PNM. The success of the PNM's revived racial appeal was signaled by a win in one of the two predominantly Black Tobago constituencies. The NAR, with its Tobago base, won in the smaller island's second constituency by a very thin margin. The UNC won nineteen seats against a sixteen-seat total for the PNM, helped significantly by a movement of East Indian wage and salaried workers and small-scale businesspeople into the urbanized former strongholds of PNM's Black supporters. This, and the solid support it received among the rural Hindu constituencies, assured the party of victory at the polls.

In all of the domestic political contentions, the changing dynamics of international globalization is hardly noticed despite the profound consequences it has for the domestic political economy. The new terms of social and economic organization are accepted as necessary for "development." There is growing inequality between a privileged class that has become absorbed into a global elite of producers, managers, and skilled professionals on the one hand, and the lower-middle and lower classes who are losing social and economic ground on the other. This is explained in a discourse of modernity that rewards and valorizes those possessing the prerequisites for developmental transformation into clones of the industrialized political economies of the North Atlantic. The organization of this type of formal democratic practice, devoid of representative governance, legitimizes the role of an international elite and a globalized domestic elite at the apex of state power while rendering invisible the true nature of its exploitative authoritarianism. In the process, all semblance of sovereignty and self-determination has disappeared.

In Trinidad, the struggle for control of governance occurs within the context of the majoritarian demands of the democratic political organization. The elite is not its only beneficiaries. The mobilization of lower-class Afro-Trinidadians forced the PNM regime, dependent upon its support, to create conditions for their upward mobility. Black Tobagonians were able to exploit alliances with the regime to secure resources for economic growth. Ultimately, however, it is elite interests that prevail. Without elite support, the PNM lost power. And, despite the challenge mounted by the PNM in the elections of 2000, it is the support of the strategic elite segments of the political economy that continues to determine electoral outcomes. This has to do with the ability of this elite to use race symbolically in its exercise of disciplinary power over the masses while sustaining solidary support from among its various segments. In the new constellation of elite interests, the wage and salaried segments of the lower-middle strata have been sloughed off in the new globalized political economy. Their support for a populist PNM provided the party with an electoral boost. It was not enough, however, to ensure control of governance.

CONCLUSION

This chapter demonstrates how democratic organization can be manipulated in the service of the interests of a dominant social grouping. In Trinidad, it has produced the reconstruction and reformulation of relations among racial and socioeconomic groupings over time. In a regulating discourse of political identity, identific notions of belonging are politicized in support of elite interests. Trinidadian democracy is characterized by such regulation as an elite comprising bureaucrats, professionals, managers, intellectuals, businesspeople, and large-scale farmers, employing race as an instrument of its own power. The importance of racially defined organization in Trinidad is the role it plays in creating and sustaining the conditions for political domination, irrespective of the democratic nature of political organization.

NOTES

1. These figures are taken from the 1990 population census reported by the Central Statistical Office of Trinidad and Tobago.

2. See Harris 1976, 171–79, for a discussion of the characteristics of this reconstructed social grouping.

BIBLIOGRAPHY

Anderson, Benedict. 1983. *Imagined Communities: Reflections on the Origin and Spread of Nationalism*. London: Verso Books.

Berreman, Gerald. 1975. "Bazar Behavior: Social Identity and Social Interaction in Urban India." In *Ethnic Identity: Cultural Continuities and Change*, edited by George De Vos and Lola Romanucci-Ross, 71–105. Palo Alto, CA: Mayfield.

Bobb, Euric. 1983. "The Oil Industry: Impact on the Local Economy; Review 1982/Forecast 1983." Central Bank of Trinidad and Tobago, *Quarterly Economic Bulletin* 2, no. 1 (March): 90–98.

Chatterjee, Partha. 1986. *Nationalist Thought and the Colonial World: A Derivative Discourse*. London: Zed Books.

Clarke, Colin. 1992. "Spatial Pattern and Social Interaction among Creoles and Indians in Trinidad and Tobago." In *Trinidad Ethnicity*, edited by Kevin A. Yelvington, 116–35. London: Macmillan Caribbean.

Depres, Leo A. 1975. "Towards a Theory of Ethnic Phenomena." In *Ethnicity and Resource Competition in Plural Societies*, edited by Leo A. Depres, 186–208. The Hague: Mouton Publishers.

De Vos, George. 1975. "Ethnic Pluralism: Conflict and Accommodation." In *Ethnic Identity: Cultural Continuities and Change*, edited by George De Vos and Lola Romanucci-Ross, 5–41. Palo Alto, CA: Mayfield.

Dreyfus, Hubert L., and Paul Rabinow. 1983. *Michel Foucault: Beyond Structuralism and Hermeneutics*. 2nd ed. Chicago: University of Chicago Press.

Du Bois, W. E. B. 1949. *Color and Democracy: Colonies and Peace*. New York: Harcourt, Brace and Company.

Enloe, Cynthia H. 1973. *Ethnic Conflict and Political Development*. Boston: Little, Brown.

Foucault, Michel. 1979. *Discipline and Punish: The Birth of the Prison*. Translated by Alan Sheridan. New York: Vintage Books.

Fraser, Cary. 1994. *Ambivalent Anticolonialism: The United States and the Genesis of West Indian Independence, 1940–1964*. Westport, CT: Greenwood Press.

Government of Trinidad and Tobago. 1965. "Industrial Stabilization Act 1965." Laws of Trinidad and Tobago, Act no. 8. Port of Spain: Government Printer.

Harris, Nigel. 1976. *The End of the Third World*. Harmondsworth, Middx., England: Penguin.

Hintzen, Percy C. 1989. *The Costs of Regime Survival: Racial Mobilization, Elite Domination and Control of the State in Guyana and Trinidad.* Cambridge: Cambridge University Press.

Klass, Morton. 1991. *Singing with Sai Baba: The Politics of Revitalization in Trinidad.* Boulder, CO: Westview Press.

Lauren, Paul Gordon. 1988. *Power and Prejudice: The Politics and Diplomacy of Racial Discrimination.* Boulder, CO: Westview Press.

Obeyesekere, Gananath. 1975. "The Sinhalese-Buddhist Identity in Ceylon." In *Ethnic Identity: Cultural Continuities and Change,* edited by George De Vos and Lola Romanucci-Ross, 231–58. Palo Alto, CA: Mayfield.

Oxaal, Ivar. 1968. *Black Intellectuals Come to Power: The Rise of Creole Nationalism in Trinidad and Tobago.* Cambridge, MA: Schenkman.

Premdas, Ralph, and Harold Sitahal. 1991. "Religion and Culture: The Case of the Presbyterians in Trinidad's Stratified System." In *Social and Occupational Stratification in Contemporary Trinidad and Tobago,* edited by Selwyn D. Ryan, 337–49. Saint Augustine, Trinidad: Institute of Social and Economic Research, University of the West Indies.

Ramsaran, Dave. 1994. "Entrepreneurs in Trinidad and Tobago: A Sociological Survey." In *Entrepreneurship in the Caribbean: Culture, Structure, Conjuncture,* edited by Selwyn D. Ryan and Taimoon Stewart, 119–73. Saint Augustine, Trinidad: Institute of Social and Economic Research, University of the West Indies.

Ryan, Selwyn D. 1972. *Race and Nationalism in Trinidad and Tobago.* Toronto: University of Toronto Press.

Ryan, Selwyn D. 1989. *The Disillusioned Electorate: The Politics of Succession in Trinidad and Tobago.* Port of Spain: Inprint Caribbean.

Ryan, Selwyn D. 1991. *The Muslimeen Grab for Power: Race, Religion, and Revolution in Trinidad and Tobago.* Port of Spain: Inprint Caribbean.

Ryan, Selwyn D. 1996. *Pathways to Power: Indians and the Politics of National Unity in Trinidad and Tobago.* Saint Augustine, Trinidad: Institute of Social and Economic Research, University of the West Indies.

Segal, Daniel. 1992. "'Race' and 'Color' in Pre-Independence Trinidad and Tobago." In *Trinidad Ethnicity,* edited by Kevin A. Yelvington, 81–115. London: Macmillan Caribbean.

Segal, Ronald. 1967. *The Race War.* New York: Viking Press.

Tinker, Hugh. 1977. *Race, Conflict, and the International Order: From Empire to United Nations.* London: Macmillan.

Weber, Max. 1946. *From Max Weber: Essays in Society.* Translated by Hans Heinrich Gertz and C. Wright Mills. New York: Oxford University Press.

Yelvington, Kevin A. 1992. "Introduction: Trinidad Ethnicity." In *Trinidad Ethnicity,* edited by Kevin A. Yelvington, 1–32. London: Macmillan Caribbean.

Yelvington, Kevin A. 1995. *Producing Power: Ethnicity, Gender, and Class in a Caribbean Workplace.* Philadelphia: Temple University Press.

Chapter 8

DIASPORA, GLOBALIZATION, AND THE POLITICS OF IDENTITY

PERCY C. HINTZEN

Now one of the main reactions against the politics of racism in Britain was what I would call "Identity Politics One," the first form of identity politics. It had to do with the constitution of some defensive collective identity against the practices of racist society. It had to do with the fact that people were being blocked out of and refused an identity and identification within the majority nation, having to find some other roots on which to stand. Because people have to find some ground, some place, some position on which to stand. Blocked out of any access to an English or British identity, people had to try to discover who they were. It is the crucial moment of the rediscovery or the search for roots.
—STUART HALL, "OLD AND NEW IDENTITIES, OLD AND NEW ETHNICITIES"

DIASPORA AND MODERNITY

An ineluctable association between capitalism and race emerges in the formation of a nation-state. This relationship is not merely inevitable but necessary as a condition of modernity. It has produced what sociologist Paul Gilroy calls "a distinctive ecology of belonging" (1997, 3) that links territory to identity and, relatedly, sovereignty to belonging (1997, 3, 10). As such, under the modern condition, citizenship has become the basis of claims to the rights and of assertions of privilege.

The link between identity and the modern state emerged in the crucible of contradictions produced out of increasing heterogeneity. This occurred in the wake of an intensification of migratory flows of people, as technical and social conditions changed rapidly in the transformation to capitalism. From such changes emerged a need for new conceptions of belonging that molded disparate populations into a unified, homogeneous, national peoplehood. The changes also necessitated that a distinction be made between those who

159

could claim the rights and privileges of belonging as "citizens" and those who could not. This distinction was integrally related to the division of labor as an imperative of capitalist accumulation.[1] Thus, the development of the nation-state was characterized by the growth of racial regimes of inclusion and exclusion.[2] Diasporic consciousness emerged as a necessary condition for accommodation, in particular national spaces for those who were denied the right to national belonging, or whose rights to such were curtailed and compromised.

Diasporic identity was historically produced, particularly in the wake of the transoceanic movement of persons in service of the colonial project. Under colonialism, "stateless" territories came under the dominion of colonizing "civilized" states. Regions of the world outside "civilized" Europe were organized into bounded territories for European conquest and jurisdiction. An integral link developed between civilization and sovereign power: only the civilized could exercise sovereignty. Relatedly, only the civilized could make claims of belonging to the modern state. This explains, for example, the exclusion of the indigenous populations of the Americas from national imaginations. Thus, modernity implies a conjoining of the nation and the civilized. The latter is racially inscribed.

Racial belonging was produced and imposed by the technologies and apparatuses of the state. The former refers to the imposed categorizations of the population through censuses, for example. It also refers, inter alia, to "invented histories and traditions, ceremonies, and cultural imaginings" that are integral to the power of the state to include and exclude. By the apparatuses of the state, I refer to its instrumentalities and institutions of power organized for jurisdictional deployment over territory. These include law and policy making as well as bureaucracies (Goldberg 2002, 9). State technologies and apparatuses function for the production of peoplehood. The latter identifies those with legitimate claims of belonging. It also forms the basis for the legitimate exclusion from the materialities of the nation of those who cannot make such claims. Inevitably, this produces a cultural politics of sameness necessary for the homogenizing project of the state (Goldberg 2002, 15–16). This politics of inclusion is challenged, rejected, or ignored by the racially excluded in a "cultural politics of difference, of struggles around difference, of the production of new identities, of the appearance of new subjects on the political and cultural stage" (Hall 1996, 467).

Thus, residence in the jurisdictional space of the state does not necessarily come with claims of belonging or the contingent rights of citizenship that legitimize access to the deserved materialities of the nation. It does not lead, necessarily, to participation in the performative imageries, the poetics and aesthetics, of national identification. The resulting tension plays out around the cultural politics of inclusion and exclusion, which, in the final analysis, is racialized. Diasporic imagination is organized materially around and in response to, and participates in, the cultural politics of exclusion. This raises the need for considerable modification in the analytics of diaspora. Because diasporic identity is organized around notions of origin and longings for return, the ideas of displacement, dislocation, and uprootedness have become its dominant themes. They have acted to reify and territorialize imaginary "homelands" (see, e.g., Lemelle and Kelley 1994, 8). Such objectification is problematic on both empirical and analytical grounds. There is no Africa, or East Asia, or South Asia, or Arabia, or America to which most diasporic subjects can return. For most who participate in diasporic imaginaries, the possibility of return is foreclosed. This has less to do with generations of residence in their host countries and more with the constructed and imaginary nature of their originary homelands. The West Indies, for example, has no concrete existence. While the diasporas of Saint Kitts or Jamaica may have meaning in these two countries, they become meaningless in the diasporic construction of the societies that host their emigrants. Both become absorbed into a "West Indian" diaspora with a "homeland" that can exist only in the imagination. Thus, for many, homeland has no concrete existence. This prompted Stuart Hall to make a distinction between "open" and "closed" diasporas. The former refers to "diasporic communities, with no possibility or desire for return" (Hall 2002). This does not resolve the problem. Diasporic imagination is constitutive of the cultural politics of place deployed against nationalist imaginaries and its material implications of exclusion.[3] Its contingent representations and practices are shifting signifiers that respond to the material particularities of place. They are conditioned and framed by discourses of belonging and exclusion in national locations of residence. However, they respond to differences in the social geography of locality. Diaspora is therefore the cultural politics of the unincluded and nonincluded deployed in highly localized arenas. In this sense, diasporic imagination is organized around structural notions of difference. But structural understandings are and can never be fixed. Rather, they emerge dialogically out of conjunctural processes that are always changing. They are reflexive of the changing positionalities of individuals and collectives across time, space, and institutional formation. This is what is entailed in social mobility. In the mobile subject is found a rejection of the Cartesian self as fixed and unchanging in time and over time. The self is revealed as a product of the moment created out of conjunctural processes that are constantly in flux.

What is universal and fixed in all of this, at least in the modern condition, is the relationship between race, territory, and belonging. This relationship refers not to national but to racial identity. In the final analysis, diaspora reveals the inevitable link between race and conceptions of origin, because

the latter is racially marked. This is notwithstanding the reorganization of
the racial imaginary in the nineteenth century. The scientific fixing of race
around biology obscured the integral association between race and territory.
It did not, however, displace the relationship between racial identity and
myths of origin.[4] This is the challenge that hybridity offers up to modernity
by dislodging subjectivity from racially inscribed origin myths. The biologism
introduced to racial discourse by scientific racism came without the refutation
of Africa as the source of Blackness in the racially constructed discourse of
origins. It also deepened the signification of Blackness as the embodiment of
the uncivilized. In this imaginary construction, Black bodies are denied the
capacities (understood as rationality and reason) for full belonging in the
spaces of civilized modernity. This denial applies even in the territorialized
locations of Africa organized under statist jurisdiction.[5] The state and nation
are markers of civilization, and Blackness, understood as uncivilized, becomes
ascribed to their constitutive outsides. At the same time, Blackness becomes
the object of state regulation, control, and jurisdiction. Diasporic identity
emerges in the contradiction of exclusion and inclusion that this implies.
Blackness cannot be accommodated within the national space because of its
negation of civilization. At the same time, the imperative of its management
demands inclusion under the jurisdiction of the state. It is therefore an intru-
sive and undesirable, even though necessary and unavoidable, presence in
national spaces where civilization is imaginatively constructed and where its
materialities are deployed. At the same time, its inclusion in national peoplehood is foreclosed.

Diasporic imagination is produced out of the cultural politics of exclusion.
It is shaped by the contradictions that emerge from the concreteness of
participation in the project of modernity by those symbolically excluded on
racial grounds. Participation comes in the form of contributions, achievements,
and access to the materialities of modernity. Race is not the only structural
determinant of positionality or the sole imaginary around which claims of
belonging can be made. It is not always and singularly the basis of legitimate
access to the economic, political, social, and cultural materialities of modernity.
In other words, it is not the only basis upon which the rights of citizenship are
conferred. Claims to national belonging can also be made by birthright and
positionality derived from social, economic, cultural, and symbolic capital.[6]
For the diasporic subject, the "cultural politics of difference" is complicated
by possibilities for inclusion provided on account of acquisition of these
attributes of belonging. Such acquisition can either be denied or shorn of
racial signification. The entanglements of the racially excluded with modernity
and the possibilities they produce are what make diasporic identity ambiguous,
contradictory, polysemous, and multivalent.

Diasporic identity must also respond contextually to differences in possibilities for acquisition of the attributes of modernity over time, social geography, and social positioning. Acquisition does not always provide access to citizenship. Birth is not always a guarantor of such access even under conditions of juridical and constitutional sanction. Wealth and cultural attributes may guarantee full claims of belonging to those born outside the jurisdictional space of the state even while continuing to exclude those with claims based on birthright. Thus, diasporic imagination responds to the realities of time, locality, and positionality. This does not mean that it is inchoate. Rather, as more or less well formed, it is available to be recalled, interpreted, and reinterpreted in keeping with the conjunctures of the moment, either by individuals or by collectivities. But there is no singularity in its deployment. Within the limits imposed by racialized construction, there is no single diasporic imagination or universality in its interpretation. There are multiple diasporic imaginaries available for recall even under the single rubric of racial identity. Each becomes available in the cultural politics of difference under conditions of nationalist exclusion or ambiguous inclusion. The unifying theme of any particular diasporic imagination is the collective memory of homeland. However, there is no single corpus of memory, and no single imaginary of homeland, even for those identified singularly in ideologies of racialized inclusion and exclusion. An individual can have many claims to homeland and many diasporic imaginaries to call upon at a particular moment of racial challenge.

Diaspora functions to bridge the gap between the imperative of national belonging imposed by the modern state on the one hand, and the discourses, aesthetics, and poetics of exclusion on the other. It preserves the link between identity and territory while acknowledging, even in their contestation, the exclusionary practices of the state. Since race is integrally linked to territorial origins, then diaspora, in the final analysis, must be conceptualized racially. One may argue that whites, understood as those with originary claims to Europe, belong everywhere as the bearers of civilization and as the nation's protectors from crisis and threat (Goldberg 2002, 40). This point receives added importance because it allows for the inclusion of continental Africans in the Black diasporic imagination. In racial terms, the African continent is cast as uncivilized hinterland territories with the state as a civilizing outpost for the containment, management, and tutelage of its populations. In the discourse of modernity, continental Africans are understood to be the objects of state control and management. Even when Africans control the apparatuses of the state, they continue to be seen in historicist terms of immaturity, in continual need of the civilizing tutelage of the North. Thus, the technologies of state power in Africa remain embedded in relations of coloniality because of the persistence of relations of imperialism after the end of formal colonial governance (Grosfoguel

2003, 6). African states also retain relations of dependency characterized by forms of exploitation, subordination, and expropriation constitutive of colonialism. As a result, they continue to suffer the consequences of persistent underdevelopment.[7] As such, the incorporation of continental Africans into the modern state is just as ambiguous as, for example, Black populations in what is conventionally understood as the African diaspora. It is this ambiguity of (un)belonging that connects African subjectivity on the continent to Black diasporic consciousness organized around notions of universal Black intimacy.

Whiteness eviscerates the ambiguity of belonging that is at the critical center of diasporic identity. European immigrants to the United States could retain claims to their national spaces of origin while participating equally in American peoplehood. They become "ethnicized" Americans. Or they pass easily into the group of Americans whose associations with origins disappear completely in the construction of their identities. They become absorbed into the unambiguous peoplehood of the USA. African Americans, as Blacks, cannot make these claims to unambiguous belonging, even against European immigrants whose presence they preceded in the territorial and jurisdictional space of the American state. Nor can Native Americans.

The role of Africa in the African diasporic imaginary raises interesting questions. These revolve around the links among civilization, the state, and the nation. In its naturalist conception, the Africa that exists in the racialized imagery of modernity cannot be civilized. In its historicist version, the African represents the "historical immaturity" of the colonial subject. This calls forth a pervasive and continuing necessity for white supremacy exercised through the instrumentalities of the "postcolonial" state. This is where the idea of the "outpost" receives its analytic power. In the final analysis, racialized discourses of inclusion and exclusion, even though organized around national imageries, refer inevitably to distinctions between the civilized and the uncivilized. These determine who, deservedly, can make claims to the material benefits of modernity. If we accept the idea of diaspora as the cultural politics of difference formed and fashioned in the crucible of racialized exclusion from modernity, then we can locate the continental "African" firmly within the African diasporic imagination. This is because of the latter's centrality to the cultural politics of difference, marked by its notions of originary claims to Africa itself.[8] African nationalism and African nationhood have all emerged from the cultural politics of difference from which Africa gets its diasporic character.

Diasporic identity connects persons of African descent in a global web of racial intimacy. It occupies the sentimental center in the Black transnational political alliances employed so successfully in the various nationalist struggles against colonialism and racial segregation. In the United States, it was the cement that tied Black immigrants and African Americans together in a political alliance aimed at breaking the strictures of white exclusivity and privilege. It was the justification for Black insistence on US intervention in the British West Indies during the 1930s in support of the region's nationalist anticolonial campaign (Fraser 1994). And diasporic imagination occupied the critical center in the challenges mounted against racial supremacy at least from the second decade of the twentieth century onward. This period of struggle was ushered in by the Back to Africa movement of the Universal Negro Improvement Association (UNIA) headed by Jamaican Marcus Garvey. It continued with the Black nationalist struggle for civil rights during the 1960s and 1970s.

Diasporic identity needs to be distinguished from ethnicization, which is the process of heterogeneous cultural accommodation. It is the cultural politics of difference that responds to racial exclusion from the modern national space and its material benefits. It is framed by memories of a collective history rooted in common origins. The form, nature, and intensity of exclusionary practices differ across space, time, and social position. This explains the lack of fixity in the diasporic imagination. Diasporic identity has to respond to the conjunctures of time, place, and position. It is also conditioned by possibilities for inclusion in the racial state offered through the acquisition of nonracialized attributes of belonging. Possession of these attributes is integral to the process of cultural and social hybridization that is at the root of modernity.[9] Blacks in the territorial space of Africa, the Caribbean, North America, and Europe can successfully make material, cultural, social, and ideological claims to modernity through the acquisition of social, cultural, and economic capital. These are so integrally related to modernity, and are so constitutive of it, that they meliorate and even eviscerate representations and practices of racial exclusion for those who possess them. At the same time, racialized exclusion is indispensable to modernity because of its role in the organization of the division of labor. Claims for inclusion in the nation-state made exclusively on grounds of racial accommodation can never be entertained. This is true particularly for those with originary claims to Africa, explaining the universality and pervasiveness of Black diasporic consciousness.[10]

Thus, hybridization can complicate racialized discourses of exclusion around which diasporic identity is organized. We may understand the material expressions of diaspora as the structural politics of race.[11] Possibilities for inclusion lend themselves to a politics of deconstruction in which resources available to those who have acquired the nonracialized attributes of modernity are available to be deployed against racially constructed exclusionary practices. This deepens the ambiguities and contradictions. Diasporic identity can, at one and the same time, challenge and collude with the racial state. Such conflicting tendencies have increased significantly with the universalizing impetus of neoglobalization. By the latter, I refer to the most recent innovations in communication and organizational technology, the development of new transportation efficiencies, the emergence of seamless networks of global production, consumption, and finance, and the complex of legitimating ideologies that allow their dispersal, application, and derivative institutionalized practices. In the merger of the global and the local, there is a withering away of the jurisdictional and legal power of the nation-state. This is accompanied by the erosion of the latter's political, economic, and cultural integrity. Thus, neoglobalization contributes to an intensification and universalization of diasporic intimacy as collective identities are globalized with the weakening of national alternatives. Transnational strategies become increasingly imperative for survival and success. There is need for quick and easy accommodation to multiple locations.[12] This has exposed modernity's secret: its rootedness in the massive movement (mostly involuntary and coerced) of populations dispossessed of the rights of ownership, belonging, and self-determination. This is precisely the impetus for diasporic imagination.

Neoglobalization therefore intensifies the very contradictions of the modern racial state that have created in diasporic identity possibilities for both challenge and accommodation. It offers increasing opportunities for inclusion in the modern state through the acquisition of cultural capital. At the same time, it intensifies significantly the processes that produce dislocation from place. Social mobility and migration challenge the racial state by making racial exclusivity increasingly untenable. But dislocation intensifies the diasporic imagination as persons turn to imaginary homelands in the formation of their identities. Thus, the weakening of the racial state has produced, ironically, an intensification of racially defined diasporic identity. This has to do with the integral relationship between race and conceptions of originary homelands.

For Black immigrants to the industrialized North, globalization has brought possibilities for transformation from victim to agent. It has provided access to rights and opportunities previously foreclosed by the racially exclusionary practices of modernity. As agents, immigrants can reverse the material outcomes of exclusion through imaginative reconstruction of their subjectivities, or through engagement with political struggle for inclusion. Diasporic identity facilitates both.

But neoglobalization comes with new complications for diasporic identity. Gilroy speaks of the "ambivalence" that is produced out of the "Diasporic yearnings" of those caught up in its transnational sojourns. He locates diasporic identity in the interstices between "residence" and "origin." This is what produces its "complex and ambivalent" character. At its base is a political culture that is "remembered and remade" (Gilroy 1997, 10). These memories and cultural reformulations (or remakes) respond, I would like to argue, to localized social geographies. The North Atlantic is the actual and desired destination for the vast majority of Black immigrants. There, they become inserted into white national spaces constructed out of white imaginations of exclusive racial belonging. They join a growing number of Black immigrants, some from their own countries, who, like themselves, are responding to the intensification of conditions of neoglobalization. The development of transportation and communication technologies greatly facilitates diasporic connections to other local and national locations, to their countries of origin, and to Africa. All these contribute to an intensification of diasporic imaginaries across fragmented geographies. At the same time, immigration deepens notions of essentialized racial difference. As immigrants with non-European origins become inserted into exclusively white national spaces, they join with those historically engaged in racial confrontation. This structural politics of race contributes to a heightened sense of racial consciousness. As diasporic intimacy increases, ambiguous national affinities that meliorate racial conflict give way to the cultural politics of transnational racial identity. Immigration also produces contradictory tendencies by introducing national distinctions into racially defined communities. This is occurring at a time of increasing social mobility. Successful challenges to the exclusionary practices of race and the presence of skilled and educated immigrants within racial communities open up opportunities that were previously foreclosed on racial grounds. These together can unleash centrifugal forces introduced by increasing diversification in socioeconomic status and by diffuse attachments to different nationally and culturally defined communities.

Such conflicting tendencies of diasporic identity have become evident in the collective self-representations of West Indian immigrants in the San Francisco Bay area of northern California. West Indian identity emerges as confrontation with and negotiation of the racialized terrain of the United States. At the most basic level, West Indians are forced to define themselves, collectively and individually, in relation to and against the African American community to which they are racially bound. Their social positioning circumscribes the choices of identity available to them. The social economics of the West Indian community have been shaped by what may be termed the materialities of location. Northern California provides abundant opportunities for the successful absorption of skilled and educated West Indian immigrants. There are very few opportunities for employment available to those among them with limited education and few skills. Because of this, the West Indian immigrant community is almost exclusively middle class. This has to do with the "pull factors" of West Indian immigration that operate against the unskilled and low-skilled in northern California while favoring the qualified and educated. The overwhelming presence of Mexican, Latino, and Pacific Rim immigrants in the labor-intensive and service sectors of the California economy has had the effect of shutting out the unskilled and low-skilled West Indian. As a result, success and achievement have become central themes in West Indian diasporic identity. These are publicized in rituals and performances of West Indian identity and are inscribed in popular understandings of the West Indian diaspora.[13] Those without the social and economic capital of the middle and professional classes are marginalized, isolated, and excluded. They become invisible in the public face of the West Indian community. In this way, diasporic identity imposes the expectation of success and achievement that supports practices of selective inclusion and exclusion in the community's social reproduction.

Achievement and success can signal insertion into the national space. For West Indians in the San Francisco Bay area, such insertion is circumscribed by the exclusionary practices of race in the peoplehood of the United States. The contradiction is resolved through a cultural politics of difference that locates West Indians outside the national terrain of the United States on nationalist and cultural rather than racial grounds. In other words, the West Indian community responds to racial exclusion by fashioning its identity around notions of national origin and cultural difference. While diasporic identity emerges inevitably out of practices of racial exclusion, it can become organized around notions of belonging devoid of racial signification. In its national and cultural expression, West Indian identity becomes incompatible with notions of American belonging. This mitigates challenges to American discourses of racial exclusion. It serves also to differentiate West Indians from the racially defined identity of African Americans. Such differentiation is cast in cultural and national terms.

In their diasporic constructions, West Indians elicit popular essentialized imageries about the West Indies in the construction of their identity. They engage in symbolic displays, rituals, aesthetics, and poetics that confirm and reinforce notions of their exotic foreignness. These accommodate American racist notions of the West Indian as exotic, hypersexual, fun loving, and given to bacchanalian excesses. Deracination provides access to the materialities of American modernity. It positions West Indians firmly within the group of permanent foreigners identified with California's technological and financial success.

Diaspora can act to manage the contradiction between the imperatives of heterogeneity on the one hand and racial exclusion on the other. It does so through notions of transnational belonging. This delinks diasporic subjects from issues of nationalist concern. It creates predispositions for disengagement with racial challenges. Identification as "foreign" preserves the myth of racial purity while blunting charges of discrimination by domestic minorities. In the final analysis, diasporic identity cannot escape racial characterization by hiding behind notions of transnational belonging. Despite efforts to escape racial characterization, West Indians are forced to accommodate themselves to white racist imageries of their exoticization.

There are also forces that impel immigrants to a racial identification with domestic minorities. This has to do with the ineluctable association between race and diasporic identity. The white racial imaginary is pervasive in the construction of American peoplehood and belonging. So are notions of racial inferiority tied to myths of origin outside of Europe. Immigrants to the United States cannot escape the inevitability of this racial identification. For this reason, West Indians in the United States are marked as Black. They cannot escape the implications of racial identity. So they are forced to participate in the African American material politics of difference and in the structural politics of race. In the process, they become inserted into alternative forms of diasporic consciousness that tie them to African Americans. The post–World War II successes of African American challenges to exclusionary racial practices have opened up opportunities for upward mobility under the rubrics of "affirmative action," "civil rights," "equal opportunity," "voting rights," and so on. The West Indian middle class is particularly well placed to exploit these opportunities. This has become quite evident in California. West Indians make claims to these opportunities on racial grounds. They do so in order to exploit the significant political strength of the African American community, particularly in Los Angeles and the San Francisco Bay area. Increased access to opportunity emerged in response to massive political mobilization during the civil rights era of the 1960s and 1970s (Fisher 1992; Horne 1995; Dymally 1972; Sonenshein 1993; Wyman 1987). Black political clout in California has brought with it considerable access to public and private sector resources. The Black West Indian middle class has been able to insert itself into these racially defined spaces created by African American political power. This is reflected in the growth of the West Indian population in Los Angeles from around five hundred before 1950 to around fifty thousand by the early 1990s. Much of this growth occurred after the mid-1960s (Justus 1994, 131).

Race is the critical ingredient in gaining access to the opportunities created by African American political mobilization. Because of this, West Indians are forced into racial identification with African Americans. In this way, they are assured of protection against the exclusive claims of a white peoplehood. This complicates their diasporic identity. As a model minority, they reject racial identification and engagement with American racial politics. But diasporic engagement with African Americans demands invocation of a Black racial commonality. So West Indians accommodate themselves to two conflicting notions of diasporic consciousness. The first relates to their identity as West Indian, and the second to their identity as Black. The two are not compatible, because West Indian identity functions to signify their separation from the racialized African American. While both subjectivities are deployed against the material implications of white exclusionary practices, West Indianness becomes a means of discursive separation from the cultural, social, and nationalist politics of African Americans. Blackness, on the other hand, elicits identification with the latter's material politics. The distinction is important. While Black identity is necessary for the contestation of white supremacy, West Indian identity is symbolically deployed in collusion with it.

West Indian immigrant presence in the United States provides a concrete example of the ambiguities and contradictions of diasporic imagination that have received attention from scholars like Paul Gilroy (1997). As West Indians, these Bay Area immigrants symbolically reject racial identification with African Americans. They also relinquish claims to American peoplehood by accommodating to their role as permanent foreigners. As nonracial non-Americans, their access to the materialities of success is considerably enhanced. At the same time, West Indians cannot escape the material consequences of their racialization. This impels them into political identification with African Americans under the broad rubric of Black diasporic consciousness.

West Indian identity in the San Francisco Bay area also highlights the relationship between social positionality and diasporic imagination. West Indian middle-class status precludes participation in the poetics and aesthetics of African American Black diasporic expression, given the latter's association with historicist understandings of racial inferiority. It also precludes originary claims to Africa, given the racial implications of these claims. Thus, West Indian Black identity is confined to deployment in the materialities of institutional, local, and national politics. By this, I mean that Black (as opposed to West Indian) identity is deployed in the structural arena of political engagement with racial exclusion. West Indians join Black professional organizations, support Black causes nationally and internationally, and align with African Americans in local and national politics. They do not, however, engage in the social and cultural practices of African American subjectivity. The point here is that, like all identities, diasporic identity has to be contextualized if its ambivalences and contradictions are to be understood and explained. West Indians are Black in certain contexts, when they are engaged with the materialities of their American existence. In other contexts, they resist Black and American identification altogether.

There is a profound relationship between identity and social geography. The West Indian immigrant community in the San Francisco Bay area differs in important respects from the larger West Indian immigrant communities on the East Coast of North America. It is relatively small, numbering fewer than ten thousand. Its members are not concentrated in defined localities of homologous residential concentration. Rather, West Indians are spread throughout the region in San Francisco and Alameda Counties, in the East Bay, in Peninsula counties, and in the city of San Jose. Most came to the area from elsewhere in the West Indian diaspora rather than directly from the West Indies. Decisions to relocate are made because of offers of jobs or because of company transfers. Some move after being stationed at military bases in the area. Others come as students, studying in one of the area's colleges or universities. Many come as dependent and nondependent family members or because they are able to use their friendship networks to secure jobs. In socioeconomic terms, many are middle to upper-middle class.

The San Francisco Bay area is one of the most ethnically diverse regions in the United States and a prime location for immigrants, particularly from Asia and Latin America. Along with Los Angeles, it is the host community to a significant proportion of the 8 million foreign-born residents in California's total population of 32.4 million (1996 figures). These immigrants constitute 33 percent of all foreign-born residents in the United States and 25 percent of all California residents. Because of their numbers, immigrants and their families enjoy a high degree of visibility. This lends itself to both positive and negative assessments of their desirability, worth, and merit in the cognitive constructions of "mainstream" Americans, both white and Black. These understandings apply differentially to immigrants based on their particular countries and regions of origin.

The historical construction of difference in California has produced three broad understandings of the diasporic populations from the Global South. These understandings apply differentially to West Indians. Their Blackness allows location in the racialized space of the African American. Their "foreignness" supports location in two cognitively constructed spaces. The first is the one occupied by the "undesirable" grouping of Mexican and Latino immigrants. The second is the diasporic space of the "model minority" occupied by the Asian immigrant. West Indian identity is organized around representations and practices of this model minority. Because of this, they are not associated in the popular imagination with the "undesirables." At the same time, they have available to them a racialized Black identity.

Preexisting generalized notions of West Indianness inform West Indian diasporic identity in the San Francisco Bay area. Unlike Latinos, West Indians are identified in popular consciousness as a "model minority" characterized by ideals of success similar to the white mainstream population of the United States. This is notwithstanding the occupational similarities between the West Indian majority living mostly on the East Coast of the United States and Latino immigrants on the West Coast. Both groups are primarily low-wage service-sector workers. As a diasporic construct, the model minority is disciplining, self-regulating, and segregating. It is also racially specified, since it refers only to immigrants from the Global South. It is one element in the technology of American racial control, applying the universalistic logic of merit in the service of racial segregation and regulation. Accordingly, different racial groups are understood to get what they earn and deserve. Model minorities are understood to have overcome obstacles of poverty and migratory disruption to achieve, on merit alone, middle- and upper-middle-class socioeconomic status (Fong 1989; Yong-Jin 1994; Petersen 1966; Steinberg 1981). As a diasporic construction, the model minority receives its importance as a legitimizing trope of white supremacy because of its deployment in the structural politics of race against charges of racial (and racist) exclusivity. It highlights and celebrates possibilities for the successful meritocratic incorporation of racial minorities into the exclusive social and economic preserves of whites. It serves as a negation of claims of racism. Thus, conservative scholars have used the putative success of West Indians to refute arguments that African American poverty stems from the pervasive effects of racial discrimination (Glazer and Moynihan 1963, 35; Sowell 1978, 41). The model minority requires deracination and rejection of claims to American belonging. Because the socioeconomic incorporation of the model minority is not understood symbolically as racially transgressive in a way that it would be for national minorities, it leaves the racial order unchallenged.

Claims made about West Indian success are much more important for the part they play in the ideological terrain of race relations than for what they say about the material realities of the West Indian immigrant presence. West Indians, collectively, are not better off than African Americans (Kasinitz 1988; Butcher 1994; Farley and Allen 1987). They face the same barriers to racial inclusion. Evidence to the contrary notwithstanding, the myth of the model minority continues to persist in popular understandings of the West Indian immigrant. It receives constant reinforcement both from within and outside West Indian communities and is sustained by the practice of highlighting West Indians who have risen to positions of national prominence as examples of West Indian universal success.

The model minority myth also highlights the potential for the diasporic imagination to expose heterogeneity as the critical ingredient in the construction of modernity. It challenges and contests the racial exclusivity of the modern state and its homogeneous discourse. The racial link between immigrants and racial minorities intensifies this challenge on two counts. The first is through the links forged between the latter and the broader diaspora in ways that contest claims to national and racial exclusivity made by the nation-state. The second is by the intensification of immigrant insertion into racially exclusive arenas on grounds other than race. These immigrants are accommodated because their identities are culturally and transnationally rather than racially defined. But the fact of their accommodation cannot but break the stranglehold of racial exclusivity. Moreover, opportunities for accommodation cannot be separated from successes in the struggle waged by national minorities against racial exclusivity.

At the same time, the model minority highlights the contradictions of diasporic identity. Diaspora can collude with the state to shore up its racial character by undermining challenges to its exclusionary practices. This opens the way for the masking of the state's practices of racial exclusivity, which become hidden behind the trope of cultural inferiority applied to its racialized minorities.

In the final analysis, diasporic subjectivity bridges the gap between modernity's demands for racial heterogeneity and hybridity on the one hand, and capitalism's demand for racial exclusivity to support its imperative of a racial division of labor on the other. Neoglobalization has intensified this contradiction with a resultant deepening and widening of diasporic consciousness. But diaspora may very well be the Achilles' heel of modernity. Its intensification comes with the possibility of undermining the racial state even while it continues to serve its purpose.

NOTES

1. This argument is cogently made by David Theo Goldberg (2002, 14–35).

2. Benedict Anderson (1983) has proposed the idea of nations as "imagined communities."

3. This is a complexity that is well recognized by Stuart Hall (1999), who, with reference to the Caribbean, sees diasporic imagination as the vehicle of national inclusion because it challenges the very "binary conception of difference" upon which depends "the construction of an exclusionary frontier" (1999, 7).

4. The ambiguity and contradictory nature of hybrid subjectivity is well recognized, especially by those who study the Caribbean because of its history of both contesting and colluding with modernity. In the Caribbean and Latin America, hybridized practices have functioned universally as instruments of coloniality by naturalizing racialized hierarchies (Puri 2004; Marx 1998). Its possibilities and complexities are recognized by Stuart Hall (1999), Mary Louise Pratt (1991), and Edward Kamau Brathwaite (1971).

5. A distinction must be made here between "naturalist" and "historicist" understandings of Black inferiority. The former assumes a "prehistorical condition" that is "naturally incapable of development and so historical progress" (Goldberg 2002, 43). This has been superseded by a "historicist" discourse that relates to notions of "historical immaturity" that can be overcome through contact with and tutelage by the civilized. This allows differential incorporation of those with demonstrated attributes of reason and rationality into the arena of modern statist belonging, however circumscribed (Goldberg 2002, 36–80).

6. I use these dimensions of capital following Pierre Bourdieu (1977, 1984); see also Jonathan Turner (1991, 512–18). In Bourdieu's formulation, economic capital refers to the ownership and control of productive resources. Social capital refers to those prerequisites that determine location in the hierarchically organized status groups, aggregates, and/or categories and the social networks associated with them. Cultural capital refers to those "interpersonal skills, habits, manners, linguistic styles, educational credentials, tastes, and lifestyles" acquired by persons in their lifetime (Turner 1991, 512). Symbolic capital has to do with the recognized forms of deployment of social, cultural, and economic capital through ritualized and symbolic displays.

7. For the more orthodox formulations of dependency see, among others, Beckford 1972; Amin 1975; Amin 1976; Frank 1967; Wallerstein 1980; and Wallerstein 1984.

8. There is a seamless relationship between the political materialities of African nationalism (as anticolonialism) on the continent on the one hand, and the cultural politics of Black nationalist expressions such as Pan-Africanism, Black power, and so on, occurring outside Africa, on the other. The latter, in turn, have informed the cultural politics of Africa, such as negritude associated particularly with French West Africa, and Black consciousness in South Africa.

9. As a result, postmodern scholars propose hybridity as the inevitable challenge to the racial state and to modernity itself. See, for example, Gilroy 1993 and Bhabha 1994.

10. The case of Blackness is special because of Africa's role in transatlantic slavery and in the production of modernity. Other racialized constructions, organized around originary myths of homelands located outside of Europe and Africa, come with different implications for positioning in the space of modernity.

11. These would include African nationalism, Pan-Africanism, Black nationalism, Black power, Black consciousness, and so on.

12. Paul Gilroy (1997, 10–12) speaks somewhat pessimistically of the possibilities of this new diaspora, with the nation-state (national camp) representing its "negation." He sees in its "ambivalence" the possible transformation into an "unambiguous exile." From my own perspective, it is integrally tied to neoglobalization as the logical trajectory of modernity. The possibility of its negation through absorption in the nation-state does not rule out its transformative potential.

13. For a fuller discussion of this, see Hintzen 2001. The material for the ensuing discussion of West Indians in the San Francisco Bay area is taken from this work.

BIBLIOGRAPHY

Amin, Samir. 1975. *Accumulation on a World Scale: A Critique of the Theory of Underdevelopment*. New York: Monthly Review Press.

Amin, Samir. 1976. *Unequal Development: An Essay on the Social Formations of Peripheral Capitalism*. Translated by Brian Pearce. New York: Monthly Review Press.

Anderson, Benedict. 1983. *Imagined Communities: Reflections on the Origin and Spread of Nationalism*. London: Verso Books.

Beckford, George L. 1972. *Persistent Poverty: Underdevelopment in Plantation Economies of the Third World*. New York: Oxford University Press.

Bhabha, Homi K. 1994. *The Location of Culture*. Abingdon, Oxon., England: Routledge.

Bourdieu, Pierre. 1977. *Outline of a Theory of Practice*. Translated by Richard Nice. Cambridge: Cambridge University Press.

Bourdieu, Pierre. 1984. *Distinction: A Social Critique of the Judgement of Taste*. Translated by Richard Nice. Cambridge, MA: Harvard University Press.

Brathwaite, Edward Kamau. 1971. *The Development of Creole Society in Jamaica, 1770–1820*. Oxford: Oxford University Press.

Bryce-Laporte, Roy S., and Delores M. Mortimer, eds. 1976. *Caribbean Immigration to the United States*. Washington, DC: Research Institute on Immigration and Ethnic Studies, Smithsonian Institution.

Butcher, Kristin. 1994. "Black Immigrants in the United States: A Comparison with Native Blacks and Other Immigrants." *Industrial and Labor Relations Review* 47: 265–85.

Dymally, Mervyn M. 1972. "The Rise of Black Political Leadership in California." In *What Black Politicians Are Saying*, edited by Nathan Wright Jr., 32–43. New York: Hawthorn Books.

Farley, Reynolds, and Walter R. Allen. 1987. *The Color Line and the Quality of Life in America*. New York: Russell Sage Foundation.

Fisher, Sethard. 1992. *From Margin to Mainstream: The Social Progress of Black Americans*. 2nd ed. Lanham, MD: Rowman and Littlefield.

Fong, Colleen Valerie Jin. 1989. "Tracing the Origins of a 'Model Minority': A Study of the Depictions of Chinese Americans in Popular Magazines." PhD diss., University of Oregon.

Frank, Andre Gunder. 1967. *Capitalism and Underdevelopment in Latin America: Historical Studies of Chile and Brazil*. New York: Monthly Review Press.

Fraser, Cary. 1994. *Ambivalent Anti-Colonialism: The United States and the Genesis of West Indian Independence, 1940–1964*. Westport, CT: Greenwood Press.

Gilroy, Paul. 1993. *The Black Atlantic: Modernity and Double-Consciousness*. Cambridge, MA: Harvard University Press.

Gilroy, Paul. 1997. *Between Camps: Race and Culture in Postmodernity*. London: Goldsmiths' College, University of London.

Glazer, Nathan, and Daniel P. Moynihan. 1963. *Beyond the Melting Pot: The Negroes, Puerto Ricans, Jews, Italians, and Irish of New York City*. Cambridge, MA: MIT Press.

Goldberg, David Theo. 2002. *The Racial State*. Malden, MA: Blackwell.

Grosfoguel, Ramón. 2003. *Colonial Subjects: Puerto Ricans in a Global Perspective*. Berkeley: University of California Press.

Hall, Stuart. 1996. "What Is This 'Black' in Black Popular Culture?" In *Stuart Hall: Critical Dialogues in Cultural Studies*, edited by David Morley and Kuan-Hsing Chen, 465–75. Abingdon, Oxon., England: Routledge.

Hall, Stuart. 1999. "Thinking the Diaspora: Home-Thoughts from Abroad." *Small Axe* 3, no. 6: 1–18.

Hall, Stuart. 2000. "Old and New Identities, Old and New Ethnicities." In *Theories of Race and Racism: A Reader*, edited by Les Back and John Solomos, 199–208. Abingdon, Oxon., England: Routledge.

Hall, Stuart. 2002. "From 'Routes' to Roots." In *An Introduction to Women's Studies: Gender in a Transnational World*, edited by Inderpal Grewal and Caren Kaplan, 458–59. New York: McGraw Hill.

Hintzen, Percy C. 2001. *West Indian in the West: Self-Representations in an Immigrant Community*. New York: New York University Press.

Horne, Gerald. 1995. *Fire This Time: The Watts Uprising and the 1960s*. Charlottesville: University Press of Virginia.

Justus, Joyce Bennett. 1994. "West Indians in Los Angeles: Community and Identity." In *Imagining Home: Class, Culture, and Nationalism in the African Diaspora*, edited by Sidney Lemelle and Robin D. G. Kelley. London: Verso.

Kasinitz, Philip. 1988. "From Ghetto Elite to Service Sector: A Comparison of Two Cohorts of West Indian Immigrants to New York City." *Ethnic Groups* 7, no. 3 (December): 173–204.

Lemelle, Sidney, and Robin D. G. Kelley, eds. 1994. *Imagining Home: Class, Culture, and Nationalism in the African Diaspora*. London: Verso.

Marx, Anthony W. 1998. *Making Race and Nation: A Comparison of the United States, South Africa, and Brazil*. Cambridge: Cambridge University Press.

Petersen, William. 1966. "Success Story, Japanese-American Style." *New York Times*, January 9.

Pratt, Mary Louise. 1991. *Imperial Eyes: Travel Writing and Transculturation*. Abingdon, Oxon., England: Routledge.

Puri, Shalini. 2004. *The Caribbean Postcolonial: Social Equality, Post-Nationalism, and Cultural Hybridity*. New York: Palgrave Macmillan.

Sonenshein, Raphael J. 1993. *Politics in Black and White: Race and Power in Los Angeles*. Princeton, NJ: Princeton University Press.

Sowell, Thomas. 1978. "Three Black Histories." In *American Ethnic Groups*, edited by Thomas Sowell and Lynn D. Collins. Washington, DC: Urban Institute.

Steinberg, Stephen. 1981. *The Ethnic Myth: Race, Ethnicity, and Class in America*. Boston: Beacon Press.

Turner, Jonathan H. 1991. *The Structure of Sociological Theory*. Belmont, CA: Wadsworth.

Wallerstein, Immanuel. 1974. *The Modern World-System I: Capitalist Agriculture and the Origins of the European World-Economy in the Sixteenth Century*. New York: Academic Press.

Wallerstein, Immanuel. 1980. *The Modern World-System II: Mercantilism and the Consolidation of the European World-Economy, 1600–1750*. New York: Academic Press.

Wallerstein, Immanuel. 1984. *The Politics of the World-Economy: The States, the Movements and the Civilizations*. Cambridge, MA: Harvard University Press.

Wyman, B. 1987. "Roots: The Origins of Black Politics in the East Bay." *East Bay Express*, August 7.

Yong-Jin, Won. 1994. "'Model Minority' Strategy and Asian Americans' Tactics." *Korea Journal* 34, no. 2: 57–66.

Chapter 9

NATIONALISM AND THE INVENTION
OF DEVELOPMENT

Modernity and the Cultural Politics of Resistance

PERCY C. HINTZEN

COLONIAL NOSTALGIA AND THE
POSTCOLONIAL PARADOX

As the current crisis of globalization intensifies and economic, material, social, and political conditions deteriorate for many in the Global South, comparisons with the era of colonial rule are inevitable. The idea of descent into chaos with the departure of the colonial power has been almost *the* guiding idea governing understandings of the neocolonial era from the inception. In 1915, it informed and justified US intervention in Haiti, the first postcolonial Black republic (Trouillot 1990, 100–102; Millspaugh 1970, 38). Now, two centuries after Haiti's independence, images of chaos in the former colonies have led to what Lance Selfa sees as a "new respectability for colonialism" (2002, 9), pointing to assessments of the latter by columnists like Max Boot writing in the *Weekly Standard* (2002). Boot proposed the "sort of enlightened foreign administration once provided by self-confident Englishmen in jodhpurs and pith helmets" as a resolution to the postcolonial crisis. And, from a different perspective, ideas circulated during the era of colonialism about a possible future direction for countries under the colonial yolk are receiving fresh consideration.[1]

The crises of the postcolonial era and reflections about a past consciously experienced as colonialism have produced certain predispositions toward nostalgia. This is especially true for those who, on the surface, have derived the most benefits from colonialism's passing, benefits acquired particularly from the acquisition of the cultural capital of education, knowledge, skills, and capabilities as the basis of their power and authority.[2] Debates among these elites about the benefits of colonialism are pervasive. On September 4, 2005, for example, a Nigerian named Jerome Awala called for a return to colonialism on an internet forum citing a number of officials in his country who had done the same (*Punch* Opinion Poll 2005). Nigerians seemed "not capable of ruling themselves," given the evidence of the deterioration of public resources, public utilities, and public services with the end of colonial rule. His posting received immediate and numerous responses including one from "Dai" pointing out the "surprising" pervasiveness of the call for recolonization in Africa and citing the specific examples of Sierra Leone and Liberia in the aftermath of those two countries' civil turmoil. That postcolonial elites who may otherwise not have access to power, wealth, or status speculate about "recolonization" may seem profoundly paradoxical unless the current postcolonial era of globalization is viewed in its proper context. It speaks to a particular paradox of postcolonialism in which the poor and the powerless (those who have benefited the least from independence) are the ones whose commitment to the nationalist project remain most steadfast in the face of doubt and nostalgia among its elite beneficiaries.

The paradox of elite nostalgia and their counterintuitive uncertainty about the postcolonial condition cannot be resolved by a simple return to colonialism. First, this would undermine their elite status and its associated material benefits. Second, their elite status and material benefits are anticipated when viewed from the perspective of an ideology of progress contained in historicist narratives of modernity that pervade the worldviews around which these narratives are constructed. For one thing, these narratives come with the presumption of the developmental superiority of sovereign self-governance (self-rule) over colonial rule. Sovereignty becomes a condition of political modernity (Mill 1975).[3] And for the modern self, political modernity is its self-confirmation. Thus, governance becomes a necessary and absolute condition of the modern self. This gives rise to the paradox of elite nostalgia for the colonial past in the face of a cultural politics of anticolonialism, in various anti-Western and nativistic guises, among the urban and rural poor.[4] Why would the current condition of sovereignty, understood as progress, elicit a longing for a less than desirable past among the elite? The answer lies precisely in the integral way in which notions of material progress rest at the center of the historicist narrative. For the elite, self-governance in the face of material backwardness and decline becomes a contradiction in terms. How then can a modern self, constructed around the narrative of historicism, exist under conditions of a premodern political economy? The answer lies in the existence of modern enclaves within the persistent poverty of underdevelopment in the territorial spaces over which the elites exercise authorial power. These enclaves are linked in an intricate web of connections to global modern metropoles to which the elites can claim to belong by virtue of their modern attributes.[5] Because, as the historicist argument goes, the granting of sovereignty was premature, this modern elite, under the postcolonial condition, come to be identically positioned as the governing elite in the erstwhile colonial order: those who are the bearers of modernity. In this way, they are able to make sense out of their nostalgia without relinquishing claims to their own modern selfhood. Nostalgia reveals and confirms the historical immaturity of those among the formerly colonized with little or none of the attributes of cultural, social, and/ or economic capital.[6] The leadership of the few (elites) who have managed to acquire the attributes of modernity, understood in the historicist terms of progress, becomes transformed in their own eyes into a neocolonial form of patriarchy. Viewed in these terms, nostalgia reproduces and retains historicist discourse in its refutation of all national claims to modern selfhood. This gives legitimacy to the denial of the full participation of the national elite in the Global South in the affairs of the modern global political economy as equals.[7]

The dilemma for the postcolonial elite is that modern subjecthood is not merely rooted in the acquisition of modern capital (cultural, social, and economic). It is also forged out of the Enlightenment values of reason and rationality. To be modern is to be constituted by forms of post-Enlightenment civility. The racial and cultural links between the postcolonial elite and the masses, the very links out of which nationalism was forged, make futile any elite claims to modern selfhood when such claims are made on the historicist grounds of a modern/premodern distinction between themselves and the masses. The profound irony is that self-governance entails highlighting and emphasizing racial and cultural ties to the very masses from whom the elites must seek to separate themselves as a condition of their modern selfhood. The conditions under which a national peoplehood is forged serve to negate the claims the elites may have to modernity. They become hoisted by their own petard in a narrative of historicism that cannot escape its racial and cultural grounding. Their presumed "civility," notwithstanding their accomplishments, is cast in this narrative as nothing but a form of mimicry. It reveals "a reformed recognizable Other, *as a subject of difference that is almost the same (as a modern subject), but not quite*" (Bhabha 1994, 86). As such, the acquisition of reason and rationality by this elite Other is cast as insufficient for the historical task of their transition to modernity. Those emerging from colonization, notwithstanding the display by the few of modern attributes, are best suited for "subjugation," albeit under new conditions of globalization relying on "neocolonial" technologies of "indirect" rule. The postcolonial elite continue to lack the prerequisites for modern "citizenship" (Chakrabarty 2000, 32). Current conditions of crisis and decline provide confirmation that the formerly colonized were best suited for one or another form of suzerainty under the tutelage, regulation, and discipline of a white colonizer. Thus, their attempt at citizenship was premature, and nostalgia (for colonialism?) serves as its confirmation.

Postcolonial nationalism (as the argument goes), in its guise as modernity, produces nothing less than the sublation of a fundamental difference between modern subjectivity and its premodern antecedent in which the postcolonial remains mired. This is underscored by the artificiality of international relations. Here, the principle of equality among nations is easily rejected, in fact as well as in practice. Thus, nostalgia is the anticipated result of the inevitable "historical failure of the nation to come to its own" (Guha 1988, 43). It derives from the recognition by the once colonized of the superiority of colonial subjecthood. Current attempts at sovereignty have produced nothing more than premodern "underdevelopment."

FROM NATURAL HISTORY TO ECONOMICS

The particular version of historicist reason outlined in the previous section does not come without its challenges. Many have pointed to the ambiguities contained in its interior logic. The "failure" or "inadequacy" of the nationalist project can be conceded without their attribution to the developmental inferiority of postcolonial subjecthood. There is no necessary connection between failure and inferiority, as is assumed by historicist thought (Chakrabarty 2000, 31). The modern postcolonial condition, however materially underdeveloped, need not ensue from a "lack" or "absence" of the attributes of the modern subject.[8] The failure of the modern postcolonial project, notwithstanding the modern subjectivity out of which it is wrought, may lie elsewhere. The proof may rest in the continued commitment of the subaltern to the nationalist project of sovereignty, notwithstanding their rejection of a modernity cast in the historicist narrative of progress toward a Euro-American future. The critical feature of modernity may not be the forms of capital inscribed by colonial Europe but rather the Enlightenment values of liberty and equality. Modern subjecthood may ensue from the entanglement of these with tradition. Thus, the attempt by the elite to make claims to modern subjecthood on terms set by European coloniality is bound to fail on grounds of their patent artificiality. What needs to be contested, therefore, are not the fallacious claims of the failure of the colonized to acquire modern subjecthood, but the claims to an exclusive modernity made by Europe and its progeny. This is precisely the cultural politics of the subaltern.

Until the 1980s, beginning with the work of scholars engaged with subaltern studies (Guha and Spivak 1988; Prakash 1994), efforts by scholars from the

Global South to explain the failure of the postcolony remained trapped in the narrative of historicism. To justify their claims to modern subjecthood, many of these scholars enacted a shift in scholarly analysis from history to economics in a new historicist narrative of developmentalism. They authored new narratives of progress that positioned the colonial and postcolonial subject firmly in the domain of modernity. In doing so, they set out to challenge claims of their own "uncivilized" premodernity by turning to economics to explain postcolonial failure. While history posited a natural developmental order, the new discipline of economics saw state intervention as an impediment to the rational choices made by individuals and firms as the prerequisite for maximum efficiency in the functioning of the marketplace (Ricardo 1821; A. Smith 1937).[9] Material crises and poor economies could be seen to result from inappropriate forms of state intervention, including the intervention of the colonial state. Armed with the knowledge produced by the new discipline, scholars of the Global South embraced the logic of historical materialism in their analytics to explain the anomaly of an underdevelopment constituted by modern subjects. Many turned to Marxist analysis, specifically its argument that economic crisis was an inevitable outcome of modern capitalism. Marxism severed the association between the modern individual and conditions of economic plenitude or affluence. Indeed, it proposed the prerequisite imperative of a universal modern abstract individual as a condition for transition to modern capitalist forms. Hence, modern subjecthood could precede modern social formations. Whether colonialism was positioned in the modern or premodern epoch became irrelevant to claims for modern subjecthood. Theories of imperialism proposed by John Hobson (1948) and Vladimir Lenin (1996) cast European colonial expansion in economic terms as an inevitable outcome of capitalism. Lenin identified imperialism as "the highest stage of capitalism," the phrase he chose as the title of what was originally a pamphlet written in 1916. When Raúl Prebisch and others at the United Nations Economic Commission for Latin America argued that underdevelopment in the Global South was the product of relations of exploitation with the Global Metropolitan North, this new "dependency theory" was taken up by Marxists such as Andre Gunder Frank, who saw "these relations [to be] an essential part of the capitalist system on a world scale as a whole" (1972, 3). Dependency theorists, along with world systems theorists, placed colonialism and postcolonial formations firmly in the arena of modern capitalism (Wallerstein 1997). Accordingly, an integral link was established between colonialism and modern capitalism. These new formulations served to position the colonial subject squarely in the domain of the modern, imbued with modern subjectivity, since modern capitalist formations (and thus colonialism and postcolonialism) could not come into history outside of a "totalizing unity" fashioned out of the "dissolution of the hierarchies of birth [and by] sovereignty of the individual" (Chakrabarty 2000, 49). This totalizing "unity," as a fundamental condition of the equality located at the heart of modern progressive liberalism, negates the claims of the historical immaturity of the colonized.

The notions of equality, embedded in modern social formations of which colonialism is part, comes up against the historical discourse of difference through which the colonial Other is forged out of the historical immaturity of the "primitive." The suturing of modernity to European cultural and social forms and to the material conditions of metropolitan Europe served to highlight the differences between the colonizer and colonized and to cast them in historicist terms of civilization and savagery. These differences were so manifest that they became central to the development of the new discipline of anthropology in the nineteenth century. They sparked a subfield of inquiry in colonialism known as "cultural pluralism" (Furnivall 1948; M. G. Smith 1965; Despres 1967). Marxist economics provided a way out of this dilemma by relegating these differences to the realm of epiphenomenon in its presumption of a division of labor. Through Marxism, the colonial Other became transformed into a product of the distorted discourses of the state. Colonized subjectivity became a superstructural manifestation of "false consciousness." The true historical character of the colonized as an exploited proletariat in modern capitalist forms of the division of labor became transformed through the distortions of the colonial superstructure. The latter rendered invisible the base of structural order of the modern state constituted by capitalist relations of production.[10] In this manner, the colonized "native" came to be understood as nothing more than a product of colonial ideology and an epiphenomenal manifestation of the modern proletariat (Amin 1982, 1976). Colonialism was thus transformed into a "special case" of capitalism, or the product of its inevitable global development as imperialism. As a proletariat, the colonized thus were reconstructed into modern subjects.

Once Marxist scholars located colonialism, as a social formation, in the epoch of modern capitalism, then colonial immiseration could be explained. This was the basis for the shift away from history to economics. Thus, economics was invoked to explain the anomaly of modern subjecthood and uneven development. Immiseration could now be laid on the doorstep of capitalist exploitation and explained as the result of the appropriation of "surplus value" by the colonial capitalists. History, on the other hand, considered immiseration as a mark of inferiority.

The problem for Marxism rested in its economic determinism. While resolving the contradiction inherent in claims by poor and powerless colonial subjects to modernity, Marxism was unable to resolve new problems that emerged from the direction taken by anticolonial nationalism. If the colonized were members of the modern proletariat, then, following Marxist historical deterministic arguments, the movements of colonial liberation were destined universally to take the form of anticapitalist revolutionary struggles. This prediction ("post-diction," because it occurred in hindsight) proved false. As many nationalist movements took on capitalist and even neocolonial forms, scholars of the Global South were again faced with a dilemma. They had either to reject prior assertions of colonialism as a capitalist formation, or to move away from Marxism's deterministic presumptions. It is in opting for the latter that historicist narratives became reiterated and reinscribed in postcolonial studies. In a subtle shift away from Marxist economic determinism, scholars from the Global South began to argue that as a social formation, colonialism and the postcolony were overdetermined; that is, they were produced from "a fusion or merging of different processes and contradictions which nevertheless retain their own effectivity" (Hall 1996b, 231; see also Laclau 1971; Frank 1972). This allowed for the persistence of traditional identities and social formations even under conditions of capitalist modernity.[11] The colonial and postcolonial state was now understood to be "overdetermined." Overdetermination can be employed to explain the presence and participation of "primitive" traditional cultures in modern economic practices (Furnivall 1948; M. G. Smith 1965; Despres 1967). This was certainly the thrust of this argumentation for scholars working on colonialism and early postcolonial forms (M. G. Smith 1965; Kuper and Smith 1971; Furnivall 1948; Despres 1967). More recent scholarship, however, has turned the tables on these formulations by employing the idea of overdetermination in arguments for a modernized colonial subject under conditions of economic backwardness in the postcolony. As such, economic historicism can be retained as an explanation for "underdevelopment" without compromising claims for the modern subjecthood of the colonized and formerly colonized.[12] The notion of "overdetermination" allows for the separation of the economic, social, and cultural conditions of colonialism. In this way, it can support arguments for the participation of modern subjects in premodern economic formations. In an "overdetermined" postcolony, universal modernity does not necessarily presuppose universal modern economic conditions. The "ethic" of modernity, already universal, can be denied its material expression because "right-bearing individuals . . . seeking to maximize their own well-being" are prevented from putting their "energies and powers of reason to the task" (Comaroff and Comaroff 1991, 61). This is at the root of the nationalist anticolonial narrative. The "rationality" and "reason" of the (modern) colonial subject, expressed in a "desire to be modern" (Chakrabarty 2000, 36), may become constrained by the materialities of the colonial political economy. The postcolony may inherit such constraints as legacies of its colonial past.

The "desire to be modern" cannot be explained away as the "colonization of consciousness" (Comaroff and Comaroff 1991) or as an artificiality and anomaly inscribed upon the consciousness of a premodern self. It emerges almost as a natural product of rationality and reason when, according to Dipesh Chakrabarty (2000), it comes into contact with the values of the Enlightenment. Thus, nationalism, as an expression of this desire, can be understood only as a product and manifestation of a preexisting modern subjectivity. By this reasoning, the failure of the modern postcolonial project, as manifest in its manifold crises, cannot be attributed to the "lack" or "absence" of modern selfhood. It has to rest elsewhere. This is where economics, with its focus on the material, was reinscribed in postcolonial thought through a new historicist discourse of "uneven development." History and economics were conjoined in this new discourse. If colonialism was a constraining force on the economy, then the postcolonial project had to have, as its central mission, the eradication of these colonial constraints. Inscribed in the role of the postcolonial state was the scientific management of accumulation to ensure transition from "underdevelopment" to "development" as the modern material condition. The pedagogies of the state came to be organized around ideas of the acquisition of financial resources for investment and of the management and control of labor. Economics were transformed into a historicist narrative of growth and development and of the material conditions necessitated by them. The role of the state was to produce, organize, and manage economic growth and development.

The narratives of economic historicism are organized around notions of a colonial past characterized by conditions of material impoverishment. These narratives of colonial formation, understood as overdetermined, evoke nothing but memories of repression and frustrated desires to be modern among the colonized. The past is fashioned in terms of material deprivation in tales of enslavement, struggles for better wages and working conditions, colonial economic monopolies and exclusivity, economic discrimination, and white supremacy. The endemic crises and deterioration typical of most postcolonial economies can undermine these nationalist assertions. They can form the bases for challenges mounted against the nation-state and its pedagogy of development. This would be the threat posed by nostalgia, were it not for the paradox of its absence among those whose experience of deprivation is most acute and its presence among the elite beneficiaries of the postcolonial condition. Nostalgia may well be a longing for "something else" among those whose interests are served through the pedagogical deployment of economic historicism by the state. Its absence among those whose material deprivation is most acute lends added support to this assertion. Perhaps the ties between forms of economic progress and modern subjecthood are merely contingent, and it is the "something else" that binds the two together in the modern arena of nationhood. Thus, nostalgia comes with possibilities for revelation of that which is rendered invisible by the foregrounding of the economy and the privileging of the material in the new discourse of economic historicism. The latter may be revealed to be nothing but a profound distortion of modernity's constitutive elements. Nostalgia may signal a longing for what remains hidden, but what is critically present even though rendered invisible by modern nationalist discourse. In other words, modernity may have little to do with the economic conditions of mass production and consumption with which it seems to be inextricably tied.

CHALLENGING HISTORICIST DISCOURSE:
THE MOVE FROM PEDAGOGY TO THE PERFORMATIVE

Marxist analysis exposes a fundamental contradiction between the two imperatives of capitalist modernity: capitalism's imperative for a division of labor on the one hand, and modernity's imperative for a citizenship constituted of universal abstract individuals on the other. The contradiction ensues from capitalism's need for the production of difference in service of the division of labor. This is pitted against modernity's imperative for the citizen-subject, constituted by the Enlightenment values of individual equality and freedom. This may be considered to be the fundamental contradiction of capitalist modernity. For Marxists, it is the motive force for revolutionary transformation. Scholars of imperialism see colonial imperial expansion as the instrumentality through which the contradiction was contained, at least temporarily, at the national level (Amin 1976). Within the colonial formation, the crisis was contained through the deployment of historicist narratives of difference that, according to Homi Bhabha (1994, 152–54), produced naturalizing divisions between enlightened modern subjects and categorical "others" located at differing degrees of distance from rationality and reason. Through this process of "othering," the latter's claims to modern subjectivity are denied altogether or are, at best, conditionally and ambiguously accommodated. Bhabha sees these historicist narratives as being deployed "pedagogically." As such, they fundamentally distort modernity by rendering invisible the "signifying processes of cultural identification" integral to the production of modern subjectivities. Bhabha locates these processes in the realm of the "performative" (Kristeva 1986), that space of the (modern) nation where rests the "powerful repository of cultural knowledge that erases the rationalist and progressivist logics of the 'canonical' nation" (Bhabha 1994, 53; Kristeva 1986). The crisis of the postcolony, productive of nostalgia, may therefore rest with the "canonical nation" as a discursive construct of the state apparatus and its technologies. This canon may misrepresent the postcolonial crisis as a failure of ethically and morally modern subjects to "become modern" in material terms. In other words, the crisis may ensue from a failure to apply the appropriate technical solutions to the problem. This justifies the deepening of the "rule of experts" (Mitchell 2002). The explanatory power of historical materialism and economic knowledge is deployed to explain this failure. What is needed, after all, is merely to follow the historical path and apply the technical knowledge of the already developed northern metropolitan countries. But the rejection of this path by those most dispossessed in the Global South and the nostalgic longings among historical materialism's beneficiaries point to deep and significant challenges to these narratives of modernity. They expose longings, however unconscious, for a modern condition that is freed from the imperative of a perpetual cycle of growth and material accumulation. In the paradox of their respective positions, they may be revealing and publicizing the centrality of the performative arena in modernity's construct, the very arena that is denied and negated in historicist notions of economic progress.

Thus, the nostalgia of the elite may derive from the profound antihistoricism of the performative. It may reveal the fundamental contradiction between the historicizing narrative of material progress and the "repositories of cultural knowledge" out of which modern cultural subjects are fashioned. Located outside the domain of the modern nation-state, modern cultural subjectivity may gain expression through oppositional cultural politics.[13] One may argue for the universality of modern cultural subjectivity, because cultural politics is always and everywhere deployed against the state. The performative, out of which nostalgia is forged, is located on the same plane of culture identified by Jean Comaroff and John Comaroff as

> the space of signifying practice, the semantic ground on which human beings seek to construct and represent themselves and others—and, hence, society and history. As this suggests, it is not merely a pot of mes-sages, a repertoire of signs to be flashed across a neutral mental screen. It has form as well as content; is born in action as well as thought; is a product of human creativity as well as mimesis; and, above all, is em-powered. But it is not all empowered in the same way, or all of the time. (Comaroff and Comaroff 1991, 21–22)

There are fundamental differences between these forms of modern cultural subjecthood and categories of subjectification that emerge out of the pedagogies of the state. The groupings produced by the latter are perpetually organized in political struggle for hegemony. The modern cultural subject becomes interpellated in positionalities constitutive of a more or less comprehensive and coherent world view that emerges out of state pedagogies. These serve the function of the division of labor. They take the form of differences organized around race, class, gender, language, ethnicity, tribe, and other forms of state-produced differentiation. They derive from ideologies of difference and are manifest in political struggles for hegemony.[14] Such struggles occur as much "within" the individual as within and among groups occupying different social positionalities. This is so because the individual subject that is produced pedagogically out of "the rationalist and progressivist logics of the 'canonical' nation" (Bhabha 1994, 153) is constituted as a "totalizing unity" inserted into mutually exclusive categories of differentiation (such as race, gender, class, tribe, religion, etc.). In reality, however, the modern subject is the product of multiple subjectivities occupying different (and even contradictory) social positionalities (as, for example, positionalities organized around relations of race, gender, occupation, status, etc.). The totalizing impetus of the canonical nation gives rise to conflicting pulls within the individual experienced as an internal "struggle." In reality, however, the modern individual subject is connected in a seamless web of culture (the performative) that is interpellated in the different social positionalities produced out of the pedagogies of the canonical nation. For the issue at hand, however, the relevant critical distinction is the one between national subjectification, discursively produced by state technology, and cultural subjectivity produced within the domain of the performative. There is, of course, a profound relationship between the two. In the final analysis, the struggles of cultural politics are directed at controlling "the cultural terms in which the world is ordered and, within it, power legitimized." (Comaroff and Comaroff 1991, 21). It is a struggle of the modern cultural self against the nation, its totalizing subjectifications, and its historicist narratives. The pedagogical gains entrance into nationalist constructions through the entanglement of the modern cultural subject with forms of subjectification that derive from the canonical nation. For example, the rooting of racial, tribal, ethnic, religious, and other pedagogically produced identities in "traditional" cultural forms acts to insert the latter, as performatives, into the national canon when they become the basis for nationalist assertions. The creole nationalism of the Caribbean, the various iterations of African socialism, and the various forms assumed by the postcolonial modern nationalist canon stem directly from the particularities of the relationship between the pedagogical and the performative in the production of the modern subject. The constantly changing outcomes of this relationship determine who secures control of the apparatus and technologies of the state and the "constructs and conventions" that "come to be shared and naturalized throughout a political community." (Comaroff and Comaroff 1991, 24). This is what constitutes "hegemony." It emerges out of struggles aimed at propagating the interests of one social group throughout society and coordinating such interests "with the general interests of other groups and the life of the state as a whole" (Hall 1996a, 423). As such, the production of the national canon of identity and its pedagogical deployment cannot escape its rootings in the performative arenas of culture. The apparatus and technologies of the state effect a distortion by transforming these cultural forms into totalizing differences and by creating new forms of distinctions (such as class and gender) that render invisible the networks of cultural performatives in which we are all entangled.

The argument being made here is that the modern nation is produced canonically by a statist discourse of economic progress and modern citizenship, the latter constituted by the liberal Enlightenment values of reason and rationality. The performative is discursively located outside the space of modernity. It is the domain of the premodern and the primitive. This exclusion becomes the source of nostalgia for a history that predates the modern nationalist post-colony. But it is a history "of the present," since the performative is integral to the production of modern subjectivities.

There are several varied "cultures of modernity" located both within and outside of the discursively produced arena of the modern nation-state.[15] They come into *political* play as hegemonic discourses and ideologies deployed through the instrumentalities of the state on the one hand, and as counterdiscourses and counterideologies posing different degrees of challenge to the state on the other. Modernity turns out to be nothing more than the deployment of the cultural forms of those with claims to being modern. What make these claims "modern," however, is their imbrication with the values of the Enlightenment that have become universalized through the European colonial project (Chakrabarty 2000).[16] Modern subjectivities are nonetheless cast in a different mold for those whose cultures are forged outside of the historical experience of western Europe. For these, the process of "othering" acts to deny their modernity. This is not at all the case for the cultural performatives derived from western Europe. Public/private and state/civil distinctions act here to insulate western European subjects from any claim of "premodern" immaturity. Their performatives are accommodated and explained within modernity's trope of "freedom," which permits expressions of cultural difference within the ambit of the modern nation. Thus, modernity is able to accommodate different cultural forms under the totalizing rubric of whiteness. These include ethnic, national, regional, and religious forms that exist within the national boundaries of nations organized around the pedagogical construct of whiteness. This is not the case for cultural "others." Their performatives are denied a place in the expressive spaces of modernity. Nostalgia may be a response to such denial and a manifestation of cultural repression. Through nostalgia, cultural performatives can be safely located in a "primitive" past. But as desire seeking expression, nostalgia is invariably directed against the national canon, understood to be the source of cultural repression. In the postcolony, it emerges in response to the totalizing and homogenizing impulse of the state experienced most intensely under a regime of economic historicism with its drive for growth and progress.

Thus, nostalgia is produced in the postcolony in response to the totalizing impetus of a historicist discourse of development economics that is incapable of accommodating the cultural performatives of former colonial subjects. The "othering" processes of categorization, now made necessary in the postcolony by the need for the scientific management of economic rationality, act to exclude "native" cultural subjectivities from the domain of the modern and to deny their expression in the construction of citizenship in the postcolony. This applies with particular force to categories of the "poor," the "rural," and the "peasant." All three emerge in modern economic thought as the embodied manifestations of "uneven development." They become significations of the "lack" or "absence" of *modern attributes* for development transformation. Their "desire to be modern" is denied realization by this "lack" or "absence." They are assumed to affect negatively the process of "becoming" a modern state. For this reason, they are targeted for management, organization, regulation, discipline, control, and containment. In this sense, they become an "invention" of modernity's discourse as "nonmodern" subjects. This process of invention was quite deliberative:

> Almost by fiat, two-thirds of the world's peoples were transformed into poor subjects in 1948 when the World Bank defined as poor those countries with an annual per capita income below $100. And if the problem was one of insufficient income, the solution was clearly economic growth. (Escobar 1995, 23–25)

The invention of the poor was necessarily and synergistically tied to processes of capital formation and the various factors associated with it: technology, population and resources, monetary and fiscal policies, industrialization and agricultural development, and commerce (Escobar 1995, 40). The production of these nonmodern subjects and the specification of the terms of transition to modernity posed a dilemma for the postcolony. Their management and organization demanded their incorporation into the modern nation as citizens. Such incorporation was articulated in the cultural linkages between themselves and the elite modernizers. In other words, *political modernity*, understood as the development of a cohesive citizenship, had to be culturally specified and organized around the performatives of those excluded from the modern economic arena because of "lack" or "absence" of modern attributes. This antinomy produced a form of schizophrenia among the elite, who found themselves squeezed between the economic rationalities of the modern and the cultural performatives of the premodern. The link between the performatives of those cast as premodern and the postcolonial nation negated elite claims to modern subjecthood, since the latter rested on the presumption of a modern civilized rational subject. Thus, the narratives of modernity and nationalism had to contain or resolve the dilemma produced by the extension of citizenship to the "subaltern." The exclusive role of the state as the instrument of economic development and the hegemony of the economic modernists became the twin bases for managing the contradictions, at least temporarily.

My argument follows in the wake of scholars such as Homi Bhabha (1994), Dipesh Chakrabarty (2000), Edward Said (1993), and Paul Gilroy (1993), all of whom see modern subjectivities as firmly rooted in what Bhabha calls the "performative." These scholars argue against the totalizing historicism of imperialism and the modern state. Through the instrumentalities of these totalizing discourses, the "subaltern" is positioned outside of the space of modernity. Discourse functions pedagogically (in Bhabha's formulation) as a technology of the modern state for the production of subordination. It is through these technologies that the "canonical nation" is constructed. In the production of subordination and exclusion, they render invisible the constituted modernity of the subaltern's subjectivity. The subaltern comes to be located on the constitutive outside of the canonical nation. This preserves intact the construction of the modern nation as one particular form of European (bourgeois) modernity. Progress is to be measured against the latter, as the ideal. But in the final analysis, European modernity is *culturally* constituted. This has led Chakrabarty (2000) to call for a discursive and analytic "provincialization" of Europe. Such provincialization, he argues, would reveal the cultural particularity that hides behind the distortions of a universalized and historicized modern political economy. It is the particularity of "white supremacy" in another guise. This is not to deny the universal significance of the Enlightenment values of freedom and equality in modernity's formation. Indeed, such values may be its distinctive features. But they are interpolated into different and existing cultural milieus. It is in this manner that modern subjectivities might be considered to be overdetermined. And an examination of such overdetermination and its different forms of articulation may well expose the different and multitudinous expressions assumed by modern subjectivities. Historical materialism denies such differences in its totalizing distortions, a denial necessitated by capitalism's imperatives of a racial and global division of labor.

The postcolonial dilemma emerges from the need to incorporate the subaltern into the modern state under the imperative of a division of labor. Anticolonial nationalism was organized through the cultural politics of resistance. It challenged colonial modernist and historicist discourse on cultural grounds. Such challenges were organized not as rejection of European modernity and its historicist implications but under conditions of its reaffirmation and even intensification, even though on economic grounds. The *politics* of nationalism was organized around the Enlightenment values of freedom and equality in what Antonio Gramsci would term a "war of maneuver." It was directed at the absolute replacement of the colonizers. Thus, it was a challenge mounted by "new forces" aimed at obtaining "a definitive (strategic) victory" (Gramsci 1971, 233). The "new" social forces of anticolonial nationalism were those of the subaltern. Their cultures and "world views," formerly excluded from modern colonial space, came to be positioned at the ideological center of the independence movements. Their *political* inclusion, however, was not accompanied by moral and ethical claims for their equality. The idea of their historical immaturity and inferiority was retained in nationalist discourse. New legitimizing and normalizing canons of subaltern subordination were organized around discourses of economic development.

The contradiction between modern political subjecthood, and economic inferiority and immaturity, was resolved in nationalist narratives by highlighting colonial anti-Enlightenment practices of exclusion. These exclusionary practices were posited as being responsible for the "failure" of the subaltern to realize their need for equality and the materialities of modernity. While independence achieved the former, the latter had to await the transformative agenda of the postcolonial state. Equal participation in the modern economy could not be achieved without sovereignty and independence. In this way, the objective of the postcolonial state was transformed into the acquisition of modern European cultural, political, and economic forms. In the nationalist canon, the granting of independence signified the realization of political modernity and the creation of the instrumentalities for economic modernity. In the process, the cultural agenda of European modernity became shrouded in discourses of nationalist aspirations. Otherwise, it would have come into conflict with the "cultural politics" of the nationalist movement around which the struggle against European domination was organized. Thus, while resolving the political problem, the postcolony introduced new dilemmas for progress by telescoping the performative into modern political organization as the basis of a national peoplehood. The "plane of culture" had to be regulated and disciplined as an imperative of the postcolonial modernist project. In other words, modern nationalist pedagogy, as its imperative, had to formalize cultural politics under the canons of the modernist postcolonial state (Crichlow 2005).[17] To do so, the invention of the modern postnationalist state was organized around tropes of economic (material) development. The prevailing narrative was one of political freedom (sovereignty and democracy) as the prerequisite for an economic rationality organized in the interests the (formerly) colonized. The expectation of betterment through the acquisition of the materialities of the colonial and colonizing middle classes brought the subaltern into this nationalist project. In this way, the rationality of economic development came to be inscribed at the pedagogical root of a totalizing and subordinating agenda of the postcolonial "canonical nation" (Crichlow 2005). While the postcolony was politically organized around the cultural politics of the performative, it incorporated historicist modernist discourse by privileging and publicizing the economy as the arena of statist organization. The ideological distortion shifted from notions of racial and cultural immaturity and inferiority to normalizing discourses organized around the absence or "lack" of the economic prerequisites for transition to modernity at the individual, socioeconomic, and nationalist levels. This shift occurred through the invention of development economics. Sir Arthur Lewis played a central role in this transformation and in the production of the new economic narrative. Through its material historicism, new categories of the poor, the peasant, and the village were invented. These became the objects of scientific knowledge, intervention, regulation, management, and discipline (Escobar 1995, 21–54).

Economic development was transformed into an instrumentality through which an unfolding process of state control of the subaltern was formalized. The new discipline emerged at the conjuncture of history when colonialism was under challenge, not only from the colonized but also from a newly assertive United States. It was accompanied by the formation of new international institutions that would eventually organize and manage a postcolonial global economy. It produced new justifications for the global division of labor as new assertions of modern citizenship were emerging in anticolonial national movements that challenged notions of racial and cultural immaturity. The United States was at the center of this reformulation, signaling a shift in the global geographic center of power and away from the discourse of colonialism. It was fitting, therefore, that the official announcement of the shift came from the first post–World War II American president. On January 20, 1949, President Harry Truman, in his inaugural speech before Congress, used the phrase "underdeveloped areas" for the first time. In doing so, he located countries of the world along a continuum measured by their level of production. Gross national product per capita was catapulted to become the standard measure of modernity (Sachs 1996, 239–40). In July of the same year, the International Bank for Reconstruction and Development, in one of its first forays into the "developing areas," proposed a program of a "multitude [of] improvements and reforms" for the economy of Colombia. The program emphasized the need for "careful planning, organization, and allocation of resources" through a "detailed set of prescriptions, including goals, quantifiable targets, investment needs, design criteria, methodologies, and time sequences" (Escobar 1995, 24–26). The new economism retained all of the discursive features of the old historicism.

The developed and the underdeveloped replaced civilization and savagery in the discursive divide of modernist thinking. As historicism, it posited narrow economic rationalities of production as the fundamental condition of modernity. Modern selfhood was now measured by evidence of economic acquisition.

The task for the new developmental economists of the Global South was to explain the absence of economic progress in their respective countries in terms other than immaturity or the "lack" or "absence" of rationality and reason. They took their cues from the anticolonialism inscribed in nationalist narratives. Rather than the immaturity of the colonized, the colonial system itself was cast as an impediment to modernity, now defined in terms of economic growth and development. For Arthur Lewis, the problem of underdevelopment had little to do with a "premodern" colonial subject. It rested with the practice of colonialism in maintaining a strict division of labor necessitated by the imperatives of ensuring a supply of cheap raw agricultural commodities and mineral products for the metropolitan center and of protecting metropolitan industry from colonial competition. Lewis, an unmitigated nationalist, challenged British colonial policy on these very grounds. He advocated strenuously for the industrialization of the West Indies as the means of breaking Britain's stranglehold on the aspirations of its colonial subjects to be modern. He interpreted the inevitable colonial opposition to West Indian industrialization as proof that the intent of British colonial policy was to protect its industries at the expense of the interests and desires of the colonized (Lewis 1949; Farrell 1980, 37). These interests and desires would inevitably produce modern political economies.

Arguments for industrialization of the colonies proposed by Lewis and other emergent development economists occupied the critical center in postcolonial thought. They recast the role of the state to be the instrument of national development and individual betterment. Under the state's formalizing control, everyone was to be its beneficiaries. What appeared disadvantageous in the first blush of classical economics were the very pillars upon which the transition to development was to be mounted. The challenge to traditional economics was mounted particularly in assessments of the role of "cheap labor." The colonial economic surplus was acquired through the comparative advantage of such labor. It was the principal basis for the organization of colonial exploitation and the primary cause of underdevelopment. Lewis assumed that the concentration on primary production produced a "large supply of surplus labor" that would become available once released from colonial control. This supply of labor could be easily absorbed into manufacturing for export. The colonial surplus produced by it would be transferred to domestic accumulation, with an increase in labor efficiency accompanying an increase in the rates of profits and savings. This was a fundamental condition of developmental transition according to the new mantra of development economics. Lewis extended his thesis to regions beyond the West Indies, such as Africa, with deep reservoirs of cheap labor in large "subsistence" sectors. Thus, the problem of underdevelopment came to rest squarely on the shoulders of a poor rural peasantry and an agro-proletariat. It was to be resolved by the introduction of modern industry to absorb these rural producers at significantly increased levels of labor productivity. They had to be managed and controlled. For evidence, Lewis turned to the experience of Britain during the industrial revolution (Lewis 1979).

Under nationalist control, cheap labor was transformed by Lewis into an instrument of development once there was a shift from the production of primary commodities to production for "the export of labour intensive manufactured goods to metropolitan markets" (Farrell 1980, 53; see also Lewis 1949). For the West Indies, the export of manufactured goods would eliminate the constraints of small markets and low market demand. In this new historicist "developmentalist" formulation, what was "lacking" or "absent" among the colonized were not the capacities and rationalities for economic liberalization (these were already present in the colonial middle class) but the capital, technology, and skills needed for the transition to economic modernity. Thus, the new developmentalist postcolonial state came to be defined around its role in labor mobilization, in attracting investment capital denied under colonialism, in formulating and providing fiscal and other incentives for investors, and in providing direct and indirect (infrastructural) support to attract industries. In combination, these measures would provide the basis for the absorption of the surplus labor released from inefficient rural agricultural production. The role of government was "quite feasibly" extended into the ownership and operation of modern industrial enterprises (Lewis 1949). Thus, the organization and management of the economy and participation in modern forms of production of goods and services became the defining features of the postcolonial state. From the new national canon organized around the ideology of economic developmentalism, a new pedagogy of difference emerged that distinguished between the postcolonial urban elite and the "poor," the "rural," and the "peasant." This new "historical narrative of difference" cast the acquisition of the cultural and economic capital of the Global North as the imperative for economic transformation to modernity. The role of the elite as possessors of this capital was to organize and run the postcolonial state as the primary instrument of modernity.

Economic historicism is the ideology of the modern nationalist elite. As a hegemonic formation, it derives its moral and social authority from a consensus over the desirability of individual material betterment and economic development organized under conditions of national sovereignty and citizenship (if not liberal democracy). The postcolonial state is the instrumentality through which this desire for modernity is realized. Notwithstanding their fundamental disagreements, all variants of postcolonial and anti-imperialist ideology are constituted by an identical historical materialism grounded in similar notions of economic development. They are all statist in character. As such, they are firmly embedded in the pedagogy of the "canonical nation" and its hegemonic and ideological constructs of economic development (Baran 1952; Frank 1967; Emmanuel 1972; Amin 1976; Thomas 1974).

The dilemma posed by postcolonial nationalism is its instantiation through the "empowerment" of culture. The nationalist movement brings "cultural politics" into the arena of power contentions. Such politics was the basis for challenging colonial power and ousting colonial rulership. As such, it was more akin to Gramsci's "war of maneuver." With the postcolonial state comes a fundamental transformation that closely resembles what Gramsci calls a "war of position." Stuart Hall summarizes Gramsci's formulation of this "transition from one form of politics to another." It occurs

in the emergence of modern mass democracy, a complexification in the role of the state and an unprecedented elaboration in the structures and processes of "civil hegemony." What Gramsci is pointing to, here, is partly the diversification of social antagonisms, the "dispersal" of power, which occurs in societies where hegemony is sustained, not exclusively through the enforced instrumentality of the state, but rather, it is grounded in the relations and institutions of civil society. In such societies, [political struggles are organized around] the voluntary associations, relations and institutions of civil society—schooling, the family, churches and religious life, cultural organizations, so-called private relations, gender, sexual and ethnic identities, etc. (Hall 1996a, 428)

This "complexification in the role and organization of the state" is organized around the deployment of two forms of power according to Jean Comaroff and John Comaroff (1991). The first relates to the exercise of "control over the production, circulation and consumption of signs and objects, over the making of both subjectivities and realities" by the state (1991, 22). In the postcolony, this "agentive" power is directed at the production of categories of economic actors and their differentiation in terms of their relationship to the modernist economic project. In this sense, what is being "empowered" are the western European modernist Enlightenment and economic values carried by the postcolonial elite. But the "empowerment of culture" in its political iteration incorporates "forms of everyday life" that are "hidden" proliferations existing "outside the realm of institutional politics, saturating such things as aesthetics and ethics, built form and bodily representation, medical knowledge and mundane usage" (Comaroff and Comaroff 1991, 22). This is where Bhabha's performative "signifying processes of cultural identification" enter into the domain of state power contentions as national subjectivities. It is, according to the Comaroffs, a "nonagentive" deployment of power. Its significance in the postcolony derives from the role it plays in hegemony. The association of economic development with historicist thinking and the interests of the former colonizers leaves economic historicism perpetually open to rejection. Radical economics openly challenges and exposes this association in its notion of neocolonialism. The inscription of ideas of freedom, equality, and social justice is not enough to eviscerate this association, especially in the absence of their realization in the material realm. Postcolonial politics, on the other hand, emerges out of the ascendance of the cultural significations of the formerly colonized. The culture of the colonizer does not disappear, however. It hides behind the historicist discourse of economic modernization. The performative signifiers of the postcolonial economic elite come to assume European culture forms and their derivatives. In this way, the latter become associated with economic modernity. For this reason, the economic struggle is engaged culturally, and vice versa. By this I mean that cultural politics might be organized around struggles over the incorporation or rejection of economic modernity. By the same token, hegemonic imposition of the ideology of economic modernism might come with challenges to "native" culture. In other words, cultural politics places economic modernism under constant challenge.

Notwithstanding statist organization around the economic canon, there is a perpetual struggle in the postcolony over the constitutive elements of the nation. At any one time, these elements are organized around the formation of a modernist nationalist alliance. This alliance, or what Hall, following Gramsci, terms a "historic bloc," comprises "leading elements [that] may be only one fraction of the dominant economic class" (Hall 1996a, 424). It is formed by the "winning over" of "strata of the subaltern and dominated classes . . . by specific concessions and compromises [and results in] the forging of 'expansive universalizing alliances'" (Hall 1996a, 424). Postcolonial hegemony is organized around the formation of this historic bloc. It emerges out of the deployment of power. In its "agentive" form, such power must serve the functional imperative of the postcolonial state "to raise the great mass of the population to a particular cultural and moral level which corresponds to the needs of the productive forces for development, and hence to the interests of the ruling class" (Gramsci 1971, 258). It is deployed through the promise of personal economic betterment. This becomes one of the bases of mass participation in the historic bloc.

There is another "nonagentive" form of power whose deployment is critical to the formation of the historic bloc. It acts through the inscription of the cultural form of the "dominated and subaltern classes" into the production of a national subjectivity. It serves to incorporate these classes into the national imaginary. Such incorporation is critical to the tasks of creating "national popular unity" and forming a "collective will" (Gramsci 1971, 182; Hall 1996a, 423). It makes possible the "coordination of the interests" of the "leading elements" of the elite with the popular interests of the dominated and subaltern classes. It produces and is produced by shared subjectivities that root the elite in the performatives of the subaltern and dominated classes. This rooting makes possible their "universalizing alliance."

The two forms of power exist in constant tension. The potential conflict that such tension can produce is mitigated by mass accommodation to economic development. When its promise of economic modernization and betterment fails, then nonagentive power may be deployed through the reiteration of "native" cultural forms, the "invention of tradition," and the rejection of "European" canons and performative culture. This is an ongoing struggle that produces constantly shifting "historic blocs of alliances" of "different specific social conformation and configuration" (Hall 1996a, 424). It occurs both within the historic bloc among its constituent elements, and through challenges mounted by social groups not included within its formation. It is a struggle for ascendance in the complex organization of national subjectivity. The struggle occurs among groupings organized around diverse cultural performatives. These can be inherited from colonial cultural struggles between the colonizer and the colonized, and/or they may reflect the diverse groupings of the colonized. They may also be produced out of new cultural forms that enter into the national domain through immigration, diasporic identity, or new penetrations from the Global North.

Thus, in the postcolony, European cultural forms retain their salience under the aegis of the historicist discourse of economic development. But the *political* incorporation of the Enlightenment values of freedom and equality into the nationalist canon also creates the conditions for the penetration of "native" performatives into the domain of state power contestations. Both are necessary for the production of a coherent modern citizenship and the development of a modern national imaginary. Thus, while white European civility, as the yardstick of modernity, was becoming transformed into the signifying practices of economic modernity, native subjectivities were being accommodated in the space of modern civil society. All of this has contributed to a postcolonial modernity that is overdetermined. "Pasts, encountered by capital as antecedents but not as belonging to its own life-process" (Chakrabarty 2000, 250), have become integral to its formation. Notwithstanding efforts at their negation, the participation of "native cultures" in the production of modernity has been exposed in postcolonial formation. Economic modernism has failed the task of totalization.

The performatives of the "pasts" produce constant challenges to economic historicism in their roles as the motive forces of change deployed against colonial and imperialist repressive orders. These "traditions" have become springboards for the exercise of "nonagentive" power. In this regard, culture holds sway. Tradition has come to inhabit our modern selfhood as anachronistic dispositions that "retain a power to haunt and deliver the shock of the uncanny" (Chakrabarty 2000, 252). It contains the possibilities for an alternative "imagination" because of its location outside of material history and within the performative domain of the "history of practice" (Chakrabarty 2000, 176). This is what is experienced as nostalgia. It emerges out of the heterodoxy of the practices of living that are pitted against the orthodoxy of the state and against the discourse of the canonical nation. It rejects the homogenizing impulse of the modern state.

Nostalgia, therefore, reveals a modernist agenda against the historicist state. It challenges material historicism in its current iteration as corporate globalism. Such a challenge emerges in the struggles over postcolonial modernity. As the promise of economic development fades for the subaltern and the dominated, modern postcolonial nationalism is freed from the totalizing and naturalizing distortions of its economic discourse. Modern postcolonial leadership becomes increasingly liberated from its shackles as the "signifying processes of cultural identification" move to the fore. Such a shift comes with the possibility of a "takeoff" to humanist development organized around the "history of practice." Cultural communities can acquire "the power to determine and control their preferred economic and political paths" (Cavanagh and Mander 2002, 107). And modernity can be freed from its bourgeois, liberal, capitalist distortions, which have proven so devastating to the human condition and an impediment to the realization of the Enlightenment values of freedom and equality. Nostalgia may be one manifestation of the diverse ways in which bourgeois capitalism and its historicism are being rejected.

NOTES

1. This perhaps more than anything else provided the rationale for the March 17–18, 2005, conference titled "Governance, Institutions and Economic Growth: Reflections on Sir Arthur Lewis's Theory of Economic Growth" at the University of the West Indies, Mona, Jamaica.

2. Cultural capital, following Pierre Bourdieu (1990, 124–25), relates to acquired knowledge, information, skills, habits, styles, and other modes and manners of behavior (Turner 1991, 512).

3. John Stuart Mill (1975, 278, 409–23), writing in the 1850s, argued against self-government for the colonies precisely on the basis of the historical immaturity of the colonized populations of India and Africa.

4. This is the very point made by Michel-Rolph Trouillot (1990) in his exegesis of Haitian political history. It is evident everywhere: for instance, in Rastafarianism in the Caribbean, and in the mass appeal of "Islamic fundamentalism" in the Middle East, which is now a response to what is generally believed to be the complicity of the elite in the region with globalization, considered to be a new form of coloniality.

5. Immigration laws and statutes of the countries of the North Atlantic that provide legal residence and citizenship to the skilled, qualified, and wealthy and that provide their children with access to educational institutions; the right of professionals and managers in the international public and private sectors to work anywhere their companies and institutions are located; and the freedom of the wealthy to acquire assets in countries other than their own, are all examples of the ways in which the national elites are involved in the web of global connections.

6. I use these terms following Pierre Bourdieu (1977) and Jonathan H. Turner (1991, 512–18). In Turner's formulation, economic capital refers to the ownership and control of productive resources. Social capital refers to those prerequisites that determine location in the hierarchically organized status groups, aggregates and/or categories, and the social networks associated with them. Cultural capital refers to those "interpersonal skills, habits, manners, linguistic styles, educational credentials, tastes, and lifestyles" acquired by persons in their lifetime (Turner 1991, 512). Symbolic capital has to do with the recognized forms of deployment of social, cultural, and economic capital through ritualized and symbolic displays.

7. This is evident in the roles these elites play in international affairs reflected, for example, in the organization of the United Nations Security Council and in the restriction of permanent membership with veto power to the United States, Great Britain, France, Russia, and China. It is also evident in the roles played by the North Atlantic in international public policy through the International Monetary Fund, the World Bank, and the World Trade Organization and in the domination by the G7 countries of the United States, Japan, Britain, France, Germany, Italy, and Canada (and, for a while, the G8 including Russia) in world affairs. China's persistent and insistent rejection of the terms of historicism may explain its ability to participate at the highest levels in the institutions of global power.

8. From the historicist perspective, it is this "lack" or "absence" that locates the colonized in the space of modernity's prehistory and that has confined them to "an imaginary 'waiting room' of history" (Chakrabarty 2000, 8).

9. Adam Smith (1937) proposed the "invisible hand" of the marketplace as the basis for economic efficiency manifest in the maximization of value. David Ricardo (1821) challenged mercantilist practices by positing comparative advantage as an argument for trade that is free from state regulation and intervention. These "economic" arguments may be viewed against arguments for a natural historical progress proposed initially by scholars such as Georg Wilhelm Friedrich Hegel (2004), for example, and particularly Herbert Spencer (1882–1898), who argued that the fittest were those who prevailed in historical competition, as indicated by their exercise of power and their acquisition of wealth. Thus, weakness and poverty were seen as indications of inferiority.

10. Karl Marx (1853), for example, writing on India, saw colonialism in a positive light as an instrument for the historical transformation of the backward areas to modern capitalism. Subsequent classical Marxists such as Bill Warren, following in this vein,

welcomed international capitalist penetration into the Global South for the very reason of its transformative potential. Scholars such as Ernesto Laclau (1971) grappled with the anomaly of underdevelopment in modern formations by proposing notions of bimodal forms in which capitalist and precapitalist modes of production exist side by side. Other scholars such as Paul Baran (1952) used the Prussian experience to argue that precapitalist forms can serve the interests of the capitalist state.

11. The work of the cultural pluralists such as Michael Garfield Smith (1965) and some identified with the dependency school such as Walter Rodney (1973) and Samir Amin (1989) are all versions of the work of scholars who pointed in this direction. Non-Marxist challenges to both formulations were mounted in the West Indies by scholars such as Lloyd Braithwaite (1953), who argued that the colonized of the West Indies were modern subjects organized hierarchically across positions of socioeconomic status.

12. The point here is that the postcolony could only have been produced by modernized colonial subjects.

13. This is revealed in many distinct social geographies and positionalities such as Rastafarianism, hip-hop, dance-hall, creole nationalist performatives, and so on.

14. This notion of ideology is consistent with Laclau's (1971) and Hall's (1981) adoption of the ideas of Louis Althusser. Individuals are understood to be "interpellated" into social positionalities organized around "images, concepts, and premises which provide the frameworks through which we represent, interpret, understand and 'make sense' of some aspect of social existence" (Hall 1981, 31; see also Larrain 1996, 48–51).

15. For example, "indigenous" communities are universally considered to be located outside of the modern domain. Groups marked as racially or ethnically inferior to the dominant group are ambiguously or partially incorporated into the modern space. These include non-European racial and cultural minorities in the Global North, and members of social groups positioned lower down in the status order in the Global South because of limited possession of the cultural and symbolic capital of modernity.

16. In other words, modern subjectivities are "overdetermined" and hybridized. However, their singular characteristic is that they all contain elements of Enlightenment values in their performatives.

17. Michaeline Crichlow (2005) makes this critical point in formulating a historical anthropology of Jamaican rural smallholders. Her distinction between formalization and informalization in the economic arena of rural production mirrors the distinction being made here in the political arena.

BIBLIOGRAPHY

Amin, Samir. 1976. *Unequal Development: An Essay on the Social Formations of Peripheral Capitalism*. Translated by Brian Pearce. New York: Monthly Review Press.

Amin, Samir. 1982. "Crisis, Nationalism, and Socialism." In *Dynamics of Global Crisis*, by Samir Amin, Giovanni Arrighi, Andre Gunder Frank, and Immanuel Wallerstein, 167–232. New York: Monthly Review Press.

Amin, Samir. 1989. *Eurocentrism*. New York: Monthly Review Press.

Baran, Paul A. 1952. "On the Political Economy of Backwardness." *Manchester School* 20, no. 1 (January): 66–84.

Bhabha, Homi K. 1994. *The Location of Culture.* Abingdon, Oxon., England: Routledge.

Boot, Max. 2002. "Lessons of a Nuclear North Korea." *Weekly Standard* 8, no. 7 (October).

Bourdieu, Pierre. 1977. *Outline of a Theory of Practice.* Translated by Richard Nice. Cambridge: Cambridge University Press.

Bourdieu, Pierre. 1990. *The Logic of Practice.* Translated by Richard Nice. Stanford, CA: Stanford University Press.

Braithwaite, Lloyd. 1953. "Social Stratification in Trinidad: A Preliminary Analysis." *Social and Economic Studies* 2, no. 2: 5–175.

Cavanagh, John, and Jerry Mander, eds. 2002. *Alternatives to Economic Globalization: A Better World Is Possible; A Report of the International Forum on Globalization.* San Francisco: Berrett-Koehler.

Chakrabarty, Dipesh. 2000. *Provincializing Europe: Postcolonial Thought and Historical Difference.* Princeton, NJ: Princeton University Press.

Comaroff, Jean, and John Comaroff. 1991. *Of Revelation and Revolution.* Vol. 1, *Christianity, Colonialism, and Consciousness in South Africa.* Chicago: University of Chicago Press.

Crichlow, Michaeline A. 2005. *Negotiating Caribbean Freedom: Peasants and the State in Development.* Lanham, MD: Lexington Books.

Despres, Leo A. 1967. *Cultural Pluralism and Nationalist Politics in British Guiana.* Chicago: Rand McNally.

Emmanuel, Arghiri. 1972. *Unequal Exchange: A Study of the Imperialism of Trade.* Translated by Brian Pearce. New York: Monthly Review Press.

Escobar, Arturo. 1995. *Encountering Development: The Making and Unmaking of the Third World.* Princeton, NJ: Princeton University Press.

Farrell, Terrence. 1980. "Arthur Lewis and the Case for Caribbean Industrialisation." *Social and Economic Studies* 29, no. 4 (December): 52–75.

Frank, Andre Gunder. 1967. *Capitalism and Underdevelopment in Latin America: Historical Studies of Chile and Brazil.* New York: Monthly Review Press.

Frank, Andre Gunder. 1972. "The Development of Underdevelopment." In *Dependence and Underdevelopment: Latin America's Political Economy,* by James D. Cockcroft, Andre Gunder Frank, and Dale L. Johnson, 3–18. Garden City, NY: Anchor Books.

Furnivall, John Sydenham. 1948. *Colonial Policy and Practice: A Comparative Study of Burma and Netherlands India.* Cambridge: Cambridge University Press.

Gilroy, Paul. 1993. *The Black Atlantic: Modernity and Double-Consciousness.* Cambridge, MA: Harvard University Press.

Gilroy, Paul. 1997. *Between Camps: Race and Culture in Postmodernity.* London: Goldsmiths' College, University of London.

Gramsci, Antonio. 1971. *Selections from the Prison Notebooks.* Translated by Quintin Hoare and Geoffrey Nowell Smith. New York: International Publishers.

Guha, Ranajit. 1988. "On Some Aspects of the Historiography of Colonial India." In *Selected Subaltern Studies,* edited by Ranajit Guha and Gayatri Chakravorty Spivak, 37–44. New York: Oxford University Press.

Guha, Ranajit, and Gayatri Chakravorty Spivak, eds. 1988. *Selected Subaltern Studies.* New York: Oxford University Press.

Hall, Stuart. 1996a. "Gramsci's Relevance for the Study of Race and Ethnicity." In *Stuart Hall: Critical Dialogues in Cultural Studies,* edited by David Morley and Kuan-Hsing Chen, 411–40. Abingdon, Oxon., England: Routledge.

Hall, Stuart. 1996b. "The Meaning of New Times." In *Stuart Hall: Critical Dialogues in Cultural Studies*, edited by David Morley and Kuan-Hsing Chen, 223–37. Abingdon, Oxon., England: Routledge.

Hall, Stuart. 1981. "The Whites of Their Eyes: Racist Ideologies and the Media." In *Silver Linings: Some Strategies for the Eighties*, edited by George Bridges and Rosalind Brunt, 28–52. London: Lawrence and Wishart.

Hegel, Georg Wilhelm Friedrich. 2004. *Hegel's Preface to the Phenomenology of Spirit*. Translated by Yirmiyahu Yovel. Princeton, NJ: Princeton University Press.

Hobson, John A. 1948. *Imperialism*. Rev. ed. London: George Allen and Unwin.

Kristeva, Julia. 1986. "Women's Time." In *The Kristeva Reader*, edited by Toril Moi, 187–213. Oxford: Blackwell.

Kuper, Leo, and M. G. Smith, eds. 1971. *Pluralism in Africa*. Berkeley: University of California Press.

Laclau, Ernesto. 1971. "Feudalism and Capitalism in Latin America." *New Left Review* 67 (May–June): 19–38.

Larrain, Jorge. 1996. "Stuart Hall and the Marxist Concept of Ideology." In *Stuart Hall: Critical Dialogues in Cultural Studies*, edited by David Morley and Kuan-Hsing Chen, 47–70. Abingdon, Oxon., England: Routledge.

Lenin, Vladimir Ilyich. 1996. *Imperialism: The Highest Stage of Capitalism*. London: Pluto Press.

Lewis, Arthur. 1949. "The Industrialization of the British West Indies." *Caribbean Economic Review* 11, no. 1: 1–53.

Lewis, Arthur. 1954. "Economic Development with Unlimited Supplies of Labour." *Manchester School* 22, no. 2 (May): 139–91.

Lewis, Arthur. 1979. "The Dual Economy Revisited." *Manchester School* 47, no. 3 (September): 211–29.

Marx, Karl. 1853. "The British Rule in India." *New York Daily Tribune*, June 25.

Mill, John Stuart. 1975. *Three Essays*. Oxford: Oxford University Press.

Millspaugh, Arthur Chester. 1970. *Haiti under American Control, 1915–1930*. Westport, CT: Negro Universities Press.

Mitchell, Timothy. 2002. *Rule of Experts: Egypt, Techno-Politics, Modernity*. Berkeley: University of California Press.

Prakash, Gyan. 1994. "Subaltern Studies as Postcolonial Criticism." *American Historical Review* 99, no. 5 (December): 1475–90.

Punch Opinion Poll. 2005. September 4. http://vote.sparklit.com/comments.spark?contentID =863667&action=viewTopic&commentID=28766923&pollID=817504.

Ricardo, David. 1821. *On the Principles of Political Economy and Taxation*. 3rd ed. London: John Murray.

Rodney, Walter. 1973. *How Europe Underdeveloped Africa*. London: Bogle-l'Ouverture.

Sachs, Wolfgang. 1996. "Neo-Development: 'Global Ecological Management.'" In *The Case Against the Global Economy: And for a Turn toward the Local*, edited by Jerry Mander and Edward Goldsmith, 239–52. San Francisco: Sierra Club Books.

Said, Edward. 1993. *Culture and Imperialism*. New York: Vintage Books.

Selfa, Lance. 2002. "Why Is Colonialism Respectable Again?" *Socialist Worker*, May 10. http:// www.socialistworker.org/2002-1/406/406_09_ColonialismBack.shtml.

Smith, Adam. 1937. *The Wealth of Nations*. New York: Modern Library.

Smith, Michael Garfield. 1965. *The Plural Society in the British West Indies*. Berkeley: University of California Press.

Spencer, Herbert. 1882–1898. *The Principles of Sociology*. 3 vols. London: Williams and Norgate.

Thomas, Clive Y. 1974. *Dependence and Transformation: The Economics of the Transition to Socialism*. New York: Monthly Review Press.

Trouillot, Michel-Rolph. 1990. *Haiti: State against Nation; The Origins and Legacy of Duvalierism*. New York: Monthly Review Press.

Turner, Jonathan H. 1991. *The Structure of Sociological Theory*. Belmont, CA: Wadsworth.

Wallerstein, Immanuel. 1974. *The Modern World-System I: Capitalist Agriculture and the Origins of the European World-Economy in the Sixteenth Century*. New York: Academic Press.

Wallerstein, Immanuel. 1980. *The Modern World-System II: Mercantilism and the Consolidation of the European World-Economy, 1600–1750*. New York: Academic Press.

Chapter 10

DEVELOPMENTALISM AND THE POSTCOLONIAL CRISIS IN THE ANGLOPHONE CARIBBEAN

PERCY C. HINTZEN

INTRODUCTION

Notwithstanding the putative initial successes of the national development model, its vulnerabilities were patently evident from the inception in the West Indies. Forms of elite domination organized around instruments of coercion, control, and co-optation; a descent into racial and clientelistic politics; the intensification of more damaging forms dependency; insertion into globalized "big power" conflicts as surrogates; the devastation of neoliberal globalization; inter alia, have collectively and separately exposed the failure of state-centered forms of developmentalism. At the same time, there have been glimmers of hope in experiments of participatory democracy (Grenada), populism and accountability (Barbados), anticapitalism (Guyana, Grenada, Jamaica), effective and practical regionalism (the Organization of Eastern Caribbean States), and tricontinentalism (Third Worldism) almost at the root of Caribbean postcolonialism, just to name a few. These have all succumbed to and their possibilities been stymied by the realpolitik of postcolonialism and its perpetual crises.

There are new opportunities opening up in the wake of the emergence of new, powerful actors from the Global South: China, India, Brazil, and South Africa. This development has the potential to refashion global power and simultaneously reduce the vulnerabilities that have stymied the development of alternative political economies. This chapter will examine forms of West Indian practice, snuffed out in postcolonial formation, that might otherwise have served genuine popular interests consistent with the need for sustainability, human security, and universal rights. Can these new global reformulations open up spaces in the region to produce alternative forms of political economy consistent with such interests?

THE PROBLEM OF NATIONAL DEVELOPMENT

Economic development and liberal representative democracy are the twin towers (decidedly chosen) of postcolonial sovereignty. On the one hand, they both have powerful semiotic significance as symbols of modern acquisition. On the other, contained within them are practices linked to global topographies of power that conscript postcolonies and their populations to forms of human degradation. There is a form of decomposition that ensues from this dilemma.[1] The state becomes a conduit, through forms of exception, to global resources. Alternatively, those who are denied access to economic, political, and social rights develop alternative practices in their pursuit.[2]

The stage was set in the role that political and economic development, as technologies of rule, played in postcolonial state formation. The first created the conditions for the technicalization of the state so as to efficiently meet and service demands imposed by global forces (Ferguson 2006, 86) to the exclusion of the vast majority from effective participation in formal governance. This led to "the rule of experts."[3] Economic development embeds the postcolonial economy even more firmly into global topographies of power. The role of the state is reduced to harnessing, in one form or another, what is "usable" for global interests. These include people, resources, and activities with the imperative of their transformation into global utilities. Otherwise, they become marginalized and ignored as "anomalies or pathologies" (Bergeron 2006, 31; see also Scott 1998, 88).

W. Arthur Lewis, as an unmitigated nationalist, is the quintessential narrator of this form of postcolonial practice. He was one of the central figures in the institutionalization of postcolonial statist practice, universally (Tignor 2006). Modernization was the challenge for postcolonial development and the justification Lewis used in his argument against reliance on exports of cheap primary commodities to satisfy the needs of capitalist industrial production in colonial centers. This, he argued, was an impediment to modernization because it demanded guarantees of a cheap supply of labor. He challenged British colonial policy on these grounds because it conflicted with the demands of industrialization, which he saw as the singular necessary condition of modernization (A. Lewis 1949; Farrell 1980). Economic development became integrally linked to modernization, predicated upon national self-determination and independence from Europe. It was to be delivered by a proactive postcolonial state supported by international organizations controlled and directed by "development scholars." The role of the state was to secure capital investments through the use of fiscal and other incentives and to ensure and support the conditions for developing the requisite human capital for industrial development and global trade (A. Lewis 1949).

Lewis's seminal work on the role of industrialization, published in 1949, both informed and inspired the debate about the organization of the postcolonial economy in the West Indies. A proactive state, under the control and direction of "development scholars," would be tasked with creating the conditions for "the export of labour intensive manufactured goods to metropolitan markets" (Farrell 1980, 53). This would be accomplished by the transfer of the large supply of cheap labor, freed from colonial commodity production, to the manufacturing sector. The role of the developmentalist postcolonial state was to secure and generate the conditions for capital investment by guaranteeing needed supplies of capital, technology, and skills through the use of fiscal and other incentives for export-led industrialization. Cheap surplus labor, freed from commodity production, would provide the former colonies with a comparative advantage in global trade. Lewis saw it as "quite feasible for the government to start and run" industries, while developing and utilizing the needed skills that served as critical resource inputs to industrial development (1949, 53). The activist state was to ensure conditions of capital accumulation through taxation and keeping wages and consumption down, by providing education and training. He saw "administrative efficiency" as the crucial element of industrial development. In return for cuts in "excessive incomes," the middle classes would gain in administrative and political power. Higher productivity, low wages and salaries, and higher taxes would produce higher growth rates and increased employment in the manufacturing sector.

In this narration, the postcolonial state is positioned as an acting subject within a global system (Bergeron 2006, 29). It is represented as the sole instrument of a form of "development" whose singular goal is socioeconomic "convergence" with the industrialized West. National development was conceived as an integral component of the global political economy (Ferguson 2006, 182–83). This constitutes a totalizing discourse of power that distorts the true realities of the postcolony. It renders invisible the true conditions of development.

We need to depart from the masculinist representations of postcolonial political economy that have dominated West Indian scholarship, particularly in economics and political science. Perhaps our focus on the colonial/postcolonial divide is misplaced and productive of a form of distortion. Independence, through its concern with sovereignty, has been an economic and political project that positions the state at the center of rights and representation. It denies the perpetual struggle against the state for participation and true representation, and it renders invisible the struggles for rights occurring outside of statist practice. The colonial/postcolonial divide excludes a focus on "forms of everyday life" existing "outside the realm of institutional politics" (Comaroff and Comaroff 1991, 22). Homi Bhabha locates these in the arena of the performative as "signifying processes of cultural identification" (1994, 153). They come into constant conflict with state power and/or act as bases for "nonagentive" deployment against the "agentive" power of the state (Comaroff and Comaroff 1991, 22). The latter is exercised in the service of the modernizing agenda of developmental convergence. If we shift focus to the "nonagentive," then the nationalist (as opposed to statist) impetus can be understood, in the final analysis, as part of an ongoing struggle for empowerment through efforts aimed at the expansion of rights and freedom demanded by diverse communities of interests. It is a struggle over representation, not through forms of "representative democracy" but for guarantees by members of diverse communities of the right to participate effectively in state practice, decision-making, and self-governance on their own terms. It is an engagement in a cultural "politics of representation." Such insertions of the formerly colonized into power contentions over governance (i.e., over control of the state apparatus) and peoplehood (i.e., over who constitutes the "nation") produced the postcolonial state. But the attempt to incorporate nonagentive power into statist practice faltered under the totalizing discourse of development and postcolonial statist practice in the process of "transition from one form of politics to another" (Hall 1996, 428). It led to a "diversification of social antagonisms" and a "dispersal" of nonagentive power. Political struggles became organized around "voluntary associations, relations and institutions of civil society—schooling, the family, churches and religious life, cultural organizations, so-called private relations, gender, sexual and ethnic identities, etc." (Hall 1996, 428). This is the tactic of hegemony imposed through forms of national subjectification, discursively produced by state technology and deployed against the cultural subjectivities produced within the domain of the performative. Members of diverse communities are perpetually engaged in struggles for empowerment, rights, and freedom against the deleterious impositions of statist power and against its forms of control and regulation.

DEVELOPMENT AS STRUGGLE

The totalizing narrative of the national development model that ties statist practice to modernization and inserts it into global topographies of power needs to be rejected. In its place, development must be seen as a struggle by communities of interests to preserve, maintain, deepen, and expand spaces of freedom in which they exercise and realize rights. When freedom, rights, and development are integrally linked in the practice of governance (both through and outside statist practice), there is, according to Nobel laureate Amartya Sen, an inevitable expansion of "economic opportunities, political liberties, social powers, and the enabling conditions of good health, basic education, and the encouragement and cultivation of initiatives" (2000, 5). Development rests on the capabilities of each citizen to exercise their "freedom to participate in the social, political, and economic life of the community" (Sen 2000, 4).[4] This comes into constant conflict with the hegemonic practice of imposing universalized uniformity through governing practice. The exercise of freedom must be located in the grounded realities of diverse groups, communities, families, and individuals. Development is the process of expanding the capabilities that allow people to "lead the kind of life that they have reason to value" (Sen 2000, 10). This struggle for development does not emerge out of a desire for convergence with the West through a process of industrialization. It emerges out of the different goals and desires embedded in diverse cultures, communities, families, and individuals. It is engaged perpetually against the totalizing imperatives of centralized authority. It is a struggle without guarantees.

How does this "turn to culture" inform our analysis of West Indian development? If the focus is to be on the state, it directs our attention to the way its practice restricts, expands, or allows the exercise of freedom and the development of capabilities to live the diverse lives that people "have reason to value." It is not the product of policies and practices of the postcolonial state. Rather, it is realized in the "intricate forms of social and moral order" that people develop in support of their rights to freedom and development (Ferguson 2006, 38–42).

This approach allows us to trace West Indian development back to the colonial plantation and the role played by the enslaved in its realization. Development under conditions of plantation enslavement was occurring both outside and within the formalized system of colonial plantation authority. In the first instance, it was made possible in the spaces of freedom allowed for social behavior and cultural practices that were "unusable" for colonial capitalism. In the second instance, it was possible when the development of capabilities for the exercise of freedom was a necessary condition of plantation production. From this perspective, we need to see freedom not as the opposite of enslavement but as the capability, however limited, to acquire those things that one has "reason to value." Development occurs in the process of their expansion.

Caribbean cultural formation, religious practice, and forms of religiosity, as modes of development, occurred outside the domain of control, regulation, and surveillance of the colonial slave-holding state. This is why culture is dismissed in development discourse and scholarship. It is understood to exist outside of political economy, given the latter's engagement with production, consumption, and material accumulation. Culture enters this domain as a commodity in global circulation, as, for example, in the tourist industry and in the fetishization of exoticized cultural artifacts. But, as the scholarship of Maarit Forde convincingly demonstrates, Caribbean religious practice is firmly located inside the political economy of Caribbean modern formations in response to the changing conditions of modernity. It is engaged in the production and reproduction of modern affective transnational networks that have reformulated institutional relations in keeping with the changing demands of modernity (Laitinen-Forde 2002; Forde 2012, 2019). Caribbean cultural and religious forms, developed outside and in opposition to the plantation political economy, have been the bedrocks upon which rests Caribbean development practice.

There is an integral link between the development of capabilities for modern forms of production and the expansion of spaces of freedom for effective participation in the formal political economy. Eric Williams (1944) examined the role slave production played in creating the conditions for the industrial revolution. But this could only have been made possible through the acquisition of forms of productive and modern rationalities. What this suggests is that modern industrial capitalism emerged out of the rationalities of the enslaved. These capabilities are integrally linked to freedom.[5] This may be the very point of the narration of the Haitian revolution by C. L. R. James (1963). The figure of Toussaint L'Ouverture is rendered much more meaningful if understood metonymically, as signification of a developing slave rationality that demanded the negation of slavery itself. In time, the new productive capabilities of the enslaved led to increasing efficiencies that gave rise to new technical and social conditions of production. Out of these conditions emerged a new class of industrial capitalists engaged in new forms industrial production that were incompatible with slavery itself (Williams 1944). The emancipation of the enslaved in the wake of these developments was, for them, in effect, a significant expansion of the spaces of freedom in the arenas of production and consumption. In other words, development was understood as an expansion of the spaces of freedom to acquire and choose the capabilities to live a life one "has reason to value." In the exercise of their expanded freedom, the formerly enslaved left the plantation en masse for own-account ownership of plots of land for peasant production or to engage in proletarian forms of "free" labor. In the process, the former slaves were transformed into a landholding peasantry and into urban and rural proletarian wage laborers. The cultural and religious forms they had developed during the period of enslavement combined with the freedoms they exercised as peasant and proletariat to enable them to eventually mount successful challenges to colonial authority itself. This is the essence of Caribbean development, understood as a struggle for freedom.

CLASS AND CARIBBEAN DEVELOPMENT

The Caribbean social strata of workers and rural farmers is a product of the
capabilities developed out of the needs of plantation slavery and indentureship
combined with cultural and religious practices developed outside the domain
of plantation authority. Their culture and capabilities are the bedrocks of
Caribbean development. The interests of the non–capital owning skilled and
professional salaried workers who constitute the Caribbean's middle strata,
and of its capital-owning middle and upper strata, are integrally linked to and
dependent upon global networks of power that constrict, constrain, contain,
and deny access to rights and the exercise of freedom. Members of the upper
and middle strata are likewise tied to and dependent upon the state. They
use their access to state resources to establish and maintain international and
national networks through which their material needs are satisfied and their
freedom to pursue them is maintained and expanded. They are also heavily
dependent upon the state for the development of their capabilities. They use
conditions of exception, understood here as the ability to depart from legal and
constitutionally defined avenues, "to intervene in the logics of ruling and being
ruled" (Ong 2006, 5) in order to gain access to state resources—in other words,
to function "outside of the law." They engage in pervasive practices of corruption,
cronyism, and nepotism, which have become normalized in the region. The
conditions of their emergence were forged not by cultural formations outside
of state authority or by the development of capabilities that can be deployed
in the exercise and expansion of freedom, but by their role as functionaries of
the colonial state and of the system of merchant plantocracy, either directly or
indirectly. They are the quintessential products of a "colonization of culture."
This does not mean that members of these strata have not been the agents of
development. However, their interests are tied to the integral role of the state in
its exercise of constitutional and legal contractual authority to receive foreign
assistance and foreign loans, to provide legal frameworks and the legal bases
for foreign investment, and to receive formal recognition as a sovereign unit in
international relations (Ferguson 2006, 50–88). These provide the conditions
upon which the well-being of the middle and upper strata depends. In other
words, their interests are *internationally* inscribed in a transnational apparatus
of governmentality (Ferguson 2006, 93). They use their capabilities in service
of the demands of powerful global actors. At the same time, they retain strong
cultural linkages to the lower strata. This forces them to engage in forms of
decomposition in which their technical and skill capabilities and their social
positioning are divorced from culture. And they practice a form of cultural
bifurcation inscribed in both the popular and the formal. They engage in forms
of cultural switching. Their authority, exercised in support of the statist and

global interests from which they derive considerable material benefits (cultural and social capital), is heavily embedded in formal cultural practice. At the same time, they live in a quotidian world of cultural networks and affective ties organized by and through nonagentive power. They are able to "move" in both worlds, and to enjoy the freedoms and capabilities provided by both. They are engaged in the heterodoxy of the practices of living while using their capabilities in the service of statist orthodoxy and its homogenizing impulse (Chakrabarty 2000).

The capacity of the middle strata to engage in cultural switching explains Caribbean postcolonial national formation. Nationalist challenges to colonialism emerged out of the capabilities and cultural forms of urban working classes and rural producers to which the middle strata were culturally linked. But statist imperatives imposed themselves on the nationalist movement in its "transition" from the nationalist struggle against the colonial state to postcolonial state formation (Hall 1996, 428). The struggle was organized around what Homi Bhabha called the "signifying processes of cultural identification" in "nonagentive" deployments of power (1994, 153). Nationalist politics represented the insertion of the cultural significations of the formerly colonized into the domain of power contentions over governance (i.e., over control of the state apparatus) and peoplehood (i.e., over the interests to be served by statist power). But modern state formation comes with its own conditions that predetermine middle-class control of its apparatus and, through such, control of governing practice. National development was proposed as the sole condition of betterment for those previously excluded, on cultural grounds, from participation in economic and political domains of agentive power. And betterment became the justification used to discipline and control the empowerment of culture as a necessary condition for meeting the accumulative demands of global industrial capital.

The conditions for the transfer of state authority to the middle and upper strata were forged in agitation for better working conditions by the urban proletariat and rural producers. The major thrust by the nationalist movement occurred during the global depression of the 1930s. Proletarian workers and rural producers used the conditions of the depression to their benefit in their ongoing struggle for the expansion of social, economic, political, and cultural rights. They did so in numerous ways including through a series of labor riots mounted throughout most of the British West Indian colonies that disrupted colonial order. A commission of inquiry, convened to examine the causes of the riots, introduced a program of welfare reform and labor legislation that conscripted the colonial state to the service of the economic, political, and social interests of the lower strata (G. K. Lewis 1968, 90–93; West India Royal Commission 1945). The commission's actions also provided active support for trade union organization. This set the stage for the strengthening of statist authority and control through the "complexification" of the role of the state in an unprecedented elaboration of the structures and processes of "civil hegemony" (Hall 1996, 428). The British colonial state authorities accomplished this by the wholesale importation into the colonies of "the multifarious institutions, official and unofficial, which characterize British public life" (West India Royal Commission 1945, 94, 108). The Colonial Development and Welfare Organization was established; it functioned, prototypically, in positioning the West Indian postcolonial state to perform its instrumental role as the guarantor of material betterment (G. K. Lewis 1968, 91). The recommendations of the commission of inquiry laid the groundwork for the development and expansion of representative governments elected through universal adult suffrage. The British Colonial Office, which had established the commission, thus created the conditions whereby the peasant/proletariat became subjected even more intensely to the disciplining power of the state apparatus. Culture became the object of the "agentive" technologies of power through its incorporation into statist organization via middle-strata authority. It was the thread that united the interests of the peasant/proletariat, the middle strata of the colonized, and the creole national capitalists through the hegemonic deployment of creole nationalism.

DEVELOPMENT AND CREOLE NATIONALISM

Postcolonial formations brought the struggle of the diverse communities of interests directly into the arena of statist organization, where they were able to make demands on its practice. These demands were met in a number of ways. The most pervasive were patron-client networks of relations through which state or state-derived resources were transferred in exchange both for support and for mobilization against groups making competing claims for such resources. In Guyana and Trinidad, they were organized in racially specified cultural networks. In Grenada, they were organized through ties to rural producers. In Jamaica, they were organized in a network of relations between political leaders and competing local urban and rural communities. As a characteristic feature of governing practice, these clientelistic networks became sources of empowerment for diverse groups. The lower strata used them to force political authorities to expand the arenas of freedom in and through which they were able to enjoy greater rights. In Guyana, Grenada, and Jamaica, they forced statist practice into new forms of international alliances that supported socialist, anticapitalist, and anti-imperialist experiments. In Trinidad, they secured guarantees of massive transfers of state oil-derived surpluses to the Black working class (Hintzen 2018). In Barbados, patronage resources were secured by the lower strata through the extraction of guarantees of "basic needs" by the development of clientelistic populism whereby electoral support went to the political party with the best agenda and record of protecting and expanding rights. These demands imposed upon the mercantile elite the requirement to transfer surpluses to the state to meet working-class demands in exchange for state protection of their economic interests (Marshall 2001, 269–300).

State policy and practice was therefore forced to respond to the demand for rights made by diverse communities of interests engaged in networks of relations with the postcolonial political elite. They were not driven exclusively, as proposed and argued by development theorists such as W. Arthur Lewis, by strategies of industrialization aimed at achieving convergence with the global industrialized northern metropole. Their insertion into networks of statist practice came with significant consequences for international relations and for national mercantile, commercial, and manufacturing interests, specifically the domestic private sector. In Guyana, Grenada, and Jamaica, lower-strata demands and the "switching" strategies of segments of the middle strata working as functionaries in the state apparatus led to reformulations in patterns of international relations through the development of political and economic alliances with the socialist bloc of countries including the Soviet Union and Eastern Europe, Cuba, and China. They also led to engagements in new forms of "South-South," "Third World," and "tricontinental" anticolonial and postcolonial alliances (Young 2001, 1–11).[6] All these were accompanied by the development of international and regional networks of migratory flows to Britain initially, and then to North America, and through interterritorial flows to capitalize on the ebbs and flows of opportunities for access to and expansion of rights elsewhere. Such movements occurred among all strata of West Indian society.

THE METROPOLE STRIKES BACK

The struggle by the diverse communities of interests in their effort to expand the arenas of freedom in which they could realize their rights to development was engaged under conditions of statist insertions in global neocolonial topographies of power. International alliances with the socialist bloc of countries managed to stave off for a time some of the deleterious consequences that stemmed from lower-strata impositions on state policy. But the postcolonial state was firmly and ineluctably embedded in these topographies, with the socialist and tricontinental blocs providing only temporary and limited fillip. And the consequences were devastating to lower-strata efforts to transform the state into an instrumentality for the expansion of rights and freedom. To meet the conditions of development demanded by the diverse communities, the state was forced to challenge local capital and the global capitalist interests in which it was embedded. This was not the case in Barbados, where the state was able to exchange the protection of domestic merchant, commercial, and financial capital against global intrusions. The revenue transfers that the state obtained in exchange provided the fiscal foundation that allowed it to meet the basic needs of the diverse groups making claims against it. This was the basis upon which Barbadian clientelistic populism rested. What was generally the case, however, was that development, understood as the expansion of rights and freedom for the diverse cultural communities of interests, inevitably came up against the terms of operation of foreign capital and its national system of material and infrastructural support. The preemptive strategy for postcolonial governments was to reformulate the pattern of global alignments in which they were involved. Guyana, Jamaica, and Grenada went the furthest in efforts to do so. They strengthened considerably their political, economic, and strategic alliances with Cuba and Eastern Europe and became deeply involved in tricontinental "Third World" engagements, particularly with Africa. The consequences proved devastating. There was a retaliatory withdrawal of investments, reductions in bilateral and multilateral transfers, and capital flight. In Jamaica, new and punitive terms of access to foreign exchange, foreign investment, and foreign loans were imposed, particularly by the IMF and World Bank, during the latter half of the 1970s. Initial rejection of these terms, followed by eventual capitulation, produced a severe economic crisis. The ruling progressive People's National Party lost support in the wake of the crisis after a significant decline in its ability to meet development needs. In 1980, the party was defeated in national elections by the pro-Western opposition, which campaigned on strict accommodation of globalized neoliberalism (Manley 1982, 1987; Stephens and Stephens 1987). The consequences of retaliatory and punitive measures were even more devastating in Guyana, resulting in severe forms of material deprivation that lasted from the mid-1970s until well into the first decade of the twenty-first century, even after the country capitulated to the demands of global capital interests. In Grenada, the roots of the country's first postcolonial leader, Eric Gairy, in the peasantry and rural proletariat prompted him to impose forms of resource transfers that were labeled "unconstitutional" and "corrupt" when judged against the terms of statist legalities. Conditions of access to effective forms of representation in governance by the subaltern, when combined with inevitable demands for the expansion of economic rights, could not be constitutionally accommodated. This set the stage for the region's most profound break with postcolonial statist practice. In 1979, the New Jewel Movement seized power in the first and (thus far) only violent overthrow of a democratically elected government in the British West Indies. The People's Revolutionary Government (PRG) garnered enormous popular support despite its suspension of the Westminster-based constitution and its refusal to hold elections. It attempted a practice of "participatory democracy" to ensure the direct participation of the country's diverse population in governance. This opened up new possibilities for freedom and rights. The experiment collapsed under the weight of international neocolonial pressure as well as tensions that erupted between the organizational demands of the state apparatus—a legacy of colonial governance and the legalities of Westminster democracy—and conditions for popular participation (Meeks 2014, 107–27). Neocolonial global power was reestablished through a US invasion backed by almost every single West Indian government.

Poor communities developed new forms of survival strategies. These included the intensification of international migration and increased dependence on transnational diaspora networks. Such strategies are characteristically employed throughout the West Indies (and the Global South) as responses to crises of development. The West Indian diaspora now contributes significantly to capability expansion through global transfers initiated, developed, and organized by those excluded by statist practice from political and economic rights. Remittances have become, for most of the Caribbean, the single largest source of foreign exchange earnings. This can be seen as a singular rejection of the developmentalist predications of W. Arthur Lewis that manufacturing exports can be the driving force of the modern postcolonial economy. In the entire region, account remittances outstrip foreign direct investment and official development assistance. In Guyana and Jamaica, remittances in 2003 accounted, respectively, for 16.6 percent and 12.2 percent of GDP. The figures have grown significantly since then in both absolute and relative terms. In many countries in the region, remittances exceed foreign exchange earnings from exports and from tourism. Importantly, they have become the major source of support for lower-income households. They "fill the gaps that the state development agencies have been unable to unplug" (Nurse 2004).

These diasporic networks indicate that development occurs, by and large, outside the arena of statist practice, and this has considerable positive implications for the entire economy. Like remittances, these networks enhance the ability of diverse civic publics to access needed global resources. In both Guyana and Jamaica, beginning in the 1970s, excruciating foreign exchange shortages, the burden of foreign debt, and punitive measures by bilateral and multilateral agencies placed severe constraints and restrictions on the state's capacity to function effectively. The vacuum was filled by subaltern petty traders organized in the informal sector using networks of family ties and informal communication systems. Freed from social stigma and the constraints of "respectability," these traders effectively overcame the limitations of poor transport infrastructure, substandard storage capacities, "dispersed and unpredictable demand," and "limited capital reserves" (identified by W. Arthur

Lewis [1949] as impediments to development) to meet pressing national needs. They were able to do so because of their political remoteness from dependence on the state and their freedom from the ethical constraints imposed by middle- and upper-class morality that prevented the latter's participation in the informal sector. They filled the breach in the face of the failure of an ineffectual formal sector that relied on ties to the state to function. They effectively and efficiently organized the marketing of produce from small rural farmers, the means to engage in informal foreign exchange transactions, and innovative forms of international trade. In this way, they were able to meet the demands of their countries' populations for essential products and foreign currency, both in short supply in the formal economy.

The development of small-scale informal entrepreneurship has been much more significant for the exercise of freedom and the expansion of the economic, social, and cultural rights of the diverse communities in the lower strata than efforts undertaken by the state. Petty trading has been much more successful than the state-dependent formal commercial, manufacturing, and financial sectors in creating conditions for effective development. The informal economy has provided means for subaltern women to assert their economic rights (Edwards 1980, 58). And the international exchanges and transfers in which subaltern groups are engaged have supported the development of nationally owned multinational corporations, providing opportunities for elite equity participation. In Guyana, for example, the trading practices of the lower strata and their transfers of remittances "in kind" from abroad through family and other forms of affective networks have become critical to the country's economic functioning. These transfers supported the formation of one of the very few locally owned multinational enterprises in the country. The Laparkan Group, formed in 1983, "is involved in transportation logistics, port operations, retailing, and travel industries" in a freight network that "spans across the Caribbean and Latin America." The company's air and ocean cargo operations provide "door-to-door service, customs brokerage, full documentation, import and export services, warehousing," and so on throughout the Caribbean region. Laparkan has become a regional leader in freight and cargo services.[7] Its formation was made possible by the global networks in which Guyanese petty trading is involved, by the strategies of members of the lower strata to support themselves through access to transnational resources, and by the production, distribution, and sale of domestic goods.

TRUE DEVELOPMENT AS THE EXPANSION OF
FREEDOM, RIGHTS, AND CAPABILITIES

The formalization of the statist development model that was legitimized as a rationale for postcolonial sovereignty and political independence was the necessary condition for the organization of "efficient and technically functional institutions" (including elections) to meet the demands imposed by global forces; the model did not seek to guarantee rights that are "benevolent and protective" of a diverse citizenry (Ferguson 2006, 86). The aim was to conscript all the diverse segments of the population into the statist agenda after the departure of formal colonial authority. Formal development was the means of constraining and containing the nonagentive cultural and material forces of diverse communities that were opening up spaces of freedom in which to realize the right to live the diverse lives that they had reason to value. This struggle for development is persistent and pervasive and is engaged in, through, and against statist imperatives. This is the struggle out of which true development occurs. Its realization in the postcolony was effectively curtailed and circumscribed by the global forces in which the state was inscribed. Its possibilities are enhanced when the state is forced to enter into alternative forms of global alliances that challenge colonial and neocolonial global capital. They are also enhanced by the development of capabilities and the seeking out of opportunities that exist outside of the purview of statist practice. Changes in the global architecture of power are opening up spaces of development for the West Indies by allowing new and alternative forms of global insertions free from colonial and imperial practice. They can create new possibilities for bringing the development practices of the diverse lower strata into the domain of state organization.

A group of newly emerging economies in the Global South are influencing new and significant developments in global formation with the potential to turn away from European- and North American–centered colonial and neocolonial hegemony. Their emergence is related to what David Harvey identifies as a "crisis" of "overaccumulation" in the Global North consistent with "the dialectics of imperialism" that impose a perpetual need for new markets, new investment opportunities, and new sources of raw materials (Harvey 2006, 413–45).[8] The need is satisfied increasingly in the Global South and especially by countries now conventionally identified through acronyms such as BRICS (referring to the growing alliance of Brazil, Russia, India, China, and South Africa), MIST (the newest emerging market club of Mexico, Indonesia, South Korea, and Turkey), and CIVETS (the market alliance of Colombia, Indonesia, Vietnam, Egypt, Turkey, and South Africa). The emergence of these countries reflects a "reversal of fortune" of the "aging industrial powers of North America [and] Europe" (Goldstone 2010, 31–43). This has the potential to destabilize typical and entrenched forms of neocolonial flows of global accumulation and transfers. It represents, according to Jack Goldstone, a "megatrend that will change the world" (2010, 31–43). We are now beginning to see, as a result, the development of new global networks of connections organized around new patterns of "South-South" relations. Freedom from neocolonial and imperial topographies of power comes with new opportunities for genuine development in the Global South. It can be pivotal in creating the conditions for true development. If Goldstone is correct, then this "megatrend" can offer new opportunities for West Indian governments to employ South-South "tricontinental" alliances for refashioning governing practice in ways that enhance the effective participation of the subaltern. It can provide unique opportunities for bringing into governing practice effective strategies for genuine development occurring outside of the state apparatus. Also, the overseas diaspora populations of the West Indian countries offer significant opportunities to impose upon the state new forms of development practice (Thomas 2004; Hintzen 2006, 42–45).

NOTES

1. I use the term "decomposition" following James Ferguson (2006) to indicate a condition in which movement through time (from colonialism to independence and sovereignty, for example) is not accompanied by, or does not produce, a reversal of status in the world and in socioeconomic conditions for both a country and its population.

2. I use the term "exception" following Aihwa Ong (2006) to refer to the ways in which people and things are excluded from statist calculus because of mutations in citizenship that lead to exclusions from its benefits, or through exceptions made to its legalities and constitutionalities.

3. I borrow this term from Timothy Mitchell (2002) to reference the negative and deleterious consequences, for the poor and marginalized subaltern, of the way experts implement economic policies in postcolonial states.

4. See also the United Nations' "Universal Declaration of Human Rights" at http://www .hrweb.org/legal/udhr.html; and the UN's "International Covenant on Civil and Political Rights" at http://www.hrweb.org/legal/cpr.html.

5. Of course, the acquisition of social position was always possible even within the social category of the slave. Hierarchically organized distinctions among field slaves, drivers, artisans, and house slaves were one form of social differentiation common to most slave societies.

6. The global anticolonial movement subsequently expanded into a "tricontinental politics of postcolonial critique" that combined and incorporated counterdiscursive formations from Asia, Africa, Latin America, and the Caribbean. This was first codified (or named) at the Great Havana Tricontinental conference of 1966. It signaled the development of new forms of "internationalist political identifications" in global postcolonial formation that posed "epistemological challenges" to imperialist practice (Young 2001, 1–11).

7. "Laparkan," *West Indian Encyclopedia*, westindianencyclopedia.com/wiki/Laparkan.

8. Here we are using imperialism in the Marxist sense, following Patrick Williams and Laura Chrisman (1994, 2), to mean "the globalization of the capitalist mode of production, its penetration of previously non-capitalist regions of the world, and the destruction of pre- or non-capitalist forms of social organization." Imperialism has been responsible for capitalism's "spread throughout the globe to the point where it now constitutes a truly global economy."

BIBLIOGRAPHY

Bergeron, Suzanne. 2006. *Fragments of Development: Nation, Gender, and the Space of Modernity*. Ann Arbor: University of Michigan Press.

Bhabha, Homi K. 1994. *The Location of Culture*. Abingdon, Oxon., England: Routledge.

Chakrabarty, Dipesh. 2000. *Provincializing Europe: Postcolonial Thought and Historical Difference*. Princeton, NJ: Princeton University Press.

Comaroff, Jean, and John Comaroff. 1991. *Of Revelation and Revolution*. Vol. 1, *Christianity, Colonialism, and Consciousness in South Africa*. Chicago: University of Chicago Press.

Edwards, Melvin R. 1980. "Jamaican Higglers: Their Significance and Potential." Monograph, Centre for Development Studies, University College of Swansea.

Farrell, Terrence. 1980. "Arthur Lewis and the Case for Caribbean Industrialisation." *Social and Economic Studies* 29, no. 4 (December): 52–75.

Ferguson, James. 2006. *Global Shadows: Africa in the Neoliberal World Order*. Durham, NC: Duke University Press.

Forde, Maarit. 2012. "The Moral Economy of Spiritual Work: Money and Rituals in Trinidad and Tobago." In *Obeah and Other Powers: The Politics of Caribbean Religion and Healing*, edited by Diana Paton and Maarit Forde, 198–219. Durham, NC: Duke University Press.

Forde, Maarit. 2019. "The Spiritual Baptist Religion." *Caribbean Quarterly* 65, no. 2 (April): 212–40.

Goldstone, Jack. 2010. "The New Population Bomb: The Four Megatrends That Will Change the World." *Foreign Affairs* 89, no. 1 (January–February): 31–43.

Hall, Stuart. 1996. "Gramsci's Relevance for the Study of Race and Ethnicity." In *Stuart Hall: Critical Dialogues in Cultural Studies*, edited by David Morley and Kuan-Hsing Chen, 411–40. Abingdon, Oxon., England: Routledge.

Harvey, David. 2006. *The Limits to Capital*. London: Verso.

Hintzen, Percy C. 2006. "Commentary on 'Public Bodies: . . .'" *Journal of Latin American Anthropology* 11, no. 1 (April): 42–45.

Hintzen, Percy C. 2018. "Towards a New Democracy in the Caribbean: Local Empowerment and the New Global Order." In *Beyond Westminster in the Caribbean*, edited by Brian Meeks and Kate Quinn, 173–98. Kingston, Jamaica: Ian Randle Publishers.

James, C. L. R. 1963. *The Black Jacobins: Toussaint L'Ouverture and the San Domingo Revolution*. New York: Vintage Books.

Laitinen-Forde, Maarit. 2002. "The Global Cosmology of a Local Religion: A Caribbean Twist in Discourses of Diaspora." *CLR James Journal* 9, no. 1 (Winter): 147–70.

Lewis, Arthur. 1949. "The Industrialization of the British West Indies." *Caribbean Economic Review* 11, no. 1: 1–53.

Lewis, Gordon K. 1968. *The Making of the Modern West Indies*. New York: Monthly Review Press.

Manley, Michael. 1982. *Jamaica: Struggle in the Periphery*. London: Third World Media.

Manley, Michael. 1987. *Up the Down Escalator: Development and the International Economy; A Jamaican Case Study*. Washington, DC: Howard University Press.

Marshall, Don D. 2001. "Gathering Forces: Barbados and the Viability of the National Option." In *The Empowering Impulse: The Nationalist Tradition of Barbados*, edited by Glenford D. Howe and Don D. Marshall, 269–300. Kingston, Jamaica: Canoe Press.

Meeks, Brian. 2014. *Critical Interventions in Caribbean Politics and Theory*. Jackson: University Press of Mississippi.

Mitchell, Timothy. 2002. *Rule of Experts: Egypt, Techno-Politics, Modernity*. Berkeley: University of California Press.

Nurse, Keith. 2004. "'Diaspora, Migration and Development in the Caribbean." Policy paper, Canadian Foundation for the Americas, September. https://www.focal.ca/pdf/migration _Nurse_diaspora%20migration%20development%20Caribbean_September%202004 _FPP-04-6.pdf.

Ong, Aihwa. 2006. *Neoliberalism as Exception: Mutations in Citizenship and Sovereignty*. Durham, NC: Duke University Press.

Scott, James C. 1998. *Seeing Like a State: How Certain Schemes to Improve the Human Condition Have Failed*. New Haven, CT: Yale University Press.

Sen, Amartya. 2000. *Development as Freedom*. New York: Anchor Books.

Stephens, Evelyne Huber, and John D. Stephens. 1987. *Democratic Socialism in Jamaica: The Political Movement and Social Transformation in Dependent Capitalism*. Princeton, NJ: Princeton University Press.

Thomas, Deborah A. 2004. *Modern Blackness: Nationalism, Globalization, and the Politics of Culture in Jamaica*. Durham, NC: Duke University Press.

Tignor, Robert L. 2006. *W. Arthur Lewis and the Birth of Development Economics*. Princeton, NJ: Princeton University Press.

West India Royal Commission (1938–1939). 1945. "Statement of Action Taken on the Recommendations." London: Her Majesty's Stationery Office.

Williams, Eric. 1944. *Capitalism and Slavery*. Chapel Hill: University of North Carolina Press.

Williams, Patrick, and Laura Chrisman, eds. 1994. *Colonial Discourse and Post-Colonial Theory: A Reader*. New York: Columbia University Press.

Young, Robert J. C. 2001. *Postcolonialism: An Historical Introduction*. Oxford: Blackwell.

Chapter 11

CULTURALISM, DEVELOPMENT, AND THE CRISIS OF SOCIALIST TRANSFORMATION

Identity, the State, and National Formation in Clive Thomas's Theory of Dependence

CHARISSE BURDEN-STELLY AND PERCY C. HINTZEN

DEPENDENCE AND TRANSFORMATION: AN OVERVIEW

In his 1974 text *Dependence and Transformation: The Economics of the Transition to Socialism*, Clive Thomas proposed a method for such transition in small, underdeveloped, dependent postcolonial states through what he termed "dynamic convergence."[1] It was based on the development of an organic link between indigenous forces of production, modes of production, demand, needs, resource use, and indigenous technology (Thomas 1974, 123–25). The goal was to overcome the neocolonial and dependent character of postcolonial societies through the transfer of state power to a worker-peasant alliance that would bring production relations under their control. Distribution was to be based on need and production organized around use value rather than profit as the basis of economic activity. These objectives were to be achieved through disengagement from international capitalism, which had led to "the present degree and pattern of integration of these economies in the international system [and] ... the dynamic base for generating and sustaining their underdevelopment characteristics." Dynamic convergence was proposed not as an end in itself but as a necessary prerequisite for the development of the "domestic capacity to participate in the world economy without ... being systematically subjected to exploitation through unequal exchange" (Thomas 1974, 241). His proposal was predicated on the argument that conditions of underdevelopment and economic dependence were produced by the subordination of domestic needs to those of the international market. The goal of dynamic convergence was to guarantee autonomous internal development. It was to be implemented through centralized planning aimed at the socialization of production and the elimination of the most important consequences of income differential.

Thomas was mounting a challenge to neoclassical and socialist theories of the 1960s–1970s, which saw small size as an impediment to development. He argued that this was the case only under conditions in which the governing productive framework was geared to the establishment of an indigenous form of capitalism. No such constraints would exist if the goal was for transition to socialism. He criticized these theories for being fundamentally ahistorical because they ignored the "dialectical process of the internationalization of the capitalist system," which inscribed the noncapitalist parts of the world into the global division of labor as producers of raw materials and consumers of manufactured goods through the system of international trade, resulting in the destruction of indigenous social forces (Thomas 1974, 50, 58). Under such conditions, the role of state planning was to aid the development of market forces and to support and encourage the growth and development of an indigenous industrial capitalist class. Thomas argued that this would intensify dependence on foreign technology, deepen economic disarticulation, and intensify the expropriation of surpluses and their expatriation to the owners of capital, technology, and managerial skill located in the Global North.

Thomas saw conditions of dependency and underdevelopment in small postcolonial states reflected in consumption patterns not consonant with the basic needs of the community; production patterns not oriented toward domestic consumption or the needs of the society; high export ratios; a high propensity to import; and a high foreign-to-domestic ratio in domestic investment. These were exacerbated by the technology gap between small Global South states and the industrialized states of the Global North, and compounded by the propensity of capitalist centers to transfer as little technology as possible to the Global South and, relatedly, to forge relations that promoted maximum dependence on imported inputs (Thomas 1974, 193). These led to forms of disarticulation and extraversion that perpetuated conditions of subordination of peripheral states, the underdevelopment of productive forces, and economic dependency. Thomas proposed social control of the state by a worker-peasant alliance as a condition for comprehensive planning for resource use and in the determination of demand. He was critical of import substitution industrialization (ISI) and its particular variation known as African socialism, which were pursued by postcolonial states because of their focus on the localization of management, the localization of ownership of foreign firms, state participation in economic activity through state-owned enterprises that competed with foreign firms, and the acquisition of state majority-share ownership of foreign capitalist firms. He saw these strategies as problematic because they were incompatible with the imperative of a fundamental break with capitalism and imperialism. Local resources would remain under the control of foreign decision-makers, profit repatriation would not be curtailed, and reliance on technological innovation in the industrialized countries would be maintained. As a result, the domestic economy would continue to be integrally harnessed to global capital, with the latter maintaining its control and management of labor and with domestic industrial production occurring in plants that were vertically integrated with global firms and corporations that retained the power to make decisions about pricing, output, levels of investment, and so on. Efforts to address high levels of unemployment, poverty, and the inequitable distribution of wealth and resources would inevitably fail. Thomas argued that ISI tended to reinforce patterns of divergence, especially between domestic demand and domestic resource use:

> [W]hat has been described as industrialization is essentially a process in which multinational corporations, although they produce goods with high income elasticities of demand, do so by means of imported knocked-down equipment for local assembly. Because the bulk of the value added in the production process largely lies in the imported knocked-down components, the result is that changes in domestic demand have had limited impact on domestic resource use. (Thomas 1974, 126)

With the implementation of ISI and other neoclassical forms of development, conditions of economic dependence were replicated in all sectors of the economy. Continued demand for foreign exchange earnings led to a concentration on tourism, and continued dependence on primary commodity exports and in some instances on manufacturing exports. There was need for development assistance to provide for infrastructural support. There was a focus on project planning rather than on planning for transformation (Thomas 1974, 188). Integral to ISI was the development of an indigenous capitalist class that was weak, peripheral, and sustained by international capitalist exploitation. These factors combined to intensify the insertion of peripheral economies into the system of international capitalism, and the incorporation of structurally dependent characteristics in the state apparatus. Both reproduced conditions of dependence.

The implementation of socialist policies and the transition to socialism, according to Thomas, was bound to fail if attempted in violation of the "First 'Iron Law' of Transformation," which demanded the convergence of domestic resource use and domestic demand (Thomas 1974, 133–40). This, he argued, explained the failure of Tanzania's experimentation with rural socialism through its policies of villagization (*ujamaa*) and decentralization of state authority. Specialization, increased efficiency, the expansion of productive capacity, and diversification were pursued as the means for increasing foreign exchange earnings by allowing more competitive prices for Tanzanian commodity exports. These policies continued to tie the economy to dependence on primary commodity exports under conditions of unequal exchange. Continued and intensified dependence on primary commodity exports ultimately resulted in the decline of agriculture's contribution to gross domestic product. What *ujamaa* achieved was the reorganization of cheap land and labor without the development of ties to applied research or linkages to industrially produced inputs such as chemical fertilizers and pesticides. These he identified as conditions of "modernization." The "socialist" reorganization of rural production and output turned out to be nothing more than the localization of statist control while maintaining colonial and neocolonial practice. Thomas criticized Tanzania's attempts to apply radical political theory without transforming the material base of production:

> The problem lies in the attempt to develop revolutionary political theory and practice without a concomitant expansion of the ideology for the conquest of the material environment. It is this which explains why Tanzania finds it strategically "necessary" to follow an agricultural production policy aimed at improving the primary export sector's performance. In this sense it differs little from that which preceded the experiments with socialism.... Resource flows to traditional agriculture continue to dominate, performance continues to be disappointing, and underdevelopment becomes more and more manifest. . . . The development of socialism cannot be measured independently of a simultaneous evaluation of the relations of production *and* the level of development of productive forces. (Thomas 1974, 174)

As a result, Tanzania's efforts at transformation were unsuccessful because they were based on an export-oriented strategy that was largely unresponsive to domestic demand and that failed to develop and apply indigenous science and technology to economic activity. As a result, planners and some state officials began to romanticize poverty and rural conditions of destitution—in other words, to legitimate and naturalize them. They refused to recognize and acknowledge these as "malformations of human existence" that needed to be eradicated for the betterment of the society as whole. For these reasons, *ujamaa* became incompatible with a dynamic strategy for socialist transformation and the development of the relations of production that were congruent with the productive forces of industrialization (Thomas 1974, 165–74, 261).

What the case of Tanzania and Thomas's critique of it demonstrates is that *ujamaa* and other versions of African socialism were very much inscribed in the project of political modernization, in which the state was integral as the instrument of economic development (Huntington 1968). Thomas does not escape his own criticism. His argument for effective planning ties his strategy for transformation to the very conditions he criticizes, notwithstanding the imperative of social control of the state through democratic participation by peasants and the proletariat in governance. The role of the state was essential for the imposition of the terms and conditions of economic accumulation, for the framing and fashioning of consumption patterns, and for the determination and imposition of the social costs that must be borne by the population. Thomas assumed that effective participation in governance would be the panacea for social alienation and would avert the need to resort to coercion. It would ensure the voluntary, cooperative, and participatory conditions for transformation generally, and for rural transformation particularly (Thomas 1974, 161, 252, 269). Democratic participation and decentralization were to be the conditions for determining the composition of consumption. This would resolve the contradiction produced by the disarticulation of the mode of distribution, the mode of production, the relations of production, and the domestic "techno-material" base evident in the industrialized socialist economies. This Thomas attributed to the confusion that existed between state and social ownership that he saw being replicated in small, underdeveloped economies attempting a transition to a socialist mode of production. It explained the persistence of dependence and of forms of distribution "rooted in underdevelopment" in these economies.

THE FAILURE TO TRANSFORM

In the last chapter of *Dependence and Transformation*, Thomas observes: "Despite the great contributions Third World societies have made to political theorizing and practice, it is not surprising that rarely has revolutionary political theory been matched by an equally radical vision of the capacity of the people to transform and master their environment. . . . Political revolutions should, as a matter of course, offer the people liberation from, and mastery of, their material environment" (Thomas 1974, 306). The critical question that drives our critique is, Why did his revolutionary program for the transition to socialism fail to take root? Why did countries committed to revolutionary theory and practice capitulate to market-driven strategies of development notwithstanding the latter's failure to deliver on its promises? Following Marxist orthodoxy, Thomas's manifesto was predicated on the imperative of social control of the capitalist state by a "worker/peasant alliance" that would create the conditions for dynamic convergence among socially determined domestic needs, domestic consumption patterns (domestic demand), domestic resource use, and domestic technology as the basis for transformation of the national economic system. To do so, the state had to become transformed from "the instrument of class creation" to the "object of class conquest" (Thomas 1974, 300). Thomas argued his manifesto for transformation on the prerequisite that "*a political revolution has been initiated and has succeeded in transferring state power to a worker/ peasant alliance, thereby fundamentally altering production relations so that the struggle to bring the productive forces under their control and direction, to disengage from international capitalism, and to raise the material levels of welfare of the population are the central economic issues at that stage of constructing socialism*" (Thomas 1974, 29). The transformative efficacy of popular control of the state by a worker/peasant alliance rested on the mechanistic assumption that such control would produce the conditions for the conversion of all forms of property (capitalist and precapitalist) into "social property" through the "domination of social forms of appropriation and the exclusion of exploitation of the labor of others" (Thomas 1974, 309).

For its realization, Thomas's proposal for transformation rested on the assumption of an integral and inextricable relationship between the "consciousness" (ideology) that is brought to bear by the worker/peasant alliance and their objective material interests, specified as "security from deprivation, developing a creative relationship of the people to their environment, eliminating dependency characteristics in social relations between people and bringing an end to all forms of alienation within society." The separation of the workers (assumed to be urban and organized in capitalist relations of production) from the material base of production, located in the rural areas organized (presumably) in a precapitalist mode of production, was what stood in the way of dynamic convergence based on a worker/peasant alliance. This separation set the stage for the exploitation of labor and the underdevelopment of productive forces (the techno-organizational bases of society). Workers would bring to the alliance the necessary "cultural, social, and psychological attitudes" embedded in their (capitalist) "social relations" of production. With the peasantry forming part of the alliance, social control of the material base would be ensured. Both would become liberated from their dependent capitalist (on the part of the worker) and precapitalist (on the part of the peasants) social relations of production, creating the conditions for the development of the productive forces (the techno-material base) and coterminous changes in relations of production (Thomas 1974, 291–97). This, in the final analysis, turns out to be the objective of socialist transformation.

The problems with Thomas's formulation reside on two levels, both related to its "settled" assumptions. First, in his specification of the state, there is need to disentangle its formulation from the apparatus of national governance in which it is collapsed. This would allow for a more critical analysis of the relationship between the two. Second, and relatedly, his essentialization of the categories of "worker" and "peasant" prevents examination of the social forces that have necessitated their formulation. We argue for an understanding of the state as globalized forces and processes that are integrally entangled with the apparatuses of national governance in ways that are essential to global interests organized in and through global topographies of power. For this reason, such entanglements would doom to failure any effort at disengagement and, relatedly, at socialist transformation under terms specified by Thomas. Second, we argue that the categories of worker and peasant are products of "state-effects" that produce forms of social distortion consistent with the concatenation and changing constellation of global actors in whose interests global power is exercised. By the apparatuses of national governance, we refer to the instrumentalities and institutions of authority organized for jurisdictional deployment over territory (Goldberg 2002, 9). Social control of the apparatuses of national governance and the application of revolutionary political theory, to the extent that they leave intact the state-effects of global technologies of power, cannot produce socialist transformation. In fact, the very categories engaged in the exercise of social control may be, and invariably are, products of the global processes and technologies in whose interests they are constituted. This is the point made by Michel-Rolph Trouillot in what he terms the "state-nation homology," and in his argument for an analysis of the state as "a set of practices and processes and their effects . . . whether or not they coalesce around central sites of governments" (Trouillot 2001, 137). Indeed, these "practices and processes" act on civil society and on the entire social formation through, as well as independent of and against, the apparatuses of national governance. Such a reformulation of the state, of course, opens up the possibility, as argued by Thomas, for social control of national governance to challenge and negate the state-effects that prevent the emergence of conditions for transition to socialism. But the institutions of national governance are fundamentally dependent on global resource transfers for their functioning (i.e., for regime survival) that would act, invariably and inevitably, as a check on any effort aimed at their reconstitution into instruments of transformation. There is the need, therefore, for a critical examination of the manner in which state-effects impose themselves on the governing apparatuses of the territorial nation before making a priori settled assumptions about their potential role as an instrument for socialist transformation.

There are different and changing constellations of global forces that may impinge differently on the national conditions of governance. These may produce forms of social, cultural, political, and psychological development to which the state must respond either through accommodation, co-optation, disciplining, control, or coercion. The response may depend on the relationship of these forces to the capacity of the governing apparatus (the regime) to secure resource transfers for its effective functioning. At the same time, for the forces that emerge from such developments to successfully challenge forms of governance, they themselves must be able to harness global forms of transfers by accommodating themselves to the imperatives of support. In other words, the relationship between global processes and the national apparatus of governance can produce social forces that are both a product of and a response to state-effects. This constrains the possibilities for the autochthonous development of social forces when their emergence is produced out of, or is dependent upon, these global forces. For this reason, "dynamic convergence" cannot occur when it is predicated on categories of "worker" and "peasant" that are already products of these global forces, in one way or another. Similarly, dynamic convergence cannot occur when it is organized by and directed through the national apparatus of governance, which is necessarily and imperatively ensconced in global topographies of capitalist power. Because their formulation is the product of global forces of capitalism, workers and peasants, as undifferentiated categories, can have no organic link to the material conditions of production as assumed by Thomas, an argument that we will elaborate later. If the conditions of transformation rest on these organic links, then they already exist outside of the nation-state nexus,[2] in "traditional" or "indigenous" formations, or in the emergence of new social formations (categories of social organization) that reject and/or challenge capitalist state power and national authority.

James Ferguson provides another alternative by pointing to new forms of governance in Africa based on the abandonment of people and territory that are not "usable" to global capital by the institutions of national governance (Ferguson 2006, 38–42). Under these conditions, capital "hops over . . . unusable" areas while creating enclaves over which they exercise absolute authority, free from national jurisdiction (Ferguson 2006). As global capital participates directly in the governing of "usable" areas, the role of national institutions of authority and their apparatuses is diminished, and their capacity to exercise control over the "unusable" areas becomes severely restricted. It is under these conditions that transformative possibilities open up as localities are freed from the state-effects of global power and are forced to depend upon factors, modes, and forces of production that are localized, and to reformulate consumption patterns in keeping with needs that are congruent with them. This is where "tradition" and "indigeneity" may and can be mobilized. Aihwa Ong (2006) identifies this development in neoliberal governance as forms of "exception" that apply to two groups: those directly or indirectly tied to processes of power and the exercise of authority consistent with the interests of global capital, and those who are abandoned by capital in the manner described.

The processes and practices of power that produce state-effects are what create conditions of exception from the legalities, constitutionalities, policies, and practices of national authority. The mutations in citizenship produced by these forms of exceptions and the ensuing exclusions from the benefits of statist and national processes can come with possibilities for transformation under the terms specified by Thomas (Ong 2006). They are most likely to occur under conditions of exception, exclusion, and marginalization from the system of global capital. Once people, resources, and activities are considered "unusable" because they cannot be transformed into global utilities for capital accumulation, they become marginalized and ignored as "anomalies or pathologies" (Bergeron 2006, 31; Scott 1998, 88). These are the conditions under which identities and the development of forms of consciousness (i.e., the concatenation of social, cultural, political, and psychological forms) become consistent with socialist transformation, in the spirit of Thomas's formulation. In a 1989 recasting of his thesis, presented when the process of transformation from the national development model to neoliberalism was almost complete, Thomas came to a similar conclusion in his assessment of the crisis produced by it and the consequent formation of new "identities" that it engendered:

> Allied to this development is the central role given to the state, by all classes (including those calling for privatization) in the resolution of the crisis with little attention being paid to the structure of the state and the emergence of important non-governmental organization. Yet the period has witnessed major individual-family-household responses to the crisis, independent of the state and sometimes in direct opposition to it. I refer here to such matters as the growing informalization of the economy, migration, the development of small-scale inter-island pro-ducing and trading, the proliferation of informal savings arrangements and even the increase in the number of "economic" and "political" refu-gees. While much of this reaction is "survival" oriented and therefore very immediate, there is a potential here for the revitalization of civil society which needs to be harnessed before the crisis can be overcome. (Thomas 1989)

CULTURALISM AS AN IMPEDIMENT TO TRANSFORMATION

Culturalism, Development, and the Production of Identities

What are the technologies and processes deployed to inscribe and reinscribe social formations into the project of global capital, and how can they be challenged? When the nation-state is integrally ensconced in the world system of global capital, opportunities for transformation must emerge outside of the state-effects produced by the processes and practices of state power. This is because the deployment of power and the imperatives of national governance act, together or separately, to produce forms of consciousness through discourses and pedagogies of "invented histories and traditions, ceremonies, and cultural imaginings" (Goldberg 2002). The forms of identity that emerge and the forms of consciousness out of which they are produced render invisible the diverse realities of social organization that can come into conflict with the imperatives of global capital. Charisse Burden-Stelly has identified the technologies, processes, and practices of the state exercised through their entanglements with national governance (i.e., through the nation-state nexus) as forms of "culturalism." Her analysis is focused on the manner in which Black identities and forms of organization become conscripts of the global capitalist project (Burden-Stelly 2016). She identifies "development" as a form of culturalism because it is constituted by and through the "inventions" of processes and technologies of state power and their entanglement with the national apparatus and civil society. Culturalist formations such as development are imperative to the ability of the national apparatus of governance to create consensus and generate loyalty through the (self-)regulation of conduct, as well as for the conscription of the population into the service of the interests of powerful global actors. This is accomplished through the deployment of technologies, processes, and practices of power. We see development as the product of these technologies, processes, and practices.

What integrates state processes, practices, and technologies with national formations in which they become inscribed (and this applies to the deployment of power in the capitalist world system as well as in the system of global socialism that is almost defunct) is the imperative of surplus accumulation on a global scale. This has been true in postcolonial formation, whether accumulation is realized through a capitalist world system as described by Immanuel Wallerstein (2004) or through the application of radical "anticapitalist" ideology to national formations under forms of international socialism. Wallerstein analyzed extensively the integral relationships among the state, national governance, and the production of identities (which he calls "status groups") in the world capitalist system. Burden-Stelly extends his analysis to the role played by culturalism in the formation of what Wallerstein calls "antisystemic" challenges to global capital that occur both nationally and globally (Wallerstein 2004, 67–76). Burden-Stelly identifies culturalism as a technology of power because of its effects in the elision of political economy (i.e., the manner in which culture delinks identities from their material base). She argues that such elision paves the way for the reinscription of antisystemic challenges back into the capitalist project (Burden-Stelly 2016). In other words, culturalism disarticulates identities and consciousness from the material conditions out of which they are produced. This acts to preempt the very changes in "relations of production" necessitated by Thomas's project of transformation. When identities and forms of organization are inscribed in material conditions in ways that produce challenges to state and nation (i.e., when they are specified in terms of radical political economy), culturalism, as a form of regulation, control, and exclusion, can act to legitimize and normalize the surveillance, disciplining, and punishment of the antisystemic formations that can emerge. Because these emerge outside of national formation in ways that allow them to escape the deployment of state power, culturalism acts to bring them back into the domain of state power and national authority. The development of antisystemic formations can and does occur at the global level, and these can insinuate themselves upon civil society. Burden-Stelly discusses Pan-Africanism and communist internationalism as examples of these global formations (Burden-Stelly 2016). They open up possibilities for the transformation discussed by Thomas that are foreclosed by engagement with national institutions of governance and by the location of transformative possibilities in the categories of worker and peasant. Most important for our critique, however, is the role of development, as a culturalist formation, in the reinscription of antisystemic challenges into the project of global capital.

Culturalism is central to our critique of Thomas in two ways. First, Thomas's developmentalism is firmly rooted in historicist and materialist discourses that collapse diverse realities and temporalize them into categories of problems that need to be resolved if development is to occur (Escobar 1995). This is what Johannes Fabian refers to as a "time-distancing" effect, which produces "strictly technical" classifications based on "moral-political connotations" (Fabian 1983, 75). The worker and peasant emerge in Thomas's formulation as temporalized categories associated with modes of production that explain their exploitation. Their formulation elides the complex and diverse ways that conscripts to global capital, organized into developmentalist categories, are involved in processes of capitalist accumulation. The classifications of peasant and worker emerge from culturalist assignations produced out of "moral, aesthetic, and political connotations." Because these categories are embedded in the field of power of global capital, socialist transformation on the terms of their specification becomes highly improbable. As categories and identities, they become disarticulated from the material conditions of exploitation that make their specifications (as worker and peasant) imperative. In other words, they must become something other than "worker" or "peasant," and their needs must be fashioned outside of the materialities of global capital. The conditions of their transformation cannot be produced through the planning apparatus of national institutions of governance, whose very existence is dependent upon the transfer of resources under terms specified by global capital.

The relationship among development, the production of categories, and national institutions is detailed, in the case of Colombia, by Arturo Escobar (1995). Development, according to him, is a technology of rule that relies on the institutional practices of governance to produce and formalize the "social relations, divisions of labor, and cultural forms" that are articulated with the socioeconomic and technical conditions of global capital. Ideology, as false consciousness, becomes disarticulated from objective interests embedded in what Thomas refers to as "relations of production." The role of the "superstructure" in producing forms of alienation to which our notion of disarticulation refers is recognized in the Marxist notions of "false consciousness." It is similarly recognized by Thomas, whose analysis of the crisis of underdevelopment and dependency is no different from our specification of the relationship between the national regime and global capital. However, Thomas assumes mechanistically that dynamic convergence will be produced through the articulation of the ideology of governance, the material base, and the objective interests of the worker/peasant alliance. This becomes the condition of transformation made possible when the institutions of governance come under popular (social) control. We argue that the categories of worker and peasant are products of the state-effect of global capitalist topographies of power and their integral entanglement with national forms of sovereign authority. Any effective challenge to this nation-state nexus must occur in spaces where, for one reason or another, the state-effects of global capital are attenuated enough to allow the valences of alternative representations to prevail in the understandings of self and in the production of identities. The problem, according to Escobar, is not bringing into convergence the forces, modes, and relations of production as a condition for moving through the temporalized processes of development. Forces of production are already present and available, and the capitalist "mode of production" is already pervasive, affecting every aspect of life, even if only by denying "unusable" populations living in "unusable" environments the opportunity and capabilities "to lead the kind of life that they have reason to value" (Sen 2000, 5; Escobar 1995, 214–26). Our critique rests with Thomas's specification of the objective of transformation in historicist terms of the development of the techno-material forces of production to be achieved through dynamic convergence of the mode, relations, and forces of production domestically. The objective of such transformation is reengagement with the global economic system through trade.

Our second critique of Thomas centers on his assertion that conversion will be made possible when the social control of national institutions of governance is captured by an alliance of workers and peasants, who will then assume "worker control over the objects of production and the work situation" (Thomas 1974, 297) and ensure "the spread of collective and social consumption" (Thomas 1974, 291). The problem is that these categories are culturally produced out of the very forces they are assumed to reject. Thomas's argument rests on his conviction that convergence would produce a revelation of their rootedness in material conditions. But, as Escobar has argued, these categories are the products of "power and discourse" deployed for the "mapping of people into coordinates of control" in order to "transform the conditions under which they live into a productive normalized social environment" (Escobar 1995, 156) consistent with the imperatives of global capital. What is demanded is not social control of the governing apparatus by these categories—they are constituted discursively, not materially, through forms of culturalism—but their disarticulation into "manifold and multiple selves" in the form of "radically reconstituted identities" that emerge in the spaces where the state-effects of global capitalism are not present enough to prevent the efficacy of their "disarticulating forces and tensions" (Escobar 1995, 215).

We argue, following Ferguson and Ong, that the form of governance by exception and the abandonment by global capital of unusable social ecologies provide opportunities for these anticapitalist forces. Their emergence is not independent of global alliances. Nor is the development of the techno-material forces of production, as argued by Thomas, a prerequisite. In the first instance, the possibilities for transformation may very well depend on global alliances of anticapitalist forces rather than autarkic disengagement from global processes. Andreas Hernandez documents the emergence of an "alternative vision" of social organization concatenated in, through, and by the World Social Forum, formed as a counterweight to the World Economic Forum, where the global and national conditions of capital are coordinated (Hernandez 2010, 215–29). It emerged as a "global counter movement to neoliberalism" that "connects many of the most vital popular movements struggling against the neoliberal project" (Hernandez 2010, 215–16). These movements challenge developmentalist-materialist discourses that tie human aspirations to the very material conditions of production and consumption explicit in Thomas's formulation.

The Culturalist Logics of Developmentalism and the Failure to Transform

Our critique of Thomas's 1974 manifesto demonstrates the pervasiveness of culturalism as a deployment of power and its centrality in developmental discourse. His statist assumptions overlooked the role of culturalism in the organization of economic and social activity and the integral relationship between the nation-state nexus and global capitalism. As Oliver Cromwell

Cox explains: "The modern nation itself is a product of capitalism" (1944, 463). Nationalist discourse is a form of culturalism that conscripts the modern nation-state into the global capitalist project. While Thomas understood underdevelopment as a manifestation of the international relations of exploitation, he neglected to pay due attention to the form and function of the postcolonial nation, its integral insertion into the topographies of global power, and the manner in which the cultural specification of interest groups and identities are central to such insertion. Whenever the conditions of transformation are tied to the apparatus of national governance, it forecloses any possibility of mounting antisystemic challenges to global capital. Development, in its neoclassical formulation, can thus be understood as a teleological historicist discourse and a linear progress narrative based on the capacity of the capitalist world system, through the pervasive deployment of state power throughout national and local formations, to dictate and determine economic organization, domestic capacity for growth, social betterment, and conditions of inequality. Thomas's emphasis on the development of techno-material conditions mirrors the logic of neoclassical economics and neoliberalism that posit the failure of national formations to create these conditions as the root cause of exclusion and dehumanization, and that propose industrial development (even though, in his case, under conditions of socialist transformation) as the basis for freedom, self-determination, and the international legitimation of small underdeveloped dependent states.

Historically, attempts to develop alternative global alliances in efforts aimed at challenging the global system of international capitalism became embedded in this culturalist discourse and practice of capitalist developmentalism. Third Worldism as an ideology was predicated on the idea of a strong, centralized nation-sate as the key to transformation. But rather than disengagement with the global system, as Thomas proposed, the conditions of transformation rested on the formation of alliances of "Third World" nations that would allow them to act collectively through forms of global political and economic cooperation. While the strategy for transformation is different, it is based on identical assumptions regarding the role of the institution of national governance in techno-material development. This is palpably evident in the 1961 Belgrade Declaration of the Non-Aligned Movement in its assertion that "the fruits of scientific and technological revolution [need to] be applied in all fields of economic development to hasten the achievement of international social justice" (Institute of Development Studies 1993, 5). Produced out of nationalist discourse and reproducing nationalist logics, conditions of "transformation" rooted in the materialist foundations of development can do nothing but reinscribe national formation into the domain of power of the global capitalist system, irrespective of "which class wield[s] power in the country" (Thomas

1983, 28). A "dictatorship of the proletariat" based on social control of the apparatus of national governance cannot produce socialist transformation when "the social" is constituted in ways that are not embedded in society.

It is the culturalist specification of "the social" as a product of statist processes, practices, and technologies of power that renders invisible the embeddedness of diverse existences in material relations. As the product of such processes, developmentalism becomes transformed by culturalism into forms of identity that are rooted in the historicist assumption that populations in the "underdeveloped" Global South are located in the "waiting room" of modernity because of their cultural inadequacies. These assumptions apply to every segment of underdeveloped society, including its bourgeoisie, its working class, and its peasantry. The failure of society to transform is explained by these narratives of (cultural) "lack," "absence," and "incompleteness" (Chakrabarty 2000, 27–46). The solution, as proposed by Thomas's manifesto for socialism and by Third Worldism, was the development of the forces of production and of the requisite "social and political conditions" congruent with transition. It is identical to neoclassical formulas. In this manner, development as the raison d'être of postcolonial national governance became a technology of culturalism that inscribed postcolonial formation into the project of global capitalism, whatever the "political theory" (whether radical or not) under which policies of national governance were fashioned. Culturalism, through the discourse of development, comes to be pitted against "ordinary citizens' struggles aimed at liberating themselves from the domination, exploitation and repression of the postcolonial state" (Ndlovu-Gatsheni 2012, 73). Developmentalism was transformed into an ideology that legitimized and normalized economic planning as a documentary practice of governance and as the condition of "emancipation" and "liberation." In both capitalist and socialist specifications, underdevelopment came to be represented in terms cultural lack, absences, inadequacies, and incompleteness that needed to be overcome. For Thomas, these conditions, manifest in inadequate development of the necessary "cultural, social, and psychological attitudes," explained the failure of workers and peasants to develop the prerequisites for dynamic convergence as the precondition for transformation. This is a precise example of the "time-distancing" effect of "moral-political connotations" rooted in "strictly technical" classifications, mentioned previously, that have nothing to do with the diverse realities of the lived experiences of the population.

The logic of culturalism that imbues Thomas's developmentalism ties under-development, dependency, exploitation, and the possibilities for transformation to "nationalist attitudes and politics" (Brewster and Thomas 1969, 121). National independence and self-determination become "tremendously progressive historical forces" (Thomas 1974) when they achieve liberal forms of national sovereignty. The task is to free these forces from conditions of economic dependence and underdevelopment. Thomas's conflation of the sovereign state with progress and the possibility of economic betterment prevented him from making the connection between underdevelopment and nation formation. It ultimately led him to the conclusion that nationalist formation and national sovereignty can provide the conditions under which indigenous resources can be harnessed to industrial projects and impose patterns of local demand based on locally defined needs as necessary conditions of transformation. When domestic resources and domestic demand are placed under the jurisdiction of a national apparatus of governance, they become inevitably subject to processes and technologies of global capital in which the former is embedded. In the final analysis, they become captured by the national apparatuses of governance.

Industrialization, Development, and the Nation-State Nexus

Irrespective of ideology embedded in liberalism, socialism/communism, and nonalignment, the nation-state nexus became central to development, accumulation, and growth, with industrialization as the foundation of self-determination and empowerment:

> Structural transformation, disengagement from capitalism, socialist development—all these imply industrialization in the basic sense of the progressive spreads of industrial techniques of organization and resource use into all branches of economic activity, as part of the struggle to make the material environment serve the community's needs. This relationship between industrialization and the degree of development of productive forces is readily perceived when one looks at the global distribution of industry and the marked concentration of industrial production among those countries which have solved the problem of mass poverty and have achieved self-sustaining increases in the level of material production. Indeed, this is so generally accepted a feature of international economy that high incomes and wealth are often taken as synonymous for industrialization. (Thomas 1974, 177)

Thomas understands industrialization as "a social process necessary to enable society to master the material environment in the service of its own needs" (Thomas 1974, 181). It is to be achieved through instruments of planning employed by the national apparatus of governance. This ties industrialization to the nationalist project of development, rooted in culturalism and embedded in development discourse, which achieves its legitimacy by gaining the loyalty of the population by claiming to provide the proletariat and peasantry (categories embedded in the historicism of development discourse) with the benefits of growth. In this manner, their "interests" became economically specified and tied to industrialization. The prospect for development becomes hinged to the formation of the requisite "national attitudes and politics." As it turns out, Thomas's objective of transformation was for the rearticulation of the national with the global economy. This explains the imperative of the role played by national governance in transformation, with the ultimate goal of the "develop[ment of] domestic capacity to participate in the world economy without . . . being systematically subjected to exploitation through unequal exchange" (Thomas 1974, 240–41).

Transformation was essentially directed at creating "a material basis for equality (of the national apparatus) in international cooperation" (Thomas 1974, 181) under conditions in which economic relations of dependence become eviscerated by socialist transformation. The objective, according to Thomas, was "the integration of the national economy into the world socialist economy on the basis of genuine independence and equality" (Thomas 1974, 135). Socialist transformation based on dynamic convergence at the national level was merely the precondition for "the development of an export capacity in industrial goods" that would allow the country to "earn foreign exchange." This was necessary, because trade was seen to be the "super engine of growth" once it was "no longer constrained by foreign exchange" (Thomas 1974, 134). For the capacity to trade in industrial goods, freed from conditions of economic dependence, peasants needed to become transformed into industrial workers, and workers needed to become more efficient through the development of the forces of production. Both needed to develop the political wherewithal to assume control of national institutions of power. Here, the culturalism embedded in this historicist developmentalist proposal is palpable. Peasants and workers have to develop the capability to play an effective role in global forms of accumulation. Industrialization provides the assurances of national accumulation. Social control of national governance ensures equity and the end of poverty. The irony is that the categories, social formations, and identities subsumed under "worker" and "peasant" were already involved in production for global trade. Their formations were dictated, determined, and produced by the system of global capital through its capacity to deploy state technologies of power in its own interest. Thus, we end up precisely back where we started. And this, more than anything else, explains the failure to develop a "world socialist economy," the collapse of Eurocommunism, and the abandonment of the project of "economic socialism" by countries guided by radical political theory. What we are left with is political "authoritarianism" and the persistence of "poverty and powerlessness" with which Thomas was forced to engage in his subsequent analyses (Thomas 1988). In the latter case, he conceded the need for "another" form of development for the poor and the powerless without giving ground on the issue of the role of the national apparatus of governance. In the former, he attributed the rise of authoritarianism to the underdevelopment of productive forces, working-class weakness, and the absence of "bourgeois democratic restraint." In other words, these societies are still locked in the waiting room of history.

TOWARD AN ALTERNATIVE VISION OF TRANSFORMATION

Thomas's manifesto was directed at small, dependent, underdeveloped states where the correct combination of domestic production, output, demand, need, and technology would provide the conditions for a transition to socialism as well as for the development of a competitive advantage in the world economy. He assumed that the needs of the population can be satisfied by the development of the forces of production under conditions of a socialized and decentralized state and equal integration into the international system. The national apparatus of governance remained the primary instrument of accumulation, distribution, price and wage setting, and economic organization. The possibility for different forms of development occurring outside the space of national jurisdiction and free from the deployment of state power was foreclosed. For Thomas, the problem resided not in the deployment of state technologies of power by global capital, but in the "underdevelopment" of the postcolonial elite—another culturalist assumption. It was the postcolonial elite, not the nature of the postcolonial state itself, that mobilized ideology and sentiment. He wrote:

> Given the way classes are formed in underdeveloped and dependent situations, the sense of oneness and unity that exists in the population at large has inevitably become an object of manipulation by the ruling classes of these countries. Forever preaching unity, these social classes are nevertheless *objectively* the main supports of the processes of fragmentation and disintegration of these societies. . . . The dominant social classes have historically developed and derived their ultimate support in the context of their relationship to imperialism. Their major contributions, therefore, are in the direction of a perpetuation of dependency relations. . . . [A] move in this direction must have as a basis the downfall of all such classes. (Thomas 1974, 277)

In reality, the postcolonial state, through the deployment of technologies of power, entraps populations through culturalist discourses that produce categories of people that are not embedded in society and that are inscribed in "historical relations . . . to imperialism" (Thomas 1974, 285). Even though recognizing that "social relations have historically been organized within the context of nation-states," Thomas nonetheless attributes class conflict to elite domination rather than to the processes, practices, and technologies of state power embedded in national political formations, and the way they objectively reproduce conditions of inequality and exploitation. The embeddedness of these processes, practices, and technologies in national and social formation is the necessary condition of accumulation for the capitalist world system. Immanuel Wallerstein (2004) refers to the product of this reproduction as the "axial division of labor," whereby conditions of dependency come to be based on terms of unequal exchange.

Thomas elided the diverse realities of "community" by collapsing their specification into categories of worker and peasant, which are produced out of discourses of culturalism and historicism. This explains his failure to recognize these as the products of state processes and technologies that harness local sentiment to the imperatives of postcolonial global capitalism. As social forces, they become the objects of national forms of economic planning under the guise of the social control of the national institutions of governance. In the process, according to Partha Chatterjee, "autonomous forms of imagination of the community [become] . . . overwhelmed and swamped by the history of the postcolonial state." This is "the root of . . . postcolonial misery" as the product of an "inability to think out new forms of the modern community" and of "surrender to the old forms of the modern state" (Chatterjee 1993, 11). Chatterjee recognizes this danger in the very objectives of nationally directed planning of the type proposed by Thomas:

> [I]n terms of sheer ability to be organized as an activity of mass involvement, self-help, and community endeavor, there is nothing superior to basic construction activity. It is for this reason that it has been widely used in those socialist countries (e.g., China and Cuba) where political motivation and involvement are high. . . . [F]rom a social standpoint, and in the context of comprehensive planning, there is always a cost that arises from any attempt to bring human and other resources to bear on the provision of the community's needs, and it is the social evaluation of those needs that determines the true benefits of such activities. (Thomas 1974 , 263)

This underscores the role of national formation in the production and definition of culturally defined categories. Mass involvement in the national institutions of governance through culturally defined categories cannot be the basis upon which the satisfaction of the varying needs of all the diverse constituencies can be realized. And it cannot produce the forms of consensus assumed by Thomas upon which rest the conditions for democratic governance. It can only serve to conscript the populace into the agenda of national governance by proposing consensus as a necessary condition for the satisfaction of individual and collective need. Those who resist become enemies of the state through their violation of the terms of consensus. As a culturalist discourse, development creates the condition for political motivation and involvement that rationalizes whatever costs arise in the drive toward economic growth as the product of community. Development is transformed into a new basis for the deployment of coercion and structural violence (as has been the case in China). Thomas's panacea for underdevelopment failed to take into account the ways in which the postcolonial state entraps its citizens to support ideologies of embedded liberalism, communism/socialism, and Third Worldism, deployed in ways that do not necessarily result in the betterment of their material conditions. More importantly, it failed to take into account the nonmaterial factors that drive their aspirations as human beings participating in these diverse social formations.

Political philosopher Thomas Pogge, in his consideration of the sources of world poverty and the denial and restriction of human rights, points to the injustice of "the territorial state as the preeminent mode of political organization" because of its absolute power to "check and dominate the decision-making of political subunits" (Pogge 2008, 184). He proposes a reformulation of governance into forms of vertical sovereignty "where authority is widely dispersed in the vertical dimension" and where people are able "to govern themselves through a number of political units of various sizes without any one ... occupying the traditional role of the state." As such, "political allegiance and loyalties [would] be widely dispersed over these units: neighborhood, town, country, province, state, region and world at large, without converging on any one of them as the lodestar of political identity" (Pogge 2008, 184). He proposes this as a means of accommodating the diversity of human reality and as a check on the global deployment of power in a way that provides everyone with the right to participate equally in the decision-making that affects their lives at any level. This is but one proposal to accommodate the form of transformation sought by Thomas without tethering populations to forms of authority and organization that deny them their right to self-determination on their own terms. Rather than centralized forms of national authority, what is required for transformation, according to Arturo Escobar, is for the "manifold and multiple selves" of the "underdeveloped" world to organize into "localized, pluralistic grassroot movements," using "local knowledge" and deploying "popular power" in developing "alternatives to development" that constitute a "rejection of the entire paradigm itself" (Escobar 1995, 215). As it turns out, the problem of the failure of transformation rests not with the failure to develop but rather with the project of development itself.

NOTES

1. For Thomas, underdevelopment means "the present peculiar conjunction of productive forces and production relations among the 'poor' countries, which at the prevailing levels of human technological development constitutes the objective basis of their poverty and of the growing inequalities of income and wealth which the world system of production and exchange naturally reproduces" (1974, 25).

2. We use the "nation-state nexus" to differentiate the concept from the generalized understanding of the "nation-state" as a homology. As such, we are referring to the effects of state "processes and practices" on the national apparatus of governance.

BIBLIOGRAPHY

Bergeron, Suzanne. 2006. *Fragments of Development: Nation, Gender, and the Space of Modernity*. Ann Arbor: University of Michigan Press.

Brewster, Havelock, and Clive Y. Thomas. 1969. "Aspects of the Theory of Economic Integration." *Journal of Common Market Studies* 8, no. 2 (December): 110–32.

Burden-Stelly, Charisse. 2016. "The Modern Capitalist State and the Black Challenge: Culturalism and the Elision of Political Economy." PhD diss., University of California.

Chakrabarty, Dipesh. 2000. *Provincializing Europe: Postcolonial Thought and Historical Difference*. Princeton, NJ: Princeton University Press.

Chatterjee, Partha. 1993. *The Nation and Its Fragments: Colonial and Postcolonial Histories*. Princeton, NJ: Princeton University Press.

Cox, Oliver Cromwell. 1944. "The Racial Theories of Robert E. Park and Ruth Benedict." *Journal of Negro Education* 13, no. 3: 452–63.

Escobar, Arturo. 1995. *Encountering Development: The Making and Unmaking of the Third World*. Princeton, NJ: Princeton University Press.

Fabian, Johannes. 1983. *Time and the Other: How Anthropology Makes Its Object*. New York: Columbia University Press.

Ferguson, James. 2006. *Global Shadows: Africa in the Neoliberal World Order*. Durham, NC: Duke University Press.

Goldberg, David Theo. 2002. *The Racial State*. Malden, MA: Blackwell.

Hernandez, Andreas. 2010. "Challenging Market and Religious Fundamentalisms: The Emergence of 'Ethics, Cosmovisions, and Spiritualties' in the World Social Forum." In *Contesting Development: Critical Struggles for Social Change*, edited by Philip McMichael, 215–29. New York: Routledge.

Huntington, Samuel P. 1968. *Political Order in Changing Societies*. New Haven, CT: Yale University Press.

Institute of Development Studies. 1993. "Poverty in Guyana: Finding Solutions." *Transition*, nos. 20–21.

Ndlovu-Gatsheni, Sabelo J. 2012. "Fiftieth Anniversary of Decolonisation in Africa: A Moment of Celebration or Critical Reflection?" *Third World Quarterly* 33, no. 1: 71–89.

Ong, Aihwa. 2006. *Neoliberalism as Exception: Mutations in Citizenship and Sovereignty.* Durham, NC: Duke University Press.

Pogge, Thomas. 2008. *World Poverty and Human Rights: Cosmopolitan Responsibilities and Reforms.* 2nd ed. Cambridge: Polity Press.

Scott, James. 1998. *Seeing Like a State: How Certain Schemes to Improve the Human Condition Have Failed.* New Haven, CT: Yale University Press.

Sen, Amartya. 2000. *Development as Freedom.* New York: Anchor Books.

Thomas, Clive Y. 1974. *Dependence and Transformation: The Economics of the Transition to Socialism.* New York: Monthly Review Press.

Thomas, Clive Y. 1983. "State Capitalism in Guyana: An Assessment of Burnham's Co-Operative Socialist Republic." In *Crisis in the Caribbean: Internal Transformation and External Constraints,* edited by Fitzroy Ambursley and Robin Cohen, 27–48. New York: Monthly Review Press.

Thomas, Clive Y. 1988. *The Poor and the Powerless: Economic Policy and Change in the Caribbean.* New York: Monthly Review Press.

Thomas, Clive Y. 1989. "The Economic Crisis and the Commonwealth Caribbean." Paper presented at the Economic Crisis and the Third World Countries: Impact and Response conference, Institute of Social and Economic Research, University of the West Indies, Mona, Jamaica, April.

Trouillot, Michel-Rolph. 2001. "The Anthropology of the State in the Age of Globalization: Close Encounters of the Deceptive Kind." *Current Anthropology* 42, no. 1 (February): 125–38.

Wallerstein, Immanuel. 2004. *World-Systems Analysis: An Introduction.* Durham, NC: Duke University Press.

Chapter 12

THE CARIBBEAN, FREEDOM, AND THE RUSES OF GLOBAL CAPITAL

PERCY C. HINTZEN

The modern world system was produced out of social, cultural, political, and economic forms organized and developed to accommodate massive global movements of people, resources, and ideas.[1] It established the conditions that enable people, with allegiances to different places of origin, to participate effectively where they reside and to develop ways of belonging there (Hintzen 2002). This flexible accommodation that is at the root of modern subjecthood has been rendered invisible by the ruses of European-centered racial global capitalism. The result has been a failure of theoretical, analytical, and conceptual frameworks and their outcomes in policy and practice to stem a crisis, namely modernity's seemingly inherent inability to deliver on the Enlightenment's promise of freedom, equality, and universal human rights. This crisis has plagued the modern project from its inception. Distortions produced out of the power/knowledge symbiosis have resulted in the epistemic erasure, silencing, and exclusion from the arenas of contestation of categories of people deemed inferior through the deployment of discourses of difference. These are the arenas in which technologies of subjectification, regulation, discipline, and control are formulated and produced and from which they are deployed. Such distortions relate not to Marxist notions of false consciousness but to the rendering invisible of those who are discursively excluded from the arena of civilized belonging. Such renderings emerge out of notions of their lack or inadequacy in the capacity for reason and rationality. In the final analysis, the exclusions are racialized, and racial subjectivities are inscribed in notions of territorially defined origins. In this chapter, I use the Caribbean, and particularly the Anglophone West Indies, to expose such erasure. Racial belonging was produced and imposed by the technologies and apparatuses of the state. Technologies refer, for example, to the imposed categorization of the population through censuses, or, inter alia, to "invented histories and traditions, ceremonies, and cultural imaginings" that are integral to the power of the state to include and exclude. By the apparatuses of the state, I refer to its instrumentalities and institutions of power organized for jurisdictional deployment over territory. These include law and policy making as well as bureaucracies (Goldberg 2002, 9). State technologies and apparatuses function for the production of peoplehood. The latter identifies those with legitimate claims of belonging to the nation. It also forms the basis for legitimately excluding from the materialities of the nation those who cannot make such claims. Inevitably, this produces a cultural politics of sameness necessary for the homogenizing project of the state (Goldberg 2002, 15–16). This politics of inclusion is challenged, rejected, or ignored by the racially excluded in a "cultural politics of difference, of struggles around difference, of the production of new identities, of the appearance of new subjects on the political and cultural stage" (Hall 1996c, 467).

On the surface, the Caribbean defies the logic of undifferentiated racial belonging. The legacy of the plantation is highly imbricated in every aspect of the region. This legacy has produced and sustains a syncretic, hybrid, transitory reality characterized by a corpus of values and institutions that gives the appearance of integrity and cohesion. These values and institutions are bases for the production of a recognized identity throughout the region. But the region was created, from the start, as a space of transitory impermanence after the almost total extinction of its indigenous population. Caribbean reality has emerged almost in opposition to this notion of impermanence. Nevertheless, at its core, it is forced to accommodate a never-ending (usually violent) assault by a global and international environment and a multiplicity of ever-changing cultural, social, economic, and political forces. The result is an extremely pregnable Caribbean, constantly penetrated, with flexible accommodations inscribed in its "ways of being." Such accommodations come up against the prerequisite of colonial and postcolonial capital for national cohesion and integrity. But there is nothing "authentic" about its socioculture; there is very little that has not originated from abroad. Everything is "adapted, reimagined, reinvented" (Stavans 1995, 60) to suit the needs of a domestic condition, constantly buffeted by external pressures, needs, and demands. The region's character is described by one its writers and theorists as "chaos—shock, mixture, combination, alchemy" (Taylor 1997, 136). But impermanence is at the core of what it is to be modern. Thus, innovativeness, adaptability, and the crossing of boundaries (of identity, place, and space) are innate characteristics of the modern subject.[2] These become operative in what I would like to term "the spaces and possibilities for being modern." It is in this sense that the Caribbean must be understood as the source and center of the modern world. What renders its modernity invisible is modernity's association with material progress, fashioned out of its genealogy of entanglement with capitalism. So, these "crossings" that are the fundamental condition of Caribbean (and thus modern) reality are rendered invisible by the imperatives of coloniality, understood here as the matrix of capitalist power organized through state authority and the regulation, control, and disciplining of sexuality, labor, and subjectivities (race, class, gender, and other communal identities) (Quijano 2000).

Hybridity and its association with Latin America and the Caribbean functions in a number of ways in the global matrix of capitalist power. First, it locates the two regions beyond the pale of the group of modern (and hence civilized) nations constituted by a peoplehood of national white purity. Second, it inscribes white supremacy into the construction of national belonging through the fashioning of desires for betterment into aspirations for whiteness, the latter located at the apex of the creole order. Third, hybridity is a technology of exclusion. In Latin America, this technology functions to exclude the indigenous "Indio" and the Afro-derived populations from full claims to citizenship through the nations' mestizo construction. In the Caribbean, its "mulatto" configuration acts to exclude from full citizenship those without originary claims either to Blackness or whiteness (such as, for example, South and East Asians particularly in Trinidad and Guyana, and Caribs in Dominica). Finally, it normalizes and legitimizes the exclusive privileges of a national capitalist elite that is overwhelmingly white (Hintzen 2002). But in its "spaces of possibilities and being," the Caribbean accommodates varied and plentiful diasporic presences. Caribbean identity is produced out of this myriad of people who settled in the region from almost every part of the world. They joined what was left of an indigenous population to initiate the world of the modern. This movement of people, motivated by the colonial agenda, engendered the need for multiple accommodations in keeping with the transitory character of Caribbean forms of coloniality.

Creole society in the Caribbean was produced pedagogically by the technologies of the colonial state. These technologies allocated historically constructed and racially identified groupings to exclusive socioeconomic sectors of the political economy. The creole continuum was fashioned from the insertion into slave society of two historically produced, racialized categories that, in the European hegemonic imagination, existed universally at the opposite poles of civilization. Creoleness was produced out of the idea of the confluence of these two categories. The "Afro-creole" (what is popularly considered "Black" in the region) is located at one end of the continuum. As a social category, it is the embodiment of the (changing) representations and practices of descendants of enslaved populations transported from West Africa for plantation labor. Racially constituted of "pure" descendants of Africans, their creolization is the product of a syncretic mix of traditional African culture with the cultural forms of the dominant European colonial overlords. "White creoles" or "local whites" are located at the other end of the continuum. They are descendants of plantation owners, former indentures, small-scale peasant landholders, workers, and (to a lesser degree) colonial officials with putatively "pure" European ancestry. Their creolization is the product of an ideology of purity that is at the root of white supremacy. Culturally polluted from immersion in the inferiorized space of plantation society, they are forced to relinquish their claims to purity and thus to European belonging. Given the connection of identity to territory, they developed organic ties to the colonial territory. Such ties form the basis for their claim to a privileged position in the national hierarchy. In the postcolony, their interests remained vested in the agenda of global capital, especially through their ownership of agricultural, commercial, and other business enterprises. They became the instrumentality through which neoliberal forms of globalization were inscribed into the political economies of the region. This is the group, for example, that made the choice to leave Cuba en masse once the revolution of 1959 took a decidedly anticapitalist turn. It may also be argued that the absence of a white creole presence in Guyana was responsible for the country's decidedly anticapitalist turn in its anticolonial nationalist movement, notwithstanding the movement's fragmentation into two competing racial sections (Hintzen 1989, 37–51).

Thus, creole discourse has been the bonding agent of Caribbean coloniality. It has functioned in the interest of the world system of global capital through the agency of a colonial or postcolonial state under the authority of a colonial or national elite. Creole identity serves as the glue that bonds the different, competing, and otherwise mutually exclusive interests contained within Caribbean society (Wallerstein 2004, 60–75; Stoler 2002).[3] It paved the way for the accommodation of racialized discourses of difference upon which rested the legitimacy of colonial capitalist power and exploitation. Racial difference, upon which coloniality rested, was rendered benign in the cognitive merger created and sustained by creole discourse. Competing interests and relations of exploitation and privilege became socially organized in a fluid, clinal system of racial and cultural hierarchy. This was the observation of Caribbean sociologist Lloyd Braithwaite in what has been called a "reticulated" color/class pattern of social stratification (Braithwaite 1953; Despres 1967).

With the abolition of slavery, creole identity engendered a cultural politics of exclusion that ensured the division of labor by preventing solidarities across lines of racialization. In Guyana and Trinidad, it guaranteed the continued supply of cheap and reliable agro-proletariat wage labor. Throughout the region, it created conditions for "middle minorities" of Syrians and Lebanese, Chinese, South Asians, Jews, and others to make clear distinctions between themselves and "creoles" in keeping with statist technologies of *divide et impera*. The presence of these middle minorities prevented the emergence of a group of Black and colored nationalist capitalists who, on racial grounds, may have allied with the group of peasants and proletarians. The racial and cultural hierarchical order institutionalized in creole discourse has legitimized and normalized a differential and unequal pattern of allocation of economic, cultural, symbolic, and social value. This has come to characterize Caribbean society and political economy. With creolization functioning to normalize this pattern of differential allocation, the power interests of a colonial and postcolonial elite in the service of global capital were rendered invisible.[4]

Racially inscribed patterns of allocation of value go to the core of coloniality and its ravages. The issue relates just as much to subordination and exploitation as it does to the conditions for the global survival of capital. The problematization of these patterns leads to a focus on the materialist ideologies of growth and consumption and their dependence on technologies of violence derived from notions of difference that are at the root of the modern condition. It also renders visible the realities of entanglement that make possible the ways of being that characterize the modern condition and modern forms of subjecthood. These ways of being are rendered invisible by the technologies of the modern state and by the state's apparatuses of enforcement through institutions of governance. My argument follows in the wake of scholars such as Dipesh Chakrabarty, Homi Bhabha, Edward Said, and Paul Gilroy, all of whom see modern subjectivities as firmly rooted in what Bhabha calls the performative (Chakrabarty 2000; Bhabha 1994; Said 1993). They expose the ruses of a totalizing historicism that has enraptured us with the fantasy of the possibilities for betterment and perfection through imperialism (whether colonial or postcolonial) and the modern state as its handmaiden (Chakrabarty 2000; Goldberg 2002).[5]

Creole hierarchy is also at the root of the allocation of status along a "color/class" continuum in the Caribbean (Braithwaite 1953). Through the instrumentalities of its totalizing discourses, the "subaltern" (i.e., the poor, the peasantry, and unskilled and semiskilled labor) are cast as impediments to development. Their significant presence in the Caribbean is what makes the region "underdeveloped." This preserves intact the construction of the modern nation in terms of European (bourgeois) modernity. Progress is to be measured against the latter as the ideal. But in the final analysis, European modernity is *culturally* constituted. What I mean here is that only as modern subjects can the subaltern participate in the colonial and postcolonial project, notwithstanding their "cultural" distance from an ideal European form. This realization has led Chakrabarty to call for a discursive and analytic "provincialization" of Europe (Chakrabarty 2000).[6] Only with such provincialization, he argues, can the cultural particularities that hide behind the distortions of a universalized and historicized modern capitalist political economy be revealed. These particularities are at the core of "white supremacy" in its current guise of historicist notions of underdevelopment. This is not to deny the universal significance of the Enlightenment values of freedom and equality in modernity's formation. Indeed, such values may be its distinctive features (Chakrabarty 2000). But they are interpolated into different and preexisting cultural milieus. It is in this manner that modern subjectivities might be considered overdetermined. And an examination of such overdetermination and its different forms of articulation may well expose the different and multitudinous expressions that these subjectivities assume.[7] Historical materialism, through its totalizing distortions, denies the possibility of differences in the formations of modern subjects: a denial necessitated by capitalism's imperatives of a racial and global division of labor. These differences in modern formations are ideologically represented in historicist terms as different stages of "development," and of different locations on the road to progress of those who are "not yet" or "not quite" modern.

The analytic framework above allows us to rethink the entire colonial project. It allows us to understand colonial forms of slavery in terms of the entangled realities of the slave owner and the enslaved. From this perspective, freedom emerges not as an absolute opposite of enslavement but as the spaces of being outside the domain of control, regulation, and surveillance of the technologies and apparatuses of the colonial slave-holding state. Emancipation, then, becomes the expansion of these spaces of being located within production and consumption. The possibilities for such expansion emerged out of the very conditions for surplus accumulation that made slavery a necessary imperative of colonial capitalism. Such a conclusion may well be drawn from the arguments of Eric Williams, among others, as to the role of slavery and slave production in creating the conditions for the industrial revolution (Williams 1944).[8] Surpluses from slave production could not be accumulated without the participation of the enslaved in the rational order of capitalist production. In other words, the capitalist slave economy presumed a slave rationality as producer. This very rationality, at some point, rendered slavery itself inefficient, making imperative the transformation to "free labor" and to a "free" peasantry. It also rendered the controlling technologies of the slaveholding colonial state ineffectual against the increasing accumulation by the enslaved of social and technical authority—the latter of course more than the former, given the relationship between race and social position.[9] This may be the very point of the narrative of liberation told by C. L. R. James in his accounting of the Haitian revolution (James 1963). The figure of Toussaint L'Ouverture is rendered much more meaningful if understood metonymically, as signification of a developing slave rationality that constituted the negation of slavery itself.

The idea of abduction has come into recent currency as a specification of a technology deployed as a form of erasure of the integral contribution of the colonized and racialized Other in the production of the materialities of the modern capitalist world system (Kamugisha 2006; Wynter 1992). It refers to the process and erasure of the capturing and entrapping of the bodies, cultures, ideas, territories, and so on, of the colonized through subjection to serve the dehumanizing colonial capitalist agenda of accumulation (Wynter 1992). Through abduction, the rationality (modernity) of the enslaved was attributed to the slaveholding plantocracy, thus legitimizing and normalizing colonial forms of capitalist surplus accumulation. In time, slave rationality produced a new class of industrial capitalists as its increasing efficiencies gave rise to new technical and social conditions of production that became incompatible with slavery itself, a point made by Eric Williams (1944). With the transformation to this new form of capital, the spaces of freedom for the formerly enslaved in the arenas of production and consumption became significantly expanded. Two manifestations of such expansion could be found in the shift by the formerly enslaved from plantation to "plot" and to proletarian wage earner. The collapse of the slaveholding planter class gave rise to new opportunities for these former slaves as some were transformed into a landholding peasantry. Others were mobilized to satisfy the demands of a growing urban and rural proletarian sector. This was an essential prerequisite for an emergent transterritorial form of capital employing more efficient methods of agro-industrial production. At the same time, however, the inefficiencies of the slave plantation were inherited by the new group of peasants, reducing the former slaves to subsistence or near subsistence. For them, liberation from slave forms of capitalist production came with marginalization and location "outside" of the modern political economy.

The incorporation of the proletarian wage earner into the new political economy came with its own dilemmas of class exploitation under new regimes of historicist subordination. The emerging order of industrial capitalism rested upon a symbiotic relationship between this new (or newly expanded) grouping and the peasantry, with the latter serving as a "reserve army" of surplus labor and as a basis for its subsistence. Both acted to depress the price of labor as a necessary condition for the intensification of surplus accumulation. The role of women for reproduction in the rural areas was integral to this process of capital accumulation. It freed the men for work in the wage-labor sectors without affecting rural subsistence production. Thus, the existence of a subsistence rural peasantry was critical to the process of abduction of the labor power of the formerly enslaved. It rendered visible their "separation" from the modern and efficient capitalist mode of production. Because they were "inefficient" subsistence producers, the rationality of rural peasants as modern civilized subjects could now be denied. Such denial extended to the urban and rural proletariat, given its organic (and racial) connection to the group of peasant producers. This highlights the artificiality of the distinction between the peasantry and proletariat, given the symbiotic relationship between rural subsistence and wage labor. Significantly, both became available for participation in international circuits of labor, such as for the building of the Panama Canal, for work in the sugar industry in Cuba, and for wage labor in Europe and the United States (Knight 1990, 288–90). Thus, labor organization in the colonies followed the path of the growing internationalization of industrial capital out of latter's need for a significant expansion of markets and of inputs to satisfy growing economies of scale. Like the condition of slavery, the economic rationality of the proletariat upon which rested the conditions for industrial capitalist accumulation was once again abducted by the colonial state. Such rationality was attributed to the new class of absentee industrial capitalists and to the growing national capitalist class of merchants, traders, and petty industrialists.

Abduction also signifies the entrapment of colonized identities within the ideological domain of colonial knowledge. Their colonial subjection is produced in the cultural conjunctures out of which their hybridized creoleness was wrought. As overdetermined, their identities are interpolated by the morality, ethics, and habitus of the European colonizers. This is the base upon which rests the hierarchy of colonial society and the inscription of white supremacy. Both color and class are ordered by the presumed attributes of Europe and the "pure" European. Judgment of worth, allocation of value, and determination of deserved status follow upon proximity to these ideals. These serve as the pedagogical ruses of coloniality.

At the same time, however, what is brought to the modern project by the subaltern is not permanently or totally lost to the claims of the national capitalist project and its civilizing mission. "Things," bodies, and attributes that are not needed for capitalist production and accumulation can be retained as markers of inferiority to be deployed as signifiers of "savagery." Others may remain free from colonial surveillance, regulation, and control for the same reason. Some, because of their necessary relationship to conditions of survival not available through colonial allocation, may be left alone or even supported and encouraged. After emancipation in the West Indies, these were inserted the arena of politics (i.e., into what is opened up in the public arena) through an "empowerment" of culture. Such "empowerment" fed the nationalist movement by bringing "cultural politics" into the domain of power contentions. It became the basis for challenging colonial power and ending colonial forms of *political* governance. Thus, the "empowerment of culture" became critical to what Stuart Hall, following Gramsci, termed a "transition from one form of politics to another." The transition was accompanied by "complexification" in the role of the state and an unprecedented elaboration in the structures and processes of "civil hegemony" (Hall 1996a, 428).

The empowerment of culture emerging out of emancipation was typical of the multitude of challenges to colonial rule as spaces of freedom began to open up in the arena of politics. According to Jean Comaroff and John Comaroff, this had implications for state power. Typically, state power is deployed in the exercise of "control over the production, circulation and consumption of signs and objects, over the making of both subjectivities and realities" (Comaroff and Comaroff 1991, 22). In the colony, this "agentive" power is directed at the production of categories of economic actors and their differentiation for the specification of their relationship to the modernist economic project. In this sense, what is being "empowered" are the western European modernist Enlightenment and economic values that are inscribed in the subjectivities of the colonized. At the same time, however, the "empowerment of culture," in its political iteration, incorporates "forms of everyday life" that are "hidden" proliferations existing "outside the realm of institutional politics, saturating such things as aesthetics and ethics, built form and bodily representation, medical knowledge and mundane usage" (Comaroff and Comaroff 1991). This is where Bhabha's performative "signifying processes of cultural identification" enter into the domain of state power contentions as national subjectivities, identified by the Comaroffs as a "nonagentive" deployment of power. Nationalist politics represented the insertion of the cultural significations of the formerly colonized into the domain of power contentions over governance (i.e., over control of the state apparatus) and peoplehood (i.e., over the technologies of imposed categorizations). But nationalism is overdetermined by its colonial roots, which resurface in a developmentalist guise with promises of material betterment. This is precisely what is conveyed by the idea of coloniality. It refers to the persistence of colonial forms in postcolonial nationalist formation. The desire for betterment, while specified in the arena of political economy, is engaged culturally. In other words, it is the driving force behind the commitment to nationalism by those who were previously excluded, on cultural grounds, from participation in the economic and political domains of bourgeois freedom. Development therefore becomes a technology deployed by the nationalist state to discipline and control the empowerment of culture in satisfaction of the accumulative demands of global industrial capital. In the final analysis, the goal and promise of material betterment become the sole bases of identification, as sovereign citizens, with the liberal capitalist nation. Cultural politics becomes the means through which access to the material benefits of citizenship is organized.

Developmentalism serves to explain the formative role played by trade union agitation for better working conditions in the nationalist movement. It also explains the ebbs and flows of anticolonial mobilization with the spirals of growth and recession in global capitalism. The major thrust of the nationalist movement occurred during the global depression of the 1930s. The decline in material conditions led to a series of labor riots throughout most of the British West Indian colonies. A commission of inquiry convened to examine the causes of the riots introduced a program of welfare reform and labor legislation that increased significantly the role of the colonial state in economic allocation (Lewis 1968, 90–93; West India Royal Commission 1945). It did so through the development of welfare reform and labor legislation that provided active support for trade union organization. It proposed replicating "the multifarious institutions, official and unofficial which characterize British public life" in the colonies (West India Royal Commission 1945, 94, 108). The Colonial Development and Welfare Organization was introduced for such replication. The shift to a welfarist agenda was clearly a response to the dilemmas of proletarianization. The expansion of the domains of freedom in the arenas of production, consumption, and politics produced by the latter demanded new technologies of control. This set the stage for the development of the West Indian postcolonial state as the instrumentality for material betterment (Lewis 1968, 91). Ultimately, efforts to implement the recommendations of the commission led to the development and expansion of representative governments elected through universal adult suffrage. Clearly, the Colonial Office in Britain was responding to challenges to British authority by redirecting the material demands of the peasant/proletariat to the state apparatus, where they became the object of the latter's "agentive" modes of power. This was in response to the growth in "nonagentive" power deployed "culturally" through the mobilization of the subaltern.

The empowerment of culture, in the form of creole nationalism, united the interests of the peasant/proletariat, the middle strata of the colonized, and the creole national capitalists. All were integrally connected to the circuits of global capital. The peasant/proletariat had become increasingly inserted into the circuits of global labor circulation in the Panama Canal, Cuba, Europe, and the United States. Indeed, the Depression and its consequences in the shrinking of opportunities for participation in these global circuits contributed significantly to the riots of the 1930s (Knight 1990). But peasant/proletarian participation in these global circuits of labor also acted to make possible their role in the development and circulation of liberal forms of statist ideologies and their transmission to the West Indies. This was the case, for example, for West Indian seamen, who became the embodiment of the "crossings" that characterized colonial identity formation. By the end of the nineteenth century, for example, one-fifth of Britain's seamen were born outside of that country and comprised West Indians as well as non-English Europeans, Africans, Asians, and North and South Americans (Cobley 2003). In 1901, according to the British census, there were more than 1,300 West Indian seamen working on British vessels (Cobley

2003). These seamen participated significantly in efforts to legalize trade unions and to raise wages, particularly in the port cities of Cardiff, Liverpool, and London. They were also pivotal in the formation of the trade union movement in the British West Indies as well as the region's earliest political associations. In this manner, they became conduits for the transmission of the ideas of liberal nationalism, in the formulation of which they were integral participants with their white proletarian counterparts in Britain. Given the differences in cultural formation between Britain and its colonies, what was transmitted was an agenda for proletarian representation in the arena of governance aimed at increasing their share of the distribution of surplus. The state, as an instrument of surplus distribution, thus became tied to capitalist accumulation. The colonized middle strata were also integrally connected to development of the liberal nationalist state in Great Britain. While, for the proletariat, the issue was freedom, the ideological interests of members of these strata were organized around that of equality. Their roots lay in the group of free coloreds who existed under colonial slavery, rendering freedom less of an object than participation in an anticolonial agenda. Thus the challenge posed by members of these middle strata to colonialism was aimed at its exclusionary practices, particularly in the arena of governance. Their demands were consistently for inclusion in the colonial apparatus of governance and for access to the habitus of the colonial elite. Even before the abolition of slavery, they were organized in efforts to fight legal restrictions on their civil and political rights. Once these restrictions were removed, their concern shifted to financial security and class standing. In other words, their political activity was consistently directed at gaining equal standing with whites. What this implied was a challenge to the system of white supremacy. This is what connected their "politics" to that of the subaltern peasant/proletariat. The "empowerment of culture" resulting from emancipation and proletarianization of necessity brought race into the arena of political contention, since culture was racially inscribed (MacDonald 1986, 36–41). What was being denied in the racial pedagogies of the colonial state were the cultural and social entanglements of the colonizer and the colonized. Such entanglements were most evident among the middle strata, with racial difference deployed as the technology of denial. The latter received its force from the idea of the middle strata's "racial" connection to the subaltern. Such connection was the operative basis for denial of their participation in the political governance of the colony and in the social habitus of the colonizer. Finally, the group of national capitalists, exclusively white under colonialism and directly connected to colonial capital, were able to make legitimate claims, through creole identity, to the developing national peoplehood emerging out of the anticolonial movement. They became the embodied link between capitalist production and nationalist interests.

Thus, in their "ways of being," the colonizer and the colonized were involved in an intricate web of relations on many grounds. This web incorporated the hierarchies of class as well as the divisions of race, gender, and territory. Importantly, it incorporated the gendered but nonetheless intimate divisions between production and reproduction. These networks of relations spanned the divisions between the West Indian colony and its European metropole, other colonial territories, and North America. The connection between colony and metropole was largely responsible for the introduction of liberal forms of bourgeois nationalism into the West Indian colonies. This transfer was facilitated by the sedimentation of colonial forms in the technologies of the postcolonial state. By the time adult suffrage was introduced in the West Indian colonies, the lower class was firmly organized into political and labor bureaucracies dominated by middle-class leadership. Mass participation in the politics of governance occurred at the very moment of a shift in global hegemony from colonial Europe to the United States. This shift was presaged in the West Indies even before the end of World War II. Following a decision by the United States to provide destroyers to Britain in exchange for the right to locate military bases in Britain's West Indian colonies, US involvement in the region was exercised through the Anglo-American Caribbean Commission, established in 1942 as part of a "bases for destroyers" agreement. American participation in colonial affairs was accompanied by intense criticism of Britain's colonial policies (Fraser 1994, 55–89). Such criticism was quite consistent with the shift away from racial forms of colonial subjection to neocolonial forms with their roots in the idea of "underdevelopment." American criticism of colonial practice provided ideological support to the racial challenge to governance being mounted by the nationalist movement and to the latter's thrust for material betterment. Ties to the United States came with the promise of growth and development. As a result, nationalist leaders in the West Indies quickly began to establish links of support with North American political and economic interests in their local political campaigns (Fraser 1994, 110–17). These relations set the stage for the intensification of the integration of the West Indies into the political economy of global capital.

Economic development thus was inscribed into the agentive power of the state as the instrumentality through which new technologies of state control of the subaltern, now a "free peasantry" and "free labor," were formalized. The new discipline emerged at a time when colonialism was under challenge not only from the colonized but also from a newly assertive United States. It was accompanied by the formation of new international institutions, which would eventually organize and manage a postcolonial global economy, and it produced new justifications for the global division of labor as new assertions of modern citizenship were emerging in anticolonial national movements that challenged the old notions of racial and cultural immaturity upon which colonialism rested. The United States was at the center of this reformulation, signaling a shift in global hegemonic power away from European colonial centers. It was fitting, therefore, that the official announcement of the shift came from the first post–World War II US president. On January 20, 1949, President Harry Truman, in his inaugural speech before Congress, used the phrase "underdeveloped areas" to describe the countries and territories of the world located outside of Europe and the North Atlantic. It was the first time that these areas were defined with reference to material and economic progress. In doing so, he instantiated a new hierarchy of countries along a continuum measured by economic production. With this conceptualization, gross national product per capita became the new standard measure of modernity (Sachs 1996, 239–52). In July of the same year, the International Bank for Reconstruction and Development, in one of its first forays into these "developing areas," proposed a program of "multitude improvements and reforms" for the economy of Colombia. The program emphasized the need for "careful planning, organization, and allocation of resources" through a "detailed set of prescriptions, including goals, quantifiable targets, investment needs, design criteria, methodologies, and time sequences (Escobar 1995, 24–26). This new economism retained all the discursive features of the old colonial forms rooted in racial inferiority. The developed and the underdeveloped replaced civilization and savagery in the divide between the "modern" and "premodern." As development, it posited the narrow economic rationalities of production as the fundamental condition of modernity. Modern selfhood was now measured by evidence of economic acquisition.

The two forms of power, agentive and nonagentive, exist in constant tension. The potential conflict that such tension can produce is mitigated by mass accommodation to economic development. When its promise of economic modernization and betterment fails, then nonagentive power may be deployed through the reiteration of "native" cultural forms, the "invention of tradition," and the rejection of "European" canons. There is an ongoing struggle that produces constantly shifting "historic blocs of alliances" of "different specific social conformation and configuration" (Hall 1996a, 424). This struggle occurs within the historic bloc of ruling interests, among its constituent elements, and through challenges mounted by social groups not included within its formation. It is a struggle for ascendance in the complex organization of national subjectivity. It can reflect legacies of colonial cultural struggles between the colonizer and the colonized and/or can take place among those organized into cultural formations of diverse groupings of the colonized. The struggle may also be engaged by members of new cultural formations who enter into the national domain through immigration, diasporic identity, or new penetrations from the Global North.[10]

The postcolonial history of the Caribbean reflects the shifting alliances linked to the promises and possibilities of material betterment and their failures. In Guyana, Jamaica, and Grenada, all with significant peasant populations, immediate postcolonial formations led to forms of state socialism that retained capitalist rationalities while effecting strategies of state-directed redistribution. These state formations came with considerable ambiguities, ambivalences, and contradictions. As the conditions of state accumulation declined precipitously, new forms of consensus began to emerge that produced new formations in the historic bloc of alliances. The decline was directly related to the undermining of historical linkages with global capital as the state began to challenge the latter's accumulative interests. This provoked a new thrust to reestablish and strengthen such ties. In Jamaica, it led the group of national capitalists to reassert their alliances with a managerial and professional grouping tied to both national and global capital, and with petty traders from the grouping of the peasant/ proletariat. These traders emerged to fill a gap produced by material shortages stemming from a foreign exchange crisis linked directly to the weakening of the country's ties to global capital. The crisis led small landowners to waver in their support for the nationalist project. They resorted to productive rationalities not integrally tied capitalist production (Crichlow 2005). In Grenada, new alliances led to the erosion of forms of production based on an independent peasantry producing for national and international markets mediated by the state. Peasant production came to be replaced increasingly by wage and salaried work in a burgeoning tourist industry organized by global capitalist investors. With the intensification of proletarianization came popular commitment to capitalist rationality in production (US Department of State 2006). In Guyana, the crisis produced by efforts to separate from global capital led to an alliance of the class of national capitalists with the cash-crop peasantry and a reintroduction of foreign extractive capital into the historic bloc of alliances (Hintzen 2001). These developments parallel, and in some instances preceded, new state formations occurring globally, including in Europe and North America.

The Caribbean remains the pivotal center of the modern world because, when shorn of its material ethos, modernity is the condition of "flexible accommodation" of people, resources, and ideas from all parts of the world in multiple geographies. And as a region of birth of the modern world system, the Caribbean is where conditions for its maintenance are most manifest and where the possibilities for its transformation are located. This is notwithstanding the Caribbean's diminished role in the production of the material resources upon which global accumulation depends. Nonetheless, the region continues to signal changes in forms of modern organization. Today, it is experiencing rapid movement away from a pattern of global relations centered on Europe (even eastern Europe) and North America to that focused on the Global South.

What is indicated is the possibility for new centers of capitalist accumulation to displace the old. At the same time, however, the region continues to point to the unsustainability of global capital. This is evident in its perpetual condition of crisis and in the challenges the region always poses by the "empowerment of culture." Global capital's reliance on forms of identity that are ideologically produced is constantly challenged by such empowerment of culture. Thus far, such challenges have been contained, controlled, and disciplined by ruses of capitalism that have fashioned desire into fetishized pleasures. The region is ravaged by North American forms of consumerism. And national consensus as to the role of the state in development remains strong.

The forms of freedom unleashed by the rationality of West Indian labor under slavery have become enraptured by development and its promises. But, without constant expansion and without the accommodation of those making cultural demands, capitalism is open to rejection. And these tendencies have been constant features of the Caribbean political economy, as is exemplified by Cuba, and by Caribbean forms of socialism that were features of statist organization in Guyana, Jamaica, and Grenada. Socialist governments have sought to appropriate the economic surpluses of global capital for popular redistribution. The tendency has also been evident in cultural movements such as Rastafarianism that have challenged the very materialist logic of accumulation. But even under conditions of infinite possibilities for surplus accumulation and for expansion of the domains of freedom and equality for the subaltern, the capitalist world system contains within it the seeds of its own destruction. Accommodation of demands stemming from the empowerment of culture can only come about under conditions that threaten the very division of labor upon which capitalist accumulation rests. Without such accommodation, the system is open to rejection on cultural grounds. Both tendencies are features of current formations of the world system of capitalism.

NOTES

1. I use the term "modern world system" following Immanuel Wallerstein to indicate a global capitalist world economy with origins in sixteenth-century Europe and the Americas (including the Caribbean). It refers to a global integrated system of production dependent on "an axial division of labor . . . and multiple political centers and multiple cultures." See Wallerstein 2004 for a full elaboration of this system.

2. I use the term "crossings" following the work of M. Jacqui Alexander, particularly elaborated upon in her published series of essays *Pedagogies of Crossing* (2005).

3. Here I would like to separate "interests" that emerge out of the relationship between ideology and "relations of production" from the "ways of being" characterized by the entanglement of these ideologically positioned groupings as modern subjects. For a discussion of ideology along these lines, see Wallerstein 2004, 60–75. I relied on the work

of Ann Laura Stoler (2002) as the basis for my distinction between colonialist identity and "ways of being" under colonial regimes.

4. These elites accomplished this by, for example, creating the impression of "nationalist" control of the domestic economy and "nationalist" alliances with global capital and participation in its accumulation.

5. By historicism, I refer to the notion of historical progress applied synchronically to racially, culturally, and nationally defined populations that positions them in a hierarchical development order while acknowledging the possibilities for the lesser developed to progress (Chakrabarty 2000; Goldberg 2002).

6. Here, once more, we use "distortion" to refer to the product of ideology that renders invisible the "true" conditions of social reality through the latter's representation in hierarchical terms that normalize and universalize the interests of a dominant ruling historical bloc (Hall 1996a).

7. Here I follow the definition of "overdetermination" employed by Stuart Hall (1996a).

8. Of course, the acquisition of social position was always possible even within the social category of the slave. Hierarchically organized distinctions among field slaves, drivers, artisans, and house slaves were one form of social differentiation common to most slave societies.

9. For a conceptual elaboration of "abduction," see Kamugisha 2006, chap. 1; see also Wynter 1992.

10. Such formations may include, for example, American forms of Black identity including the Black Muslims.

BIBLIOGRAPHY

Alexander, M. Jacqui. 2005. *Pedagogies of Crossing: Meditations on Feminism, Sexual Politics, Memory, and the Sacred*. Durham, NC: Duke University Press.

Bhabha, Homi K. 1994. *The Location of Culture*. Abingdon, Oxon., England: Routledge.

Braithwaite, Lloyd. 1953. "Social Stratification in Trinidad: A Preliminary Analysis." *Social and Economic Studies* 2, no. 2: 5–175.

Chakrabarty, Dipesh. 2000. *Provincializing Europe: Postcolonial Thought and Historical Difference*. Princeton, NJ: Princeton University Press.

Cobley, Alan Gregor. 2003. "That Turbulent Soil: Seafarers, the 'Black Atlantic,' and the Shaping of Afro-Caribbean Identity." In *Seascapes, Littoral Cultures, and Trans-Oceanic Exchanges*, conference proceedings, edited by Debbie Ann Doyle and Brandon Schneider. Washington, DC: Library of Congress.

Comaroff, Jean, and John Comaroff. 1991. *Of Revelation and Revolution*. Vol. 1, *Christianity, Colonialism, and Consciousness in South Africa*. Chicago: University of Chicago Press.

Crichlow, Michaeline A. 2005. *Negotiating Caribbean Freedom: Peasants and the State in Development*. Lanham, MD: Lexington Books.

Despres, Leo A. 1967. *Cultural Pluralism and Nationalist Politics in British Guiana*. Chicago: Rand McNally.

Escobar, Arturo. 1995. *Encountering Development: The Making and Unmaking of the Third World*. Princeton, NJ: Princeton University Press.

Fraser, Cary. 1994. *Ambivalent Anti-Colonialism: The United States and the Genesis of West Indian Independence, 1940–1964.* Westport, CT: Greenwood Press.

Gilroy, Paul. 1993. *The Black Atlantic: Modernity and Double-Consciousness.* Cambridge, MA: Harvard University Press.

Goldberg, David Theo. 2002. *The Racial State.* Malden, MA: Blackwell.

Hall, Stuart. 1996a. "Gramsci's Relevance for the Study of Race and Ethnicity." In *Stuart Hall: Critical Dialogues in Cultural Studies*, edited by David Morley and Kuan-Hsing Chen, 411–40. Abingdon, Oxon., England: Routledge.

Hall, Stuart. 1996b. "The Meaning of New Times." In *Stuart Hall: Critical Dialogues in Cultural Studies*, edited by David Morley and Kuan-Hsing Chen, 223–37. Abingdon, Oxon., England: Routledge.

Hall, Stuart. 1996c. "What Is This 'Black' in Black Popular Culture?" In *Stuart Hall: Critical Dialogues in Cultural Studies*, edited by David Morley and Kuan-Hsing Chen, 465–75. Abingdon, Oxon., England: Routledge.

Hintzen, Percy C. 1989. *The Costs of Regime Survival: Racial Mobilization, Elite Domination and Control of the State in Guyana and Trinidad.* Cambridge: Cambridge University Press.

Hintzen, Percy C. 2001. "Cheddi Jagan (1918–97): Charisma and Guyana's Response to Western Capitalism." In *Caribbean Charisma: Reflections on Leadership, Legitimacy, and Populist Politics*, edited by Anton Allahar, 121–54. Boulder, CO: Lynne Rienner.

Hintzen, Percy C. 2002. "The Caribbean: Race and Creole Ethnicity." In *A Companion to Racial and Ethnic Studies*, edited by David Theo Goldberg and John Solomos, 475–94. Malden, MA: Blackwell.

James, C. L. R. 1963. *The Black Jacobins: Toussaint L'Ouverture and the San Domingo Revolution.* New York: Vintage Books.

Kamugisha, Aaron. 2006. "Abducting Western Civilization: Coloniality, Citizenship and Liberation in the Caribbean Intellectual Tradition." PhD diss., York University.

Knight, Franklin W. 1990. *The Caribbean: The Genesis of a Fragmented Nationalism.* 2nd ed. Oxford: Oxford University Press.

Lewis, Gordon K. 1968. *The Making of the Modern West Indies.* New York: Monthly Review Press.

MacDonald, Scott B. 1986. *Trinidad and Tobago: Democracy and Development in the Caribbean.* New York: Praeger.

Quijano, Anibal. 2000. "Coloniality of Power and Eurocentrism in Latin America." *International Sociology* 15, no. 2: 217–34.

Sachs, Wolfgang. 1996. "Neo-Development: 'Global Ecological Management.'" In *The Case Against the Global Economy: And for a Turn toward the Local*, edited by Jerry Mander and Edward Goldsmith, 239–52. San Francisco: Sierra Club Books.

Said, Edward. 1993. *Culture and Imperialism.* New York: Vintage Books.

Stavans, Ilan. 1995. *The Hispanic Condition: The Future Power of a People.* New York: HarperCollins.

Stoler, Ann Laura. 2002. *Carnal Knowledge and Imperial Power: Race and the Intimate in Colonial Rule.* Berkeley: University of California Press.

Taylor, Lucien. 1997. "Créolité Bites: A Conversation with Patrick Chamoiseau, Raphaël Confiant, and Jean Bernabé." *Transition*, no. 74: 124–61.

US Department of State. 2006. "Background Note: Grenada." Washington, DC: Department
    of State, Bureau of Western Hemisphere Affairs.

Wallerstein, Immanuel. 1974. *The Modern World-System I: Capitalist Agriculture and the
    Origins of the European World-Economy in the Sixteenth Century.* New York: Academic
    Press.

Wallerstein, Immanuel. 1980. *The Modern World-System II: Mercantilism and the
    Consolidation of the European World-Economy, 1600–1750.* New York: Academic Press.

Wallerstein, Immanuel. 2004. *World-Systems Analysis: An Introduction.* Durham, NC: Duke
    University Press.

West India Royal Commission. 1945. "West India Royal Commission Report." London: Her
    Majesty's Stationery Office.

Williams, Eric. 1944. *Capitalism and Slavery.* Chapel Hill: University of North Carolina Press.

Williams, Eric. 1974. "Economic Transformation and the Role and Vision of the PNM."
    Address to the Sixteenth Annual Convention of the People's National Movement, Port of
    Spain, Trinidad.

Wynter, Sylvia. 1992. "Beyond the Categories of the Master Conception: The Counterdoctrine
    of the Jamesian Poiesis." In *C. L. R. James's Caribbean*, edited by Paget Henry and Paul
    Buhle, 63–91. Durham, NC: Duke University Press.

Chapter 13

TOWARDS A NEW DEMOCRACY IN THE CARIBBEAN

Local Empowerment and the New Global Order

PERCY C. HINTZEN

INTRODUCTION

Governance, whether democratic or not, is exercised as an entangled set of institutional and bureaucratic practices aimed at ordering and directing people and their relationships to other people and to things (Escobar 1995, 107–9). It must be judged by its "far reaching effects" on the governed—what I choose to term its "instrument effects" (Escobar 1995, 107–9). It is in these effects that the intent of sovereign power is both revealed and realized. And intent is closely aligned with the constitutive interests of the *effective* participants in governance.

The West Indies is inscribed in global entanglements effectuated in "interlinked transnational formations" through which the local, the national, and the global coalesce (Ferguson 2006, 103–12). The role of postcolonial West Indian governance has been confined almost exclusively to establishing and guaranteeing contractual legal authority to legitimate the extractive work of transnational firms, to fashioning institutional practice consistent with the needs of the market in the formal economy, to establishing and running the legal order (from which many are exempted), to organizing political parties, to co-opting and controlling public interest groups, and to disciplining public discussion and opinion. All of these respond to demands placed upon national governing authority by powerful international interests. The problem that this chapter addresses relates to the manner in which these interlinkages, both historically and currently, explain the region's practices of governance, irrespective of form. Our focus on the Westminster model, universally adopted by all of the former British colonies in the Caribbean region, makes analytical sense because it allows for the disentanglement of form and practice through a focus on democracy. However closely it does or does not adhere to its British provenance, there is considerable convergence in the practice of governance throughout the region.

Representative democracy in the West Indies is practiced in and through networks of neocolonial and imperialist relations that provide the regime and its governing apparatus with global legitimacy. This has preempted possibilities of escape from the limitations and constraints imposed by these networks, including attempts at state-directed expansion of human capabilities necessary for guarantees of rights and freedoms. In the absence of alternative forms of direct participation, any attempt at such expansion can come at considerable cost to political freedom. Alternatively, when attempts are made within the framework of representative governance to incorporate subaltern interests in governing practice, the result is often political crisis. There is, therefore, a disjuncture between representative practice and the ability of national apparatuses of governance to expand people's substantive freedoms and the human capabilities needed for their exercise. Conversely, when demands for freedom and capabilities impose themselves upon representative practice, there is no hesitation to curtail them.

The fundamental concern of this chapter is with the manner in which the interests of global actors, including nationals acting on the global stage, affect governing practices, and their consequences, positive or negative, on stated goals of governance, particularly as these relate to the interests of local communities and constituencies. In the final analysis, the intent is to explore the compatibility between such practices and the conditions for genuine development. Such an examination is not inconsistent with the declarative assertions of West Indian postcolonial governments in their nationalist demands for democratic transformation from colonial governance. The problem for the West Indies that the Westminster model was to resolve, at least at the level of discourse, was that of freedom. Postcolonial governance implied the expansion of freedom to the colonized subjects as an escape from conditions of colonial commandment (Mbembe 2001, 34–35).[1] This was not merely an end in itself, but was understood to be the "principal means of development" (Sen 2000). This is important because "development" has been the singular and universal goal of West Indian governance (as it has been for all forms of postcolonial governance). It legitimizes all forms of governing practice (Harris 1976).[2]

This brings into question the constitution of the state and its relationship to national governance. Michel-Rolph Trouillot has pointed to the fallacy in our claims of an integral connection between the two in assertions of a "nation-state homology." He insists upon an understanding of the state as "a set of practices and processes and their effects … whether or not they coalesce around central sites of governments" (Trouillot 2001, 137). The point of such a departure from convention is to direct our attention away from the form of governance in order to explain the manner in which "state-effects" are imposed on its practice. Our concern is with "novel articulations of social power" (Robinson 2014).[3] As such, we must of necessity take into account these state-effects, independent of the authority exercised through the apparatus of national governance.

WESTMINSTER, DEMOCRACY, AND DEVELOPMENT

By the Westminster model, I make reference here, most fundamentally, to a codified system of laws and governance contained in a written constitution, a sovereign head of state, a cabinet led by the head of government, a bicameral or unicameral parliament with one branch comprising members elected by local constituencies in a general election, a parliamentary opposition, an independent judiciary, archived minutes of meetings, and an independent civil service. Postcolonial adoption of the formalities of the Westminster model has been the instrumentality through which nationalist concentration was consolidated in the British West Indies. As I will argue, this provided the necessary condition for continued participation in global topographies of neocolonial and imperialist power as the legitimizing practice of postcolonial formation.

Democracy is presented universally as a particular and desirable ideal form of governance. Almost universally in postcolonial formation, it has provided the instrumental link between (political) freedom and development. Nobel Prize–winning economist Amartya Sen has made an explicit and normative link among the three. Democracy, he maintains, as an "institutional arrangement," must be rooted in "the exercise of people's freedoms through the liberty to participate in social choice and in the making of public decisions" (Sen 2000, 4–5). Ideally, the result of its practice must be the achievement and expansion of "economic opportunities, political liberties, social powers, and the enabling conditions of good health, basic education, and the encouragement and cultivation of initiatives" (Sen 2000, 4–5). When judged by this yardstick, in varying degrees and under different registers, democratic practice has failed in the West Indies. Indeed, there has been no necessary connection between "democracy" and "development." For most of the former British colonies in the West Indies, notwithstanding their impressive scores on various democracy indexes and rankings (to which they point with pride), their populations have not escaped the maladies of recurring, even perpetual, universal global crises that have intensified with the shift in emphasis from "national development" to neoliberal-induced forms of globalization. The explanation for these failures rests with how development has been specified, universally and for West

Indian governments, as "convergence" with the modern industrialized Global North. This imperative has become inscribed upon the practice of governance, converting its goals almost exclusively to the pursuit of growth in production, consumption, and accumulation, producing the postcolonial dilemma of failure of both development and democracy. The result has been a decomposition of freedom, rights, and development.

The quest for development convergence has imposed in the space of post-colonial governance a form of decomposition in which rights that are integral to democratic practice are understood to exist independently of conditions for development transformation. The two are sequentially rather than integrally linked (Ferguson 2006, 176–82).[4] By convention, both can be realized only through forms of modernity not yet achieved in "developing" societies. In "underdeveloped societies," democracy, in practice, can hinder the progress of development. As such, it must be placed in a lockbox for the future. Modernity, and therefore freedom, comes at the end of the process of development. This legitimizes forms of exclusion from democratic practice through the denial of the rights of participation of those seen as impediments to progress. It explains the divergence between formal democracy, institutionalized through the Westminster model in the West Indies, and its practice. The former becomes transformed into a mere legitimizing discourse of nationalism argued around guarantees of those very rights, understood to have been denied by colonial governance. This, in a fundamental way, was the charge made against colo-nization and the basis for nationalist demands for independence. But once development, specified as convergence, became integral to nationalist objec-tives, freedom and the guarantees of fundamental rights had to be curtailed. Given this dilemma, the question to be asked of postcolonial governance turns on the issue of congruence between development goals and guarantees of fundamental rights. The stated goal of convergence with Western industri-alized modernity becomes irrelevant, or relevant only under conditions of such congruence.

GOVERNANCE, RIGHTS, AND EXCEPTION

As is currently practiced, there is an ideological distortion that ties development and democratic discourse together. Both, as ideologies, are imposed by global conditions and global interests in ways that explain their failure. This brings into focus the inevitable connection between the local and the global, which has been called "glocalization" (Steger 2009, 42; Robertson 1995, 25–44),[5] as an essential characteristic of colonial and postcolonial formation in the Caribbean. Here, I refer to the manner in which local communities become inserted into global spaces. What is at stake is whether or not, and how, such insertion can provide opportunities to enhance individual and collective rights to freedom and development.

Governance, then, must be judged on the basis of the link it creates among conditions of freedom, determination of rights, and the practice of development consistent with Sen's formulation mentioned earlier. The goals of freedom and democracy, inscribed in the discourse of independence and in the objectives of the Westminster form, would require a fundamental shift in the objectives of development from "convergence" with the industrialized North to guarantees of "a standard of living adequate for health and well being including food, clothing, housing and medical care and necessary social services, and the right to security in the event of unemployment" (Sen 2000). By these sets of standards, governance in the West Indies has failed to meet its "desired" objectives. Effective pursuit of the rights and capabilities for development and freedom by subaltern social groups[6] has come to depend on harnessing opportunities existing outside of and in opposition to the official and formal system of "democratic" governance. The poor and powerless have become exceptions to government guarantees of "rights" and excluded from the benefits of citizenship. While engaged with the established structures of political representation, they are excluded from effective participation. This is one form of exception (Ong 2006, 5).[7] The other references forms of privilege exercised by the governing elites and the interest groups they represent that exempt both from compliance with constitutionality and the rule of law.

The problem exists on two levels. The first has to do with the incongruence between participation and representation built into the Westminster model (and its modifications and deviations). As a liberal practice, Westminster democracy relies on mobilization for support through diffuse claims of representation that do not come with the guarantee of rights, even when there is strict adherence to the principle of "one person one vote" (Hintzen 1989).[8] The limitations placed on *effective* participation in governance by the subaltern have allowed members of the middle and upper strata of West Indian society to use conditions of exception, understood here as their ability to depart from legality and constitutionality, "to intervene in the logics of ruling and being ruled" (Ong 2006, 5) in order to gain access to state resources—in other words, to function "outside of the law." They engage in pervasive practices of corruption, cronyism, and nepotism, which have become normalized in the region. The lower strata, as the overwhelming majority, by and large are without these opportunities, except indirectly through forms of patronage and clientelism (Stone 1973; Edie 1991). They are forced to create their own conditions for economic opportunity, their own extrajudicial forms of political practice (including riots), and their own forms of social welfare and protective security. For them, "societal arrangements," formed and fashioned to satisfy social needs through the guarantee of economic and political rights, occur outside of state practice.

Members of the upper and middle strata use their access to the state (i.e., to processes and practices of global power whether exercised through the apparatuses of national governance or through global presences) to establish and maintain international and national networks through which their material needs are satisfied and their freedoms to pursue them are maintained and expanded.

Postcolonial development in the West Indies has been disconnected, piecemeal, uneven (as it relates to the various sectors of society), ad hoc, and reversible. Development is practiced as a problem of technicality and efficiency consistent with understandings derived through the regime's engagements with "transnational topographies of power" (Ferguson 2006, 89–99). Rather than a mechanism for bringing the grounded realities of diverse social groups, families, and individuals into effective representation in governing practice, governance is directed toward the coordination of societal arrangements and institutional practices in keeping with the imperatives of these engagements (Ferguson 2006, 95–99). This has imposed a universalized uniformity in governing practices throughout the region, legitimized as they are in discourses of political freedom and economic development. Civil society, as the object of statist intervention, is restricted to "societal arrangements and institutional practices" that accord with goals imposed through participation in international topographies of power. The role of government is reduced to harnessing, in one form or another, what is "usable" for global interests. As pointed out by Suzanne Bergeron, following James Scott, "people and activities that do not fit into the model are left out of the frame and turned into anomalies or pathologies that need to be transformed: they are either ignored or eliminated with the result in the loss of freedom, social dislocation, alienation, and environmental degradation" (Bergeron 2006, 31; Scott 1998, 88).

The struggle for national independence occurred in the West Indies through the formation of political parties, labor unions, clientelistic networks, ethnic and communal organizations, and the like, which were fashioned into "civil society." An inherent structural incapacity is built into liberal democratic practice to accommodate the diverse forms out of which these are constituted on their own terms (Wallerstein 2004).[9] Thus, in the West Indies, "democratic governance" has been used systematically to deny, constrain, and limit the conditions of true development. From the inception, formalized "independence" gave the postcolonial state constitutional and legal contractual authority to receive foreign assistance and foreign loans, to provide legal frameworks and the legal bases for foreign investments, and to receive formal recognition as a sovereign unit in international relations (Ferguson 2006, 50–88). In other words, the postcolonial Caribbean was *internationally* inscribed in a transnational apparatus of governmentality in which governments are unable to "exercise the range of powers we usually associate with a sovereign nation-state" (Ferguson 2006, 93). Thus, "good government" became the exercise of effective means of meeting the demands of powerful global actors. All the diverse segments of the population had to become conscripted into such an exercise. When the interests of powerful global actors conflicted with the rights of segments of the national population, good government came into conflict with "government that is good." Good government, in its practice, came to rely on "efficient and technically functional institutions" (including elections) aimed at meeting demands imposed by global forces rather than aimed at guaranteeing rights that are "benevolent and protective" of a diverse citizenry (Ferguson 2006, 86). Segments of the national population have become differentially constrained and contained by the demands of global interests. This is not to say that there is an inevitable conflict between these demands and the political and economic rights of local segments of the population. Given the nature and character of the formation of Caribbean political economy (and that of postcolonies in general), the acquisition of rights by domestic social groups, families, and individuals rests integrally with the access they have to both local and global resources that the government is not in a position to guarantee. Those excluded by the governing apparatus, through forms of exception, are left to develop their own strategies for securing such access.

THE STRUGGLE FOR MEANINGFUL RIGHTS AND RECOGNITION

It is certainly not the case that "development," understood here as guarantees of economic rights, has not occurred in the Caribbean; quite the opposite. But access to its conditions is class differentiated in the face of the state-effects of exclusion and privilege. If freedom, rights, and development are to become aligned in governing practice, there needs to be an examination of the strategies adopted by subaltern groups to secure, guarantee, and produce development change *on their own terms*. Because the economic rights of the middle and upper strata are fashioned, formulated, constrained, and constricted by the demands of global actors, members of these strata have become instantiated in global interests that have stymied possibilities for true development (Ong 2006, 31–52; Mamdani 2009).[10]

At the same time, there have been periods in the early phases of postcolonial practice when technical and social conditions at the global and local levels have combined with the interests of global actors to open up possibilities for the pursuit of subaltern rights. During the "national development" phase of preindependence, the popular mobilization of workers and peasants along with party organization combined with the needs of foreign investors for labor and with Cold War contestation to produce "thick social investments" in the former colonies. This created a space for accommodation by the region's political elite of demands for economic, political, and civil rights made by the working classes and peasantry. "Far-reaching investments" in social welfare, education, health, housing, and so on became conditions for popular support in the immediate pre- and postindependence period (McMichael 2010; Ferguson 2006, 197). But such accommodation came with considerable inefficiencies and high remuneration and transaction costs that not only affected surplus accumulation but also were unsustainable. The imperative was always there to curtail these accommodations, and when they became excessive, to intervene for preemption or prevention. In many instances, there were modifications in the formal arrangements of the Westminster model. As a result, the lower strata were forced into a perpetual struggle for economic development and political rights.

SUBALTERN STRUGGLES AND CURTAILMENTS IN DEMOCRATIC PRACTICE

Anticolonial mobilization for independence in the former British colonies was inserted into and supported by transnational anticapitalist networks, including the radical wing of the British Labour Party, the World Federation of Trade Unions (WFTU), the Red International of Labor Unions (through which the Communist International, or Comintern, under the control of the Soviet Union, channeled organizational and ideological support), the Negro Bureau of the Red International of Labor Unions, and the International Trade Union Committee of Negro Workers (an offshoot of the Red International of Labor Unions). The West Indian working class and peasantry, by providing the mass base for such mobilization, were inserted into international anticapitalist movements, which through their socialist ideology were making explicit the links among capitalism, class exploitation, and colonialism. As a result, anticapitalism became the crucible in which the subaltern's struggle for political and economic rights was forged. The Caribbean Labour Congress (CLC), formed by middle-class leaders who had cultivated ties with the British Labour Party, became an instrumental conduit for such insertion (Howe 1993, 84–89). Labor mobilization escalated into violence throughout the West Indies during the 1930s in protests against low wages, colonial neglect of the welfare of workers, substandard housing, subhuman working and sanitary conditions, and denial of the absence of worker participation in decision-making on the terms and conditions of their labor through collective bargaining (Bolland 1995; Fraser 1994, 37–50). The British Colonial Office responded by introducing "representative government" with the promise of full independence. In exchange for governance and participation in the global system of sovereign nations, middle-class creole leaders of the nationalist movement used their control of organizations of mass mobilization, now converted into political parties and trade unions, to co-opt, regulate, and control the subaltern and to harness their members to the interests of global capital (Hintzen 1993). Representative governments allowed these elites to legitimize their claims as representatives of the "will of the people." In exercising this "will," understood in terms of the need for development, they entered into a new pattern of neocolonial domination and dependency. In the process, the neocolonial reality was rendered invisible under the symbolic camouflage of the exercise of the sovereign right of international association (Hintzen 1997).

But what was being represented was neither the "general will" nor the economic interests of the mass supporters of the political elite. In the process of "democratic transition," sectarian interests, organized through the forging of ties of race and clientelism, were pitted against each other in political competition, while insertion into emerging neocolonial capitalist networks, increasingly centered around the United States, was justified as the sole means of development. And development, in its statist narration, can be realized only through programs of convergence with the industrialized North. In Guyana, racial fracturing orchestrated by the colonial state just before independence resulted in a split in the radical nationalist People's Progressive Party into politically organized racial segments. This significantly compromised and weakened working-class mobilization, which had managed, quite successfully, to secure the expansion of economic, political, social, and cultural rights denied by colonial governance. Under the guise of "democracy," and exploiting the racial fissure, the British handed effective power to political leaders of the country's white and "near-white" merchant class, representing less than 5 percent of Guyana's population. With the goal of ensuring capitalist control of postcolonial formation, the British Colonial Office decided to make a fundamental shift away from locally elected constituency representation (one of the central pillars of the Westminster model) to proportional representation based on percentages of the national vote. This forced an alliance between leaders of the Black racial faction and political representatives of the minority white and near-white local capitalist faction under conditions that gave the latter absolute control of economic and development policy (Hintzen 1989; Hintzen and Premdas 1983). With their struggle for economic rights compromised by "democratic" representation, members of the Black lower strata rejected democratic legitimacy to support their political leaders in successful efforts to gain exclusive control of the national apparatus of governance through "undemocratic" and "fraudulent" practices. This they saw as the only way to escape the clutches of global capital instantiated through the practice of proportional representation (Hintzen and Premdas 1983). It was only through electoral fraud that their political representatives were able to jettison their alliance with representatives of the domestic capitalist class. But fissures between the Black and Asian Indian working class prevented the reemergence of a multiracial, class-based challenge to imperialism, which had proved so successful earlier. What it did allow, however, was a realignment of the country's international relations through a shift to Cuba, the Soviet Union and its Warsaw Pact allies, and China.

In Trinidad and Tobago, North American and European Black radical assertions combined with mass dissatisfaction over rights in the 1960s to fuel a widespread "Black power" rebellion against the extant form of Westminster governance in 1970. It was sparked by "exceptions" granted to a group of powerful elites tied to international capital and exclusions of the Black working class from effective participation in governance. As part of its successful effort to retain power, the ruling party was forced to institutionalize massive expansions of clientelistic transfers. Like in Guyana, the stage for a racially mounted challenge was set in colonial-era attempts to resolve fundamental problems that inhered in the practice of Westminster liberal democracy by gerrymandering the boundaries of the constituencies to favor the ruling party after its leaders made commitments to pro-capitalist and pro-Western policies just prior to the granting of independence in 1962. In the wake of the rebellion, the ruling party's racial supporters were able to secure massive social transfers out of state surpluses. Mass mobilization against the government opened the floodgates to claims to political rights by different sectors of society, including Asian Indians and the population of the sister island of Tobago.

In Guyana, the turn to the Soviet bloc intensified the political and economic crisis in the wake of punitive retaliation by Western capital, which significantly reduced the global transfers upon which the Guyanese political economy depended. This led to the emergence of new multiracial radical challenges to the regime that provoked it to resort to repressive violence and, eventually, to a reinsertion into the network of global capital and a renunciation of socialist aspirations (Hintzen 2001). In Trinidad, while the Black challenge to the regime effectuated considerable changes in the pattern of ethnic representation in governance, it failed to resolve the crisis of effective participation that continues to haunt the country's society to this day. The reason for the failure was that the clientelistic response of the state was conditioned on an intensification of its participation in global capitalist networks (Ryan 1991, 1996).

The critical assertion here is that conditions for development cannot be separated from global processes and international entanglements that both constrain and support its realization. While in Guyana radical mobilization against global capitalist interests was undermined by racial loyalties, in Trinidad the Black working class was able to expand its access to global transfers in exchange for the resumption of support for the ruling party. Both came at the expense of democratic practice and political freedoms. And both failed to produce genuine development or expanded rights for the subaltern. In Jamaica, subaltern assertions of rights were meliorated, accommodated, and regulated through patronage networks through which transfers to the urban and rural poor were made (Stone 1973; Edie 1991). New possibilities for effective development opened up when the regime shifted its patterns of global alliances to Cuba, Eastern Europe, and the tricontinental "Third World" beginning in 1972. The shift allowed the People's National Party (PNP), under the leadership of democratic socialist Michael Manley, to make far-reaching social investments in poor communities. New conditions were placed on foreign investors to ensure domestic retention of a larger share of the economic surplus. The shift was in response to radicalized working-class demand for economic and political rights.

This discussion of Guyana, Trinidad, and Jamaica highlights the inability of formal democracy to create the conditions for access to economic rights and political freedom in postcolonial practice because of the inscription of the postcolony in global topographies of capitalist power and in global forms of capitalist transfers. Under such inscription, demands for economic rights become circumscribed. They cannot be accommodated under conditions in which freedom, rights, and development are conjoined. Inevitably, efforts to satisfy subaltern demands lead to the further curtailment of access to political and economic rights by the regime because such rights come into conflict with the perpetual and endless need by both global and national capital for surplus accumulation. Such curtailment occurred in Jamaica in the face of retaliatory withdrawals of investments, reductions in bilateral and multilateral transfers, and capital flight. The resulting economic crisis prevented the realization of the promise of reallocation. The progressive anticapitalist ruling party lost support in the wake of the crisis, and in 1980, it lost power to its pro-American, pro-capitalist, and pro-Western counterpart (Manley 1982, 1987). This intensified the hardships faced by the poor. In Guyana, Black working-class radicalism produced an identical shift in the country's global alliances to Cuba, Eastern Europe, and the tricontinental "Third World" beginning in 1975. The ensuing and inevitable international economic retaliation came with the constriction of access to global resource transfers. This produced a crisis by undermining the material base of society in ways that forced the regime, eventually, to become unquestionably instituted in postcolonial imperialist networks of the globalized capitalist system. In Trinidad, the state's clientelistic response to the demands of its racial supporters was made during a time when the country enjoyed access to significant oil revenues from newly discovered reserves, thanks to increasing oil prices in global markets; oil-producing states were able to dictate their terms of trade. The country's subaltern Black population was able to barter support for the ruling regime in exchange for considerable access to these resources. This became the basis for the significant expansion of their economic capabilities. But these transfers were tied to the vagaries of the international oil market. For the lowest strata of society, they proved inadequate, even in the best of circumstances, and this strata continues to be subjected to perpetual crises that ebb and flow with the rise and fall of global oil prices.

SUBALTERN DEVELOPMENT AND DISENTANGLEMENT FROM GOVERNANCE

Possibilities for the expansion of political and economic rights open up for the subaltern when a crisis occurs that affects the ability of the regime to access needed global resources. In both Guyana and Jamaica beginning in the 1970s, excruciating foreign exchange shortages, the burden of foreign debt, and punitive measures by bilateral and multilateral agencies placed severe constraints on the capacity of the institutions of national governance to function effectively. The vacuum was filled, partly but significantly, by subaltern petty traders organized in the informal sector using networks of family ties and informal communication systems. Freed by social stigma from constraints of "respectability," these traders effectively overcame the limitations of dispersed and unpredictable demand and limited capital reserves to meet pressing national needs. They were able to do so because of their political remoteness from dependence on the state and their freedom from ethical constraints imposed by middle- and upper-class morality that prevented the latter's participation in the informal (and need I say illegal) sector. They were able to meet the demands of their countries' populations for essential products and foreign currency, both in short supply in the formal economy. The transnational networks in which these petty traders remain involved extend to members of overseas diaspora populations, who are sources of significant material transfers that occur outside of statist practice. The development of small-scale informal entrepreneurship has been much more significant for enhancing the economic capabilities of the subaltern than efforts to do the same undertaken by the state. Petty trading has been more successful than the state-dependent formal commercial sector in creating opportunities for the effective development of the lower strata. The informal economy has also provided means for subaltern women to assert their economic rights (Edwards 1980, 58).

While existing outside of the space of governing practice, petty traders and diaspora populations living abroad bring the concerns of those who are excluded and those in the networks in which they participate into the arena of state decision-making (Thomas 2004; Hintzen 2006, 42–45).[11] This offers significant opportunities for the reconstitution of governing practice because of the increasing dependence of the national governing apparatus and the local private sector on the network of global transfers in which they are engaged. In Guyana, for example, the trading practices of the subaltern and the transfers of financial and "in kind" remittances from abroad through family and other affective networks have become critical to the country's economic functioning. They have supported the formation of one of the very few locally owned multinational enterprises in the country. The Laparkan Group of companies, formed in 1983, has become a regional leader in freight and cargo services.[12]

PROSPECTS FOR A NEW DEMOCRACY

The question becomes whether changes in the structure of global relations offer opportunities for a reconstitution of forms of governance in ways that can accommodate the different and diverse strategies of development employed by those located outside the ambit of national authority under conditions in which the state-effects of global capital are less imposing on their conditions of freedom. David Harvey identifies a "crisis" of "overaccumulation" in the Global North consistent with "the dialectics of imperialism" that impose a perpetual need for new markets, new investment opportunities, and new sources of raw materials (Harvey 2006, 413–45). In response to this crisis, global capital has been developing new efficiencies and new strategies for reducing remuneration and transaction costs and, relatedly, its dependence on national governmental authority. One of the consequences of these reductions is the direct engagement of capital investors in the governing of "usable" localized areas and workers in the Global South (Ferguson 2006, 38–42). They "hop over" unusable areas while reducing their commitment to the agendas of governing regimes aimed at sustaining support from strategic sectors of the population through transfers and allocations. With the reduction of transfers from the global system, the role of national institutions of authority and their capacity to exercise control over "unusable" areas and people have become significantly diminished. People and territories that are not "usable" to global capital are being abandoned (Ferguson 2006, 38–42).

There is also an important unintended consequence of the crisis of overaccumulation in the Global North. Conditions engendered by the shift in production and investment to the Global South have led to new challenges to Euro-American global interests. New patterns of global allocation have created opportunities for the emergence of new blocs of countries that are growing in

power. They are known by acronyms such as BRICS (referring to the growing
alliance of Brazil, Russia, India, China, and South Africa), MIST (the newest emerging market club of Mexico, Indonesia, South Korea, and Turkey),
and CIVETS (the market alliance of Colombia, Indonesia, Vietnam, Egypt,
Turkey, and South Africa). Their emergence portends a "reversal of fortune"
of the "aging industrial powers of North America [and] Europe" (Goldstone
2010). It comes with the potential to destabilize typical and entrenched forms
of neocolonial statist power. This represents, according to Jack Goldstone, a
"megatrend that will change the world." We are now beginning to see, as a result,
the development of new global networks of connections organized around new
patterns of "South-South" relations. Freedom from neocolonial and imperial
topographies of power can come with new opportunities for genuine development in the Global South. It can be pivotal in creating the conditions for new
forms of governing practice freed from colonial and imperialist impositions
(Goldstone 2010). The point here is not that the interests of these emerging
multipolar centers of global and economic power would predispose them to
support the type of developmental and democratic transformation consistent
with the guarantees and expansion of rights and freedoms used here as the
yardstick for democratic success. Their interests are inextricably tied to a newly
reconstituted global capitalist economy characterized by increasing intensities
in capital formation and transnational flows (Robinson 2014). It is not their
strength but rather their relative weakness that restricts their capacity to impose
conditions of governance on national apparatuses of authority. When this is
combined with declining neocolonial power, it can open up spaces for genuine
development and democracy in the Global South. Such spaces emerge in the
confluence of a trifecta of Western relative decline, the relative weakness of
emerging powers, and the growing incapacity of national apparatuses of governance to exercise authority over segments of their populations and swathes
of their territory. If Goldstone is correct, then the "megatrend" can offer new
opportunities for refashioning governing practice in ways that enhance the
effective participation of the subaltern. It can provide unique opportunities
for bringing into governing practice effective strategies for genuine development that are occurring outside of both state practices and processes and the
authority of national governance. It can allow for the expansion of capabilities
that are instrumental for guarantees of political and economic rights.

GLOCALIZATION AND COUNTERHEGEMONIC
TRANSNATIONAL NETWORKS

My argument thus far is that opportunities for effective development and genuine democracy are opened up by global processes and state-effects occurring

outside the space of governance, or by possibilities provided by global actors who are relatively free from the state-effects of global capitalist power. This is especially true for transnational social movements currently engaged in forms of "counterhegemonic globalization" (Evans 2007, 420–42) aimed at "complex deterritorialization and reterritorializaton of political authority" (Held and McGrew 2007, 363). These movements are pitted against the very hegemonic forces of transnational domination in which forms of representative democracy in the Caribbean are inscribed.

Possibilities for democratic and development transformation at the local level may, in part, emerge through global alliances with anticapitalist forces. Andreas Hernandez documents the emergence of an "alternative vision" of social organization centered on the formation of the World Social Forum as a counterweight to the World Economic Forum, the organization through which the global and national conditions of capital are coordinated (Hernandez 2010). The World Social Forum emerged as a "global counter movement to neoliberalism," which "connects many of the most vital popular movements struggling against the neoliberal project" (Hernandez 2010). These movements challenge developmentalist-materialist discourses that tie human aspirations to the very material conditions of capitalist production and consumption offered up in postcolonial formation as the sole condition of development.

The most significant of these, and with particular relevance for Caribbean development, have been labor movements, women's movements, and environmental/indigenous movements. The historical impact of global labor on the expansion of political and economic rights and capabilities for the Caribbean subaltern has been well documented and already discussed. Almost all of the leaders emerging during the first phase of West Indian nationalism successfully employed links to radical movements in Britain to support labor agitation in their respective territories. They successfully employed the class appeal of radical socialism to gain traction with the urban and rural colonized proletariat and peasantry (Hernandez 2010). The failure of postcolonial representative democracy was predicated on its transformation into the instrumentality, inscribed through the goal of developmental convergence, for the regulation, disciplining, and conscription of popular support for the service of imperial capital.

TRANSNATIONAL WOMEN'S MOVEMENTS

Transnational women's movements have played a significant role in the expansion of political and economic rights in the Caribbean. Universally, networks organized around transnational feminism and employing "class and gender struggles" have demonstrated their "creative ability to transform and reinterpret [gender concepts] to fit local circumstances" (Evans 2007, 431). Successful participation in these global networks by women in the region is evident in the growing numbers of women's organizations that are challenging the neocolonial script. They include the influential Red Thread Women in Guyana, who are mounting persistent challenges to statist forms of exception and exclusion. The penetration of feminist and gender struggles into the scholarship of the region has been particularly important. The establishment of the multicampus Institute for Gender and Development Studies at the University of the West Indies is one outcome of these struggles. In 2014, a former director of this institute was the principal of the university's Cave Hill campus; another was deputy principal of its Saint Augustine campus. And a third was the principal of the university's fourth campus, which caters to students in countries of the region without a main campus. The female-to-male ratio of students enrolled in the university was 80:20 at the Mona campus and 60:40 at the Saint Augustine campus, attesting to the significant strides made in women's access to higher education. Women's access to rights has paid dividends in their increased representation in governance, including, at the time of writing (2014), two prime ministers, one leader of the opposition, one former prime minister, one former executive president, and one former governor. Notwithstanding these successes, the mere replacement of men by women does not necessarily signal economic or political transformation. As Chandra Talpade Mohanty and Aihwa Ong have pointed out, global liberal feminist networks have done much to conscript women in the upper and middle strata of the Global South into the project of capitalist modernity (Mohanty 2004; Ong 2006, 31–52). It is only through the engagement of women in counterhegemonic global networks that new horizons of possibility for such transformation can emerge.

THE GLOBAL INDIGENOUS MOVEMENT

The global indigenous movement has also created new possibilities for the expansion of rights to subaltern populations in Guyana, Dominica, and Saint Vincent. Indigeneity, with its moral claim to territory, continues to act as a bulwark against the national apparatus of liberal representative democracy. In Dominica, Karifuna descendants of the indigenous Caribs inserted in regional networks of indigenous peoples in Latin America and the Caribbean organized to challenge postcolonial practice and have successfully challenged statist practices of exclusion, marginalization, and displacement in their ongoing struggles for autonomy. They forced the country's courts to grant them exclusive occupation of a "Carib Territory" (Gregoire, Henderson, and Kanem 1996, 107–71). Parallel movements have emerged among Carib-descended populations in Saint Vincent and the Grenadines. In 1999, nine indigenous groups in Guyana came together to formulate a comprehensive strategy to "redefine prevailing political, legal, economic, and cultural relations with the state and thereby to transcend four centuries of colonial domination and institutionalized racism that *remain firmly entrenched in Guyanese law, policy, and practice*" (La Rose and MacKay 1999).

What these examples suggest is that in the West Indies there is "a rein-vigoration of the conditions by which local communities regain the power to determine and control their preferred economic and political paths" (Cavanagh and Mander 2004). This portends new possibilities for changes in governing practice that may guarantee "community self-reliance, public health, equity, accountability, and democracy" under circumstances in which people "control the conditions of their life" (Cavanagh and Mander 2004).

There is need, therefore, to focus on examples in which those who are excluded by exception are creating opportunities for democratic and devel-opmental transformation. Scholars writing from spaces of direct involvement in these processes are already charting this course. Journalist Dayo Olopade (2014) has identified new forms of social organization in Africa located out-side the forces of the state, nation, and capital. People abandoned by national governments are becoming organized around family, innovative technology, the sustainable use of the natural environment, alternative forms of commerce, and youth formations for the "mapping" of new identities and communities. Case studies in an edited volume by Philip McMichael (2010) document the struggles of local communities in Asia, Africa, and Latin America by people who are challenging national authorities and state processes and practices fashioned out of the forces of global capitalism.

The point of this selective discussion is to support the argument that conditions of effective development occur outside the framework of forms of governance instantiated in representative democratic practice, where the state-effects of its entangled relationship with global topographies of power are minimal. Western liberal democracy, specifically its Westminster model, justifies and legitimizes the false notion of a national sovereignty that is integrally linked to the idea of the consolidation of national authority over territory and domestic affairs. This notion was formed and fashioned in the crucible of the demand imposed by capitalist and precapitalist forms of global accumulation (Lauren 1988). The relationship between national sovereignty and international relations renders invisible the very effects of state processes and practices on territories under national jurisdiction. Globalized state forces, national forms of institutional authority, "civil society," and localized social formations are all inscribed in a "world economy" of entangled relations. Genuine democracy and development rest upon the possibilities for disentangling and disarticulating these global relationships. Political philosopher Thomas Pogge points to the injustice of "the territorial state as the preeminent mode of political organization" because of its absolute power to "check and dominate the decision-making of political subunits" (2008, 184). For the purpose of this analysis, we need to emphasize the entangled relationship among the state, national authority, and local social formations and the absolute dependence of national governance upon global transfers. When such transfers are curtailed or diminished, it weakens the power of national authority to "dominate decision-making." This is when spaces of possibility can open up for alternative visions of sovereignty. As centralized forms of national authority lose their capacity to dominate decision-making, possibilities for transformation emerge for the "manifold and multiple selves" of the "underdeveloped" who are organizing in "localized, pluralistic grassroots movements," using "local knowledge" and deploying "popular power" in developing "alternatives to development" that constitute a "rejection of the entire paradigm itself" (Escobar 1995, 215). These movements may produce conditions in which, according to Pogge, people are able "to govern themselves through a number of political units of various sizes without any one . . . occupying the traditional role of the state." As such, "political allegiance and loyalties [would] be widely dispersed over these units: neighborhood, town, country, province, state, region and world at large, without converging on any one of them as the lodestar of political identity" (Pogge 1995, 184). Pogge advances this as a means of accommodating the diversity of human reality and as a check on the global deployment of power in a way that provides people with the right to participate equally in decision-making that affects their lives at any level. This is but one proposal to accommodate the form of democratic and developmental transformation consistent with the right to self-determination and to genuine "development as freedom." The goal here is to remove the constraints and limitations imposed by forms of statist practice inscribed in neocolonial and imperialist cartographies of power. Changes in the global architecture of international relations discussed previously are opening up possibilities for such removal.

NOTES

1. I use the term "colonial commandment" following Achille Mbembe (2001, 34–35). It refers to the rationality for colonial governance rooted in a form of white supremacy based on forms of violence that imbued colonial exclusive sovereignty with the "right to dispose."

2. See, for example, the discussion of postcolonial practice and its relationship to economic development in Nigel Harris (1976).

3. This term is taken from William Robinson (2014) in his discussion of new possibilities opening up for challenging global capital.

4. See, for example, James Ferguson, who proposes a relationship between time and status in development discourse (2006, esp. 176–82).

5. The term refers to the complex interaction of the global and the local and the fact that global processes always take place in contexts (Steger 2009, 42; see also Robertson 1995, 25–44).

6. By "subaltern" I refer to social groups who are excluded from a society's established structures for political representation, the means by which people have a voice in their society.

7. I have taken the term "exception" from Aihwa Ong (2006). It refers to the practice of governing authorities to deny segments of the population access to the rights and benefits they deserve as citizens. It also refers to the exemption of the privileged from legality and the rule of law.

8. In the Caribbean, constituencies were manipulated in Guyana and Trinidad before independence to ensure that representatives of the creole middle and upper strata inherited colonial power (Hintzen 1989). Politics are characterized by pervasive practices of voter fraud (most notably in Guyana), vote buying, and clientelism.

9. It is a critique that is reflected in the assessment of the emergence of liberalism by Immanuel Wallerstein (2004, chap. 1).

10. Global feminists, for example, use universal forms of "sister solidarity" to impose forms of feminism on the Global South that legitimize and strengthen imperialistic interventions (Ong 2006, 31–52). Diasporic populations in the Global North use claims of "ethnicity" to intervene in countries with which they have absolutely no connection in ways that can jeopardize efforts at national reconciliation and accommodation (Ong 2006, 53–71), while "human rights" groups can intervene in national conflicts as "saviors" in ways that are totally inappropriate to the situation, that violate the rights of segments of the population, that intensify conflicts, and that create conditions for the violation of state sovereignty (Mamdani 2010).

11. The real possibilities for transformation were observed by Deborah Thomas (2004). The manner in which statist discourse can conscript the diaspora into its agenda is discussed in Hintzen 2006.

12. "Laparkan," *West Indian Encyclopedia*, westindianencyclopedia.com/wiki/Laparkan.

BIBLIOGRAPHY

Bergeron, Suzanne. 2006. *Fragments of Development: Nation, Gender, and the Space of Modernity*. Ann Arbor: University of Michigan Press.

Bolland, O. Nigel. 1995. *On the March: Labour Rebellions in the British Caribbean, 1934–1939*. Kingston, Jamaica: Ian Randle Publishers.

Cavanagh, John, and Jerry Mander, eds. 2004. *Alternatives to Economic Globalization: A Better World Is Possible; A Report of the International Forum on Globalization*. 2nd ed. San Francisco: Berrett-Koehler.

Edie, Carlene J. 1991. *Democracy by Default: Dependency and Clientelism in Jamaica*. Boulder, CO: Lynne Rienner.

Edwards, Melvin R. 1980. "Jamaican Higglers: Their Significance and Potential." Monograph, Centre for Development Studies, University College of Swansea.

Escobar, Arturo. 1995. *Encountering Development: The Making and Unmaking of the Third World*. Princeton, NJ: Princeton University Press.

Evans, Peter. 2007. "Counterhegemonic Globalization: Transnational Social Movements in the Contemporary Global Political Economy." In *The Globalization and Development Reader: Perspectives on Development and Global Change*, edited by J. Timmons Roberts, Amy Bellone Hite, and Nitsan Chorev, 420–42. Oxford: Blackwell.

Ferguson, James. 2006. *Global Shadows: Africa in the Neoliberal World Order*. Durham, NC: Duke University Press.

Fraser, Cary. 1994. *Ambivalent Anti-Colonialism: The United States and the Genesis of West Indian Independence, 1940–1964*. Westport, CT: Greenwood Press.

Goldstone, Jack. 2010. "The New Population Bomb: The Four Megatrends That Will Change the World." *Foreign Affairs* 89, no. 1 (January–February): 31–43.

Gregoire, Crispin, Patrick Henderson, and Natalia Kanem. 1996. "Karifuna: The Caribs of Dominica." In *Ethnic Minorities in Caribbean Society*, edited by Rhoda E. Reddock, 107–71. Saint Augustine, Trinidad: Institute of Social and Economic Research, University of the West Indies.

Harris, Nigel. 1976. *The End of the Third World*. Harmondsworth, Middx., England: Penguin.

Harvey, David. 2006. *The Limits to Capital*. London: Verso.

Held, David, and Anthony McGrew. 2007. "Towards Cosmopolitan Social Democracy." In *The Globalization and Development Reader: Perspectives on Development and Global Change*, edited by J. Timmons Roberts, Amy Bellone Hite, and Nitsan Chorev. Oxford: Blackwell.

Hernandez, Andreas. 2010. "Challenging Market and Religious Fundamentalisms: The Emergence of 'Ethics, Cosmovisions, and Spiritualties' in the World Social Forum." In *Contesting Development: Critical Struggles for Social Change*, edited by Philip McMichael, 215–29. New York: Routledge.

Hintzen, Percy C. 1989. *The Costs of Regime Survival: Racial Mobilization, Elite Domination and Control of the State in Guyana and Trinidad*. Cambridge: Cambridge University Press.

Hintzen, Percy C. 1993. "Democracy and Middle-Class Domination in the West Indies." In *Democracy in the West Indies: Myths and Realities*, edited by Carlene J. Edie, 9–24. Boulder, CO: Westview Press.

Hintzen, Percy C. 1997. "Reproducing Domination: Identity and Legitimacy Constructs in the West Indies." *Social Identities* 3, no. 1: 47–75.

Hintzen, Percy C. 2001. "Cheddi Jagan (1918–97): Charisma and Guyana's Response to Western Capitalism." In *Caribbean Charisma: Reflections on Leadership, Legitimacy, and Populist Politics*, edited by Anton Allahar, 121–54. Boulder, CO: Lynne Rienner.

Hintzen, Percy C. 2006. "Commentary on 'Public Bodies: . . .'" *Journal of Latin American Anthropology* 11, no. 1 (April): 42–45.

Hintzen, Percy C., and Ralph Premdas. 1983. "Race, Ideology, and Power in Guyana." *Journal of Commonwealth and Comparative Politics* 21, no. 2: 175–94.

Howe, Stephen. 1993. *Anticolonialism in British Politics: The Left and the End of Empire, 1918–1964*. Oxford: Clarendon Press.

La Rose, Jean, and Fergus MacKay. 1999. "Our Land, Our Life, Our Culture: The Indigenous Movement in Guyana." *Cultural Survival Quarterly* 23, no. 4 (Winter): 29–34.

Lauren, Paul Gordon. 1988. *Power and Prejudice: The Politics and Diplomacy of Racial Discrimination*. Boulder, CO: Westview Press.

Mamdani, Mahmood. 2009. *Saviors and Survivors: Darfur, Politics, and the War on Terror*. New York: Random House.

Manley, Michael. 1982. *Jamaica: Struggle in the Periphery*. London: Third World Media.

Manley, Michael. 1987. *Up the Down Escalator: Development and the International Economy; A Jamaican Case Study*. Washington, DC: Howard University Press.

Mbembe, Achille. 2001. *On the Postcolony*. Berkeley: University of California Press.

McMichael, Philip, ed. 2010. *Contesting Development: Critical Struggles for Social Change*. New York: Routledge.

Mohanty, Chandra Talpade. 2004. "'Under Western Eyes' Revisited: Feminist Solidarity through Anticapitalist Struggles." In *Feminism without Borders: Decolonizing Theory, Practicing Solidarity*, by Chandra Talpade Mohanty, 221–51. Durham, NC: Duke University Press.

Olopade, Dayo. 2014. *The Bright Continent: Breaking Rules and Making Change in Modern Africa*. Boston: Houghton Mifflin Harcourt.

Ong, Aihwa. 2006. *Neoliberalism as Exception: Mutations in Citizenship and Sovereignty*. Durham, NC: Duke University Press.

Pogge, Thomas. 2008. *World Poverty and Human Rights: Cosmopolitan Responsibilities and Reforms*. 2nd ed. Cambridge: Polity Press.

Robertson, Roland. 1995. "Glocalization: Time-Space and Homogeneity-Heterogeneity." In *Global Modernities*, edited by Mike Featherstone, Scott Lash, and Roland Robertson, 25–44. London: Sage.

Robinson, William I. 2014. *Global Capitalism and the Crisis of Humanity*. New York: Cambridge University Press.

Ryan, Selwyn D. 1991. *The Muslimeen Grab for Power: Race, Religion, and Revolution in Trinidad and Tobago*. Port of Spain: Inprint Caribbean.

Ryan, Selwyn D. 1996. *Pathways to Power: Indians and the Politics of National Unity in Trinidad and Tobago*. Saint Augustine, Trinidad: Institute of Social and Economic Research, University of West Indies.

Scott, James C. 1998. *Seeing Like a State: How Certain Schemes to Improve the Human Condition Have Failed*. New Haven, CT: Yale University Press.

Sen, Amartya. 2000. *Development as Freedom*. New York: Anchor Books.

Steger, Manfred B. 2002. *Globalism: The New Market Ideology*. Lanham, MD: Rowman and Littlefield.

Steger, Manfred B. 2009. *Globalisms: The Great Ideological Struggle of the Twenty-First Century*. 3rd ed. Lanham, MD: Rowman and Littlefield.

Stone, Carl. 1973. *Class, Race, and Political Behaviour in Urban Jamaica*. Mona, Jamaica: Institute of Social and Economic Research, University of the West Indies.

Thomas, Deborah A. 2004. *Modern Blackness: Nationalism, Globalization, and the Politics of Culture in Jamaica*. Durham, NC: Duke University Press.

Trouillot, Michel-Rolph. 2001. "The Anthropology of the State in the Age of Globalization: Close Encounters of the Deceptive Kind." *Current Anthropology* 42, no. 1 (February): 125–38.

Wallerstein, Immanuel. 2004. *World-Systems Analysis: An Introduction*. Durham, NC: Duke University Press.

BETWEEN CULTURE AND POLITICAL ECONOMY

Percy Hintzen as Theorist of Racial Capitalism

CHARISSE BURDEN-STELLY

In my dissertation, "The Modern Capitalist State and the Black Challenge: Culturalism and the Elision of Political Economy" (Burden-Stelly 2016), for which Percy Hintzen served as the adviser, I levied a trenchant critique of what I called "culturalism," an antiradical regime of meaning-making in which Blackness is culturally specified and abstracted from material, political, economic, and structural conditions of dispossession. The result of culturalist hegemony in contemporary analyses of the Black condition and theories of the African diaspora, I argued, has been twofold. First, historical materialist critique, critical political economy, and Black anticapitalist thinkers have been marginalized. Second, culture has been politicized as the dominant mode of organizing against oppression and the primary intellectual focus of fields like Africana studies. Although I did not employ the language then, what drove my interrogation was an interest *racial capitalism*, specifically its modern US specifications, and especially its effects on twentieth-century Black radical individuals, institutional arrangements, and intellectual production. The development of my thought along these lines, especially my methodology, is indebted to Hintzen's influence and scholarship: a combination of neo-Marxism, politics, economics, philosophy, and political and historical sociology allowed me to bring regimes of racial governance, capitalist social relations, institutional formation, and epistemology into a single focus. Since finishing my dissertation, I have become even more interested in a specific regime of racial capitalism, what I call *modern US racial capitalism*, defined as a war-driven racially hierarchical political economy constituting white supremacist accumulation, dependent extraction, imperial expropriation, labor superexploitation, property-by-dispossession, and coercive debt regimes (Burden-Stelly 2020). Multiple texts collected in this volume, as well as Hintzen's underrated tome, *The Costs of Regime Survival: Racial Mobilization, Elite Domination and Control of the State in Guyana and Trinidad* (1989), informed and shaped not only my dissertation but also my intervention into the discourse of racial capitalism.

In 2000, a second edition of Cedric Robinson's *Black Marxism: The Making of the Black Radical Tradition* was published with a new preface and a foreword by Robin D. G. Kelley. Since then, "racial capitalism" has taken off across the humanities and social sciences as a conceptual framework to understand the mutually constitutive nature of racialization and capitalist exploitation on a global scale, in specific localities, in discrete historical moments, in the entrenchment of the carceral state, and in the era of neoliberalization and permanent war (Johnson and Lubin 2017). For Cedric Robinson, racial capitalism describes how "the development, organization, and expansion of capitalist society pursued essentially racial directions, [and] so too did social ideology. As a material force, then," he further asserts, "it could be expected that racialism would inevitably permeate the social structures emergent from capitalism" (Robinson 2000, 2). In popularizing the concept of racial capitalism, Robinson opened up space to consider how, throughout the twentieth century, a number of Black anticapitalist thinkers articulated a synonymous framework in their interrogations of the Negro Question, Black self-determination, and the conjunctures of imperialism and the color line. In placing the history, conditions, and experiences of African descendants at the center of their analyses and critiques of capitalist accumulation, scholars such as W. E. B. Du Bois, Claudia Jones, James Ford, Esther V. Cooper Jackson, Walter Rodney, and James Boggs, among many others, approximated theories of racial capitalism. Percy Hintzen can easily be added to this list of scholar-activists. His work is particularly germane to persons interested in the political economy, culture, and ideology of racial capitalism, and the social relations and epistemologies emanating therefrom. While scholars in disciplines from sociology to political science either left the state by the wayside in their studies of transterritorial and supranational regimes of governance, movements of people and goods, and cultural circulations; or remained entrapped in a nation-state framework that neglected the internationalist, world-systemic, and global realities of culture and political economy, Hintzen's work on the Caribbean (not to mention Africa and Latin America) has consistently offered a methodology for expertly avoiding such pitfalls. This "blueprint" for the study of racial capitalism is evident in several of the chapters collected in this volume.

In the coauthored essay "Culturalism, Development, and the Crisis of Socialist Transformation," Burden-Stelly and Hintzen take Clive Thomas's *Dependence and Transformation: The Economics of the Transition to Socialism* as a starting point to put forth a fundamental critique of the nation-state, the basic unit of the capitalist world system, as an impediment to socialist transformation. Such a critique is necessary because, as Hintzen powerfully notes in "Diaspora, Globalization, and the Politics of Identity": "An ineluctable association between capitalism and race emerges in the formation of a nation-state. This relationship is not merely inevitable but necessary as a condition of modernity." Given its entrapment in global capitalism, the postcolonial state form, even under the guise of socialism, transforms diverse populations into objects of nationalized economic planning that, instead of improving their economic conditions, perpetuates their subjection to global capitalist imperatives. "The state as globalized forces and processes," Burden-Stelly and Hintzen argue, "are integrally entangled with the apparatuses of national governance in ways that are essential to global interests organized in and through global topographies of power." It is these entanglements that "would doom to failure any effort at disengagement and, relatedly, at socialist transformation under terms specified by Thomas." Socialist transformation, then, is not impeded merely by a failure to develop or by relations of dependency, but rather by the statist and culturalist discourse of development itself, which sets to work new forms of state coercion and structural violence. Hintzen in particular illuminates that the maintenance of categories like "worker" and "peasant"—"products of state processes and technologies"—are instrumental in "elid[ing] the diverse realities of 'community'" and "harness[ing] local sentiment to the imperatives of postcolonial global capitalism." As such, he urges the accommodation of diverse populations, on their own terms, and localized knowledge production in the apparatus of decision-making to check the deployment of global power and reject the entire discursive and material development project. In doing so, he reveals not only the rhizomatic inscriptions of racial capitalism in the postcolonial nation-state, but also a possible way forward.

The groundwork for this argument is laid in essays such as "Rethinking Democracy in the Postnationalist State" and "Rethinking Democracy in the Postnationalist State: The Case of Trinidad and Tobago." In the former, Hintzen contends that development introduced new ideological and material justifications for inequality by positioning postcolonial elites as the class that was essential to throwing off the fetters of colonialism. The pretext for this class domination was the elite's technical, managerial, and bureaucratic acumen. Such discourse condemned the poor and working classes for failing to adopt the correct attitude and skill to facilitate development transformation. In the latter piece, Hintzen applies this analysis to the postcolonial reality of Trinidad and Tobago based on its distinctive history constituting Spanish colonial heritage, an elite class of domestic French planters, a large population of East Indian and Pakistani Muslims and Hindus who originally came to the island as indentured servants and a portion of whom ascended into the business-owning middle strata, and a significant Black population stratified by class and color. Here, the politicization of Black identity, coupled with the Westminster model of government and the political relegation of East Indians due to their concentration in the agricultural sector, allowed Black and colored elites to "fashion an ideology of creole nationalism" that provided the basis for their control of the state apparatus. This was notwithstanding that "the nationalist movement was neither 'nationalist' nor 'Black'" but rather "the embodiment of a strategic reorganization of the noncapitalist and nonfarming educated, bureaucratic, and professional elite." This aggregated social class "had little to do with the social, cultural, or economic interests of its Black lower-strata supporters except through the delivery of politically strategic patronage." Together, these writings illustrate how the Afro-creole elite sutured development discourse and racial politics to conscript the mass-based anticolonial agenda to their exclusive class interests. Such interests facilitated, and were maintained by, the reproduction of a globalized political economy rooted in neocolonial racial capitalism.

At the same time, Hintzen asserts in "Developmentalism and the Postcolonial Crisis in the Anglophone Caribbean" that challenges to capitalist-led development by, inter alia, experiments in participatory democracy, populism, regionalism, tricontinentalism, and anticapitalism have been inspirational but were ultimately undermined by the "realpolitik of postcolonialism and its perpetual crises." These failures are due in large part to the postcolonial state's imperative of securing global resources like capital investments and foreign exchange with the aim of industrialization and modernization as a road to socioeconomic convergence with Western countries. These goals require the repression of struggles against the state for participation and forms of representation that result in material betterment—insurgencies that occur largely outside of statist practice. The challenge to racial capitalism, then, is fundamentally incompatible with the specifications of the postcolonial nation-state because the "struggle for development does not emerge out of a desire for convergence with the West through a process of industrialization. It emerges out of the different goals and desires embedded in diverse cultures, communities, families, and individuals. It is engaged perpetually against the totalizing imperatives of centralized authority. It is a struggle without guarantees." In these writings, Hintzen deftly maneuvers between the national and the international, political economy and ideology, race and class, domination and contestation, to reveal the centrality of racial capitalism to the "Caribbean postcolonial" (Puri 2004)—and vice versa. In doing so, he makes an immense methodological and theoretical contribution to the study of these phenomena.

Taking on these insights from the angle of creole politics, discourse, and identity, Hintzen illuminates in "Afro-Creole Nationalism as Elite Domination" the ways that US-led neocolonialism and global capitalist hegemony were integral to the empowerment of postcolonial Afro-creole elites who were willing to accommodate economic relations and antidemocratic political structures conducive to the continued penetration of international capital. As a result, the aspirations of the lower strata—the key force in the struggle against colonialism and racial capitalism—and the international decolonial networks of solidarity established by this group of workers and peasants were repressed. This violence made the imposition of neoliberal restructuring in the context of the debt crisis more swift, enduring, and destructive. Similarly, in "Race and Creole Ethnicity in the Caribbean," Hintzen dissects the colonial foundations of creole identity and discourse. A tool of nationalist elites, creole identity sutures racial discourse to the consolidation of power and economic exploitation, which are the bases of muting differences and smoothing out competing interests among this group. Privilege and access organized along the lines of cultural, color, and class hierarchies impose a form of liberal-democratic consensus that subsumes and obscures the ravages of racial capitalism and its effects on the majority of the population. Likewise, "Creoleness and Nationalism in Guyanese Anticolonialism and Postcolonial Formation" zooms in on Guyana to explicate the ways that colonial relations were reproduced through racialized competition for power and control of the state's governing apparatus. This competition between African and Asian Indian populations, which dovetailed with the anti-Indian position of the creole elite, challenged the homogenizing tendencies of the postcolonial state and undermined the formidable class-based anticapitalist, anti-imperialist nationalist movement. Such race-based antagonism buoyed the domination of a pro-capitalist, pro-US creole elite, which, Hintzen explains, "was an instantiation and iteration of a coloniality that was being transformed with the emergence of North America as the new center of metropolitan capitalism. Hence, the United States was an active agent in its deployment." As such, the creole elite was supported and maintained through international capital and various discourses, including anticommunism and the restoration of democracy, that legitimated intervention. In these representative examples, creoleness, and its relationship to class formation, culturalist discourse, the domination of international capital, and racial ideology, provides invaluable insight into racial capitalism—and its rootedness in regimes of antiradicalism like anticommunism—as an enduring reality in the Caribbean.

One of Hintzen's most important scholarly contributions is his explication of the turn from developmentalism to neoliberalization and the hegemony of structural adjustment programs (SAPs). He does so in the context of elite class formation and the entrapment of the Caribbean postcolonial state in international capitalist imperatives. Here, he is unparalleled in bringing into sharp relief the entanglements of political economy, ideology, racial formation, and cultural narration in the reproduction and maintenance of racial capitalism.

Developmentalism, an essential technology of racial capitalism after World War II, was grounded in the racial ordering of states based on ideologies of "modern" and "backward" that legitimated domination and control by those deemed modern and justified their intervention in the social, political, and economic lives of those conceived as racially and economically backward. "Development policy, in its application," Hintzen explains, "pertain[ed] exclusively, and not surprisingly, to those countries that [lay] outside the North Atlantic.... The descendants of Western Europe ... [were] located at the top of a development pyramid." He adds: "The position of each on the pyramid relate[d] to its degrees of closeness to the Western European ideal, defined in terms of all or a combination of moral, ethical, charactological, and genetic traits" (Hintzen 1995a, 56). The idea was that modernization and high standards of living could be achieved in the underdeveloped world if a particular path set out by Western powers generally, and the United States particularly, was strictly followed. Any resistance was interpreted as indisputable evidence of the irredeemable inferiority of racialized/backward populations and nations and was used to explain and rationalize the resource and income gap between North and South (Hintzen 1995a, 58).

At the same time, developmentalism demanded the organization of centralized state power in postcolonial states not only to manage the implementation of modernization and development but also to maintain political order, understood as the ability to adhere to and abide by the dictates of international capitalist institutions, policies, and practices. State-organized corporatism created an elite comprising nonproletarian workers and an "aristocracy of labor" (political parties and industrial unions) controlled by "professional and intellectual elites" (Hintzen 1995b) that operated in the interest of international capital. Hintzen writes:

> This is what explains the historical and almost universal emergence of an elite social grouping from among the non-proletarian wage and salaried occupational categories. This emergent elite was historically produced out of colonial social formations.... Their professional and intellectual leadership was involved, simultaneously, in formalising proletarian organisation into trade unions, political parties, insurgent armies, and guerilla groups. These became the bases of mobilisation against colonial domination. The legitimising ideology of the professional and intellectual leadership was anti-colonial or anti-imperial nationalism. While the appeal was for liberation from colonial domination, the goal was control of the bureaucratic apparatus of colonial government ... [which had] become the primary instrument of accumulation and domination. (Hintzen 1995b)

In other words, the former anticolonial nationalists morphed into the elite class, which implemented developmental policies that would ostensibly bring them closer to the material conditions of wealth enjoyed in the dominant capitalist nations. This is not least because "the upper and middle strata are integrally tied to and dependent upon the state" *and* upon international capital for all forms of access, including "states of exception" that allow them to employ "corruption, cronyism, and nepotism" in efforts to garner and maintain material and cultural resources. Hintzen brilliantly assesses this reality in "Developmentalism and the Postcolonial Crisis in the Anglophone Caribbean":

> [T]heir interests are tied to the integral role of the state in its exercise of constitutional and legal contractual authority to receive foreign assistance and foreign loans, to provide legal frameworks and the legal bases for foreign investment, and to receive formal recognition as a sovereign unit in international relations. These provide the conditions upon which the well-being of the middle and upper strata depends. In other words, their interests are *internationally* inscribed in a transnational apparatus of governmentality. They use their capabilities in service of the demands of powerful global actors.... Their authority, exercised in support of the statist and global interests from which they derive considerable material benefits (cultural and social capital), is heavily embedded in formal cultural practice. At the same time, they live in a quotidian world of cultural networks and affective ties organized by and through non-agentive power. They are able to "move" in both worlds, and to enjoy the freedoms and capabilities provided by both.

Ultimately, power, authority, and control of the state rested in the meritocratic and technical claim of the upper and middle strata to cultural superiority—read proximity to Western values, ethics, and imperatives—as the agents of modernization and development.

The political economy, racial logics, and class-based objectives of developmentalism created the conditions for the neoliberal turn in racial capitalism as the oil shocks of 1973–1974 and 1979–1980 and the Mexican debt default of 1982 shattered the international order organized around the developmentalist state. These events inaugurated a new regime of accumulation, exploitation, and expropriation predicated on international governance. SAPs were the most effective instrumentality of global capital. Hintzen explains, in "Structural Adjustment and the New International Middle Class":

> There is an essential link between programs of structural adjustment and international interventionism.... The former entails a dissolution

of the nationalist elite alliance of professionals, intellectuals, and non-proletarian wage and salary workers. It also entails the dissolution of the welfarist structure of statist organization. The consequences are a ... curtailment of efforts at income redistribution to proletarian workers and the semiproletarian peasantry.... Nationalist ideology was replaced with support for programs of international interdependence that are consistent with the changing demands of international manufacturing and finance capital. The groundwork for programs of transformation in keeping with these demands was laid by international political and economic intervention in the form of structural adjustment.

"Interdependence" served as an ideology of racial capitalism insofar as these "processes of integration and interaction [produced] unevenly distributed rights, obligations, and burdens" that were "entrenched and stabilized" through appeals to racial difference. The "structural and embedded" processes and "institutional arrangements" of international manufacturing and finance capital "create[d] the international conditions of ongoing imperial domination" (Getachew 2019, 20, 32, 33). The ideology of interdependence dovetailed with the material realities of the global debt crisis, including doubled import commodity prices, quadruped oil prices, massive increases in imports, and severely depressed export prices and volumes (Arrighi 1991, 64). What resulted were conditionalities imposed by the International Monetary Fund and World Bank as prerequisites for foreign exchange and development assistance. This form of "global governance without global government" (Stiglitz 2002) provided the conditions under which powerful financial and commercial interests—in collaboration with international institutions and banks—were able to dictate policies throughout the Caribbean, and the Global South more broadly, that facilitated increased capitalist penetration and exploitation. "Solvency," another ideological innovation of racial capitalist restructuring, became the new development mantra, with governments in the developed core squeezing developing countries into the repayment of their debt obligations to maintain their "creditworthiness" by adopting a set of policies that would allow them to service their debt—to the detriment of serving their populations. Hintzen's analysis of developmentalism, the neoliberal turn, and SAPs in the Caribbean offers a deep understanding of the interrelationship between the postcolonial state and international capital, the material realities and ideological underpinnings of domination, and the cultural politics of class formation that constitutes racial capitalism.

Hintzen intimates in the prologue of this volume that as a Guyana-born, Barbados-raised subject, his sensitivity to racial injustice, imperialism, and militarism at the intersection of British coloniality and US capitalist hegemony has made him skeptical "that the postcolonial arc bent in the direction of a transformative agenda for justice." As such, throughout his career, he has applied his unique training in political sociology, politics, economics, philosophy, and Marxist analysis to studying, critiquing, and attempting to reshape the arc of the postcolonial. His uncanny ability to bring together the local, national, and global contours of political economy, class, race, culture, ideology, and state formation positions him as one of the most careful and sophisticated scholars of racial capitalism. His body of work, only a fraction of which is collected in *Reproducing Domination: On the Caribbean Postcolonial State*, makes an essential, though heretofore underrated, contribution to this growing subfield.

BIBLIOGRAPHY

Arrighi, Giovanni. 1991. "World Income Inequalities and the Future of Socialism." *New Left Review* 189 (September–October): 39–65.

Burden-Stelly, Charisse. 2020. "On Bankers and Empire: Racial Capitalism, Anitblackness, and Antiradicalism." *Small Axe* 24, no. 2 (July): 175–86.

Burden-Stelly, Charisse. 2016. "The Modern Capitalist State and the Black Challenge: Culturalism and the Elision of Political Economy." PhD diss., University of California.

Getachew, Adom. 2019. *Worldmaking after Empire: The Rise and Fall of Self-Determination.* Princeton, NJ: Princeton University Press.

Hintzen, Percy C. 1989. *The Costs of Regime Survival: Racial Mobilization, Elite Domination and Control of the State in Guyana and Trinidad.* Cambridge: Cambridge University Press.

Hintzen, Percy C. 1995a. "Racism in Foreign Policy and Development Programs." In *The Color of Hunger: Race and Hunger in National and International Perspective,* edited by David L. L. Shields, 55–70. Lanham, MD: Rowman and Littlefield.

Hintzen, Percy C. 1995b. "Structural Adjustment and the New International Middle Class." *Transition,* no. 24 (February): 52–74. University of Guyana Press.

Johnson, Gaye Theresa, and Alex Lubin. 2017. *Futures of Black Radicalism.* London: Verso.

Puri, Shalini. 2004. *The Caribbean Postcolonial: Social Equality, Post-Nationalism, and Cultural Hybridity.* New York: Palgrave Macmillan.

Robinson, Cedric J. 2000. *Black Marxism: The Making of the Black Radical Tradition.* Chapel Hill: University of North Carolina Press.

Stiglitz, Joseph E. 2002. *Globalization and Its Discontents.* New York: W. W. Norton.

PUBLICATIONS BY PERCY C. HINTZEN

BOOKS

Reproducing Domination: On the Caribbean Postcolonial State. Jackson: University Press of Mississippi, 2022. (Primary author and coeditor with Aaron Kamugisha and Charisse Burden-Stelly.)

Global Circuits of Blackness: Interrogating the African Diaspora. Urbana: University of Illinois Press, 2010. (Coeditor with Jean Muteba Rahier and Felipe Smith.)

Problematizing Blackness: Self-Ethnographies by Black Immigrants to the United States. Abingdon, Oxon., England: Routledge, 2003. (Coedited with Jean Muteba Rahier.)

West Indian in the West: Self-Representations in an Immigrant Community. New York: New York University Press, 2001.

The Costs of Regime Survival: Racial Mobilization, Elite Domination and Control of the State in Guyana and Trinidad. Cambridge: Cambridge University Press, 1989.

SPECIAL ISSUES OF JOURNALS

"Applying a Caribbean Perspective to an Analysis of HIV/AIDS." *Global Public Health* 14, no. 11 (2019). (Coedited with John Vertovec, Elena Cyrus, Mark Padilla, and Nelson Varas-Díaz.)

ARTICLES AND CHAPTERS

"The Caribbean: Horizons of Possibilities for a Future without Guarantees." In *Re-Ordering Caribbean Futures in the Fires of Global Change*, edited by Richard Bernal, Patricia Northover, Hamid Ghany, and Natalie Dietrich Jones. Kingston, Jamaica: Ian Randle Publishers, 2021.

"Poverty." In *Keywords for Health Humanities*, edited by Priscilla Wald, Sari Altschuler, and Jonathan Metzi. New York: New York University Press, 2021.

"Diaspora, Affective Ties, and the New Global Order: Caribbean Implications." In *Pan-Caribbean Integration: Beyond CARICOM*, edited by Patsy Lewis, Terri-Ann Gilbert-Roberts, and Jessica Byron, 28–46. Abingdon, Oxon., England: Routledge, 2019.

"Epilogue: The Political Economy of Music and Sound." In *Sounds of Vacation: Political Economies of Caribbean Tourism*, edited by Jocelyne Guilbault and Timothy Rommen, 193–206. Durham, NC: Duke University Press, 2019.

"The EU, CARIFORUM and CELAC: A New Development Alliance?" In *EU Development Policies: Between Norms and Geopolitics*, edited by Sarah L. Beringer, Sylvia Maier, and Markus Thiel, 135–54. Cham, Switzerland: Palgrave Macmillan, 2019.

"Introduction to the Special Issue: Applying a Caribbean Perspective to an Analysis of HIV/AIDS." *Global Public Health* 14, no. 11 (2019): 1547–56. (Coauthored with John Vertovec, Elena Cyrus, Mark Padilla, and Nelson Varas-Díaz.)

"Precarity and the HIV/AIDS Pandemic in the Caribbean: Structural Stigma, Constitutionality, Legality in Development Practice." *Global Public Health* 14, no. 11 (2019): 1624–38.

"Rethinking Identity, National Sovereignty, and the State: Reviewing Some Critical Contributions." *Social Identities* 24, no. 1 (2018): 39–47.

"Towards a New Democracy in the Caribbean: Local Empowerment and the New Global Order." In *Beyond Westminster in the Caribbean*, edited by Brian Meeks and Kate Quinn, 173–98. Kingston, Jamaica: Ian Randle Publishers, 2018.

"Culturalism, Development, and the Crisis of Socialist Transformation: Identity, the State, and National Formation in Thomas's Theory of Dependence." *CLR James Journal* 22, nos. 1–2 (Fall 2016): 191–214. (Coauthored with Charisse Burden-Stelly.)

"After Modernization: Globalization and the African Dilemma." In *Modernization as Spectacle in Africa*, edited by Peter J. Bloom, Takyiwaa Manuh, and Stephan F. Miescher, 19–39. Bloomington: Indiana University Press, 2014.

"Introduction: Theorizing the African Diaspora; Metaphor, Miscognition, and Self-Recognition." In *Global Circuits of Blackness: Interrogating the African Diaspora*, edited by Jean Muteba Rahier, Percy C. Hintzen, and Felipe Smith, ix–xxvi. Urbana: University of Illinois Press, 2010. (Coauthored with Jean Muteba Rahier.)

"Commentary on Berg's 'Homeland and Belonging among Cubans in Spain.'" *Journal of Latin American and Caribbean Anthropology* 14, no. 2 (November 2009): 293–96.

"Desire and the Enrapture of Capitalist Consumption: Product Red, Africa, and the Crisis of Sustainability." *Journal of Pan African Studies* 2, no. 6 (September 2008): 77–91.

"Jagan, Janet." In *Encyclopedia of Latin American History and Culture*, 2nd ed., edited by Jay Kinsbruner and Erick Langer. Detroit: Gale, 2008.

"Diaspora, Globalization and the Politics of Identity." In *Culture, Politics, Race and Diaspora: The Thought of Stuart Hall*, edited by Brian Meeks, 233–86. Kingston, Jamaica: Ian Randle Publishers, 2006. Reprinted in *Les diasporas dans le monde contemporain*, edited by William Berthomière and Christine Chivallon, 107–24. Paris: Éditions Karthala, 2006. Reprinted in *Diversidade, espaço e relações étnico-raciais: O negro na geografia do Brasil*, edited by Ronato Emerson dos Santos. Belo Horizonte, Brazil: Autêntica, 2007.

"Commentary on 'Public Bodies: . . .'" *Journal of Latin American Anthropology* 11, no. 1 (April 2006): 42–45.

"Globalisation and Diasporic Identity among West Indians." In *Globalisation, Diaspora and Caribbean Popular Culture*, edited by Christine G. T. Ho and Keith Nurse, 3–23. Kingston, Jamaica: Ian Randle Publishers, 2005.

"Nationalism and the Invention of Development: Modernity and the Cultural Politics of Resistance." *Social and Economic Studies* 54, no 3 (September 2005): 66–96.

"Imagining Home: Race and the West Indian Diaspora in the San Francisco Bay Area."
Journal of Latin American Anthropology 9, no. 2: 289–318. Reprinted in *Global Circuits
of Blackness: Interrogating the African Diaspora*, edited by Jean Muteba Rahier, Percy C.
Hintzen, and Felipe Smith, 49–73. Urbana: University of Illinois Press, 2010.

"Creoleness and Nationalism in Guyanese Anticolonialism and Postcolonial Formation."
Small Axe 8, no. 1 (March 2004): 106–22.

"Rethinking Democracy in the Post-Nationalist State: The Case of Trinidad and Tobago."
In *Modern Political Culture in the Caribbean*, edited by Holger Henke and Fred Reno,
395–423. Mona, Jamaica: University of the West Indies Press, 2004.

"From Structural Politics to the Politics of Deconstruction: Self-Ethnographies
Problematizing Blackness." In *Problematizing Blackness: Self-Ethnographies by Black
Immigrants to the United States*, edited by Percy C Hintzen and Jean Muteba Rahier, 1–20.
Abingdon, Oxon., England: Routledge, 2003. (Coauthored with Jean Muteba Rahier.)

"Race, Ideology, and International Relations: Sovereignty and the Disciplining of Guyana's
Working Class." In *Living at the Borderlines: Issues in Caribbean Sovereignty and
Development*, edited by Cynthia Barrow-Giles and Don D. Marshall, 414–40. Kingston,
Jamaica: Ian Randle Publishers, 2003. Reprinted in *Unmasking the State: Politics, Society
and Economy in Guyana, 1992–2015*, edited by Arif Bulkan and D. Alissa Trotz, 178–208.
Kingston, Jamaica: Ian Randle Publishers, 2019.

"Whiteness, Desire, Sexuality, and the Production of Black Subjectivities in British Guiana,
Barbados, and the United States." In *Problematizing Blackness: Self-Ethnographies by Black
Immigrants to the United States*, edited by Percy C. Hintzen and Jean Muteba Rahier,
129–68. Abingdon, Oxon., England: Routledge, 2003.

"The Caribbean: Race and Creole Ethnicity." In *A Companion to Racial and Ethnic Studies*,
edited by David Theo Goldberg and John Solomos, 475–94. Malden, MA: Blackwell,
2002.

"Guyana Today: Politics, Race, and Crisis in Guyana." *Diaspora* (February–March 2002):
82–86.

"Race and Creole Ethnicity in the Caribbean." In *Questioning Creole: Creolisation Discourses
in Caribbean Culture*," edited by Verene A. Shepherd and Glen L. Richards, 92–110.
Kingston, Jamaica: Ian Randle Publishers, 2002.

"Afro-Creole Nationalism as Elite Domination: The English-Speaking West Indies." In
Foreign Policy and the Black (Inter)National Interest, edited by Charles P. Henry, 185–218.
Albany: State University of New York Press, 2001.

"Cheddi Jagan (1918–97): Charisma and Guyana's Response to Western Capitalism." In
Caribbean Charisma: Reflections on Leadership, Legitimacy, and Populist Politics, edited
by Anton Allahar, 121–54. Boulder, CO: Lynne Rienner, 2001.

"Rethinking Democracy in the Postnationalist State." In *New Caribbean Thought: A Reader*,
edited by Brian Meeks and Folke Lindahl, 104–26. Mona, Jamaica: University of the West
Indies Press, 2001. Reprinted in modified form in *Humanities and Social Sciences in East
and Central Africa: Theory and Practice*, edited by Isaria N. Kimambo. Dar es Salaam: Dar
es Salaam University Press, 2003.

"Identity, Arena, and Performance: Being West Indian in the San Francisco Bay Area." In
Representations of Blackness and the Performance of Identities, edited by Jean Muteba
Rahier, 123–46. Westport, CT: Greenwood Press, 2000.

"Identity, Nationalism and Elite Domination: The English Speaking West Indies." In *Ethnic Cleavage and Closure in the Caribbean Diaspora: Essays on Race, Ethnicity and Class*, edited by Prem Misir, 78–110. New York: Caribbean Diaspora University Press, 2000.

"Adapting to Segregation: African American Strategies in the Post Welfare Environment." *Harvard Journal of African American Public Policy* 4 (1998): 45–48.

"Democracy on Trial: The December 1997 Elections in Guyana and Its Aftermath." *Caribbean Studies Newsletter* 25, no. 3 (September–October 1998): 13–16.

"Guyana." In *Latin American and Caribbean Contemporary Record: 1989–1990*, vol. 9, edited by Eduardo A. Gamarra. New York: Holmes and Meier, 1997.

"Reproducing Domination: Identity and Legitimacy Constructs in the West Indies." *Social Identities* 3, no. 1 (1997): 47–75.

"Conversation: Racial Formation in Contemporary American National Identity." *Social Identities* 2, no. 1 (February 1996): 161–91. (Coauthored with David Theo Goldberg, Richard Ford, Angie Chabram-Dernersesian, and Herman Gray.)

"Racism in Foreign Policy and Development Programs." In *The Color of Hunger: Race and Hunger in National and International Perspective*, edited by David L. L. Shields, 55–70. Lanham, MD: Rowman and Littlefield, 1995.

"Socioeconomic Obstacles to HIV Prevention and Treatment in Developing Countries: The Roles of the International Monetary Fund and the World Bank." *AIDS* 9, no. 6 (June 1995): 539–46. (Coauthored with Peter Lurie and Robert A. Lowe.) Reprinted in *HIV and AIDS in Africa: Beyond Epidemiology*, edited by Ezekiel Kalipeni, Susan Craddock, Joseph R. Oppong, and Jayati Ghosh, 204–12. Malden, MA: Blackwell, 2004.

"Structural Adjustment and the New International Middle Class." *Transition*, no. 24 (February 1995): 53–73. University of Guyana Press.

"Democratic Processes and Middle-Class Domination in the West Indies." In *Democracy in the Caribbean: Myths and Realities*, edited by Carlene J. Edie. Westport, CT: Praeger, 1994.

"Race and International Relations: History and the Making of Modern Haiti." *International Journal of Comparative Race and Ethnic Relations* 1, no. 2 (1994): 32–48.

"Trinidad and Tobago: Democracy and Racial Politics." In *Democracy in the Caribbean: Myths and Realities*, edited by Carlene J. Edie. Westport, CT: Praeger, 1994.

"Alternatives in the Caribbean." *Christianity and Crisis* 51, no. 19 (January 1992).

"Guyana: Cheddi Jagan, President." *Current Leaders of Nations*. North Wales, PA: Current Leaders Publishing Company, 1992.

"Arthur Lewis and the Development of Middle Class Ideology." In *Sir Arthur Lewis: An Economic and Political Portrait*, edited by Ralph Premdas and Eric St. Cyr, 107–15. Mona, Jamaica: Institute of Social and Economic Research, University of the West Indies, 1991.

"Ethnicity y clase social en la politica Caribena postcolonial." In *El Caribe hacia el 2000: Desafios y opciones*, edited by Andrés Serbin and Anthony Bryan. Caracas: Editorial Nueva Sociedad, 1991.

"Guyana." In *Latin American and Caribbean Contemporary Record*, vol. 8: *1988–1989*, edited by James Malloy and Eduardo A. Gamarra. New York: Holmes and Meier, 1990.

"Guyana." In *Latin American and Caribbean Contemporary Record*, vol. 6: *1986–1987*, edited by Abraham Lowenthal. New York: Holmes and Meier, 1989.

In *Dictionary of Latin American and Caribbean Political Biography*, edited by Robert J. Alexander. Westport, CT: Greenwood Press, 1988. (Coauthored with Marvin Will, fifty-seven biographic entries on leaders of the Anglophone Caribbean.)

In *Dictionary of Latin American and Caribbean Political Biography*, edited by Robert J.
Alexander. Westport, CT: Greenwood Press, 1988. (Fourteen biographic entries on
Haitian leaders.)

"Ethnicity, Class, and International Capitalist Penetration in Guyana and Trinidad." *Social
and Economic Studies* 34, no. 3 (September 1985): 107–63.

"Race and Class in Less Developed Countries: The Cases of Guyana and Trinidad."
Transition, no. 9 (1984).

"Race, Class and Development: Toward an Explanation of Poverty and Repression in Less
Developed Countries." *Plural Societies* 15 (1984): 193–219. (Coauthored with Ralph
Premdas.)

"Bases of Elite Support for a Regime: Race, Ideology, and Clientelism as Bases for Leaders in
Guyana and Trinidad." *Comparative Political Studies* 16, no. 3 (Fall 1983): 363–91.

"Race, Ideology, and Power in Guyana." *Journal of Commonwealth and Comparative Politics*
21, no. 2 (July 1983): 175–94. (Coauthored with Ralph Premdas.)

"Guyana: Coercion and Control in Political Change." *Journal of Interamerican Studies
and World Affairs* 24, no. 3 (August 1982): 337–54. (Coauthored with Ralph Premdas.)
Reprinted in *The Enigma of Ethnicity: An Analysis of Race in the Caribbean and the
World*, edited by Ralph Premdas, 181–96. Saint Augustine, Trinidad: University of the
West Indies Press, 1993.

"Industrialism or Development: Alternative Choices for Developing Countries." *Release* 1,
no. 1 (January 1978).

"Myth, Ideology, and Crisis in Plantation Society: The Guyanese Example." Working Papers
in Caribbean Society, series A, no. 4. University of the West Indies, Saint Augustine,
Trinidad, October–November 1978.

"The Colonial Foundations of Race Relations and Ethnic Politics in Guyana." *Guyana
Journal of Sociology* 1, no. 1 (1975).

MEDIA AND POPULAR PUBLICATIONS

"Sociology's Plight: The Global Majority, Racial Capitalism, and the Burden of Historicism."
Sociology, Capitalism, and the Impossibility of Racial Justice: Forum on Sociology,
Miami Institute for the Social Sciences, May 31, 2021. https://www.miamisocialsciences
.org/home/pdc8en801y27tmp6arcmc929j1cs5s.

Carbon Bomb: Exxon, The World Bank, and One of the Biggest Oil Discoveries of Our Time.
YouTube, premiered October 16, 2020. https://www.youtube.com/watch?v=chmOg
YB7DGk. (Contributing author.)

"HIV/AIDS: A Disease of Globalized Capitalism." *Global African Worker*, February 18, 2020.
https://www.globalafricanworker.com/content/hivaids-disease-globalized-capitalism.

"Kamala Harris, Guyana, and Unrealized Metaphor." *Stabroek News* (Georgetown, Guyana),
November 12, 2020. https://www.stabroeknews.com/2020/11/12/features/in-the-diaspora
/kamala-harris-guyana-and-unrealized-metaphor/.

"Oil Aspirations and the Curse of Neocolonial Governance." *Stabroek News* (Georgetown,
Guyana), January 20, 2020. https://www.stabroeknews.com/2020/01/20/features/in-the
-diaspora/oil-aspirations-and-the-curse-of-neocolonial-governance/.

"Bombing Rubble May Obscure the Real Kenya." *Newsday*, August 16, 1998.

"The Cooperative Republic in Guyana." *Stabroek News*, March 3–15, 1995. Two series of eleven talks on the Cooperative Republic of Guyana, Radio Rorima and Guyana Broadcasting Service Series on Living History.

"Commentary Symposium: The Democrats in the White House." *Socialist Review* 22, no. 3 (July–September 1992).

Op-ed articles in major national and international newspapers on an ongoing basis as a writer for the Pacific News Service news agency.

INDEX

abduction, 8, 249–50

Abeng (Black radical group), 36

absentee owners, 91, 250

accommodation, 58, 75, 122–26, 137, 160, 197, 214, 227, 244, 255, 257

accommodation coalition, 150

Adams, Grantley, 26, 46–47, 54, 125

Adams, Tom, 66

Africa, 9; alliances with, 214; Black elites, 135; Blackness and, 108; creole identity and, 111; nationalist movements in, 60, 164; rejection of, 104; state power and, 163–64. *See also* diaspora

African Americans, 49, 51, 164–65, 168–71

African purity, 126

African socialism, 222–25

African Society for Cultural Relations with Independent Africa (ASCRIA), 36, 111, 126–27

Afro-creole identity: class relations and, 26; domination and, 36–37; formation of, 245–46; hierarchy and, 102; neocolonialism and, xiii–xv, 9; in Trinidad, 110, 154; white supremacy and, 20–21. *See also* creole identity

Afro-creole nationalism, 5–9; class basis of, 52–55; development and, 34; formation of, 20, 22–23; in Guyana, 112; as middle-class elite domination, 24–28, 37, 43–70, 147, 285–86; neocolonialism and, 55–56; in Trinidad, 135–57. *See also* anticolonial nationalism; creole nationalism; national-ist discourse

agricultural commodities, 68, 81, 89, 193

agricultural sector, 146, 223–24. *See also* peasant lower class

Alexander, M. Jacqui, 257n2

Algeria, 60

alienation, 232

Allfrey, Phyllis Shand, 58

alliances, global, 72, 164–65, 212–14, 233–34, 255–56, 270–71

Althusser, Louis, 200n14

amalgamation, 106–9. *See also* creole identity

American Committee for Ethiopia, 21, 47

Amerindians, 114–15, 120

Amin, Samir, 73, 200n11

Anderson, Benedict, 39n4, 102, 173n2

Anglo-American Caribbean Commission, 50, 254

Angola, 60

anthropology, 182

anti-Blackness, 9

anticapitalism, xi–xiv, 126–31, 268, 286

anticolonial nationalism, xi–xiii, 4–6, 12–14; anticapitalism and, 182–83; class and, 211; creole discourse and, 104–5; cultural politics of resistance and, 190–91; in early twentieth century, 43–49; elite domination and, 5–9, 12–38, 90; equality and, 97–98; globalization and, 63–70; goals of, 87; inequality and, 86–87; liberation and, 13; as neocolonial construction, 141–56; race and, 24–28; rights and, 264; Soviet Union sup-port for, 27, 46, 51; trade unions and, 251–53;

ABOUT THE EDITORS

Percy C. Hintzen is currently professor of global and sociocultural studies at Florida International University and Professor Emeritus of African American studies at the University of California, Berkeley. He is a postcolonial scholar with a focus on Caribbean political economy, postcolonial studies, and the African diaspora.

Charisse Burden-Stelly is associate professor of African American studies at Wayne State University and the 2021–2022 visiting scholar in the Race and Capitalism Project at the University of Chicago. She is coauthor, with Gerald Horne, of *W. E. B. Du Bois: A Life in American History* and coeditor with Jodi Dean of *Organize, Fight, Win: Black Communist Women's Political Writing.* Burden-Stelly's book *Black Scare/Red Scare* is forthcoming from the University of Chicago Press. She has published numerous edited volume chapters, and her writings appear in peer-reviewed journals including *Small Axe, Souls, Du Bois Review, Socialism and Democracy,* the *International Journal of Africana Studies,* the *Journal of Intersectionality,* and the *CLR James Journal.* Her public scholarship can be found in venues such as the *Monthly Review,* the *Boston Review, Black Perspectives,* and the *Black Agenda Report.*

Aaron Kamugisha is Ruth Simmons Professor of Africana Studies at Smith College. He is editor of six books and five special issues of journals on Caribbean and Africana thought, and the author of *Beyond Coloniality: Citizenship and Freedom in the Caribbean Intellectual Tradition* (Indiana University Press, 2019).

CPSIA information can be obtained
at www.ICGtesting.com
Printed in the USA
BVHW042052251022
650195BV00005B/10